WHY RELIGIONS SPREAD

Books by Robert L. Montgomery

The Diffusion of Religions: A Sociological Perspective

Introduction to the Sociology of Missions

The Lopsided Spread of Christianity

The Spread of Religions: A Social Scientific Theory Based on the Spread of Buddhism, Christianity, and Islam (First Edition)

WHY RELIGIONS SPREAD

The Expansion of Buddhism, Christianity, and Islam with Implications for Missions

SECOND EDITION

ROBERT L. MONTGOMERY

Copyright © 2012 Robert L. Montgomery

ISBN: 978-0-615-63702-0
All Rights Reserved.

Printed by Lightning Source

Graphic Designer: Laura Gaines
Cover design by Laura and Thom Gaines
Electron Graphics
www.electron-graphics.com

Biblical excerpts taken from *New Revised Standard Version Bible,* copyright 1989, Division of Christian Education of the National Council of Churches of Christ in the United States of America. Used by permission.

Dedicated to
Mary Taylor Todd,
my college sweetheart in 1950
and my wife since 2008

CONTENTS

PREFACE TO THE SECOND EDITION xiii
PREFACE TO THE FIRST EDITION xv

INTRODUCTION A
Background, Definitions, Historical Overview, and Acknowledgments . . . 1

INTRODUCTION B
Theoretical Framework and Methodology 19

PART I
RELIGIOUS CONTENT FACTORS

CHAPTER 1
Beliefs and the Spread of Religions 39

CHAPTER 2
Moral Guidance, Moral Energy, and the Spread of Religions 73

CHAPTER 3
Gathering, Organization, and the Spread of Religions 111

Contents

PART II A
MACRO SECULAR SOCIAL FACTORS

CHAPTER 4
Internal Social Conditions in Receiving Societies and the Spread
  of Religions 147

CHAPTER 5
Intersocietal Relationships and the Spread of Religions. 193

PART II B
MICRO SECULAR SOCIAL FACTORS

CHAPTER 6
Social Relationships and the Spread of Religions 231

CHAPTER 7
Motivations and the Spread of Religions 257

PART III
ADDITIONAL APPLICATIONS OF THE ANALYSIS

CHAPTER 8
The Spread of Irreligion 293

CHAPTER 9
Looking Forward 343

CHAPTER 10
Implications for Missions 379

REFERENCES 425
NAME INDEX 445
SUBJECT INDEX 451

WHY RELIGIONS SPREAD

PREFACE TO THE SECOND EDITION

My original reasons for writing this book have not changed. My primary goal remains to set forth some of the major categories or sets of reasons why people have responded to the three most widely spreading religions. I isolate seven major factors or categories. The basic purpose of doing this is found in the last chapter (Chapter 10), which considers the implications of these categories for missions. I regard the variety in responses to religions introduced from the outside to be the most important missiological question to be investigated.

I still seek to use a social scientific approach, which I explain in the following Preface and Introductions, but I recognize that for some people this approach seems out of place in the study of religion and history. However, I still think that the social sciences are a useful tool for analysis, even in the complex fields of religion and history. My use of "theory" is in the narrow sense, as used in the social sciences for "explanation" or "reasons for." I can also consider my "causes" as simply "categories of reasons." I still believe that formal propositions can be used to sharpen the argument. In this Second Edition I have not only corrected a number of errors found in the First Edition and added some new material, but I have also endeavored to present the material in a clearer form.

My original purpose for self-publishing has also not changed. It was to make the book available to more readers at a lower cost, since the offer to publish by an established publishing company would make the book available only in hardback. Finally, with the new title that does not use the phrase "a social scientific theory," I hope to appeal to a somewhat wider audience.

The following Preface to the First Edition describes how the question of the variety of responses to religions introduced from the outside presented itself to me. While I believe that the First Edition of this book continues to be useful, this Second Edition should be even more useful for those seeking to clarify the categories or types of factors contributing to the spread of religions and how to plan missions in relation to these factors.

PREFACE TO THE FIRST EDITION

Working as a Christian missionary in Taiwan I encountered a surprising and puzzling phenomenon: a set of highly contrasting responses by social groups to the Christian message. A variety of responses to mission work are usually taken for granted, but the contrast I encountered was quite great. The minority aboriginal people of Taiwan, existing in some ten language groups, believed the Christian message in large numbers (most of them before I arrived on the field), whereas the response of the majority population was relatively small. The large majority of the aboriginal people became Christian, whereas in the majority population less than 10 percent of the population is Christian.

As a son of missionary parents in China growing up in the 1930s, I was accustomed to the large-scale rejection of Christianity, similar to the response of the majority population in Taiwan. I should note that there has been a dramatic reversal in China of this largely negative response just in the last few decades, which has only added to my curiosity. Another major contrast in response that I had noted while in Taiwan was between Korea and Japan. In the twentieth century, there was a large-scale reception of the Christian message in Korea, but in Japan in the same time period and also extending back several centuries there was a major rejection. I also considered other religions and realized that at least two—Buddhism and Islam—had spread widely, but also had experienced varying responses.

Because of these experiences and broad observations, I determined to see what understanding I could gain from the social sciences as to why there were such variations in responses to religions introduced from the outside. Many people might question applying secular social scientific methods to the study of religion, much less to the study of conversion or the spread of religions. I therefore wish to set forth here my theological and philosophical views regarding science in general and the social sciences in particular.

The fact is that religions and societies are bound up with each other. Regarding the spread or transmission of religious faith, many people overlook the obvious effect of the family on the spread or transmission of religious faith. The family is a social institution that is studied extensively in the social sciences. In addition to the influence of families, social groups and whole societies have an influence in determining religious identities. Thus, in a theological sense, there is no secular realm. God is in and works through all things.

Because of the work of God in all things, including social relations, I believe that there is a larger or more comprehensive theological explanation than a sociological explanation for why religions spread in varied ways. A theological explanation of the spread of religions includes both a particular understanding of God and of human nature. To maintain the distinction between theological and sociological understandings, some would prefer to speak of the theological explanation as an "interpretation" and reserve "explanation" for scientific theory. I will not quibble over these terms, but basically my belief is that God works through social conditions to bring about faith and that social conditions can be studied social scientifically. Thus I am among those who see the scientific approach, which rules out any theological reasoning—not the same as ruling out personal belief that God works in the world and in human life—as an important tool or means of bringing clarity to thought, including theological thought, about the human side of religion. Because of this view, I decided to work to develop a sociology of missions or a theoretical understanding of the spread of religions that would stand up under social scientific inquiry.

Like the sixteenth- and seventeenth-century scientists, I believe that science—they called it natural philosophy—is a gift of God to help us understand and use God's creation for good. Nature and human life are neither purely random nor mechanical but operate on the basis of probability and in patterns that can be discerned. Of course, the possibility of and actual misuse of nature (and mistreatment of humans) was increased by the increased knowledge of nature and the technology that resulted from such knowledge. Even science itself, or the scientific method, has been used as a supposed basis for denying the existence of God. I am opposed to such an ideological view of science, which can be termed "scientism"—a kind of expanded belief in science that does not recognize its limited view of reality (Stenmark 2003). In other words, I believe that there is superempirical reality, which is beyond the ability of science to study (except the human reaction to superempirical reality). However, in spite of the limitation of science to the examination of empirical reality, there are few people who would want to return to the days before modern science or even to the more recent past, for example, before the discovery of antibiotics.

About one hundred and fifty years after the initiation of the modern scientific movement, sometimes referred to as the institutionalization of science, occurred first in Italy and then primarily in England and France, the methods of the "experimenters" were increasingly applied to the study of human behavior. This resulted in the birth of the social sciences in the nineteenth century. By then, and continuing to the present, scientific activity is rarely given a theological purpose, as it was earlier. However, I continue to apply the same rationale of the seventeenth-century experimenters to the work of the social sciences, namely to learn more about God's work in the world. With the social sciences, learning the works of God through science means not only learning about nature, but also about human history. If God is working among humans, as I believe, then in scientific study of human behavior and societies we can learn something about God's activity in history.

Even if scientific work can have a theological purpose, as I believe it does, it has to leave theology out of its theorizing, methodologies, and conclusions. I believe theology has the duty to wrestle with and incorporate the valid results of scientific work. Of course, this is an ongoing task since scientific findings are constantly being challenged and changed by scientists, and theories are modified or set aside. In other words, the validity of scientific theories, and even the facts on which they are based, need to be under constant scrutiny and adjustment. I believe the special power of scientific work comes from this openness to public challenge and constant elaboration. Theology cannot be challenged in the same way because of its basic dependence on faith, as in "the assurance of things hoped for, the conviction of things not seen" (Hebrews 11:1). Furthermore, I believe that this faith is in response to the authoritative revelation of the Bible. However, I wanted a theoretical understanding of the spread of religions that would stand up under social scientific inquiry, regardless of the inquirer's faith or nonfaith. I expected future elaboration and adjustment of the understanding, but I wanted to make a beginning in an area where few sociologists of religion have entered. Of course, I did not think that a social scientific theory could replace, only throw light on, a theological understanding of the Mission of God in the world as revealed in the Bible.

Even though science does not answer to revelatory authority, I believe that it can serve as a corrective, a kind of judgment, on human thinking, which includes human thinking and behavior in response to and in reflection upon revelation. To correct and improve thought about missions, thereby having an impact on mission planning, was a major impetus to my pursuit of a social scientific study of missions.

There have already been important developments in the area of employing the social sciences in theological thought and Christian activity. For some time, theologians and missiologists have recognized the value of psychology and anthropology in understanding pastoral work, conversion, and response to the Christian message around the world. I refer to the inclusion of pastoral psychology in theological training beginning soon after World War II and of anthropological studies into mission training, especially in Roman Catholic and evangelical schools. Walter Conn (1986a, 1986b, 1987) and Lewis Rambo (1993, 1999, 2003) provide examples of the incorporation of psychology in understanding of conversion, an essential part of missions. In anthropology, a group of scholars, mostly both missiologists and anthropologists (McGavran 1957 [1955]; Luzbetak 1963; Tippett 1971; Kraft 1979; Hiebert 1985; Tabor 2000), led the way in using anthropology in understanding missions. In addition, missiologists have compiled comprehensive statistics on the religions of the world (Barrett 1982; Barrett, Kurian, and Johnson 2001; Barrett and Johnson 2001; Johnstone and Mandryk 2001). Their work is continually being updated. However, so far at least, sociology of religion in contrast to anthropology has had comparatively little influence in the study of missions or missiology. In Europe, people have made greater use of sociology to study missions, as witness the work of Roger Mehl (1970 [1965]) and the journal, *Le Fait Missionnaire* or *Social Sciences and Missions*, now edited by Eric Morier-Genoud and Wendy Urban-Mead.

The social sciences are normally understood to include the major fields of political science, economics, anthropology, psychology, and sociology. What has made the balanced use of these fields especially difficult is that they are highly specialized and have numerous subfields, including applied fields such as communications, management, social work, and community development. The division of these special fields from one another is exacerbated by the fact that each one has its own professional organizations, professional ladders, social networks, and publications. My own view is that these fields are complementary, with each having important contributions to make to knowledge of human life in societies. However, I found sociology especially useful for my goal of understanding the spread of religions because of its focus on human life in groups combined with a drive to go beyond description and develop theory or explanations of behavior.

As I pursued my special interest in the sociology of religion, I came to realize that sociology, including sociology of religion, along with the other social sciences, had fallen under the influence of scientism with its "imperialistic claims" for science. This in itself was not too serious for scientific work since faith and nonfaith are irrelevant to its methodologies. However, I found that the theoretical drive of sociology, as opposed to the more descriptive approach of anthropology and history, tended to isolate much of sociological work. For example, I noticed how sociology books were often relegated to the back of many bookstores.

I have been encouraged by recent developments in the field of sociology, represented by a "turn toward culture," which offsets sociology's isolation. What this means is that many sociologists are emphasizing now that human beings are to a great extent driven by a search for meaning. There are too many scholars to mention in this connection, but I think especially of Robert Wuthnow (1989), Jeffrey Alexander (2003), Christian Smith (2003B, 2010), Rodney Stark (2001, 2003), John R. Hall (2009), and James Davison Hunter (1991, 2010).

Cultures, of course, express this search for meaning. I believe that this is one reason cultural anthropology, as opposed to sociology, has had the greatest impact among missionaries as well as in the general public. This is not to mention the fact that the "thick descriptions" of anthropology are more interesting than the abstract and seemingly irrelevant theories of some sociology. Accompanying the turn toward culture in sociology has been the "new paradigm" (Warner 1997) in sociology of religion and the important and interesting work of Rodney Stark (1996, 2001, 2003) and associates, for example, in *Acts of Faith* (Stark and Finke (2000). A major contribution of the new paradigm and by Stark in particular has been to emphasize the influence of the content of religions on world history, a view that has had a major influence on me. Fenggang Yang (2006) has been especially active in applying the new paradigm to the study of the dramatic religious changes in China.

Before I describe the results of my social scientific study in the following introductions, I should include my perspective on the large field of the humanities, which has a somewhat problematic relationship with the social sciences. The humanities are a demonstration of the power and attraction of the human search for meaning, and they continue to have an important place in human thought even though they are highly influenced by the natural and social sciences. The humanities have numerous fields, including philosophy, literature, history, and art, all of which may well use or incorporate scientific studies and knowledge. Nevertheless, the humanities, unlike the sciences, give a foundational place to normative views, namely opinions and evaluations that cannot be scientifically demonstrated. History, in particular, has come to make much use of the social sciences. Other fields use scientific analyses, such as the professional fields of journalism and counseling. However, in the end, these fields are based in the humanities because of their overall normative approach. I believe in the importance of the humanities and their great contribution to thinking, knowledge, and a full orbed life. I don't think it is possible to live without them, because our lives are based on our beliefs and values. I owe much to the work of the philosopher of religion, Mikael Stenmark (2001) for his work on scientism. He shows that scientism imperialistically claims that all true knowledge is scientific knowledge, thus driving the humanities and certainly religion from the knowledge field. However, humans have refused to live by such claims.

Even though he sought incorrectly as a social scientist to define the super empirical reality of God, Emile Durkheim (1965 [1915]:479) noted long ago that we always have to go beyond science in human thought, and that it is religion that provides people with the strength to live. Recently, Christian Smith (2003b) has made clear that living by faith is simply the way we all live, and that all thought and knowledge, including science, is founded on beliefs that can be expressed as narratives. However, science necessarily does its work without reference to its normative base. That is, beliefs and opinions should be irrelevant to forming its theories and obtaining its findings.

In the end, the humanities must be more comprehensive than the sciences in the sense of needing to incorporate scientific knowledge, while science cannot incorporate the humanities except as human data. Theology (and philosophy) especially must be comprehensive in approach since theology is thought about God, whose will and action incorporate all reality, including the empirical reality with which science deals. Science, by definition, can make no statements about God, except in the indirect sense that statements about creation or humanity can be statements about God and God's activity. I call this "indirect theology." This puts science in a very humble position in relation to theology, but nevertheless because of the clarification science brings to empirical reality, theology must take account of and incorporate the valid explanations of science, as incomplete as they may be.

This brings me to an important complicating factor that affects human life, including religion. Even though I believe that God is working in history, I also believe that there is much in human thought and behavior that resists and opposes God. In this regard, it is encouraging that even sociology must take up the question of evil, as it is understood in culture (Alexander 2003). In the end, however, theology must evaluate or make judgments about the "works of God" and the "works of human opposition" in a way that the social sciences cannot be evaluative. However, the social sciences can be very useful in order for such judgments or evaluations to be based on reality rather than wishful thinking or superficial opinion.

As long as I have mentioned human opposition to God, I should say that my view of religion is that it incorporates both a search for and resistance to God. (I will discuss my social scientific definition of religion in Introduction A.) Religions, including my own, seem to specialize in building "halfway houses" to God. Church buildings, institutions, rituals, and organizations can easily become such halfway houses when they are conceived as satisfying or fulfilling the human response to God. We go so far and then decide that we have done enough to "get us into heaven." This is where a basic tendency of religion to be an exchange or an attempt to bargain with God appears. This form of religion then becomes a barrier rather than a way to God based on God's grace.

The social scientists Rodney Stark and William Sims Bainbridge (1996 [1987]) have in fact brought out this exchange element in religion in their *Theory of Religion*. However, rewards in religion do not have to be approached on an exchange or earned basis only. Here language fails us by its ambiguities. Rewards in religion (which, incidentally, are continuously offered in the Bible) can be approached either as earned or unearned compensation. In other words, according to the Bible, the true rewards of faith are outcome rewards, not earned rewards. The struggle between grace and law is an old one, and even if we settle it intellectually, it continues within us psychologically. At any rate, the very institutionalization of religion incorporates opposition to God and so often has included the attempt of religions to rely on coercion to sustain themselves and to eliminate competition. In the most extreme form, the reliance on human constructed concepts and institutions in religion has resulted in the attempt to eliminate by force all who do not comply. The result has been crusades and terrorism in the name of God.

Beyond simply in bad religion (the halfway or bargain-based religion), resistance to God may be expressed simply in direct rejection of all religion and a naked elevation of the self as central to life. The self is set against a God who is seen as unreasonably demanding and exclusive and requiring an intolerant and authoritarian religion. This form of resistance has found expression largely in the modern era, beginning in the West. This has been the "secularism" (ideological) part of the secularization movement.

Although the social sciences cannot theologically evaluate the good and bad in religion, it is possible to analyze many causes and effects in religious change in the world. This brings me to state my view as to what is distinctive about scientific knowledge. It is found both in its subject matter—the empirical—and its method of gaining knowledge. Entire books are written on this subject, but it is enough for me to say here that science is different because it limits itself to what can be known through systematic observation of empirical reality and therefore its studies can be replicated or falsified. Thus, it is important to recognize that science is a self-limiting discipline. There is a basic empiricism, although this is often too narrowly defined as excluding any consideration of faith and inner states of mind, such as attitudes and motives. It may not be possible to observe inner attitudes such as faith and love in their basic or total reality, but expressions of them can certainly be observed and therefore incorporated in scientific studies. Methodology is the key element in scientific study, which must be public and able to be replicated. Replication requires that methodology be plain. It is important to add what is often forgotten: Scientific study is not aimed primarily at description, as important as it is for exploration of a subject, but it is aimed primarily at theory or explanation. This is made especially clear in sociology, and that is why I like the term *sociology of missions:* It implies a special interest in theory.

The heavy emphasis on empirical data, clear methodology, replication, and theory all set limits to scientific knowledge and set it apart from the humanities. However, as limited as it is, it is a powerful tool and punctures many a bubble of opinion and wishful thought, and I might add, beliefs based on such thought. In regard to understanding the normative basis for the scientific approach, I recommend Robert Merton's (1973 [1942]: 267-278, 286-324, 383-412) "ethos of science." It includes universalism, communism (not the political ideology), disinterestedness, organized skepticism, originality, and humility (the last two added later) (Montgomery 1999: xviii-xix). I believe that Christian theology supports this ethos of science and it is this ethos that enables science to function as a corrective or judgmental force in human thought, including theological thought.

In regard to my overall theology, I believe that God has decided to use human beings (in spite of their various oppositions) to accomplish his purposes. Therefore, the study of human religions—what affects them and what they affect—is a study of both "God's works" and of human opposition to those works. Theology needs this kind of knowledge. Also theology is needed to give the larger picture of the meaning of religions and everything else, but without good social scientific work the larger picture of theology will be distorted by incorporating inaccurate knowledge and biased and false opinions.

Since I am interested in a social scientific theory of the spread of religions, I must add that social scientific theory is about relating social facts in cause-and-effect relationships. There are broader approaches to the concept of theory that use the terms *paradigm* and *model,* but I believe that it is useful here to keep a rather narrow view of theory on which subsequently broader perspectives or paradigms may be built. Thus theory means not simply describing the spread of religions, but explaining it. Again, description along with its categories and typologies is important and needed, but the basic drive of science, and sociology in the social sciences, is to produce theory or explanation.

In the end and practically speaking, because we are humans and live normatively, the sharp distinction I try to maintain between the social sciences and the normative views found in the humanities and in personal life undoubtedly breaks down at certain points. This is especially true of personal faith. Nevertheless, it is best for me, having been trained in theology as well as the social sciences, to seek to maintain a sharp distinction between the two. Readers can probably perceive my normative views, but I will seek to specify them as such when I express them. In the last chapter I will also demonstrate how it is possible to incorporate a social scientific perspective into a theological perspective. Basically, I am seeking to establish social scientific theory about the spread of religions and, at the same time, to show how such theory has important implications for the practice of missions.

Let me hasten to add, however, that I (and I believe most people who work in the field of missiology) want to remain open to additional theoretical work, not only from sociology of religion, but from other social scientific fields represented by psychology, anthropology, political science, and economics, as long as this work is based on empirical data and is controlled for both anti and pro religious bias. One of the ways I seek to remain open to elaboration is to establish a theoretical framework that can be filled out and to which new sections can be added. I present this framework in Introduction B and it forms the basic structure of the book. However, before presenting the theoretical framework, I will present a general background for my examination of the spread of religions in Introduction A. Let us leave the philosophy and theology behind this book as presented in the two Prefaces and proceed to a more specific guide to the book, in the following Introductions A and B.

INTRODUCTION A

BACKGROUND, DEFINITIONS, HISTORICAL OVERVIEW, AND ACKNOWLEDGMENTS

Social scientists have given very little attention to explaining the spread of religions, and so there is little theory on which to build. One of the reasons for this neglect is the tendency among both scholars and adherents of religions to consider religions, especially the world religions, as more or less fixed entities rather than having spread to where they presently exist. People tend to assume that particular religions are native to certain areas rather than having spread to where they now exist. This ahistorical approach has lead to the neglect of considering why and how religions have spread. Even when detailed histories have been written, particularly of Buddhism, Christianity, and Islam, the emphasis has been on describing where they are rather than explaining why they are there.

The tendency to regard Christianity a Western religion meant that its dramatic spread in the world in the last decades of the twentieth century was little noticed by either scholars or the general public, as pointed out by Philip Jenkins (2002). One of the few exceptions among sociologists to examine the spread of religions is Rodney Stark. Initially, he (1996) developed theory on why religious movements succeed or fail. Specifically he (1995; 1997 [1996]; 2001) considered the spread of Christianity in its first three hundred years and also the important effects of monotheism, one of which is missions. This represents one of the rare considerations by a sociologist of the spread of any religions.

Before presenting the theoretical framework in Introduction B that forms the structure for the book, I will state some important definitions and assumptions.

DEFINITIONS

In trying to define religion, let us recognize that among early humans and even in tribal and traditional societies up to recent times there was little consciousness of something distinct called *religion*. This was because people took for granted the pervasive reality of the supernatural or superempirical. Thus, in ancient languages there was no word for religion. The present world religions have roots extending into the past for some three millennia, and even much further if one considers some of the basic psychological or nonhistorical elements of religions. The consciousness of the historical religions to which people could be converted, however, only began to emerge some three millennia ago and acceptance or conversions to particular religions only began to take place regularly some two millennia ago. This came about with increasing contacts between peoples, but especially with the appearance of Judaism and Christianity, religions that called for exclusive loyalty to God. They believed God had revealed himself to humans in a special way and expected the human response of faith and love. In the East, other religions like Buddhism had already begun to have followers but never expected their exclusive loyalty like the biblically based religions.

Carl Ernst (2003:39-47), after pointing to the Latin origin of the word *religion,* in the sense of a "painstaking sense of duty" (still a common notion), presents Augustine's Christian contribution in *Of True Religion* (390 CE). Augustine conceived of religion as (1) only in the singular, not in the multiple sense: (2) having a strong doctrinal content, not simply being a matter of obligatory practices: and (3) having its authority as properly resting in the Christian Church and the revelation through Christ. By the time of Hugo Grotius's book, *On the Truth of the Christian Religion* (1627), other religions are recognized, but Christianity is considered "the unsurpassing choice."

It is primarily the encounter of Europe with the rest of the world that set the terms of debate about which religion has the truth. It has been pointed out, for example, that "the concept of Buddhism was created about three centuries ago to identify what we now know to be a pan-Asian religious tradition that dates back some twenty-five hundred years" (Reynolds and Hallisey (1989 [1987]: 3). Currently, the social sciences exist in the context of religious diversity and have the difficult task of trying to come to some common understanding of religion, and by extension, the spread of religions, which has been largely ignored. This means that the concept of religion is something of a social construct, perhaps not as unrealistic as the construct of race, but nevertheless a reification or an acceptance of something as external reality when it exists only in the mind. The concept of society also has this quality. It is religious organizations and institutions that do the most to give external reality to religions, as well as society itself.

I have found the approach of Stark, who has been working on a sociology of gods, very useful. He (2001:15) defines religions as "explanations of the meaning of existence based on supernatural assumptions and including statements about the nature of the supernatural." This is a very straightforward, substantive definition that defines religion by its content rather than simply by its function, as much of sociology has tended to do. It also distinguishes as did

Durkheim (1965 [1915]:58) religion from magic, which has no theology and no church, only clients. Interestingly, ideologies, especially antireligious ideologies seeking to severely control or even eliminate religions, often begin to function like religions, including spreading like religions. This was apparent with Fascism, but especially with Marxism, which has spread widely. Even scientism may be considered an ideology that has spread widely—scientism actually being a part of Marxism (or Marxism one expression of it) but also existing as a separate ideology primarily among intellectuals. The rise and spread of irreligion and its ideological expressions require special attention (see Chapter 8) because of certain parallels to the spread of a religion. Modern irreligion draws heavily on scientism and modern concepts of the individual. Surprisingly, modern irreligion developed in the context of the Christian religion in Europe and has spread to some extent with Christianity but also in competition with it.

Stark (2001:10) admits that there are "Godless religions" which consider the supernatural as a substance or an essence. Immanuel Kant (1724–1804), along with other intellectuals in the West, and various Eastern religions, such as "official" Buddhism and Taoism, have advanced such religions that refer to the supernatural, but not to a personal God. Many people prefer to think of the supernatural as an impersonal substance, a force, or the ground of being. ("Let the Force be with you.") These kinds of religions that are heavily philosophical have spread very little and are therefore not of much concern in this book. I believe that the most sociologically useful approach to forming theory about religions and the spread of religions is based on recognizing that a key element in religion is belief in a divine being or beings—at least that will be my approach. I should add that I like Christian Smith's (2003:98) approach to defining religion in terms of the superempirical (rather than simply the supernatural) because the Divine may be believed to be in and throughout the natural, interpenetrating with it (immanent), as well as being above and beyond it (transcendent). His definition is: "religions are sets of beliefs, symbols, and practices about the reality of superempirical orders that make claims to organize and guide human life." In either case, in the minds of many religious people, the Divine is in both the natural and empirical, as well as the supernatural and superempirical. In the end the religions that have spread widely are those that believe in a divine being and (as will be seen) a special being through whom access is gained to the Divine and to salvation.

I use *spread* as equivalent to the traditional social scientific term, *diffusion*. I (1996, 1999) have discussed the concept of diffusion at some length in other books. Everett Rogers (1995:12), who reviewed and summarized diffusion theory, acknowledges that very little attention has been paid to the diffusion of ideas, including religions and ideologies, as opposed to technology. Some people have associated diffusion with some of the discredited theories that attributed the origins of human culture to a few selected cultures (Perry 1992:487). For my purposes, the term *spread* is sufficient to refer to religions moving from one society to another by propagation that results from some form of recruitment or the acceptance of religious identities not previously held. Arnold (2006 [1896]: 1) at the beginning of his study of the spread of Islam accepted Muller's definition of a missionary religion as one...

> ...in which the spreading of the truth and the conversion of unbelievers are raised to the rank of a sacred duty by the founder or his immediate successors... It is the spirit of truth in the hearts of believers which cannot rest, unless it manifests itself in thought, word and deed, which is not satisfied till it

has carried its message to every human soul, till what it believes to be the truth is accepted as the truth by all members of the human family.

In previous books (1999, 2002) I have discussed the diffusion or spreading process—knowledge, persuasion, decision, implementation, and confirmation. This process is important, and its study should certainly be included in sociology of missions. However, because of the need to focus, in this book I will not discuss the process, but simply recognize that the spread of religions may be blocked or reversed before the process has affected a large proportion of a population. There may often be a long delay between the spread of initial knowledge and the final confirmation. An empirical review of religions reveals that most religions have spread to some extent (otherwise they would hardly be known), but that only a few religions have spread quite widely across numerous sociocultural boundaries.

Before looking at which religions have spread widely, I will note that my theory of the spread of religions does not include a consideration of spread or diffusion of religions by migration or what Chris Park (1994:100) calls relocation diffusion in contrast to expansion diffusion. In relocation diffusion "the number of people who adopt the innovation grows by direct contact, usually in situ." The spread of religions by migration is an important historical phenomenon that has had a major effect in world history, but this effect has depended on what kind of religion has migrated. As an historical fact and in the current world situation, religions have spread to numerous new places by migration or relocation, and in some cases (Hanciles 2003) this has aided the spread of religions to new peoples, but not necessarily.

The Jewish Diaspora is perhaps the most famous case of the spread of a religion by migration rather than propagation. Zoroastrianism spread from Iran to India by migration. In both cases,

Judaism and Zoroastrianism did not spread to any great extent to surrounding people in new settings. Of course, European Christians migrated to the Americas in large, numbers and Christianity did spread to a considerable extent to Native Americans, although also with great resistance. The difference is that Christianity, in contrast to Zoroastrianism and Judaism, is a missionary religion that usually actively aims to convert people.

Today Muslims and followers of various Eastern religions are migrating to Europe and North America, and in both cases some conversions are taking place. This is true because there is a missionary spirit present in both Islam and Eastern religions and because there is freedom to convert in Western democracies. Thus, the difference between relocation diffusion and expansion diffusion is that, unlike the former, in the latter the religion specifically reaches out to convert new people who then change their religious identities. This is also known pejoratively as proselytizing because of its association for many with intolerance. At any rate, this type of spreading has characterized so-called missionary religions and so is quite distinct from spread simply through migration. Migration of religion deserves separate attention as an historical phenomenon, but I will stress the fact that the spreading religions considered are those that cross both sociocultural boundaries and geographical boundaries, primarily through propagation and recruitment, resulting in acceptance of religious identities not previously held. The rejection by intellectuals of intolerance (and therefore proselytizing, which they consider intolerant) has undoubtedly contributed to the neglect of the study of missions by social scientists. Of course, I reject the view that proselytizing has to be associated with intolerance and hold that to assume this is an antireligious bias.

I must note that the spread of religions through migrations is taking place on a fairly large scale as people migrate from all over the world to the West. Some, though not most, of these migrations are even missionary motivated. The study of immigrant religions (C.F. Warner 1998; Yang 1999; Kwon, Kim, and Warner; 2001; Ebaugh and Chafetz 2000, 2002; Guest 2003; Carnes and Yang 2004) has become a major subfield in the sociology of religion. Although I am sorry that equal attention has not been given to the spread of religions through the sending out of missionaries overseas, immigrant religions themselves are having considerable missionary effect in making conversions among immigrants who were either irreligious or merely nominally religious in their homelands. Nevertheless, a major task of immigrant religions is preserving the faith and other aspects of culture that immigrants bring with them. Of course, the practical difficulty and expense in carrying out overseas studies and the availability of immigrant groups for scholars in America help a great deal to account for the focus upon immigrant religions as opposed to overseas religions.

Technically, the spread of religions by immigrant groups could occupy a certain section of my theoretical framework. Since this subject is receiving major consideration elsewhere, I have chosen not to focus on immigrant religion as such. Instead, I have chosen to focus my study on the spread of religions across socio-cultural borders—which are usually also geographical borders—by propagation leading to the change of religious identities in new locations. In other words, I am considering primarily why religions have spread or not spread across borders through propagation and ensuing acceptance of new religious identities. The growth of religions is a related, but different, subject since growth is often within geographical or social borders.

My study overlaps with studies of conversion. However, since my perspective is that of sociology of religion rather than psychology of religion, my emphasis is on change of individuals and groups in their religious attachments and identities as religions spread across borders. A recent study of "conversion careers" by Henri Gooren (2010) suggests that *recruitment* is a better term to use in the spread of religions than *conversion*. I accept this suggestion although in the increasingly individualistic modern world, the spread of religions is actually increasingly marked by conversions of individuals that follow a "conversion career." However, I use a minimal definition of conversion that is simply acceptance of or change in religious identity. I recognize the followers of a religion on the basis of their self-identification and not on the basis of any self-reported religious experience, nor an externally applied standard of orthodoxy. I also recognize that self-identification with a religion may be relatively superficial, given on the spur of the moment, affirmed out of habit, or simply with the desire to contrast oneself with those of another religion. However, self-identification with a particular religion is a mark of the extent of that religion's public presence in the world.

HISTORICAL OVERVIEW OF THE SPREAD OF RELIGIONS

For most of human history, the largest part of which is unrecorded, human beings followed various primal religions in which the spiritual and the superempirical were a seamless part of life. The history of religions began to be recorded only in the most recent millennia Before the Common Era (BCE) when religious specialists organized and sacred sites and temples were constructed. At the same time, individuals and families continued the long practiced veneration of household deities and ancestors.

Robert Bellah (1969 [1964]:67-83) has identified these early religions as primitive and archaic religions, the first two of five stages of religion: primitive, archaic, historic, early modern, and modern. In the first two stages (or if you prefer "types") of religion, the supernatural was taken for granted and, as already noted, there was actually no concept of religion as a separate entity. This is still the case in many of the older societies of the world. In these societies people today often identify themselves as followers of a distinctive religion simply because they think it is expected of them in the modern world, or they may identify themselves in opposition to a new religion being introduced from the outside. In a number of traditional societies, in fact, people may combine beliefs and practice rituals from several religions. Whoever or whatever is worshipped does not require exclusive loyalty as is the case in Judaism, Christianity, and Islam. Even where religions record members, people may maintain multiple memberships.

We can study the phenomenon of the large-scale spreading of religions only as occurring over approximately the last 2,250 years, dating from the sending out by the Emperor Asoka of teachers of the Dhamma, referring to the moral teachings of Buddhism. Approximately two millennia ago, followers of particular religions began to travel widely, but especially the Biblical religions of Judaism and Christianity began calling for exclusive loyalty to God. The adherents of most religions today are biased in favor of considering their own religion as native to their area. Other religions are labeled as foreign. This perspective even influenced scholars of religions, who in any case do not like the idea of efforts being made to convert others resulting in the change of the religions that are the object of their study! Arguments are made to support the territorial view of religions based on the fact that certain religions have been in particular areas longer than other religions. However, most people do not recognize that their religion was introduced to their society from the outside only in the last two thousand years and in many cases much more recently. For example, European Christians and their descendents in North America have largely forgotten that Christianity was brought to them by missionaries. Only until recently, both within and outside of the West, people considered Christianity a Western religion when actually its origins were Middle Eastern. Reading the Bible and noticing the way of life in it should convince most people that Christianity is decidedly not a Western religion, but now we have the added fact that the majority of Christians live outside of the West.

Buddhism was introduced from the outside to the over 150 countries where it exists apart from India. Islam was introduced from the outside everywhere it exists apart from the small part of Arabia where it originated. Even Hinduism was introduced from the outside to people in much of India and certainly in Southeast Asia. The supposedly "foreign" religion of Christianity has been in India for close to two thousand years, much longer, for example, than the "native" religion of Sikhism. I believe it is time to recognize that the ideas of "native" and "foreign" religions are primarily polemical tools.

The basic facts are that the world religions are all new in comparison to the long history of humanity, that consciousness of a religious identity emerged primarily only in the last two thousand years (and is still not in the consciousness of many people), and that there is increasing religious interchange in a shrinking world. Given these facts, I find it useful to begin with the assumption that all religions are capable of spreading, at least to some extent. From an individual perspective in a world where people increasingly have freedom to choose their religion under religiously diverse conditions, I also assume that anyone has the potential of choosing any religion. In the Western industrialized world today, we see people choosing to follow what they consider a primal religion or a religion that they think is similar to one followed by their pre-Christian forebears. In addition, increasingly people are learning about religions from other parts of the world and choosing to follow these religions or combine elements from them with what they consider their native religion (Woodhead, Heelas, Davie 2003). Perhaps most important, for the last few centuries, beginning in the West, people are choosing to follow no organized religion, and some even to disbelieve in any superempirical reality or divinity. As already noted, irreligion has spread alongside religion. Societies are becoming increasingly religiously diverse, with the freedom to choose any religion or no religion. I assume that all religions and irreligion(s) are able to spread, at least to some extent, and that anyone is a potential follower of any religion or some form of no religion. These assumptions open our view to all religions, as well as to those who reject all religions. A theory of the spread of religions, just as a theory of religions, should not rule out any religion nor form of irreligion from its view.

However, having said all of this about the current situation, there remains an important historical fact that influences my choice of data to analyze and to use as evidence for theoretical statements. This fact may seem to be in conflict with the modern phenomenon that all religions and irreligion are able to spread, at least to some extent, and that anyone has the potential of choosing any religion or no religion. However, such freedom of choice is primarily a modern development. The historical fact is that in the last two thousand years not all religions have spread equally, and people have not chosen all religions or no religion in equal numbers. In fact, three religions—Buddhism, Christianity, and Islam, in historical order of their appearance—have spread much more widely and to a much greater variety of societies than any other religions up to the present. My approach, therefore, will be to develop theory on the basis of the spread of these three religions and secondarily to relate theory to what is taking place in modern societies. Typically, the social sciences focus on what is taking place in modern societies; but when it comes to understanding the spread of religions, including in the modern era, I believe it is necessary to consider primarily what has happened over the last two thousand years.

Writing toward the end of the nineteenth century, Thomas Arnold (2006 [1896]:1) accepted the view of the missiologist Max Muller that Buddhism, Christianity, and Islam were missionary religions in contrast to Judaism, Brahmanism (Hinduism), and Zoroastrianism, which were classified as nonmissionary. He undertook to describe the spread of Islam through peaceful preaching, but neither he nor anyone else to the present has attempted to explain why Buddhism, Christianity, and Islam became missionary religions and spread so successfully.

It is true that Buddhism spread almost entirely in Asia with little direct competition with Christianity and Islam for many centuries. Its major competitors were Hinduism in South and Southeast Asia and Taoism (not so much Confucianism) in China. Although Buddhism was almost eliminated from its land of origin, it spread widely throughout Southeast Asia, Central Asia, and East Asia. Hinduism spread throughout South Asia and was a rival for a time to Buddhism in Southeast Asia. However, it lost out to Buddhism in Southeast Asia, with the exception of some parts of Indonesia. Also, Hinduism failed to spread at all to Central Asia and East Asia, with the exception of India's northern neighbor Nepal. Hinduism has about twice as many adherents as Buddhism (970 to 474 million, Johnson, Barrett, and Crossing 2012), but our study is of the spread of religions not simply their size. The vast majority of Hindus today are limited to India (93 percent) whereas Buddhists are widely scattered over 150 nations, and in general Buddhism has been more successful in winning followers in the West than Hinduism (Jaffarian 2003). The religions of China spread in East Asia, but little elsewhere. Thus Buddhism proved to be the least ethnically bound of the Asian religions and that is the intrinsic characteristic of religions that spread. We will try to see why. Although Buddhism spread almost entirely in Asia before the modern era, in the last century and a half it has spread in various forms with other Eastern religions to the West; so in the end the difference is relative, not absolute, between Buddhism and other Asian religions, especially Hinduism. Thus, Buddhism is in a somewhat different category from Christianity and Islam, and it is not continuing to spread as rapidly as either of them. However, certain parallels remain, as will be seen.

Christianity and Islam have had more contact with one another than either has had with Buddhism. They are the two largest religions in the world (about 2.3 and 1.6 billion followers respectively, Johnson, Barrett, and Crossing 2012). Although Christianity spread from the Middle East eastward to Iran, Central Asia, India, and China (Moffett 1992; Montgomery 2002), it spread primarily throughout the Mediterranean Basin in its first three hundred years and then in a second stage lasting some seven hundred years, northward to the European peoples. After a period from approximately 1000 to 1500 CE in which the spread of Christianity ebbed, it gradually renewed its expansion, initially accompanying European expansion. It spread from Europe to the Americas and to various places in the Pacific, Africa, and Asia in a third great stage of diffusion that gained greater momentum in the nineteenth century and continued in the twentieth century. Finally, after the middle of the twentieth century and the collapse of colonialism, Christianity began a fourth great stage of expansion so that by the turn of the twenty-first century 60 percent of Christians lived outside of Europe and North America. Clearly, Christianity has ceased to be merely a Western religion.

Islam spread from the Middle East in all directions but primarily eastward to Central Asia and Northern India and westward to the Atlantic. It spread northward to parts of Europe from which it was later driven, but it remained in Anatolia and parts of the Balkans. It also spread southward to East, West, and South Africa. Its farthest spread was to Southeast Asia, where Indonesia became the nation with the largest Muslim population. More than fifty nations have a majority Muslim population and a great diversity of languages, ethnic groups, and ideological and sectarian groups are included within Islam (Ernst 2003:16), just as in Christianity. In the last half century, Islam has spread considerably by immigration and to some extent by propagation to Europe where twelve-to-seventeen million Muslims live, and to North America where there are over five million.

This brief historical review of the more extensive missionary spread of Buddhism, Christianity, and Islam than all other religions is important background for the present study. In addition, the modern spread of irreligion challenges me to apply the theory to this modern phenomenon (Chapter 9). However, the major task for any theory of the spread of religions is to explain why the three religions I have identified spread to so many more societies than any other religions, and also why there have been major variations in how these religions spread. They were received rather openly on the one hand but firmly rejected on the other hand. When received they have been changed—and in some cases changed rather drastically, especially if they were received under pressure. Thus it is important for this analysis that each of these three religions has many versions, so much so that they could be referred to as Buddhisms, Christianities, and Islams. The variations in the spread of each of the different versions of these religions give important clues for theory.

Stark (2001) has pointed out that Hinduism (the mother religion of Buddhism) and Judaism (the mother religion of Christianity and Islam) both spread and are spreading in the present. However, neither Hinduism nor Judaism nor any of the other major world religions have spread to as wide a variety of societies as Buddhism, Christianity, and Islam. If it is agreed that these three religions have spread more widely than other religions, then the important theoretical problem is to explain why. My approach is to examine (1) how the faith and practice of the religions affected their spread; and (2) why the secular or nonreligious social conditions affecting each of the three religions either blocked or facilitated their spread.

The three spreading religions are usually not grouped together, Buddhism having come from Hinduism and being based primarily in Asia, and Christianity and Islam having a common origin from Judaism and being originally based in the Middle East. (Islam was also influenced by Christianity.) The grouping together of the three widely spreading religions will require comparisons that are usually not made but also yield some results that have not previously been recognized—all this because we are examining something rarely studied, the spread of religions.

In summary, as I approached the problem of developing a theoretical framework for explaining the spread of religions, I found that the analysis required a concentration on clarifying why Buddhism, Christianity, and Islam were able to spread so widely compared to other religions. Aiding the analysis is the fact that the three religions had numerous failures as well as successes in spreading. There is much to compare within each of the religions, as well as between them.

ACKNOWLEDGMENT OF INTELLECTUAL CONTRIBUTIONS

I acknowledge many scholars in my references, but I would like to mention some of the social scientists that I have found helpful in developing theory related to the spread of religions, although I am not attempting to rank them in the importance of their influence. In regard to beliefs, Stephen Sharot's (2001, 2002) analysis of the world religions in terms of their elite and popular versions helped me tremendously. Sharot demonstrated the attraction of popular religions to large numbers of nonelite people who try to cope with the numerous problems of life and who yearn for Divine compassion and help. This stimulated me to consider how the three spreading religions were able to offer people some of the same options as offered in popular religion, in particular, access to God through relationship with a person who links the immanent and the transcendent.

I have already mentioned Stark's (2001, 2003) contribution to my giving attention to the influence of religious content on the spread of religions. Rational-choice theory (Stark and Bainbridge 1996 [1987]; Young 1997), with its emphasis on the tendency of human beings to choose what is perceived to be beneficial to them, has certainly influenced my analysis of the spread of religions. However, I recognize that religious benefits or rewards may be perceived in different ways, some of which can even seem to be contradictory. For example, benefits may be perceived more or less extrinsically or they may be seen as intrinsic or inherent to religious faith. Also, rewards may be viewed as earned or as unearned gifts.

I appreciate Christian Smith's (2003b) criticism of the rational-choice approach when it appears to overemphasize exchange or achieving a reward as a motive for faith. However, I believe that a form of the rational-choice approach fits within his "cultural approach" that emphasizes human personhood, motivation, and action within moral orders. I would add the element of gratitude to the sense of obligation that he emphasizes as important in morality. Smith (2010) greatly expanded his views in his book, *What is a Person?: Rethinking Humanity, Social Life, and the Moral Good from the Person Up*, a book which I found very helpful in understanding the human capacity for moral formation.

I continue to find very helpful the work of social identity or social-category theorists, beginning with Henri Tajfel (1972, 1974, 1981; Hogg and Abrams 1988, 1993). Like rational choice theorists and Smith in the "turn toward culture," Tajfel and those who have come after him have been willing to struggle with the factor of motivation. They have emphasized the tendency for humans to seek to acquire and maintain social identities that contribute to self-esteem ("positive self-evaluation" in rational choice theory). This will be taken up especially in Chapter 7.

In earlier books (1996, 1999, 2002), I made greater reference to diffusion theory and the work of Everett Rogers (1995) than in this book. However, in principle I believe that diffusion theory and theory of the spread of religions dovetail. The emphasis in diffusion theory has been on the diffusion of technology and not of ideologies and religions. One particular point where studies of these two types of diffusion should overlap is in relation to "opinion leaders." I expect future work to bring together results from both kinds of studies.

Most recently, I found the work of Randall Collins (2004) on "interaction ritual chains" very useful. In particular, he opened my eyes to recognize the power of religious symbolism that is used in both informal and formal religious interchange to produce what he calls "emotional energy." Collins shows that emotional energy is produced by many different kinds of ritual interactions. However, I realized in thinking of my own religion and in observing others around the world, that worship, especially, produces much emotional energy and that the desire for emotional energy is a powerful motive in drawing people into religious groups.

There are many other scholars who have contributed to my thinking. I refer to them throughout the text; but, of course, I must take personal responsibility for all the views expressed in the book.

INTRODUCTION B

THEORETICAL FRAMEWORK AND METHODOLOGY

There are many reasons why religions spread. However, in this book I set forth a theoretical outline or framework in order to indicate the various categories or types of reasons for religions to spread. A framework allows for further development within each of the delineated sections or topics. In fact, the framework itself may be given new shape by adding new sections or subsections. For example, toward the end of my study I decided to add the difficult topic of religion and morality taken up in Chapter 2.

Some social scientists give the impression that religions can only be studied as dependent variables or only as phenomena affected by social conditions. A sociologist explicitly told me this when I was in graduate school. Some might substitute *primarily* for *only*. A review of social scientific studies of religions shows that such studies often focus only on how outside social forces affect religions. In fact, it has been a special contribution of the social sciences to demonstrate how religions reflect the societies around them. This is based on the fact that all religions become embedded in societies and cultures so that it is impossible for them not to reflect to a great extent the sociocultural influences surrounding them. A simple illustration is that human language is shared with others, and therefore religious language will be highly influenced by the cultures in which the religions exist. At the same time, languages of introduced religions will affect the languages into which they are translated along with the cultures of those languages. Nevertheless, as religions have spread, they have very clearly taken on characteristics of the societies and cultures to which they spread. These are the types of changes social scientists have primarily investigated, rather than why the religions spread in the first place or how they influenced the societies to which they spread.

In the Preface to the First Edition, I stated that recognizing socio-cultural factors, as both influencing and being influenced by religions should not be a problem for religious people who believe that God works through humans, who clearly are social beings. A theologian might even assert that a sovereign God works in and through all aspects of society, and even further, that the incarnation of God as a human being indicates the willingness of God to enter the flow of human history and be subject to the many limitations and influences of created existence. It was because of this belief that much of my (1991, 1996, 1999, 2002) work to the present has been to examine social conditions that have affected the spread of religions. One of the reasons I emphasized the influence of social conditions on the spread of religion is that I thought these forces had been ignored by many religious people like myself, particularly those directly involved in the spread of religions through missions.

In my 1991 article and 1996 book I gave special attention to intersocietal relations of domination and subordination in the spread of Buddhism, Christianity, and Islam, holding constant internal social conditions in receiving societies. However, in a later study (2002) of the lopsided spread of Christianity (spreading largely westward instead of eastward), I examined a set of factors: (1) missionary motivation; (2)

geographical factors; (3) intersocietal relationships; (4) sociocultural characteristics of receiving societies; and (5) individual perceptions of recipients. I found that religious motives and mission activity itself (factor 1), as necessary as they were, and geographical factors (factor 2) could not account for the failure of Christianity to spread eastward to the same extent that it spread westward. However, I found that the two macro level factors (3 and 4) and the micro level factor (5) all came into play. In particular, I found that the social and religious diversity in the Roman Empire and among the small Asian and European societies provided a more receptive arena for Christianity than the more highly controlled societies to the East (Persia, India, and China.) In both books I showed that the macro level factors of either intersocietal relations (1996) or internal social conditions and intersocietal relations (2002) were linked to micro level factors of individual perceptions and motives in the recipient populations, especially motives related to self-esteem and social identity.

In spite of my previous emphasis in my studies on macro and micro nonreligious social factors in influencing the spread of religions, more recently I came to realize that I needed to expand my consideration to include more of the internal content factors of religions along with external social factors. My own personal religious commitments and my theological interests made me want to look initially at secular social factors in my sociological considerations.

I should have remembered Max Weber, one of the major founders of the social sciences. Recognizing that religions are profoundly affected by their socio-cultural contexts, he was willing to consider religions as more than simply dependent variables in societies. However, his successors in sociology tended not to follow his example in this and in other ways, especially in his attention to history. Weber (1958 [1904]; 1972 [1922]; 1967 [1946]) clearly recognized the two-way interaction of religions with their surrounding societies extending throughout history. Most recently, Stark (2001, 2003) has moved against the stream in sociology by demonstrating the influence of the belief content of religions on numerous historical phenomena, including the spread of religions. Other social scientists, particularly those studying the relationship of religion to politics (cf. Freston 2001; Jelen and Wilcox 2002) are also taking seriously the influence of religious beliefs on societies. Christian Smith (2003b, 2010) has provided a rationale for the underlying importance of belief and morality in all of human behavior, as have other sociologists such as Wuthnow (1987) and Alexander (2003) in taking the "turn toward culture."

In particular, Stark (2001, 2003) shows the powerful impact of monotheism in history. He also shows that many aspects of social change cannot be understood apart from the influence of religion. Such changes as reformations, science, the end of slavery, witch-hunts, and persecutions can be either positive or negative. Religion served as a necessary, though not sufficient, cause for these phenomena. Although a necessary cause is not in itself the same as a sufficient cause for a phenomenon (although it can be), it is a basic requirement without which the phenomenon would not occur. It was Stark's approach that emboldened me to look more carefully at the content of religions for causes influencing their spread. I came to the conclusion that it was because of their content that the three religions—Buddhism, Christianity, and Islam—were prone to spread. Nevertheless, in addition, external social forces continued to be important factors in facilitating or blocking their spread.

Thus the theoretical framework set forth in the book has two basic parts: (1) religious content factors that are necessary for the spread of religions; and (2) secular social factors that can change the course of the spread of religions, though not cause their spread in the first place.

The two parts—religious content and secular social conditions—are in fact interacting. Religious belief, morality, and religious organization are influenced by secular social conditions and vice versa; but the two types of factors can be seen as causes that originate primarily from religions, on the one hand, and from secular social conditions on the other.

On the basis of my previous work and my new attention to religious content factors, I constructed the theoretical framework that forms the outline for the main part of this book or Chapters 1–7. At this point, I will introduce the Two Parts with their Sub-Parts that make up the theoretical framework.

THE TWO PARTS

Part I of the theoretical framework has to do with religious content factors that influenced the spread of religions. These are not theological factors even though there are theological interpretations that can be given to them. They are the empirical or observable aspects of religions, all of which also incorporate the inner aspects of human life found in human thought and emotion. They also all involve human social life. In other words, even though they are religious factors, in this study they are looked at in a secular or nonreligious way.

Part II of the theoretical framework has to do with social factors that are not religious content. I am calling them secular social factors in contrast to the religious content factors. They also have a theological interpretation, but they do not arise directly from religions. Both the religious content factors and the secular social factors are looked at with the secular approach of science.

Since the scientific approach is secular, it makes no reference to God as a cause or as working in the spread of any religion. Nevertheless, if people believe that God does work through human beings and their socio-cultural conditions and also that humans may either work with or against God, then these believers should have no objections to joining the general scientific community in examining the observable or empirical factors affecting the spread of religions. This means that there can be a secular study of religion even though there is no basically secular realm in the view of faith; the methodology can be secular. Theological interpretations may be added later. This is exactly what I have done.

In considering the spread of religions or considering religions in general, observable factors are of two kinds: (1) those that belong to the human side of religions, considered in Part I; and (2) those that belong simply to human life in general apart from religions, but which nevertheless have important influences on and from religions, considered in Part II. As already noted, many social scientists tend not to recognize that religions themselves may be considered as causal forces rather than being simply recipients of influence from outside conditions. This matches the opposite tendency of some religious people to recognize only that God acts directly in religious affairs, ignoring the work of God through humans and secular affairs. Therefore, the theory presented in this book contains consideration of the effect both of religious factors and secular factors (both considered through the secular method of the social sciences). I have named the two parts Religious Content Factors and Secular Social Factors. The former are the factors that may be observed in religions, which are necessary for their spread; and the latter are factors that are discerned in societies at large, which either hinder or facilitate the spread of religions.

THE SEVEN FACTORS

Within each of the Two Parts (Religious Content Factors and Secular

Social Factors), I selected what appeared to me to be key factors, recognizing that these key factors incorporated other factors too many to delineate and investigate for a single volume. My hope is that the factors set forth in the seven chapters will be expanded and supplemented in the future.

Under Part I, religious content influencing the spread of religions, I identified three major factors: (1) beliefs—Chapter 1; (2) moral guidance and energy—Chapter 2; and (3) gathering and organization —Chapter 3. Although these are three distinct aspects of the religious content of the spreading religions, they are closely interconnected. They are also closely connected to surrounding socio-cultural conditions. Some examples of interacting internal religious factors and external sociocultural are conditions: beliefs involve language and other cultural expressions; religious morality incorporates local norms; and religious organizations bring local forms and practices into religions. At the same time, religious beliefs, morality, and organizations also influence social actions and the forming of cultures. In fact, I seek to show that without their internal religious content factors, the three missionary religions examined (Buddhism, Christianity, and Islam) would not have spread and contributed to the forming of distinct cultures. The same three religious content factors are not as strongly represented or represented differently in those religions that did not spread as widely.

Regarding Part II, while religious content factors are necessary for the spread of religions, secular social causes have an additional important impact on spreading religions, as I have shown in previous research. They are more varied and therefore occupy a larger part or more sections of the theoretical framework and of the book. Under secular social factors influencing the spread of religions, I identified four factors. These four factors are divided between those on the macro or large-scale level (Part II A) and those on the micro or individual level

(Part II B). The levels are clearly interrelated and the individual must be seen in the context of the social, but it is useful to approach these influences from above and below, so to speak. The two levels, macro and micro, are actually interacting; and it is almost impossible to refer to one without implicating connections to the other. Researchers can also distinguish a middle or meso level. In many respects, the religious content factors of the first three chapters are on the meso social level. This is because the beliefs, morality, and organizations of religions are shared by groups that occupy a position between societal (macro) and individual (micro) levels. The religious content or meso level factors, then, are covered in the first three chapters, which belong to Part I.

The secular social factors of Part II A and B affecting the spread of religions are dealt with in four chapters. The macro level of social factors is divided between internal social conditions in receiving societies (Chapter 4) and intersocietal relationships between receiving and sending societies and between receiving and other, usually nearby, societies (Chapter 5). The micro level is divided between individual social relations (Chapter 6) and individual motivations based on perceptions (Chapter 7).

Religious content factors and secular social factors, with their respective sub-parts, provide an outline or a framework that can be expanded and elaborated. In this sense, this outline awaits critical evaluation both in social scientific and religious studies. The latter includes studies of religions and missiology. To facilitate such evaluation, I have developed a series of theoretical propositions for the framework. The analysis in each of the seven types of factors actually includes a number of additional theoretical statements, but the propositions seek to provide at least the main thrust of the argument. I will state these propositions below.

One of the disadvantages of looking in turn at multiple factors that caused the three religions to spread widely is that there is a certain amount of repetition as each religion is taken up in each chapter. I seek to avoid repetition by emphasizing different aspects of each religion in succeeding chapters and different conditions affecting each religion, but some repetition seems unavoidable, for which I ask indulgence.

THEORETICAL PROPOSITIONS

To demonstrate the theoretical potential of the framework, I make propositions to reflect the major points in each section of the framework that is presented in each chapter. I will list these propositions below, but they are also placed in each of the succeeding chapters. By making these propositions, I hope to encourage at least two advancements in the study of the spread of religions: (1) attention to theory construction as opposed to endless descriptive studies; and (2) attention to the variety of religious and social factors that influence the spread of religions. Of course, specific propositions also give better targets for criticism and refutation or elaboration, which is all to the good. Such propositions have been useful for providing criticism or elaboration in recent writings in the sociology of religion (e.g. Stark and Bainbridge 1996 [1987]; Stark and Finke 2000), even though most of the propositions in these books do not deal directly with the spread of religions.

PART I
RELIGIOUS CONTENT FACTORS

1. Beliefs (Chapter 1)

1.1 *The three widely spreading religions build on the source of the widespread influence of popular religion, which is its immanent, accessible, and tangible means of contact with transcendent sources of power for help in* *coping with the difficulties of life.*

1.2 *The most powerful religious belief factor affecting the spread of religions is the presentation of a single human figure who becomes a means of access to the divine and to salvation through the offer of compassion.*

2. Moral Guidance and Moral Energy (Chapter 2)

2.1 *To spread widely, religions must offer moral guidance and moral energy.*

2.2 *To spread widely, religions must offer salvation equally to all individuals thus emphasizing egalitarianism.*

2.3 *To spread widely, religions must emphasize compassion for all people.*

3. Gathering and Organization Factors (Chapter 3)

3.1 *Religions with voluntary organizations to which people make personal commitments are necessary for religions to spread, while religions with involuntary and/ or transient followers will not ordinarily spread.*

3.2 *Religions are able to spread widely because they organize open gatherings in which people can interact around important symbols of the divine that provide solidarity and emotional energy for life.*

3.3 *Religions spread only when there are carriers to take the religions to new people in new areas.*

PART II A
MACRO SECULAR SOCIAL FACTORS

4. Social Conditions in Receiving Societies (Chapter 4)

4.1 *In order for a religion to spread successfully, people in a receiving society must have the opportunity to choose* *to be identified with a new religion.*

4.2 *Religions spread more easily to relatively small preliterate societies without official religions than to large complex societies with established literate religions that have strong links to governments.*

4.3 *New religions may spread in large societies where a particular religion has not yet been made monopolistic, and thus where there is relative religious diversity.*

4.4 *The spread of new religions can be greatly accelerated or blocked by governmental power, depending on whether governments seek or approve of a new religion or already have an established alliance with a religion.*

4.5 *The association of religions with coercive power leads to covert and overt resistance from within and outside of religions.*

5. Intersocietal Relationships (Chapter 5)

5.1 *Domination or threat from a sending society of a religion toward a receiving society creates resistance to the spreading religion, which may result in rejection or, if pressure is extreme, acceptance with significant change of the spreading religion.*

5.2 *When there is no domination or threat from a sending society, but rather from another nearby society (or societies), then a receiving society may be receptive to the spreading religion, particularly if the new religion is an aid in resisting other dominating or threatening societies.*

PART II B
MICRO SECULAR SOCIAL FACTORS

6. Social Relationships (Chapter 6)

6.1 *Social relationships can facilitate or block the spread of religions depending on the influence of those who are known and trusted and provide important emotional and material support.*

6.2 *When social relationships have been disrupted, a new religion may spread by facilitating the establishment of new relationships or a new religion may be resisted by the strengthening of former relationships.*

6.3 *Spreading religions have a universal appeal that leads to the establishment of global social networks that both aid and are aided by globalization.*

7. Motivations (Chapter 7)

7.1 *People will be receptive to or resist a new religion according to whether they perceive that it enhances or detracts from an aspect of their social identities which they value.*

7.2 *People will receive or resist a new religion according to whether they perceive that it heightens their emotional energy through ritual interactions.*

ADDITIONAL APPLICATION OF THE ANALYSIS

In addition to the Chapters 1–7 belonging to Parts I and II A and B, I apply the analysis using the seven factors to three areas in Chapters 8, 9, and 10 titled The Spread of Irreligion, Looking Forward, and Implications for Missiology.

Regarding the spread of irreligion (Chapter 8), I apply the seven factors to understand how this modern phenomenon has taken place. Nonbelief in any superempirical or supernatural being has probably existed for millennia, but in the last three centuries it has taken on movement (or multiple movement characteristics) that has helped to bring out its ideological or quasi-religious characteristics. The irreligion movement has taken many forms, so it is more accurate to speak of it as existing in a number of movements—some more radical than others. This is also analogous to the many versions of the three religions. The most radical movements have been those that have attempted to impose irreligion on populations, as in Communism, just as some have sought to impose religions on whole societies. These movements originated in Western Europe in a Christian context, where Christianity had been very authoritarian, but the irreligion movements have spread around the world.

I wrote Chapter 9 because I felt that it was important to seek to make some predictions based on the analysis. However, world social conditions have been changing rapidly; and so I considered these changing conditions first but also included the important continuing religious content influences.

In the last chapter, Chapter 10, I placed the discussion of Implications for Missiology that had been the Appendix in the First Edition. My purpose in the research of this book was to develop theory that would stand under social scientific examination, and therefore I wanted to separate clearly theological and missiological considerations from the analysis. Nevertheless, missiological considerations are never far from my heart as made plain in the Preface to the First Edition. I regard Chapter 10, therefore, as the book's climax.

A theological and missiological understanding, of course, comes to the issue of the spread of religions from the perspective of revelation (actually the interpretation of revelation). My perspective reflects my particular background and training in Reformed Protestant Theology, which continues the Biblical tradition of viewing God as working in the world through both religion and the secular social world—in short, in all things. Furthermore, I believe that religious scholars who work in the inclusive or comprehensive perspective of theology (whatever their faith or tradition), have the responsibility of incorporating valid scientific theory within their theological understandings or at least of wrestling with the results of social scientific work. Chapter 10 presents my "wrestling" as an example, which can be debated and elaborated.

METHODOLOGY

The spread of religions has taken place primarily over the last two thousand years, and so my analysis with the theoretical propositions set forth in Introduction B employs historical data from this period. My basic methodology is to use comparison of historical cases in which as much as possible the experimental method is simulated. That means making cases similar, as in experimental and control groups, except for an independent variable, which is then related to subsequent differences in the dependent variable. I have already identified the spread of the three religions as the dependent variable. There is a great deal of variation within and among them. The two parts with a total of seven factors of the theoretical framework contain the independent variables or the causes for the spread of religions.

Historical data cannot be controlled and manipulated in the same way as current data; but historical sociology has and will continue to simulate the experimental method of isolating distinct independent variables, then comparing how effects vary on the dependent variable. In experimental studies this can be done through "holding constant" or "controlling" (making the same) certain causes so that varying effects of single varying causes can be compared. For example, one may control for age and gender (consider only people of similar ages and gender) so that only the varying effects of ethnicity might be considered. At the same time, one may control for ethnicity and gender in order to look at the varying effects of age, and control for ethnicity and age to look at the varying effects of gender, and so forth. Such clarity in the use of controls is usually not possible in historical studies, but the principle of the methodology is useful in any study.

In the social sciences, theory at its basic level means statements of cause-and-effect relationships between independent and dependent variables that can be tested or at least observed empirically. Some scholars, usually not social scientific ones, object to the use of the term *variable* in historical studies with its implication of distinguishing causes and effects in solely one-way relationships, which rarely occur in history. It is true that in historical studies, circular or tautological thinking is always a danger in which cause and effect are basically not distinguishable. However, I prefer to use the term *variable* and also to speak of cause and effect in order to emphasize that there can be predominant directions of influence, and to make it easier for others to disconfirm or elaborate my conclusions.

Therefore, I state that the spread or diffusion of religions is my basic dependent variable and both internal religious content and external secular or nonreligious social conditions provide independent variables. I recognize that there are two-way causative relationships between the diffusion of religions and various religious and social conditions making it often difficult to establish primarily one-directional cause-and-effect relationships. I will try to bring two-way relationships into my analysis where appropriate. However, the lack of clarity in the direction of causes can be remedied by including time sequences in analysis. Basically, I understand that changes act upon each other in something of a spiraling effect over time. Thus, each stage in the diffusion process acts upon most of the later stages. Nevertheless, in the end, I believe there can be primary, if not single, directions of influence in historical cause-effect relationships.

In discussing the work of Weber, Talcott Parsons (1964:xxi) offers the following enlightening statement regarding the uncovering of causes in history:

> In the case of the relation between Protestantism and capitalizm, the study of the operation of religious ideas led to questions of historical interpretation. But Weber early became acutely aware, as many participants in the discussion still are not, that the problem of causation involved an analytical problem, one of the isolation of variables and the testing of their significance in situations where they could be shown to vary independently of each other. The purely "historical" method, seeking ever more detailed knowledge of the "ideal" and "material" historical antecedents of modern economic organization, is inherently circular. It was only by establishing *a methodological equivalent of experimental method* [italics mine], in which it is possible to hold certain factors constant, that even the beginnings of an escape from circularity was possible.

This explains why I am not satisfied simply with description of the spread of religions and the piling up of lists of causes. Weber used his sociological historical comparative method to look for the relationship between religious orientations and social structures, particularly economic social structures. I will be trying to use the same method, but naturally on a much smaller scale, to look for the relationships of both the contents of religions and social conditions on the one hand (the independent variables) with the particular phenomenon of the spread of religions on the other (the dependent variable).

Regarding my examination of religious content causes for the spread of religions, since I am trained in theology as well as the social sciences, it is important to state that in a social scientific study, religious content causes have to be considered in their empirical (sociological) aspects, not in aspects unavailable to observation. As a matter of fact, religious belief statements can be observed even if their inner source is not available for observation. Beliefs about God and other superempirical realities are not available for scientific examination as to their truth; but the affirmations of such beliefs are certainly observable, as are the effects of these affirmations. Thus the belief contents of different religions can be compared empirically, and comparisons can then be made in variations in subsequent phenomenon that appear to be related to differences in beliefs.

If religious belief statements can be compared (Chapter 1), then even more, religious moralities and organizations are subject to comparative observation (Chapters 2 and 3). It is essential that all of these observations and comparisons are available to anyone to examine, regardless of their religious faith. The outside socio-cultural forces (Chapters 4 through 7) that surround and penetrate religions and affect their spread have been the primary area of examination for the social sciences; and they are certainly subject to observation, albeit with the sometimes enormous difficulties of sorting out cause and effect in historical data.

PART I

RELIGIOUS CONTENT FACTORS

CHAPTER 1

BELIEFS AND THE SPREAD OF RELIGIONS

POPULAR AND ELITE RELIGIONS

Before considering the distinctive beliefs of the three widely spreading religions, I note an important clue to their success provided by the phenomenon of popular religion that is in contrast to elite religion. Actually, popular religion has its roots in earlier primal religion, prevalent among all peoples; It is elite religion that later became typical of ruling groups. Elite religion actually incorporated much of popular religion while adding elements (discussed below) to support the rule of the elite. Both types of religion are characterized by the desire for contact with the transcendent or supernatural, but popular religion in particular seeks immediate contact with the Divine to cope with life that is often mired in misery and full of uncertainties. To account for the characteristic of popular religion that is found in the three widely spreading religions, I make the Proposition:

> 1.1 *The three widely spreading religions build on the source of the widespread influence of popular religion, which is its immanent, accessible, and tangible means of contact with transcendent sources of power for help in coping with the difficulties of life.*

All of the world religions, including the three that spread most widely, have incorporated and expressed varieties of popular religion. Popular religion is apparent in tribal religions, but particularly in traditional and hierarchical societies that distinguish clearly between elite and popular statuses and in which there is a large under class. Sharot (2001:4, 36) uses the elite-popular religion distinction in his analysis of world religions. Elite religion defines the current order of nature and society as being anchored in the transcendent cosmos because in this way elites are aided in the maintenance of order and continuity in their rule. Arend Th. van Leeuwen (1964:165) defined this type of rule as an "ontocracy." In an ontocracy rulers are seen as being at the apex of a pyramid like structure and as having a direct connection to the cosmos. Orthodox doctrine, continuity, overall harmony, and official organization are typical elite religion concerns. Secular knowledge and skills are developed and used by the elite to preserve knowledge through literature and to display impressive religious rituals and monuments.

In contrast to elite religion, popular religion arises from the life of uncertainty and misery of the people at large. It therefore has the thaumaturgical goal of finding relief from suffering and misfortune and the fulfillment of practical needs for healing, but also for having children, crops, and all that contributes to survival and good fortune. Popular religion also incorporates family and clan rituals and community rites and festivals to obtain divine approval. At the same time, in contrast to the secular tendencies of elite religion, popular religion is very drawn to the search for and expression of spiritual power, partly because the people at large lack secular power and have limited resources to deal with life's problems. Festivals also express social solidarity and provide some relief from lives of toil and suffering and even a certain resistance to those who control their lives most of the time. Elites usually tolerate, foster, and even participate in popular religion partly in order to maintain social unity and order. This is behind the view of Karl Marx that religion is the opium of the people.

A particularly important feature of popular religion, as well as culture, is its attraction to outstanding persons, who may be either mythical or historical persons who are elevated to mythical stature. This characteristic of popular culture continues to the present. In their interesting and example-filled study of modern American heroes, Scott Allison and George Goethals (2011) show that heroes fill an important role in the life of their admirers. Allison and Goethals (2011: 161) develop a set of eight traits characterizing heroes and villains: Heroes are smart, resilient, strong, selfless, charismatic, caring, reliable, and inspiring, while villains, in addition to sharing the first two traits with heroes, are violent, greedy, mentally ill, immoral, egotistical, and vengeful. In the end, heroes and villains provide standards against which to measure the human moral quest. Thus, in their conclusion Allison and Goethals (2011: 207) state, "Most of us make bad moral choices as well as good ones. We need all the help we can get to act effectively and morally. Heroes blaze the trail toward competence and morality, and villains remind us of the dark side." This study of modern heroes is highly consistent with Christian Smith's (2010) understanding of the quest of persons for morality that includes personal dignity. Morality will be considered in the next chapter, but for our purposes here, it is important to note that popular religion in its search for supernatural help is particularly characterized by its search for contact with supernatural beings. Furthermore, these beings are typically envisioned in immanent and tangible form.

The pervasiveness of various forms of popular religion throughout the world indicates the strong human desire for direct contact with the divine and associated supernatural power. We shall return to the subject of popular and elite religion later as they are expressed in various religions. The point made here is that the historic existence of pervasive popular religion enables us to understand the power and attraction of the distinctive beliefs, to be discussed below, of the three widely spreading religions.

BEYOND MONOTHEISM

Stark (2001:31-113) shows the relationship of beliefs to the spread of religions. In particular he shows that monotheistic religions attempt to spread through efforts to convert nonbelievers. However, there are two major problems with the theory of the need for a religion to be monotheistic in order to spread widely. One has to do with the Asian religions of Hinduism and Buddhism and the other with Judaism.

Stark (2001:108) wrestles with the case of Hinduism. It has theistic beliefs, which at least approximate monotheism. At the same time it also presents numerous intermediaries to the Divine, not a single or even a primary intermediary. The Divinities with which most people have contacts are known as "avatars" or incarnations of the Divine. Elite Hinduism contains sophisticated philosophy, but Hinduism also expresses popular religion on a large and varied scale.

Hinduism spread throughout South Asia and to parts of Southeast Asia, and today has spread to the West, but it was eventually eclipsed by Buddhism outside of India, except for Nepal and parts of Indonesia. Today over 90 percent of Hindus live in South Asia. On the other hand, Buddhism, although "officially" nontheistic, spread to a much wider variety of societies than Hinduism in Southeast Asia, Central Asia, and East Asia. Buddhism also attracts more people in the West than Hinduism. Stark (2001:46, 47) solves this problem of the spread of the originally nontheistic Buddhism by pointing out that Buddhism became very religious or theistic as it spread. It approved and even provided for the worship of many gods, but especially for the worship of Buddha himself. This seems to solve the problem of why Buddhism spread, but not the fact that it spread much more widely than philosophically theistic Hinduism or any other Asian religion.

Buddhism shares many characteristics with Hinduism and other religions of Asia in that it has incorporated, or its followers have simultaneously practiced, other religions, especially popular religions. However, Buddhism, unlike Hinduism or any other Asian religion, offered (offers) a single major figure through whom individuals can obtain eternal salvation. Hinduism has no single founder or single savior figure. Unlike Hinduism, Jainism, Taoism, Confucianism, and Sikhism all had founders, but none are elevated to a position of a savior offering salvation universally to humanity as Buddha was elevated and as Buddha offers. Thus Buddhism is distinct from the other Asian religions in offering a single dominant figure to which to pray for salvation. The variety of individual gods offered in the popular religions of Hinduism and Taoism, as well as in popular Buddhism, could not rise to the level of the transcendent Buddha as a savior. Regarding Theravada Buddhism, in which official or monkish Buddhism is among the least theistic of all Buddhisms, Sharot (2001:154) states:

> Anthropologists appear to be in general agreement that the Buddha, gods, and spirits are all part of what Buddhists perceive as a single cosmological system... All are agreed that Buddhists conceptualize the Buddha and his teaching as superior to the spirits... Whereas Hindus have incorporated folk practices in a syncretistic fashion, Buddhists have incorporated them in stressing their separate and inferior status.

He goes on to note that there still may be a blurring in practice between "the higher level of the pantheon/cosmology and the thaumaturgical orientation [practical help and healing] of the lower levels," which helps to account for similarities between Buddhism and Hinduism, as well as with other Asian religions, particularly Taoism. However, even in popular Theravada Buddhism, Buddha remains the dominant mediator of salvation.

Melford Spiro (1982 [1970]:33), who focused on Burmese Theravada Buddhism, states:

> Although a human being, the Buddha was far from an ordinary mortal. He not only attained nirvana–an extraordinary achievement in itself–but (something which is even more unusual) achieved Buddhahood... He is a saint, supremely enlightened, proficient in knowledge and conduct, one who fares well (to ultimate Deliverance), world-knower, peerless driver of men to be tamed, teacher of the gods and of men, enlightened, the Blessed One.

It seems merely a technicality not to apply the term *Savior* to the Buddha since in popular Theravada Buddhism people pray to him. Spiro (1982 [1970]:33) adds in a note, "Although agreeing that He is not a Savior, only some Burmese agree, as we shall see, that He is not alive."

What is true of popular Theravada Buddhism in elevating Buddha is even truer of Mahayana Buddhism. The dissident group (the Mahasanghika) responsible for initiating Mahayana Buddhism elevated Buddha to a particularly high position. Kenneth Ch'en (1973 [1964]:12n) states "its main contribution to Buddhist doctrine was its concept of a transcendental Buddha who is omnipresent and omnipotent, who manifests himself in an earthly form to conform to the needs of man."

However, just as in Theravada Buddhism, the elevation of Buddha to a transcendent level prepared the way for the creation of intermediaries in popular religion. Mahayana Buddhism developed intermediaries known as bodhisattvas who delay their entrance into nirvana in order to help others reach salvation, one of the most famous being Guanyin or the Goddess of Mercy in the Far East. Nevertheless, Buddha remained as the central cosmic figure. His cosmic significance and influence is made especially strong in Mahayana Buddhism. In the end, no other religion except Buddhism was able to spread from India to the Far East and none of the other Far Eastern religions were able to spread westward to Central and South Asia or even to Southeast Asia except Buddhism, with the exception of Confucianism spreading to Vietnam. Confucianism also spread to Korea, and to Japan as a background philosophy.

Regarding the success of Buddhism being due to the special figure of Buddha, John Noss is very clear. He (1949:172) notes first that in its original form Buddhism did not find a response among the masses, but then adds:

> But the masses became interested. Not in the teaching, but the man. Original Buddhism would not have had so great an effect on the history of religion in the Orient, if the coldly rational philosophy of the sage of the Sakyas had not been mediated through a personality that could be adored. Fortunately for the future of Buddhism, its founder balanced the arahat [saint] ideal of self-salvation with the ideal of compassionate goodwill toward all living beings, and practiced that compassion himself. Thus there grew up after him a cult that took refuge in him, the compassionate as well as enlightened one, even more than it did in his teaching, so difficult to understand and practice.

Scholars, such as William Herbrechtsmeier (1993), have argued on the basis of nontheistic Buddhism that religion does not need to deal with the supernatural, and that human powers are understood differently in Asia than in the West. For example, in Asian cultures humans are believed to be able to do wondrous things that would be considered superhuman in the West. However, my argument is not that religion is necessarily theistic. Stark (2001:9,10) also recognizes nontheistic religion. Rather, my argument is that Buddhism spread widely, not only because it was religious in terms of encouraging belief in and prayer to many beings, elevated or spiritual humans, but that Buddha himself (or "[h]is transcendent spirit...thought to exist in his teachings, or dharma") provides the way to salvation that extends beyond this life (Herbrechtsmeier 1993:11). The earlier argument used by Marco Orru and Amy Wang (1992:58) against Durkheim's view of Buddhism and religious phenomena in general (as based primarily in the distinction between the sacred and the profane), I take as valid for explaining the spread of Buddhism: "Plainly, Buddha is central to Buddhism as an observed religious phenomenon; neither the four noble truths, nor the Dharma, nor the Samgha, nor the Unconditioned would have any meaning without the Buddha. We believe the evidence provided from Buddhism warrants such a claim."

Hinduism has an equally sophisticated philosophical content as Buddhism, but it does not have a single savior figure like Buddha. Stark (2001:108) notes that Hinduism is basically monotheistic, not polytheistic, because of its belief in a high God. However, in the end, Hindus have chosen "lesser" deities and incarnations (avatars) to worship. There is clearly not a single dominant "elevated" human mediator to worship, as in Buddhism, which spread much more widely. Nevertheless, it is Judaism more than any Asian religion that demonstrates most clearly that something beyond monotheism is needed for religions to break out of ethnic attachment and spread widely.

Judaism is much more clearly monotheistic than Hinduism, as much as or more than Christianity and Islam, which are partly derived from it. Stark (2001:52-59) shows that Judaism has an ability to spread by propagation, which took place especially in the Roman Empire in the early centuries of the first millennium C.E. However, Judaism has not generally shown the ability or desire over the centuries to spread by propagation, but has maintained a close attachment to Jewish ethnic identity. During this time Judaism has come under varying degrees of pressure with persecution. There is the special case of the conversion of the Turkish Khazars north of the Black Sea to Judaism (Koestler 1976), but such occurrences appear to have been rare.

In relation to the success of Christianity and Islam in spreading, Stark (2001) argues that monotheism has had a powerful effect in world history, and that monotheism is a key factor in enabling religions to break out of identification with particular ethnic and national groups, even though such identification continuously takes place. However, as already noted, monotheism alone has not been sufficient to create successful continuing diffusion, especially wide diffusion to multiple societies, such as attained by Buddhism, Christianity, and Islam. An additional factor, therefore, appears to be necessary. Given the outstanding ability of the three religions to spread, and the relative lack of diffusion through conversion by Hinduism, Judaism, and any other religion simply affirming monotheism, such as Zoroastrianism or Sikhism, I make this unusual, but most important, proposition:

> *1.2 The most powerful religious belief factor affecting the spread of religions is the presentation of a single human figure who becomes a means of access to the divine and to salvation through the offer of compassion.*

Buddha, Jesus Christ, and Muhammad are all human figures, but in one way or another they offer an immanent means of access to God. Very importantly they each have biographies that enable them to be envisioned. In spite of official Buddhist views to the contrary, Buddha has essentially come to be regarded as Divine, at least in popular Theravada Buddhism and certainly in Mahayana Buddhism. Christianity, of course, offers a clearly specified Divine-human savior, Jesus Christ, who also specifically mandated that his message of salvation be taken to the whole world. However, both Buddha and Jesus Christ shared human nature with other humans. This is made part of the redemptive power of Jesus Christ (Hebrews 5:7-10).

The theory that the spread of a religion is due to the elevation of a human figure to a position of becoming a means of access to God and salvation can be used to analyze differences in diffusion within Christianity, in which there are numerous variations in beliefs and practices. One variation is in the emphasis placed on belief in God's purpose to redeem humanity through Christ and the missionary mandate based upon this purpose, as Stark (2001:98-102) points out. This could be called a variation in the level of lifting up of the Savior figure. A result of this variation is the extensive spread of "evangelical Christianity," which emphasizes salvation through Christ, and the relative lack of diffusion of "liberal" Christianity, which rejects or reduces the unique claims regarding Christ. In addition, state Christianity, with its emphasis on formal and nominal Christianity, has also failed to spread as extensively as "evangelical Christianity," except by conquest and immigration. Additional religious factors related to the elevation of a single human figure will be considered in the next two chapters.

The greatest question regarding the elevated status of the central human figure could be raised about Muhammad, since he is seen specifically as not being Divine. However, people began to make the figure of Muhammad central to their faith soon after his death, even though many of the Arab tribes were not immediately interested in doing so. Karen Armstrong (2000:26) states:

> It was probably during the riddah wars [wars to subdue the Arab tribes to the east soon after Muhammad's death] that Muslims began to assert that Muhammad had been the last and greatest of the prophets, a claim that is not made explicitly in the Quran, as Muslims countered the challenge of these riddah prophets [prophets who were producing their own Quranic-style "revelations."]

Another and later process, which tended to emphasize the importance of Muhammad, is described by Albert Hourani (1991:70):

> Those engaged in the great controversies about where authority should lie, or about the nature of God and the Qur'an, tried to find support for their views in the life and sayings of Muhammad. Thus, during the second and third Islamic centuries (roughly the eighth and ninth centuries AD) the body of sayings attributed to the Prophet expanded.

Bernard Lewis (1994 [1993]:92) summarizes the exaltation of Muhammad:

> Thus arose the cult of personal veneration–which Muhammad himself had explicitly rejected–making him an exemplar of ethical and religious virtues, the best and noblest of mankind. To meet and outdo the miracles of Jesus and Moses, Muhammad, who had explicitly disclaimed any superhuman powers

or attributes, was made the protagonist of a cycle of wonders and marvels stretching back to his early childhood and even to before his birth.

Ernst (2003:78-84) writes of the "unique spiritual position" of Muhammad in Islam in which he is given a cosmic role that includes different emphases with different people. Among some there is an emphasis on grace and for others it is authority. A fifteenth-century Persian philosopher and prime minister "appreciated both the transcendental position of the Prophet, as recipient of divine light, and the necessity for him to be a normal man." Ernst (2003:84) summarizes:

> The history of Muslim views of Muhammad until fairly recently has been dominated by an emphasis on his cosmic role as the main intercessor for humanity. Mystical concepts of Muhammad portrayed him not only as an ethical guide but also as the pre-eternal light from which God created the world. The main shift in the past century has been, in part, a response to the stridently negative depictions of the Prophet created by European authors, though it also reflects the growth of bourgeois scientific rationalism in Muslim countries. No longer is the Prophet a mystical presence or a semi mythical figure wielding apocalyptic powers; now he is viewed as a social and political reformer who coolly dealt with corrupt pagan opponents as he set up a society that would stand as the model for human perfection on earth.

However, regarding those who have been the most active as missionaries over the centuries, the Sufis, Ernst (2003:167) states, "Sufis came to view Muhammad as the being in light whose creation preceded the creation of the universe. His mission was universal, and in his compassion he alone of all prophets would intercede on behalf of all humanity."

John Esposito (2010:43) writes of the past and contemporary Muslim regard for Muhammad:

> In his lifetime, throughout Muslim history, and today, the Prophet Muhammad is seen as the "living Quran," the embodiment of God's will in his behavior and words. Sunni Muslims (85 percent of the world's Muslims) take their name from sunnah, meaning those who follow the example of the Prophet. Muslim veneration of Muhammad explains why so many Muslims have been given the name Muhammad or names derived from it (Ahmad, Mahmud, and Amin).

Understanding Muhammad's special role and status helps us appreciate the widespread frustration, sense of humiliation, and anger of many mainstream Muslims, not just extremists, at the denigration of Muhammad and Islam.

I will note that Christians generally have not given the name of Jesus to their children, except for those in Hispanic culture, who were perhaps influenced by the practice of Muslims to name their children after Muhammad. The point here is the centrality of Muhammad in Islam, parallel to the centrality of Jesus in Christianity.

As the "seal" of all the prophets that had gone before, Muhammad is considered the last and greatest of all the prophets. In the first of the "five pillars," "the shahadah," Muhammad is always associated with Allah as his prophet and special wali (friend of God). Lamin Sanneh (1996:45) explains in detail the nature of the centrality of Muhammad in Islam and states specifically about the shahadah:

> Thus in the great shahadah, the monotheist witness of the faithful, the name of the Prophet is joined to that of God, and Muhammad becomes the gateway to obtaining God's approval. Muslims might forgive anyone for taking the name of God lightly, but not so the name of Muhammad. We evade the Muslim sense of religious truth if we avoid the figure of the Prophet in the theological insistence that it is God alone who matters. Muhammad is the believer's guarantee that God has acted, justifying the call to witness, worship, devotion, and faithfulness, Muhammad's witness is God's ultimatum, is God's witness, the particular, historical form God has ordained for the divine message to be transmitted and received, God as see-through infinity is indistinguishable from self-enthronement, in effect, for exclusive human agency. A community that adopts a God without prophetic counsel must end up with religion as group self-worship and others as alien adjuncts.

It is important that the Qur'an (Koran) is believed to have been directly dictated to Muhammad and to be exactly identical to the heavenly original that is in the heavenly language. Through the Qur'an, Muhammad becomes the most important human guide to the Divine. Sufis added the perspective that they could cultivate the state of mind or spirit of Muhammad, his interior islam, that enabled him to receive the revelation of the Qur'an. Thus Muhammad was the key to finding the unity with God sought by the Sufis (Armstrong 2000:74). It is significant that many Sufis became active in missionary work. In his study of central Asia, T. Jeremy Gunn (2003:397) states, "Sufis have had an important influence not only on the practice of Islam, but also on its initial propagation." Peter van der Veer (1994:34) points to the importance of Sufism in missionary work, "The expansion of Sufi brotherhoods was a crucial aspect of the Islamization of South Asia, since Sufism was largely coextensive with Islam until the nineteenth century." Ira Lapidus (2005 [1988]:361-64, 383) also notes the importance of Sufis in the spread of Islam in South and Southeast Asia.

Thus, paradoxically, what appears to be most significant in enabling a religion to rise above ethnic and local cultural features and to spread to new groups is the lifting up of a single human figure to a position of special significance. Perhaps this similarity between Buddhism, Christianity, and Islam (and their contrast with other religions) has not been noted by many observers and religious scholars because they give major attention to the details of religions and the many differences among them. In many ways, Buddhism has greater similarity to other Asian religions than to Christianity and Islam. Furthermore, Christianity and Islam have greater similarity to Judaism and to each other than to Asian religions. Perhaps also the special religious significance given to a human does not draw the attention of people studying religions. However, belief in the ability of a particular human being to be a means of access to the transcendent Deity and to salvation turns out to be a key factor, even a necessary factor, for a religion to spread. All three of the widely spreading religions lift up a distinct human figure for people to follow, a figure who is human, but who provides in some way a means of salvation to the individual. Of course, there are great differences between the three figures and the salvation they offer. The similarity of the three religions in regard to presenting a human figure and salvation does not mean that they form a category of religions in other regards.

Even though Weber (1967 [1946]:292) used contrasting types of religious figures and actions to compare religions, for example, "exemplary prophecy" and "emissary" or "ethical prophecy," he also warned against any easy categorizing of religions when he said:

> In no respect can one simply integrate various world religions into a chain of types, each of them signifying a new 'stage.' All the great religions are historical individualities of a highly complex nature; taken all together, they exhaust only a few of the possible combinations that could conceivably be formed from the very numerous individual factors to be considered in such historical combinations.

Such a statement gives grounds, at least, to consider that Buddhism, which has more in common with Hinduism and other Asian religions than with Christianity and Islam, and Christianity and Islam, which have more in common with Judaism than with Asian religions, might at least have a common characteristic that makes them prone to spread. The theoretical view of this chapter is that this common characteristic is the belief in a single human figure who is able to give people access to God and salvation.

OTHER RELIGIONS AND THE THREE RELIGIONS

So far we have compared the three widely spreading religions to the two mother religions, Hinduism and Judaism, in regard to whether they recognized a single special human as a means of access to God and salvation. However, there are other religions that should be considered primarily because they had single founders or central figures more clearly than Hinduism and Judaism. Other religions, particularly Confucianism, Taoism, Jainism, Zoroastrianism, and Manichaeism all have single founders. Although each case is different, in none of these religions is the founder given the status of Buddha, Jesus, or Muhammad. Confucius was a sage and teacher, not a prophet and certainly not a mediator to the divine or a bringer of salvation. His teachings did become important, not only in China, but also in Korea, Japan, and Vietnam, helping to form the "cultural area" of the Far East, but that was the extent of the spread of Confucianism. To this day it is a matter of debate whether Confucianism is even a religion.

Lao Zi, the probable founder of Taoism, is classified by Weber (1972 [1922]:55) as manifesting "exemplary" prophecy along with Buddha, in contrast to "ethical" prophecy expressed primarily in the Middle East. The "exemplary" prophets did not bring a message from a transcendent personal God who required obedience as the "ethical" prophets did, but rather gave teachings about ultimate reality to give people wisdom for living. Lao Zi was regarded primarily as a sage philosopher who taught about the impersonal Tao. When Buddhism came to China, Buddhism and Taoism were often rivals, but at the same time there were attempts to combine them and they were sometimes confused in the perceptions of people. When the followers of Taoist philosophy saw the way in which Buddhism spread, they followed the Buddhist example and elevated Lao Zi and gave him heavenly associates. This could also be seen as a propensity of popular religion. Furthermore, there were numerous other gods already present in Taoism. Although Lao Zi was (is) worshipped, he never gained the significance of Buddha as providing a means of salvation to all people.

Jainism is thought to have been founded by Nataputta Vardhamana, who was given the title, Mahavira, meaning "Great Man" or "Hero" (Noss 1949:131). Jainism and Buddhism developed in the same time period beginning in the fifth century BCE as sectarian movements in a period when nonbrahmins (ksatriyas or warriors and vaisyas or merchants and landowners) were reacting against dominant brahminism. Weber (1967 [1946]:120) explains, "We must at this point establish as a fact of fundamental importance that all the great religious doctrines of Asia are creations of intellectuals. The salvation doctrines of Buddhism and Jainism, as well as all related doctrines, were carried by an intellectual elite that had undergone training in the Vedas." Mahavira and Buddha were leaders of intellectuals who withdrew from politics, a situation that favors the development of salvation religions. In such a situation they "consider their intellectual training in its ultimate intellectual and psychological consequences far more important than their practical participation in the external affairs of the mundane world" (Weber 1967 [1946]:122). Weber goes on to say:

> Confucianism, the ethic of a powerful officialdom, rejected all doctrines of salvation. On the other hand, Jainism and Buddhism, which provide radical antitheses to Confucianist accommodation to the world, were tangible expressions of an intellectualist attitude that was utterly anti-political, pacifistic, and world-rejecting.

Mahavira and Buddha both represent "exemplary" prophecy. While Mahavira was believed to be a savior who descended from heaven to enter the womb of a woman and who was sinless and omniscient, as time passed his status was reduced or at least obscured by veneration of the savior beings (Tirthankaras) that preceded him (Noss 1949:141). Jainism, with its emphasis on asceticism or world renunciation and its philosophy of fallible human thought, has had a great influence on Indian culture, including on Mahatma Gandhi. According to my theory of the elevated human savior as influencing the spread of religions, Jainism could possibly have spread like Buddhism. However, over the period of time that Buddha was elevated to be a savior, Mahavira was not. The major difference seems to be that the salvation offered through Jainism was restricted to those who could follow ahimsa by breaking off every attachment to the world and its objects. Although also world renouncing, Buddhism's "middle way" made it possible for followers to be less ascetic and also to achieve salvation.

Staying within India, but coming many centuries forward to the fifteenth century, we come to the religion of Sikhism whose founder, Nanak, followed a tradition of teachers who stayed within Hinduism, but reacting to Islam, he emphasized the basic truth of monotheism. The Guru, Nanak, died in 1538, but appointed a successor. Even though it is said that his body disappeared after his death, he was not elevated to a position of becoming the single central figure of Sikhism. While followers increased and became increasingly militant, nine gurus followed Nanak leading to the tenth Guru, Govind Singh or Govind the Lion. He directed that there should be no more gurus, but the Granth (the writings of the gurus) should become their Guru. The Granth is worshipped as a divinity in Amritsar, the Golden Temple of the Sikhs. Although Sikhism appears at first also to have the potential to become a religion that spreads widely, it clearly does not fit the criteria of having a single figure as a means of access to God and salvation.

Continuing to examine various world religions, we come to Persia where Zoroaster, the founder of Zoroastrianism, probably lived in the seventh century BCE. Unlike Mahavira and Buddha, who represented "exemplar" prophecy, Zoroaster represented "ethical" prophecy, primarily because of his personal call from God. The religion of Zoroaster had the same source as the religion of the Vedic Aryans, from which Hinduism eventually developed. Also, Zoroastrianism probably influenced Mahayana Buddhism during its spread to Central Asia and China. However, as Weber (1967 [1946]:55, 56) notes, Zoroaster, along with Muhammad, belonged to the Near Eastern ethical prophets who looked to a "personal, transcendental and ethical god," not to the Asian exemplary prophets who looked to "superdivine, impersonal forces." The problem at this point, then, is to consider why Zoroastrianism did not spread as widely as Christianity or Islam did.

Like Muhammad, Zoroaster strongly opposed the popular religion of his day in the name of the one God, Ahura Mazda, the high God already known. The sacred book of Zoroastrianism, called the Avesta, has numerous portions. The most important of the portions is the Yasna, containing the Gathas, because it clearly is the most ancient source of information on Zoroaster's life and thought. Zoroastrianism became the religion of the Achaemenid rulers, beginning with Cyrus the Great of Biblical fame.

According to our theory of the importance of a single human being serving as means of access to God, Zoroastrianism demonstrated that it had a high potential to spread widely, but in the end failed because of a rising tide of popular religion that reduced the importance of Zoroaster. But first, regarding the high position originally accorded Zoroaster, Noss (1949:459) writes:

> A highly worshipful attitude came to be taken toward Zoroaster himself. To the adoring eyes of his later followers, that very human man, "the shepherd of the poor" who appears in the Gathas, became a godlike personage whose existence was attended by supernatural manifestations. Heaven and Hell were thrown into commotion by him. His coming was known and foretold three thousand years before by the mythical bull; and King Yima, in the golden age, gave the demons warning that their defeat was impending.

Miracles were said to attend the birth and the adult life of Zoroaster. He was venerated widely, including by the Greeks and the Romans.

All of this bode well for the spread of Zoroastrianism according to our theory. However, the old Aryan nature worship came back into the religion. Even more important for reducing the focus on Zoroaster, were the many Yazatas or angels in popular religion. Furthermore, the divinity Mithra, the god of light, came back in popular religion, along with Haoma, the god of sacred intoxication, and other foreign gods and goddesses. Zoroaster in his lifetime rejected all these divinities. After this revival of popular religion during the period of religious pluralism from the time of Alexander the Great, especially under the Parthians, Zoroastrianism was established as a rigid state religion by the Sassanid dynasty that began in 226 CE. The latter day polytheism and ceremonialism that followed Zoroaster were formalized into orthodoxy. Movements, regarded as heretical, such as Mazdakism, Mithraism, and especially Manichaeism, were strongly suppressed within Iran, but spread outside of Iran. Thus, Zoroastrianism did not become a world religion that spread as widely as Buddhism, Christianity, and Islam because popular religion diluted the original monotheism of Zoroaster and reduced the central significance of Zoroaster. Furthermore, elite and formalized Zoroastrianism also became closely identified with Iranian nationalism, particularly the Sassanid regime, and thereby lost its universal appeal. The issue of popular religion will be examined more carefully below.

Before returning to consider popular religion again, we will note that one of the heresies of Zoroastrianism, Manichaeism, spread much more widely than its mother religion. This is a phenomenon seen in the cases of Buddhism, Christianity, and Islam, which spread more widely than their mother religions of Hinduism and Judaism. Manichaeism, had the founding figure of the martyred Mani, who died in prison or, as in one version, whose body was stuffed and crucified and hung on the gates of Seleucia-Ctesiphon in Iran between 273 and 276 CE (Moffett

1992:110). Manichaeism spread both eastward and westward from Iran. Understandably, it often became confused with Christianity, especially in Central Asia. However, Mani himself faded in significance, but Manichaean theology, not any loyalty to its founder, found its way into movements (forms of Catharism, such as Bogomilianism in the Balkans and Albigensianism in France) that sought to purify or bring greater spirituality to the established Christianity using a dualistic view of the material and spiritual.

PERSISTENT POPULAR RELIGION

The phenomenon of popular religion needs further examination since it seems both to favor and to be opposed to the major belief that causes religions to spread, namely, the belief in a central human figure who gives access to God and salvation. As already noted, popular religion is especially relevant to what has been said about the spread of religions because of the tendency in it for people to seek direct and tangible contact with supernatural sources of power, especially forces that are personalized in heroes, saints, or other divine or semi-divine figures. Whereas elite religion emphasizes the transcendent with its normative order, popular religion is interested in the immanent and the possibilities of immediate aid and rewards. Thus, with its goal of seeking practical aid in desperate situations, popular religion usually tends to look to multiple supernatural figures having special powers, who are also often represented materially and artistically. These popular religions have had wide appeal as indicated by the term "popular." However, their very popularity among particular peoples and the secondary and local character of the supernatural figures worshipped have tended to make the various popular religions culture-bound. The development of the various popular religions supports the view of the significance of "elevated" human figures, often historical heroes, saints, or mythical figures, for the spread of religions, except that they tend to spread primarily within socio-cultural groupings. The figures to whom people appeal in popular religion are usually considered as being under the overall direction of a high god and to be given special or specific assignments. Thus popular religion, while aiding a religion to spread within a socio-cultural group, in the end hinders its spread to a wider variety of societies unless a central cosmic savior figure is maintained.

In China and in other countries under Confucian influence, the division between elite and popular religions was very clear. The elite supported a cult of the ruler with rituals to establish the legitimacy of the ruler and maintain the favor of heaven. At the same time, a variety of popular religions were tolerated as long as they did not initiate dangerous heterodox or sectarian thinking that would challenge the established order. In India, Hinduism maintained its elite philosophical systems while tolerating a wide variety of popular local religious expressions. Hinduism appealed to the courts of kingdoms in Southeast Asia and its literature had great prestige. However, its multiplicity of local religions combined with a comprehensive social caste system hindered its spread as a religion. In the end, Hinduism has remained rather bound to a particular culture. Of course all religions are heavily loaded with local cultural expressions, but the three spreading religions have been more successful in becoming supra cultural than other religions.

As already stated, Buddhism had the advantage of lifting up the single figure of Buddha, but at the same time its incorporation of popular religions has also hindered its spread, although not to the extent of popular religion in Hinduism. Outside of Asia in the modern era Buddhism has found greatest acceptance in its philosophical and psychological therapeutic forms, some of which it shares with Hinduism and other Asian religions. In this sense, Buddhism and

Hinduism occupy a similar position in spreading to Western countries, with Buddhism ahead because of its single elevated figure.

Zoroastrianism appears to be a religion that had the potential of spreading and did provide theological perspectives that influenced other religions, but it became highly limited by its adoption of popular religion. Furthermore, it combined with a rigid elite religion that suppressed religious innovations. State religions tend not to be missionary beyond their borders.

Of the three religions that have spread the most widely, the strongly monotheistic religions of Christianity and Islam have from their beginnings shown the greatest ability to spread rapidly across socio-cultural boundaries. However, in speaking of monotheism, Sharot (2001:40) states:

> A general impediment to the development of monotheism was the demand among the masses for tangible and accessible religious objects that could be brought into relationship with concrete life situations and influenced through magic. Not even in the essentially monotheistic faiths of Judaism and Islam were beliefs in spirits and demons permanently eliminated; the decisive consideration was whether the supreme God or the spirits and demons exerted the stronger influence on the interests of individuals in their everyday lives.

Christianity began increasingly to incorporate elements of popular religion especially after the Roman government made it illegal in the fourth century not to be a Christian. As Ramsey MacMullen (1997) has pointed out, even though paganism was outlawed, it succeeded in finding expression within Christianity, primarily in popular religion, as elite religion became allied with the state. The elite leaders of

Christianity tended to elevate Christ to the status of judge and maintainer of order, namely, Pantocrator or Lord Omnipotent. This allowed and encouraged the cult of the Virgin Mary to provide an alternative immanent means of access to God with emphasis placed on her accessibility and compassion. Mary was able to carry on the function vacated by the various goddesses of pre-Christian religions, as well as by Jesus Christ himself. Saints and tangible representations of divine power, such as statues, icons, and relics, became increasingly used. Furthermore, special weight was given to the sacraments, which were increased in number, and to which magical elements were added. It could be said that a considerable amount of Gentile "baggage" in the form of popular religion was thus brought into Christianity, which helped to provide an accessible means to the Divine in contrast to elite Christianity, which formed its alliance with state power.

Differences within Christianity appeared from the beginning, but once it was associated with state power in the fourth century, controversies over authority to determine the beliefs and practices of Christianity divided it between Eastern and Western churches, as well as between Eastern Orthodoxy and the Eastern churches belonging to Monophysitism and Nestorianism. In Europe various religious resistance movements developed over questions of authority, doctrine, and spirituality in the Church leading up to the Protestant Reformation. These often were led by elites or intellectuals. A central issue for resistant groups was what authority was legitimate in determining how to eliminate many of the elements of popular religion that had developed over the centuries. The Reformation churches believed that Roman Catholic authorities had placed themselves above Biblical authority and the authority of the Bible needed to be restored.

In the sixteenth century, both the Protestant Reformation and the Roman Catholic Reformation that was stimulated by it placed a new emphasis on the centrality of Jesus Christ. The Roman Catholic Society of Jesus became a great missionary organization. In the major Protestant churches, as people struggled over orthodoxy, the dynamism of the sixteenth century was replaced by the rigidity and formalism of scholasticism in the seventeenth century. However, the Pietistic Movement of the eighteenth century raised the issue of how people should relate experientially to Jesus Christ. The evangelical movements of the eighteenth and nineteenth centuries, which emphasized a personal experience with Jesus Christ, were a major catalyst for the modern Protestant missionary movement. In these controversies over authority in determining the central truths of Christianity, much of northern Europe broke with the earlier popular religion of Christianity that was associated particularly with Latin culture. The process of change in Christianity will be discussed further in later chapters. However, when reviewing the spread of Christianity over the last two thousand years, it can be seen that an emphasis on the centrality of Jesus Christ as the sole means of access to God is associated with acceleration in the spread of Christianity and a de-emphasis on Jesus Christ caused lack of attention to spreading the faith.

Islam, like Judaism, has not included as much popular religion as Christianity. One reason is that it did not develop the hierarchical structure separating elite clergy and religious virtuosi from the ordinary layperson that became characteristic of Christianity. In addition, there is the clear command against images in both Judaism and Islam. However, although the idols were purged from the Kaaba in Mecca and it was rededicated to Allah, the ancient sacred black rock was preserved from pre-Islamic days and made the center of the hajj or pilgrimage, one of the "five pillars" of Islam. Sharot (2001:203) comments that the esoteric study of the ulema (community of scholars) encouraged the development of popular movements with their own heroes. Hourani (1991:156-57) discusses the turn to various saints. Some of the shrines of saints that became important were those of:

> Mawlay Idris (d. 791), reputed founder of the city of Fez; Abu Midyan (c. 1126-97) at Tlemcen in western Algeria; Sidi Mahraz, patron saint of sailors, in Tunis; Ahmad al-Badawi (c. 1199-1276) at Tanta in the Egyptian delta, subject of a cult in which scholars have seen a survival in a new form of the ancient Egyptian worship of Bubastis; and 'Abd al-Qadir, after whom the Qadiri order was named in Baghdad.

Van der Veer (1994:38,39) discussing the Sufi saints and shrines in South Asia states:

> The tombs of famous saints and their descendants form a hierarchical network of shrines over a landscape they have sanctified...The saint's cult is primarily a cult of power (barakat). The Sufi saint is a miracle man who has great powers, some of which–such as healing powers–are very much in demand. It is a commonplace that people turn to Sufi shrines for solutions to practical problems, such as the desire for children or the healing of diseases. The powers of a shrine and a pir [spiritual master] family are broadcast through oral and written narratives that are spread by followers. These hagiographic tales provide answers to the problems of later generations as well as models of behavior. An especially successful medium of communicating the powers of a saint is music, especially devotional songs. Shrines draw great gatherings of people who come to hear the music and the poetry in praise of the saint and his family.

In spite of the de-emphasis on Jesus Christ and Muhammad in various times and places discussed above, their central status has been maintained in the long run so that none of the subsidiary figures could permanently replace them at the center of the faith. In addition to the tendency for Buddhism, Christianity, and Islam to adopt or produce subsidiary supernatural figures in popular forms of religion, they also had special charismatic leaders who attracted varying numbers of followers.

RELIGION AND LEADERS

Parallel to the phenomenon of popular religion with its search for intermediaries, the phenomena of religious leaders is consistent with the importance of the focus by the spreading religions on a single human who gives access to God and salvation. That is, the phenomenon of religious leadership also draws from, but at the same time can be opposed to, belief that enabled the three religions to spread.

It is no secret that religious leaders with special qualities of leadership can be very effective in drawing followers to religious groups. When Hinduism and other Eastern religions have spread to the West it has usually been through the leadership of individual "masters" or "gurus" (single human figures) who emphasized universal aspects of their teachings. A study by Kamel Ghozzi (2002) comparing the resilience and decay in ulema groups in Tunisia and Iran contributes to understanding the importance of religious leaders and of effective organizations. He points out that the emergence of a charismatic leader (the Ayatolla Khomeni) in Iran contributed to the resilience of the ulema in Iran, whereas the lack of such a religious leader in Tunisia contributed to the decay of the ulema in Tunisia, although a charismatic political leader was able to lead the nation to independence. The other two important factors for creating resilience were theological consensus and autonomy of the religious organization. The point to be made here is the importance of outstanding religious leaders who can attract people for maintaining the vitality of religions.

It could also be argued that historically the Pope, the "Vicar of Christ," has provided a central rallying point and a base for continuity in the Roman Catholic Church. Studies of churches, especially Protestant churches, at the congregational level show the key importance of effective leadership if a church is to have vitality. Among other things, religious leaders in some measure are representatives of, even substitutes for, God and the central figure who provides access to God and salvation. However, just as popular religion in itself has not been able to sustain religions indefinitely or in every circumstance, outstanding leadership alone has also not been sufficient to ensure continuity in all circumstances for religions. In fact, religious leadership, like popular religion, may well distort religion and lead it in deviant and possible destructive directions. Nevertheless, it can be seen that both strong leadership and popular religion borrow characteristics from the key belief content variable for spreading religions of a central human figure who gives access to God and salvation. More consideration will be given to leadership in Chapter 3 that takes up religious organization.

A REVERSED DIRECTION OF CAUSATION?

Some may question whether the direction of causation can be reversed so that the spread of religions causes the emergence of the central "elevated" figures. There certainly can be some two-way influences in historical phenomena without meaning that influences or effects become equally two-way or entirely circular. My argument is not that there is no reverse causation, but that the predominant influence is from having a central mediating or saving figure in the direction of spreading, rather than spreading creating the central figures.

Among the three religions, the best argument for the spread of a religion causing the elevation of its central figure (the reversal of influence) can probably be made for Buddhism. Buddhism started spreading from India when teachers of the dhamma/darma (religious law or teachings) were sent out by the Emperor Ashoka, probably some 250 years after Buddha lived. The teachers went to Sri Lanka and then Buddhism spread throughout Southeast Asia, but there was less success in spreading to Persia, the land of Zoroaster. Before it began to spread widely Buddhism was primarily a philosophical system, but as it spread Buddha was elevated. The monks in Theravada maintained the Buddha as a central figure as Buddhism spread in Southeast Asia and in Mahayana. As discussed earlier in this chapter, Buddha became a very attractive figure, which was recognized by the monks. At the same time, the exalted position of Buddha and the difficulty of the renunciations required, meant that popular religion would be maintained and even elaborated within Buddhism. However, the popular religion within Buddhism could never eliminate the attractive figure of Buddha.

In the case of Christianity, Jesus Christ was clearly central from the beginning and did not seem to have been seriously challenged as a central figure, except possibly by John the Baptist in some circles. However, John's secondary position is made clear very early (Mark 1:7,8; Acts 19:3; John 1:19-28). The reversal of influence (spread causing elevation) can be seen as the figures of popular Christianity became additional mediators between Jesus Christ and individuals. In the hierarchical church and society, it is not surprising that Christ became elevated to a position that seemed distant to the people at large. This stimulated the development of various mediating figures, such as Mary and other saints. These, in fact, took the positions previously occupied by the various divinities of popular religions. However, with the reduction in importance of these mediating figures in the sixteenth century Reformations (Protestant and Roman Catholic), Jesus Christ became more central and accessible more broadly. A major spread of Christianity has taken place since then, increasing in the nineteenth and twentieth centuries up to the present. The direction of influence from Christ at the center toward spreading seems clear, but his elevation above an immanent to primarily a transcendent position actually hindered missions.

In Islam, a certain elevation in the importance of Muhammad can be seen as Islam spread, helping to accelerate that spread. Muhammad was clearly a strong central military and political leader from the beginning and incorporated his secular leadership in a religious message of reform. However, the struggle to establish his central prophetic position among the Arab tribes after his death has already been mentioned. Although the movement toward popular religion began to take place as Islam spread, primarily in the elevation of saints, Muhammad himself was elevated further. Hourani (1991:157) states:

> In course of time the Prophet and his family came to be seen in the perspective of sainthood. The intercession of the Prophet on the Day of Judgment would, it was commonly believed, work for the salvation of those who had accepted his mission. He came to be regarded as a wali [friend of God] as well as a prophet, and his tomb at Madina was a place of prayer and petition, to be visited for itself or as an extension of the Hajj. The birthday of the Prophet (the mawlid) became an occasion of popular celebration: the practice appears to have begun to grow by the time of the Fatimid caliphs in Cairo, and it was widespread by the thirteenth and fourteenth centuries.

The ongoing struggle between Sunni and Shi'a, over the question of who represented the legitimate succession to the Prophet, is perhaps the most important historical development to keep Muhammad central in Islam. As already seen, the struggle over authority helps to make central the one each claims to represent. In Islam, there is some early reverse direction of influence in which the spread of a religion causes the elevation of its central figure. However, the focus on Muhammad as the central figure of Islam would not have been possible without his important influence in the initiation of the spread of Islam.

The evidence, then, is that there was some reverse influence in which the spread of Buddhism, Christianity, and Islam caused some elevation of their central figures. I have already noted that the development of popular religions was one of the major qualifications to the focus on single elevated human figures. This elevation actually encouraged the development of additional intermediaries in popular religions. Thus, popular religions typically result from an elevation of the central figure beyond easy access and at the same time, work to reduce the importance of the central figure, as various intermediaries are elevated. This hinders the missionary impulse of religions. However, internal struggles over authority and orthodoxy cause a renewed focus on the central figure. Thus, the reverse influence in which the spreading of a religion causes the elevation of a central figure did not nullify the fact that these religions would not have spread had they not already had central human figures, who offered a means of access to God and salvation.

CONCLUSION

This chapter begins with the recognition that religion, especially popular religion, is characterized by the desire for contact with the Divine through immanent, accessible, and tangible objects. This characteristic of the pervasive religions among humans enables us to understand the spread of Buddhism, Christianity, and Islam more widely than any of the other religions of the world. These three religions are in fact distinguished by their offer to all people a single human figure who is able to give access to the Divine and salvation. The figures offered are made immanent, accessible, and tangible in biographies and in teachings. Buddha, Jesus Christ, and Muhammad are each perceived differently, but each is said to provide a unique means of access to God and salvation.

Due to the human tendency to seek contact with God, particularly to gain Divine aid for the many problems faced by humans, people have at various times and places sought to augment the three figures of Buddha, Jesus Christ, and Muhammad with secondary intermediaries. This was (is) especially the case for Buddha and Jesus Christ who were elevated to the transcendent level and seen to be somewhat separated from human need. This made the creation of intermediaries all the more likely. Nevertheless, the fact is that the figures of Buddha, Jesus, and Muhammad have made it possible for the three religions, which focus upon them, to spread to a greater extent than any other religions.

In addition to having these three central figures, the three most widely spreading religions contained moral guidance and energy and were able to gather and organize people to a greater extent than other religions. These additional internal characteristics of the missionary religions, closely related to their beliefs about their central figure, will be considered in the next two chapters, after which the secular social factors affecting the spread of these religions will be examined.

CHAPTER 2

MORAL GUIDANCE, MORAL ENERGY, AND THE SPREAD OF RELIGIONS

RELIGIONS AND MORALITY

A second religious content factor affecting the spread of religions is morality. This factor grows out of and depends upon the subject of the first chapter, beliefs associated with the central mediator figure of the religion. In addition, as Wayne Meeks (1993:1-17) makes clear, morality is also closely related to community or religious gathering and organization, the subject of the next chapter.

I use the terms "moral" and "morality" to refer to the distinction between right and wrong or good and bad behavior. "Ethics" is closely related to "morality" and usually refers to some system based on reflection about morals that is developed to guide behavior. Other terms related to "morality" are "justice" and "just behavior." All societies maintain moral norms and standards and most religions have some connections to morality, even though in some societies, discussed below, religion and morality may be distinguished and approached separately. This makes the relationship between religions and morality complex and difficult to analyze. I am not saying that Buddhism, Christianity, and Islam spread because they had superior moralities, but at crucial times they did provide moral guidance and especially moral energy to their followers, which proved to be effective and attractive to many societies in which they spread. This will be discussed under each religion, but more needs to be said about religions and morality in general.

All societies, just as all individuals, have to deal with the problems of potential or actual immorality or deviant behavior and the maintenance of some form of justice, at least a form agreeable to the leaders or rulers. Societies and most individuals seek to exercise some kind of control of what is considered immoral or deviant behavior. However, societies and individuals usually seek to move beyond mere external control of behavior to internal direction and motivation and the creation of moral energy. This is why governments and others who exercise control seek to establish their legitimacy and moral authority and not simply rule by force. Governmental authority will be discussed in more detail in Chapter 5. At this point it is important to understand that religions are important for morality because religions relate directly through God to both authoritative or legitimate moral guidance and direction. In addition, although often unrecognized by students of religion and morality, there is a need for moral energy to follow the direction provided. These two basic aspects of morality are important for the analysis of this chapter.

Christian Smith (2003b, 2010) has argued persuasively that one of the capacities of human beings is moral awareness and judgment. He (2010: 384-433) goes on to give a complex picture of persons and moral life that depends on the fulfillment of personhood. This purpose (telos) exists in persons in spite of the brokenness that humans experience and to some extent the very failure of humans enables them to recognize what they ought to be and do. My emphasis in this chapter is that religions can and have enabled humans both to recognize successes and failures in morality and to move toward some form of fulfillment in morality. There is a contrast, however, between recognition, or knowledge, of morality and actual movement or achievement in the moral realm. Religions play a crucial role in both knowledge and achievement. Moral energy is needed for the latter.

On the one hand, there is need for continual guidance of behavior, but on the other hand there is an even greater need for the creation of motivation and energy to fulfill moral goals. It should be understood that a tension exists between giving moral guidance and giving energy to fulfill moral goals. An emphasis on moral guidance usually leads to the imposition of ethical and legal systems, whereas an emphasis on moral energy leads to giving attention to inner motivation and the human response to Divine grace, compassion, and salvation. Periodically, the moral guidance aspect of societies fails or become isolated from the sources of moral energy with the result that moral systems become rigid and atrophied. Fear and threat are then used to motivate moral behavior. This happens primarily because with the loss of moral energy people lose their motivation to simply "follow the rules." The loss of moral energy results in a breakdown of social order, as well as individual moral behavior.

Thus the central moral problem in all societies and especially individuals is not so much knowledge of what is right behavior, but the motivation and energy to carry it out. Of course, individual and social morality is much more complicated than this brief overview of them. Most large and complex societies have numerous subgroups each with their own standards of morality. Furthermore, each culture of the world with its religious (or in some cases nonreligious) background emphasizes its own moral system. However, most societies have a minimum level of morality expected of everyone and some societies are stricter than others in enforcement. When moral authority systems fail, then societies become receptive to new systems. Also they may recognize a moral guidance and energy that is better than what they have. This is a condition that provided opportunities for the three religions to spread.

Once it is recognized that the central moral problem for humans is not knowledge, but energy, then it is possible to perceive that the three widely spreading religions were able at crucial times to attract people at least partly on the basis of what they offered toward moral behavior. What they offered was not separate from, but grew out of their beliefs and especially belief in the key figure central to each religion. I identify the central beliefs of these religions affecting morality as (1) salvation offered to each individual equally and (2) compassion extended to all people. Both of these beliefs are dependent on the central figure. It is also true that what will be dealt with in the next chapter was important for advancing and making available this moral appeal. This is the fact that the three religions established religious communities to propagate and maintain their beliefs upholding their morality, even when their actual behavior contradicted their beliefs. These beliefs set moral standards and goals for individuals and societies of equal justice for all and of compassion in treatment of others. Even more important, the gifts of salvation and compassion created moral energy to fulfill the moral standards that came through the central saving figure. Of course, the actual histories of the three religions that spread widely, like all religions, show their association with immorality, moral failure, and injustice. This chapter does not attempt to assert the permanent or consistent moral superiority of the three spreading religions over other religions. The point is that they do offer guidance for behavior, but more importantly they create motivation and energy to fulfill moral goals, and these qualities have been attractive to numerous peoples. The three religions could not have spread without offering moral guidance, but especially moral energy.

We take for granted that religion and morality are always closely related, but this is not necessarily true, even for the religions that spread widely. The need for social solidarity and mutual aid through moral behavior (a major impulse behind morality) and the need for supernatural help in the affairs of life (a major religious impulse) may be acted upon separately. Bellah (1969 [1964]) describes primitive and archaic religion as both having a basically monistic view of life in which the divine, the individual, and the society are merged into a natural-divine cosmos. In that sense, moral behavior having to do with human interrelationships and religious rites are part of a whole and both contribute to social solidarity. However, people often tend to separate their religious ritual behavior and their moral behavior toward others. As societies become more complex, religion and morality tend to become even more differentiated. It is in Bellah's next stage or type of religion, historic religion, that the distinction between the transcendent and the earthly realms become clearer and a tension develops between the two. People may observe religious ceremonies while not emphasizing or even ignoring moral standards or they may keep moral standards while not emphasizing or even ignoring religious ceremonies. We see the former in much temple worship and the latter among intellectuals such as the Greek philosophers, as well as modern ethicists.

Sharot (2001:8) speaks of the "ethicalization of religious life in the world religions," which "meant that salvation became dependent on ethical behavior in this life, and this involved the emergence of notions of religious merit, sin, the division of another world (or worlds) into specialized places of reward and punishment." The ethicalization of religious life incorporated the two opposite tendencies noted above (guidance and energy), but it tended to focus on legal systems that set forth clear requirements to guide the moral life. The promise of rewards and punishments in the next life has often been used with vivid portrayals to motivate desired moral behavior, but this has not proven to be highly effective over the long term. Spiritual thought and practices have been more effective in providing the motivation and energy that the moral life requires over the long term. The three religions that spread were able to do so because they provided moral guidance, but especially moral energy to people through their beliefs and strong communities, at least initially and at various times.

RELIGIONS
OTHER THAN THE THREE SPREADING RELIGIONS

Confucianism makes perhaps the clearest distinction between morality and religion that was made in any society of the ancient world. As a result it provides an early demonstration that the formation of moral or ethical principles, as well as of religious beliefs, is an inherent human capacity, as well as need. Religion, particularly as expressed in religious ceremonies, was approved and recommended in Confucianism, but not made the basis for moral action. Rather the focus was on the fact that human beings inherently could and should maintain proper relationships with others in an ascending hierarchical order ending with the emperor. A standard or model for behavior is set in the "superior person." This early example of the secularization of morality has been carried forward or replicated in the modern world with various secular theories of social and political justice and particular theories of professional ethics, such as business, medical, counseling, educational, and research ethics (Smith et al 2003a). The result of this ancient and modern secular approach to morality is the provision of a means for intellectuals and leaders to establish and direct orderly systems, primarily though their examples, but also through enforceable rules. On the other hand, the approach of Confucianism and other basically secular systems of morality in the modern world is that they produce very little moral energy for most people, only for those in leadership–to maintain their superior moral positions and the systems they control. One result of this radical or strong distinction between morality and religion is that it leaves the way open for various forms of religion that do not conflict with the "official" morality to spread and be sustained among the people at large. This is exactly what took place in China and in Korea, where the way was opened for Buddhism to spread alongside various other forms of traditional and popular religions, while a Confucian moral system was maintained by the rulers. Modern secular societies with their various ethical systems likewise leave space for religions to spread among the people at large who are looking for moral inspiration.

Hinduism developed as a unified religious-moral social system in which the maintenance of caste became one of the main features of the social morality. The Hindu system included sophisticated philosophy and fascinating and complex mythology, which was combined with the provision or approval of the worship of numerous local deities through many rites and in community festivals. These features of Hinduism gave it deep roots in the population, but at the same time hindered its spread because of its attachment to localized expressions of religion. Buddhism was not able to survive ultimately in the Hindu monopolistic social-moral context, but it was successful initially in providing moral guidance for a period during the Maurya Dynasty and then subsequently for people outside of India, as will be seen.

Turning to the Middle East, the "ethicalization" of religious life was made particularly explicit in ancient Hebrew religion leading up to the formation of Judaism. In spite of the separation made between religious rites and morality in the popular religion of most of the surrounding peoples, the prophetic message that was preserved was clear: God made no separation between having a right relationship with God and a right relationship with others. Judaism became a missionary religion, particularly in its early days in the Roman Empire, when both its monotheism and its high ethical standards won great admiration and attracted followers. However, its efforts to maintain its distinctive identity caused a stronger emphasis to be placed on its legal system (its law) than on the grace of God that motivates morality. It failed to sustain its missionary effectiveness precisely because this emphasis caused Judaism to remain primarily attached to Jewish ethnic identity, and this could only be obtained by outsiders through fulfillment of certain ritual requirements. Nevertheless, this did not prevent Judaic standards of moral justice from having a great impact on morality in the world up to the present through the Hebrew Scriptures, the teaching and behavior of Jewish people, and also through the daughter religions of both Christianity and Islam.

The discussion so far of religion and morality and of the morality of selected religions indicates that there are broad areas of commonality in moralities among religions and societies. Nevertheless, the following discussion will focus on the three widely spreading religions and the particular ways in which their moralities aided them in spreading. The following theoretical propositions guide the analysis of how the morality of the three religions aided them in spreading:

> **2.1** *To spread widely religions must offer moral guidance and moral energy.*
> **2.2** *To spread widely religions must offer salvation equally to all individuals thus emphasizing egalitarianism.*
> **2.3** *To spread widely religions must emphasize compassion for all people.*

BUDDHISM AND MORALITY

Buddhism originally existed primarily as a sectarian religious group within the majority Hindu society, although probably Buddhist ideas had gained wide acceptance among the people, particularly in the third caste, the vaisyas, who formed the majority of the traders and merchants (Thapar 1969 [1960]). The Mauryan dynasty that arose in northern India at the end of the fourth century BCE was centered in the Aryanised region of Magadha in modern Bihar, but it included a wide variety of other peoples extending from parts of Afghanistan to much of the subcontinent of India. The Emperor Ashoka was the grandson of the founder of the dynasty, Candragupta, said to have been either a Jain or a follower of a contemporary sect of Buddhism. Ashoka ruled from 274 to 232 BCE and is credited in Buddhist sources as having converted to Buddhism as a result of the cruelty that he had inflicted on the Kalinga people during his conquest of their area. Whatever actually took place, it is apparent that Ashoka perceived the teachings of Buddhism as providing moral guidance for ruling a diverse people and creating social solidarity. He was certainly motivated by the compassion of the Buddha. The inscriptions carved on rocks during his reign describe his well-known policy of Dhamma. Thapar (1969 [1960]:305) writes:

> (Dhamma is the Prakrit form of the Sanskrit word Dharma, virtually untranslatable into English. It has been variously translated as Morality, Piety, Righteousness, etc. Since the precise nuance of the word cannot be conveyed, I prefer to keep it in the original.) It was in the conception of this policy, seen in the context of Mauryan India, that the true achievement of Asoka lay. He did not see Dhamma as piety resulting from good deeds inspired by

formal religious beliefs, but as an emphasis on social responsibility.

Even if Asoka did not see social morality as a product of religious beliefs, he did promulgate social moral policy from beliefs associated with Buddha. Various aspects of the Dhamma show the goal of Asoka to employ it for the ruling of a diverse empire. For one thing the principles of Dhamma were acceptable to people of various religious sects. Thapar (1969 [1960]:308, 309) states:

> The policy was not defined in terms of rules and regulations. It seems to have been deliberately left vague in details, and only the broad policy is given, which was to mould behavior. Of the basic principles, the one on which Asoka laid most stress and which he repeated frequently was that of toleration. Toleration according to him was of two kinds: a toleration of people themselves and also a toleration of people's beliefs and ideas...Another principle fundamental to the practice of Dhamma was nonviolence. Asoka did not insist upon it as a religious precept like the Buddhists and the Jainas, but because violence was not in keeping with social behavior...The policy of Dhamma also included measures which today would be described as "social welfare."

In keeping with what I said about the separation of Asoka's "morality" from "religion," Thapar adds, "He attacked in no uncertain terms what he described as 'useless ceremonies and sacrifices,' held as a result of superstitious beliefs." Nevertheless, he drew his moral principles from the teachings maintained by the followers of Buddha. In addition to establishing the policy of Dhamma, Asoka also established a category of officers, known as Dhamma-mahamattas, who were responsible for teaching the policy and keeping the ruler in touch with public opinion. These teachers were sent on missions to neighboring kingdoms and they are credited with taking the faith of Buddhism to Sri Lanka and other places. It turns out that Dhamma "was too vague, and perhaps too idealistic," but nevertheless, after Asoka we hear of Buddhism beginning to spread.

Buddhism competed with Hinduism in Southeast Asia for many centuries. Although the courts of the kingdoms appeared often to favor the Hindu hierarchical caste system that gave special high rank, including divinity, to rulers, Buddhism eventually became more pervasive among the diverse peoples. It is not unrealistic to believe that the egalitarian principles inherent in Buddhism (offering salvation to all) and its emphasis on compassion were more appealing to the populations at large. In addition, the rulers found in Buddhism, like Emperor Asoka, a social morality by which they could rule.

In East Asia it is instructive to note that Buddhism met in Confucianism, discussed above, an already constructed sophisticated moral system for ruling and for maintaining social solidarity. In many respects, East Asia as a whole, illustrates the fact that religion and morality can be sustained in human practice as distinct systems. It is important for our theory that Buddhism spread widely in China precisely in the period following the fall of the Han Dynasty in 220 CE when there was disillusion with the traditional Confucian moral system. This was the period when North China was taken over by Turkic rulers and many Chinese literati fled south to escape the turmoil. For nearly 300 years the country had unstable Chinese regimes south of the Yangtse River and non-Chinese states in the North. As Arthur Wright (1971 [1959]:21-64) describes it, first there was a turn toward neo-Taoism with its emphasis on naturalism and even antinomianism. However, one important development was the "investing of the old Chinese naturalistic notion of li, "order," with a new metaphysical meaning drawn from Mahayana philosophy" (Wright 1971 [1959] :47). Most important for our purpose here is recognition that a new source for moral guidance and energy was found in the imported faith. Buddhism emphasized that it "ameliorates and assuages but it does not seek [political and social] reform" (Wright 1971 [1959]:50).

In regard to the moral guidance provided by Buddha, it was recognized as being the "Middle Path" discovered by Buddha who earlier tried the two extremes of pleasure of the senses and self-mortification. The Middle Path, known as the Noble Eightfold Path, consists of right understanding, right thought, right speech, right action, right livelihood, right effort, right mindfulness, and right concentration. The constant meditation on the meaning of these eight categories "gives vision and knowledge, which leads to Calm, Insight, Enlightenment, Nirvana," thus providing a basis for ethical conduct, mental discipline and wisdom (Rahula 1959: 45, 46). The Middle Path leads to the cessation of Dukkha, a term that is difficult to translate. In addition to the ordinary meaning of "suffering," "it also includes deeper ideas such as 'imperfection', impermanence', 'emptiness', 'insubstantiality'" (Rahula 1959: 17). Here the way embodied and offered by Buddha to his followers, even if not fully understood by most, points to a way to overcome the brokenness described by Smith (2010: 75-78).

The timing was right in China for the acceptance of Buddhism with a new source of moral guidance and energy. In the meantime, in North China, Buddhism, already known by the foreign rulers coming from Central Asia, was usually preferred over the native Confucianism as a source for religious motivation and energy needed for the moral orders they sought to impose. At approximately the same time, Buddhism also spread to the three kingdoms of Korea, where it became officially recognized by the governments.

Buddhism gained many followers and was favored by rulers at different times in China and in Korea in the first millennium CE. However, in both China and Korea, Buddhism as an official ideology for the rulers was eventually replaced by Confucianism (neo-Confucianism), which had a strong influence among the literati, the advisors and bureaucrats serving the rulers. In contrast, in Japan (more like Southeast Asian societies in its acceptance of Buddhism), although Confucianism was influential, the rulers found it useful to make Buddhism the official religion. They required all people during the Tokugawa period (1600-1867) to be registered in the many Buddhist temples. However, as Mullins (1998:7) notes, the nation was not fully unified in this way. Instead, "Japanese religiosity evolved in the premodern period into a syncretistic system of 'layered obligations.'" Mullins (1998:8) observes:

> Participation in religious events and rituals was primarily motivated by the sense of duty and obligation that accompanied membership in a household and community, not by clearly defined beliefs or exclusive creeds. Over time, Shinto came to dominate rituals associated with this-worldly concerns of birth and fertility, and Buddhism the rituals associated with other-worldly concerns and care for the dead...By the time Japan embarked on its push to modernization most Japanese were integrated into this system of household (Buddhist) and communal (Shinto) religious obligations.

In this study I am not examining all of the moral guidance associated with Buddhism. The Noble Eightfold Path, for example, would need to be considered. I am only noting that Buddhism found a pervasive place throughout Asia because it contributed moral guidance, but also moral energy, to diverse societies having their own moralities. Buddhism provided a spiritual source for moral energy particularly in its doctrines of salvation for all and compassion toward all life. These doctrines were (are) personalized in the Buddha in a clearer way than in any of the other Asian religions. In Mahayana there is the additional inspiration of the bodhisattvas, who postponed their entrance into Nirvana to practice pure altruism to help needy humans. Nevertheless, in Buddhism, a major motive for morality is to gain merit and reduce the number of rebirths and gain a place in paradise. As an example, Spiro (1982 [1970]:92-113; 438-77) describes how in Theravada Buddhism merit is acquired in a number of ways, including through morality. In the long run this has not aided the vitality of Buddhism. Actually, the emphasis on gaining merit through moral behavior is found in all religions and results in reduced religious vitality and moral energy. This is because outward observances take precedence over the inner sources of morality.

Nevertheless, Buddhism at various times has maintained the inner sources of morality. A modern example of the moral energy found in Buddhism is seen in a movement based in Taiwan named "Tzu Chi" or "Ci Ji" (Ci meaning "kind," "loving" and Ji meaning "to cross over," "to help"). It has established worship centers, hospitals, and schools throughout the Island and internationally. The founder of the movement, Master Wang Chin-yun, now known as Master Cheng Yen, is a woman, born May 14, 1937 in a small town in eastern Taiwan. A pamphlet (Shaw 2007 [1997]:8) explaining the movement states that Master Cheng Yen was so moved by thoughts of social compassion that "she decided to leave her home and find a temple where she could take refuge in the Buddha." Later, she was moved by contact with three Roman Catholic nuns to "humanize Buddhism" by a "just do it" philosophy of compassion. This appears to be partly to draw on native as opposed to foreign sources for moral action and, of course, it has many similarities to Christian movements in which hospitals and schools were established worldwide. Through her dynamic leadership numerous social institutions and relief programs have developed. In the pamphlet there is a striking picture of a mosaic in the lobby of the large Tzu Chi Hospital in Hualien, Taiwan. It is of Buddha caring for a sick disciple in a manner that is strikingly like the manner of Jesus also shown in numerous pictures elsewhere. This modern Buddhist movement to "just do it" in practical acts of compassion draws followers who are not necessarily personal followers of Buddha, but the compassionate aspect of the person of Buddha is continually lifted up in the movement.

The basic empirical fact is that in the Southeastern Asia, Buddhism was the only Asian religion to spread widely and remain among the people, with the exception of Hinduism in Indonesia in Bali and some of the population in Java. Buddhism proved itself adaptable to local religious and moral systems primarily because it did not challenge local moral systems or offer a substitute moral system. Instead, Buddhism introduced a religion that fulfilled human needs for contact with the next world and for coping with the miseries of this world through a moral "Middle Way". Its major contribution to morality was its emphasis on human equality, compassion, and tolerance in social life. This emphasis in itself should not be underrated in a world in which compassion and tolerance are often very absent. This is especially true when the other two missionary religions, Christianity and Islam, have so often presented anything but a compassionate face.

CHRISTIANITY AND MORALITY

Christian morality cannot be understood apart from the close relationship of religion and morality set forth in the Hebrew Scriptures and the Jewish faith. According to this Biblical approach to morality, a person's relationship to others is a direct reflection of a person's relationship to God. Human treatment of others is a direct outgrowth of how human beings believe God treats them. This means that the worship of God cannot be separated from human treatment of other humans, since all humans are made in God's image. The basis for this basically Hebrew morality is given its ultimate expression when Jesus teaches that as we are kind to others we are being kind to him (Matthew 25:31-46) and welcoming him means welcoming God who sent him (Mark 37).

The Hebrew prophets made it very clear that God hated religious ceremonies that were not combined with right behavior (Isaiah 1:10-17) and that the Temple dedicated to the worship of God was of no value unless it produced the just behavior toward others that God wanted (Jeremiah 26). At the very formation of the nation in the wilderness, the Ten Commandments, the basic guide to moral behavior, are given as the appropriate response of gratitude for salvation from slavery. The Ten Commandments themselves are placed in two tablets, the first tablet related to religious responses to God and the second tablet related to behavior toward others. Clearly, they are not to be separated. The New Testament is full of moral guidance, but it is given as fulfillment of the guidance already given in the Hebrew Scriptures, not in contrast to it. However, the New Testament picks up certain emphases from the Hebrew Scriptures, grace and faith, and stresses them as the source of the energy (power) to act morally. All of this is based directly on the Savior figure already discussed and the gift of the Spirit given through Christ. The basic fact to keep in mind about Jesus Christ is that he did not come primarily as a teacher of morals, but as an eschatological preacher announcing the inauguration of the "last days" (Schweitzer 1968 [1906]). This fact is also recognized in the epistles, for example in Hebrews 1: 1,2. This is the basis for Christianity becoming an eschatological or millennial movement that spread the approach to morality based on grace and faith.

Christianity grew out of the context of the faith of Israel and was even considered a Jewish sect in its early period. As a minority religious group in the Roman Empire, Christians were in a very different position from the people of faith before them who were members of a nation of believers. This minority position helps to account for the great concern of Christians for the reputation of the group and their concern not to be in conflict with others for the wrong reasons. David Horrell (2002:329) writes:

> These letters [the pastoral Epistles] focus a good deal on the need for "right" conduct among members of Christian congregations, essentially meaning behavior that is decent and socially respectable according to the standards of the time. Slaves are to be obedient and submissive; women are to be silent and subject to their husbands; church leaders are to govern their own households well, keeping their children in order (see I Tim 2.8-3.12, 6:1-2; Ti 1:6-9, 2.2-10). The pastoral Epistles therefore share with other letters in the later Pauline tradition a broadly conservative social ethic that may in part be a reaction to hostility and conflict with outsiders and to the realization that the "End," the final day of the Lord, was not going to come as quickly as earlier expected (cf. Col 3:18-4.1; Eph 5.21-6.9; I Pt 2.18-3.7; 2 Pt 3.8-10). Conflict with outsiders could perhaps be lessened if Christians ensured

that they conformed as far as possible to standards of "decent" behavior. At least if they were then the objects of hostility, it would be for the name of Christ alone and not for any other reason (cf. I Pt 4.12-16).

As a missionary movement, therefore, there is an underlying assumption that most people know what is right moral behavior, even if they don't follow it. Christians want to command respect by doing what they and others know to be right. Clearly, Christianity is not about denigrating the morals of others, but about having access to God who enables people to do what is right, much of which they already know. The Apostle Peter's opening words to Cornelius and his household (Acts 10:34,35) and the Apostle Paul's message to the Athenians (Acts 17:22-31) both show a basic respect for the religious and ethical goals of their Gentile hearers. Regarding religious and moral goals, the Apostle Paul recognizes his own need to improve (Philippians 3:12) and he even encourages a kind of competition in morality:

> Let love be genuine; hate what is evil, hold fast to what is good; love one another with mutual affection; outdo one another in showing honor. Do not lag in zeal, be ardent in spirit, serve the Lord. Rejoice in hope, be patient in suffering, persevere in prayer. Contribute to the needs of the saints; extend hospitality to strangers (Romans 12:9).

This mixing of religion and morality is straight out of the Jewish tradition, but it also places an emphasis on love that was distinctively characteristic of the words of Jesus to his disciples (John 13:34,35).

Christianity did not undertake simply to replace the morality of the Roman Empire, certainly not some of the standards represented by Stoicism and Platonism. Meeks (1993:68) makes it very clear that there are many similarities between the lists of vices in both Christian and Jewish sources and contemporary pagan sources:

> Words on the root porn- and perhaps in general references to sexual misdeeds are more common in the Christian lists than in the ordinary ones. The word "idolatry" appears where, in pagan lists, one would expect "desecration" or the like. Both peculiarities are shared by Christian lists with Jewish ones of the same period. Otherwise, Christian and Jewish lists are interchangeable with those of other moralists of the time.

Nevertheless, Meeks (1993:86,87) also describes how Christian morals arise directly from Christ's act of salvation and the human reception of it. For example, the notion of proper humility, "bound to look peculiar," came directly from the crucifixion of Jesus about which they sang hymns. The "inflexible obstinacy" in refusing to give up their beliefs may not have appeared as humility to Pliny, but it follows exactly the path of Jesus in "laying down his life," which is to be followed by our laying down our life for others (I John 3:15). This verse and many others point to the most distinctive aspect of Christian morality: it flows from salvation. Christians are able to turn from the list of vices because "you were sanctified, you were justified in the name of the Lord Jesus Christ and in the Spirit of our God (I Corinthians 6:10-22). Of course, baptism marked the new status of being saved and morality is the result of living according to this new status (Meeks 1993: 93). The acquired (not achieved, but given) status was the source of the energy to live according to the revealed will of God in Jesus Christ.

Writing of the effect of Christianity in its first five hundred years, the missiologist, Kenneth Scott Latourette (1937:245) writes:

> Although the vast body of Christians entertained no thought of reconstructing society on the model of the Sermon on the Mount, the impulse emanating from Jesus was not without profound effects upon the Mediterranean world. It is something more than a convention which pictures human history as divided into the two eras Before Christ and After Christ. The advent of Jesus set in motion *vast energies* [italics mine] which placed their imprint deeply not only upon Graeco-Roman culture but also upon all the peoples and cultures which have been touched by it and its successors. Here was a new beginning. Although modified by them, Christianity was not the logical outcome of forces at work in Graeco-Roman culture, but a fresh departure, a new creation.

Clearly, it was moral behavior rather than moral teachings that in the end were most effective in spreading Christianity. This is a point made by Meeks (1993:4) in saying that talking about "morality or ethics" is talking about people. "Texts do not have an ethic; people do." Stark's (1997 [1996]:213) comment on this is "It is only as Christian texts and teachings were acted out in daily life that Christianity was able to transform the human experience so as to mitigate misery." Stark goes on to emphasize the Christian emphasis on equality among diverse groups and in family relations and also compassion in the face of cruelty and in care for the sick. Likewise, Robin Fox (1987:335) in discussing the spread of Christianity states, "In cities of growing social divisions, Christianity offered unworldly equality. It preached, and at its best it practiced, love in a world of widespread brutality."

Was there a great distinction between the approach of Christianity to the morality of the Mediterranean world and the morality of the

European tribes to the north? Although the effect might have been more dramatic in terms of becoming the foundation of a new civilization in Europe, the approach to the morality of the people was not essentially different. Thus, although Christianity brought with it many of the characteristics of Greco-Roman civilization, it did not try to replace the morality of peoples wholesale, but rather deal with moral problems piecemeal. Latourette (1938:355) describes some of the effects:

> In morals as well as in religion the effect of Christianity was marked. Indeed, since in Christianity morals and religion are theoretically inseparable, this was to be expected. Very early after conversion, peoples began to bear the ethical impress of the newly adopted religion. Among the Anglo-Saxons, many even from the ruling families entered the monastic life and submitted to its demands. Theodore, the famous missionary Archbishop of Canterbury of the seventh century, in his penitential spoke out against drunkenness, sexual offences, theft, murder, and perjury. Presumably these standards, backed by his authority, had some effect. The laws of the Haraldsson, who had so much to do with the conversion of Norway, forbade the exposure of infants (except monstrosities) and provided that at the opening of the thing [official gathering] a slave should not be sacrificed, as heretofore, but freed.

As Christianity became the official religion of the Empire and then the state religion in the many European kingdoms, a shift took place in what aspect of morality was emphasized. The Church as the major surviving institution in the West gave increasing attention to law, which is the guidance aspect of morality. Voluntary commitment of congregations of believers as the major source of moral energy was deemphasized and the Church took up the task of establishing Church law, known as Canon Law. Roman laws were a major contributor to the formation of Canon Law. The repeated imposition of celibacy on the clergy over the centuries helped to emphasize the legalistic basis of spiritual life found in the rules of imposed asceticism (Phipps 2004). Thus less attention was given to the sources of moral action, to grace, faith, and resulting voluntary commitment that provide the energy of moral action. Various orders did the most to preserve the voluntary and missionary spirit, particularly through the traveling monks, but the orders were like islands in the larger Church governed by its hierarchy and many lost their influence over time as they became sedentary and wealthy.

In the sixteenth century, the Protestant Reformation challenged the authority of the monopolistic Church, primarily by stressing the authority of the Bible over the Church and by emphasizing grace and faith over church laws with their means of acquiring merit. Nevertheless the Protestant churches, except for those coming out of the minority Radical Reformation, continued as officially established state churches. They entered into numerous military struggles to gain control of territories. Arguably, this greatly weakened the emphasis in the Protestant churches on moral energy in comparison to doctrinal and moral guidance. Grace and faith were emphasized in principle in their confessions, but orthodoxy in beliefs became the order of the day. It took the focus on personal spiritual experience with Jesus Christ in the Pietistic movement of the eighteenth century to bring back the right emphasis on moral energy based on grace as opposed to authoritarian doctrinal and moral guidance. The struggle to maintain the right emphasis has continued to the presence. Alongside the Pietistic and evangelical movements, another major reaction to imposed Christianity took place in Western Christianity. This reaction created the secularization movement and the attendant irreligion movement. This will be discussed in more detail in Chapter 10.

Returning to the start of the modern age, European countries, beginning with Portugal and Spain, began their expansion just before 1500, carrying with them the Christianity that had been brought to them. According to the view of morality already seen in the first two stages of the spread of Christianity (to the Mediterranean basin and to Europe), morality was assumed to be an outgrowth of religious faith, but by 1500 the Christian faith was highly institutionalized and governed by law. In the modern era since 1500, missionaries often spoke of taking civilization to other peoples. However, even if specific practices, such as headhunting or infanticide, were opposed as morally wrong, missionaries often admired the moral qualities of the people in receiving societies. In fact, many missionaries saw their own fellow citizens as more morally reprehensible than the indigenous people. One thinks of the missionary monk, Bartolome de Las Casas (1484-1566), who opposed the treatment of Native Americans at the hands of his fellow Spaniards. The missionaries to the Pacific Islands continually opposed the oppressive and corrupting influence of traders and whalers. Missionaries in Africa opposed both the slave trade by Westerners and Arabs and the cruel treatment of Africans, for example, in the Belgium Congo (Phipps 1991). In China, Jesuit missionaries in the court admired much about the moral system of China. James Legge (1815-1897) and missionaries in the nineteenth and twentieth centuries are also examples of Western Christians who greatly admired the morality of the Chinese classics.

After the Roman Empire and before 1500 Nestorian missionaries contacted Persia, Central Asia, India, and China and Roman Catholic missionaries contacted China under the Mongols. Nestorian Christians were an aid to the Mongols in organizing their Yasa, the Mongol law.

Islam had established itself as a major new civilization with which Christians in the Byzantine Empire had hostile relations from the founding of Islam in the seventh century. In Asia, India and China represented major centers of distinct civilizations and moral systems that had spread their influence to all surrounding countries. Islam had its own religious-moral system to be considered shortly. While Roman Catholic Christianity spread rather successfully in conjunction with coercive power to Latin America and the Philippines, in India and especially China and its neighbor Japan, Roman Catholic missionaries encountered considerable resistance. The exception to this was the warm reception of Roman Catholic missionaries in the Chinese court. However, this was followed by a rejection by the Imperial government based on disagreement between the Emperor and the Vatican in the rites controversy. (Jesuits had tried but failed to obtain Vatican approval for their incorporation of Chinese ancestral ceremonies.) By the time of the explosion of missionary efforts in the nineteenth century very little headway had been made in spreading Christianity in India, China, Japan, the Southeast Asian mainland, and Indonesia. Indonesia had actually found Islam a welcome aid against Western colonial intrusion contributing to the spread of Islam throughout the archipelago. In contrast to the majority peoples who experienced Western imperialism and colonialism (obviously immoral to them), minority groups throughout Asia often welcomed Christianity as it facilitated their aspirations for maintaining distinctive identities, but also provided them with moral systems to counter the systems imposed on them by majority societies. This receptivity to Christianity also took place in Korea in the twentieth century as Korea struggled to assert its national identity over against Japanese domination, as well as resist Shintoism with its worship of the Emperor and elevation of Japanese morality.

Western imperialism and colonialism offset the claims of Christianity that it offered an elevated moral system. In the face of outside domination Islam and the older civilizations to the east maintained and strengthened their cultural defense systems. These systems contained their own moralities supported by their traditional religions. Only in the cases of China and Korea was there a somewhat secularized ancient moral system in Confucianism that oversaw a variety of religious beliefs and practices. In the twentieth century, Communism coming out the West reinforced the secularism of China, North Korea, and Vietnam while supporting aspirations for independence from Western domination. After a period of independence from Western domination, Chinese people have become particularly open to Christianity, as in the earlier movement among Koreans.

In the sixteenth century the monopolistic religious cover provided by Roman Catholicism in Western Europe was broken by the Protestant Reformation supported by nationalistic movements, particularly in northern Europe. Following this, nations increased authoritarian government rule, but eventually reduced it and removed it in a process that began in the Netherlands and England, but extended throughout Europe with some important reversals (the Napoleonic Empire after the French Revolution in the eighteenth century, Fascism in the twentieth century.) Beginning in the eighteenth and extending into the nineteenth century, the West, at least many of its intellectuals, broke from a long-time identification with Christianity and its moral system. In the United States, initially made up primarily of immigrants from Europe, religion was formally separated from government. In addition, the nation established a government with internally separated powers. By the formal separation of religion and government, the United States was able to avoid a strong antireligious movement among the people. In fact, the opposite has taken place with the growth of religions throughout United States history and the perpetuation of a religiously infused morality (moralities).

Because of these inter-religious, antireligious, and political struggles, Christianity developed a remarkably diverse moral system that simultaneously recognized human goodness and human sin. This sophisticated moral system was implicit from the beginning in the diversity found in the Bible and in the church of the first three centuries. It recognizes that human beings apart from religion are capable of much social good, but at the same time, all human beings, including religious people (sometimes especially religious people,) are capable of much evil. Thus, Christian morality recognizes that the secular world can undertake the support of such positively good efforts as education, medical work, social welfare, and the general advancement of knowledge. Even ethics can be approached as a secular discipline. In addition, Christian morality supports the need for a number of checks against the misuse of power and knowledge, including (even especially) by people of religious faith. Individual freedoms and open opposition are encouraged. Because of these dual perspectives of the presence of good in the secular world and of weakness and failure in the religious world together with the self-criticisms they encouraged, Western societies, typically thought of as "Christian" by those outside of the West, often appear confused and chaotic. I would not identify them as "Christian," but recognize Christian influences, many of which have been quite diverse and even opposed to each other. To many in traditional societies, especially those resisting Western domination, Western societies often appear morally corrupt, degenerate, and evil. However, in addition, now after the passage of time, Christians in the West are recognizing the moral failures of the past in the religious wars, slavery, the slave trade, imperialism, colonialism, racism, and anti-Semitism leading to the Holocaust, to mention some of the major historic moral blots in Western history. Stark (2003) has pointed to the contributions of Christianity to Western history that range from witch hunts and persecutions to science and freedom.

While the mixture of moral failure and moral advancement, as well as religious decline and religious revival, has been taking place in the West, Christianity has continued to spread rapidly to new lands. The result is that in the latter part of the twentieth century, Christianity ceased to be primarily a "Western" religion. The numerous Christian groups that now exist all over the world each seeks to express the morality that they find in the Bible and particularly in Jesus Christ, while at the same time living up to the highest moral standards of their own people. However, even within Christian groups there are strong divisions of opinion over what types of behavior are acceptable for Christians. These divisions existed in the recent past over slavery and other social justice issues and they continue today, for example, over women's rights and sexual orientation. In fact, human rights throughout the world have become a matter of concern, shared by Christians and non-Christians. In the end, Christianity does not have a single moral system, but multiple moral viewpoints and in general has come to recognize that diversity of viewpoint on moral issues is necessary in order to correct social wrongs. That is, competing groups are able to call attention to the moral failures of one another and work for reform. At the same time, many Christians believe that moral wrongs contain the seeds of their own destruction and people caught in them are being self-destructive, but when given the freedom and opportunity to change will often correct themselves. Also, many Christians believe that although there is a human tendency constantly to fail morally, there is also a human tendency to seek social justice. Most importantly, in a free and competitive moral environment, a shift takes place in what is emphasized in morality, from moral guidance alone to moral energy that will result in actual moral deeds. This is because more than ever people want to see moral deeds rather than only moral words.

It should be noted that in the spread of Christianity, especially in the last two centuries, in spite of the immorality associated with imperialism and colonialism, it has exhibited great moral energy in establishing medical and educational facilities throughout the world along with carrying out programs of relief for suffering people. These efforts have benefited countless numbers of people and many of them have now been taken over and emulated, including expanded, by government and public agencies, as well as by other religious groups. Nevertheless, the efforts of Christians in imitation of Jesus Christ to relieve the suffering of individuals have been an attractive feature of Christianity to many people.

ISLAM AND MORALITY

Islam from its beginning served as a revitalization movement, as such movements have come to be understood from the work of A. F. C. Wallace (1956, 1967). That is, Islam brought unity and a new moral, social, and political order to a disunited and subordinated people existing in numerous tribes. It enabled the Arabs to throw off the domination of two advanced empires, the Byzantine and Persian Empires, and then to expand their rule to the Atlantic in the west and to Central and South Asia in the east. Islam especially appealed to non-Arab tribal peoples, plentiful then and now, whose leaders saw in it the opportunity to unite and empower their people under a new moral, social, and political order. Arab power foundered on the rocks of tribalism, rival leadership, and the upward mobility of Persians and Turks after only about a century and a half. However, Islam as a religion continued to be a means for various peoples, North Africans,

Persians, Turks, Africans to the south, Central Asians, and South and Southeast Asians to be renewed and empowered to assert their freedom from domination. Islam was able to combine the egalitarianism and authoritarianism of tribal life in a new moral order based on belief in an authoritarian, but compassionate God who offered salvation to all individuals. It kept the basic unitary view of life typical of followers of primal religions, namely that religion is fused with all of life, including the exercise of power.

Actually, the linking of religion to governing power, which also existed in the two complex societies confronted by Islam, the Empires of Persia and Byzantium, continued in many complex societies up the modern age. This matter will be considered in more detail in Chapter 6, but the point here is that Islam was formed in conjunction with the forming of a new and unified social-moral-political order. Buddhism did not ally itself with governmental power for several hundred years after Buddha. It has done so eventually most permanently in Southeast Asia. Christianity allied itself with government power after its first three hundred years, but neither Buddhism nor Christianity had as strong a unitary view of religion and government, as well as all social institutions, as Islam, where religious, social, and political leaders were often indistinguishable.

Islamic morality, like Jewish and Christian morality, is basically behavior that is an expression of religious faith. Ethics are theological ethics, not a set of rules set up apart from religion, as one might speak today of professional or medical ethics.

Ernst (2003:111) writes:

> It has been pointed out previously that the Qur'an contains relatively few clear prescriptions that could be construed as legal ordinances, although it has

frequent and abundant verses urging the believers to reflect upon the power of God as manifest in creation and in the human soul...Gratitude for God's favors and blessings is the appropriate human response, so that obedience to divine command follows naturally. Ingratitude and rejections of God (both implied by the Arabic word kufr) are intellectual errors as well as displays of arrogance. So even if the Qur'an does not provide guidance for every conceivable detail, it points to the development of a moral consciousness and human responsibility to God–to pray as if you see God, and if you do not, to know that God sees you. The subsequent working out of Islamic ethical thought begins from this point, although a number of additional authoritative texts come into play besides the Qur'an.

Ernst (2003:115) goes on to explain that "both Jewish and Islamic traditions stand in contrast with the Christian emphasis on freedom from the law, as spelled out by St. Paul in the New Testament." In Christianity, legal codes were initially left to the secular authorities, but later under monopolistic Christianity, the church developed its Canon Law using the Roman legal codes. In many respects, in modern secularized Western societies, Christianity has returned to its original pattern of leaving detailed law to the secular authorities, nevertheless with Christian input. In contrast to the generalized approach of Christianity, Islamic law as developed outside of the Qur'an "addressed politics, economics, and family, in addition to religious practice and ethical practice," all of which has had an important influence in the numerous Islamic societies.

The Islamic world of today represents a reaction to the influence of the dominant Western nations, both their colonial domination and their secularized approach to government. On the one hand there has been a reaction among the people by turning to the stricter forms of Islam from the past, in many cases creating a greater religious zeal and moral strictness than ever existed, but in this way providing some security and order in the midst of change and uncertainty. On the other hand, the success of the secularized mode of government and economic order of the West has appealed to many Islamic rulers and intellectuals. This has created enormous tensions within Islam that are yet to be worked out.

Without its moral order, Islam would not have spread. On the one hand, it offered to many societies the firm guidance of an authoritarian moral order linked to a social and political order. On the other hand, and influencing the development of moral energy was Islam's emphasis on a compassionate God and salvation available for every individual. In this way, it provided a spiritual life under the one true God and his prophet and the Divinely dictated text that could both guide and energize moral life within the new order. Although Islam went through a period in which it tolerated considerable diversity and experienced a flowering of economy, science, and civilization in general, it is now caught in a post-colonial imposed religious order that severely limits diversity. It has not been able to accept the religious view that gained dominance in the West after 1500, namely that the secular can be good and religion can be bad, because of the dual fact that God created a good world and humanity in God's image, but humans, no matter how religious, are continually subject to sin and failure. For modern radical Islamists, the separation of religion and government as practiced in modern democracies is separating God from government and much of human life. The radical Islamic view means giving religion the authority of God, instead of seeing religion as the human response to God that is full of imperfections. They are also failing to see that believers in God can express their faith within the secular world; a world separated from the control of religion, not separated from God.

The fact remains, however, that Islam through its emphasis on both the authority of God over all of life and the compassion of God (almost every Surah or chapter of the Qu'ran begins with "In the name of Allah, the Beneficent, the Merciful") has given Muslims a moral energy based in both obedience and gratitude. One area where this can be seen is in the modern organizations to relieve suffering. This can be seen as an expression of the third Pillar of Islam or zakat, namely "the making of gifts out of one's income for certain specified purposes: for the poor, the needy, the relief of debtors, the liberation of slaves, the welfare of wayfarers" (Hourani 1991: 148).

MORALITY FOR MISSION

How does the moral guidance and energy of each of the three spreading religions affect how they approach each other? This becomes an especially crucial question for Christians and Muslims, who have the clearest missionary mandates. The Christian theologian, Miroslav Volf (2011), speaks directly to this issue. First, through careful argument he affirms that Christians and Muslims worship the same God. Regarding mission, he (2011: 210) states:

> As I have argued earlier, the Christian faith is not simply about allegiance to God. It is about worshipping God through Christ, the Word becomes flesh (see Chapter 10); Christ reveals the true character of God, and Christ makes the true worship of God possible. Having a common God doesn't cancel the need for witness to Christ as the way to God.

Many Muslims feel similarly about da'wa [Muslim counterpart to Christian evangelism], as Muhammad was sent "as a universal (Messenger) to men" (Saba' 34:28).

From this basic perspective, Volf (2011:211) goes on to argue:

> I suggest that having a common God is neither here nor there when it comes to mission. But a joint affirmation that God is a loving God and that God enjoins people to love their neighbors as they love themselves [he earlier shows this as a common belief of Christians and Muslims] is critical, for it provides a basis to work out a common code of conduct as Christians engage in evangelism and Muslims in da'wa.

There is much to be said, as Volf subsequently shows, to flesh out the morality of how Christians and Muslims should meet each other that would express the morality of love that each affirms. What is significant is that there are important thinkers among both groups who are seeking to do just that.

Even though Buddhism does not have as clear a missionary mandate as Christianity and Islam, it has shown itself capable, especially in recent years of undertaking extensive work to relieve suffering, a prime example being the Tzu Chi movement initiated by Dharma Master Cheng Yen mentioned earlier in this chapter. It could be argued that some of the practical morality of seeking to relieve suffering now seen in Islam and Buddhism was directly or indirectly inspired by Christian missionary activities of the past two centuries. Much or some of the inspiration may be in reaction against Christian efforts in order to demonstrate home-grown morality. Nevertheless, the basis for extending mercy to others is found in all three religions and continues to attract followers. In the end, the religious basis for moral energy will be the basic source for moral action that goes beyond simply the offering of moral guidance.

CONCLUSION

Since morality is such a universal human concern and element in human cultures, it is difficult to demonstrate that the three religions which spread more than others owe their success to having unique moral systems. Although each of the three spreading religions contain moral teachings, they are not alone in doing so. Confucianism, for example, is primarily a moralistic philosophy, which has had great influence in the societies surrounding China, namely Korea, Japan, and Vietnam. However, in each of these societies, Confucianism left a spiritual vacuum that was at least partially filled by Buddhism, along with Taoism and its folk religious expressions. Hinduism like Buddhism encompasses moral principles, but apart from having some influence in Southeast Asia and the Himalayas in the spread of Indian culture, it was largely eclipsed there by Buddhism and was unable, like Buddhism, to spread to East Asia. As a result, Hinduism has remained primarily in South Asia as a religious-moral social system closely tied to local culture.

Judaism contains a powerful moral core that has been highly influential, especially through its daughter religions of Christianity and Islam. However, even the powerful morality of Judaism did not enable it to escape from its largely ethnic identity. What has to be considered primarily is how the morality associated with Buddhism, Christianity, and Islam may have aided in their spread in spite of many similarities with other religions and cultures in their views of moral behavior, as well as similarities in their moral failings.

The belief factor discussed in Chapter 1 is the core factor enabling the three religions to spread. Closely connected to the central figure are the beliefs in salvation available to every individual and compassion for all. These beliefs with universalistic application support moral values that gave the three religions great appeal. It meant that they did not simply offer moral guidance or instruction, but that they were able to create moral energy in grateful response to the central mediating figure and his offer of salvation and compassion. The three religions or particular versions of them were able to spread to areas where established or prevalent religious moral systems had lost their energy. For example, Buddhism spread to China, Christianity in the Roman Empire, and Islam in Persia in such periods. Also, they all spread to small societies when these societies were in need of new moral orders as they came in touch with the larger world. Nevertheless, all three of the religions at different times shifted their emphasis toward legalism in which the emphasis is on gaining merit through good behavior rather than on good behavior as an expression of gratitude. Only their central savior figure and the doctrines of salvation and compassion have prevented their complete surrender to legalism.

Of the three religions, Christianity has shown certain qualities in its morality or essentially its vision of the basis for morality that distinguishes it from the other two and all other religions, including itself at many times and places. In Christianity it is stressed in a way not done in other religions that morality is not an achievement or simply obedience to Divine authority, but a gift coming from a life redeemed by the Savior. Moral behavior is seen as intrinsically rewarding and not a means to an end. Struggle, effort, and sacrifice are required in the moral life, but they are not achievements to gain merit or a reward. In contrast to this view, in all other religions, including Christianity itself in different forms and in different periods, morality has tended to be based on fulfillment of requirements and thereby as gaining merit and reward that is extrinsic to or beyond morality itself. There seems to be a basic human fear of removing external rewards or punishments as a means of motivating moral behavior as though such a removal would weaken moral effort. Christian morality, especially when it is not part of a state religion, does not so much present a system or set of legal requirements, but rather provides an energy or power to fulfill and transform commonly accepted moral practices. It is very true, however, that Christianity and individual Christians have not been able always to fulfill this moral vision that is basically centered on faith in the grace of God found in the Savior rather than being centered on requirements, rules, and the efforts to fulfill them. This faith-based moral vision seems to run counter to basic and natural human views of the basis for motives and achievement in human life.

Once Christianity became a state religion in the fourth century, it began a process of shifting toward emphasizing the need for guidance and an imposed morality. As a society-wide institution with major political and governing responsibilities it was necessary and almost inevitable that Christianity would have to develop a legal system. In spite of the legal system, however, Christianity retained an internal dynamic so that it did not entirely lose its voluntary element, expressed primarily in the orders and later in the voluntary congregational and denominational system that has come to be dominant in secularized societies. The congregational and denominational system is rooted in the early formation of autonomous bodies throughout European society that produced monasteries, universities, guilds, and towns. Leaders of various nations, particularly in northern Europe, began to challenge the domination of monopolistic Christianity and supported the Protestant Reformation that justified their independence from religious domination. This disruption of monopolistic Christianity helped to revive and multiply voluntarism in Christianity. However, the broad distribution of voluntary groups did not finally take place until organized religion was formally separated from government. The basic dynamic of Christian morality as a gift rather than an achievement spread widely throughout Christianity along with voluntarism. This revival of the grace based and faith based morality enabled the missionary movement of the nineteenth century to explode and continue to the present.

At present Christianity faces the world as a carrier of a unique morality, even if it often fails to express it and individual Christians often fail to live by it or even understand it. Most important, no one is able to embody it at all times. However, grace based and faith based morality still breaks out in unexpected times and places, often in opposition to people who otherwise are recognized as morally good, but wrong in emphasizing morality as an achievement. Such an emphasis undercuts moral energy, replacing it with moral rigidity.

CHAPTER 3

GATHERING, ORGANIZATION, AND THE SPREAD OF RELIGIONS

All peoples practice some form of gathering. Scholars study various gathering patterns of peoples around the world, a classic example being Durkheim's (1965 [1915]) study of Australian aboriginal gatherings and their religious meanings. He used their religious life to set forth his theory of religion, even though he never went to Australia. Gatherings serve as "rites of intensification" where people reaffirm and celebrate their common values and identity and are energized to carry on their life in a difficult world. In addition to simply gathering with one another, people also form organizations to maintain continuity and accomplish goals.

Turning to the religions of the world, when Buddhism, Christianity, and Islam are examined, we discover that they gathered and organized people on a more successful and larger scale than other religions, especially the latter two. Judaism was the earliest religion that was very successful in gathering and organizing its people and it had a major influence on Christianity and Islam. However, Judaism remained primarily associated with an ethnic group. Although its beliefs are universalistic, they are not applied in a way to be readily open to all people since in effect, joining Judaism means joining an ethnic group. On the other hand, Judaism's two daughter religions, Christianity and

Islam, have been successful in crossing numerous geographical and social boundaries and initiating new groups because their gatherings were specifically open to all people. All three of the widely spreading religions, especially Christianity and Islam, not only gathered people in emotionally charged regular worship services, but also organized themselves on the basis of universalistic beliefs and moral principles (discussed in the first two chapters) that enabled them to maintain themselves over time and also to create new groups in new societies. This chapter deals with the gathering and organizing characteristic of the spreading religions, which was a necessary cause for their spread. The gathering and organizing abilities of the three religions is directly related to their beliefs.

COMMITTED, NONTRANSIENT MEMBERS

In addition to having faith in a central elevated human being who is able to give access to God and to salvation for all people, there is a certain basic level of activity or practice necessary if a religion is to spread. It is necessary for spreading religions to gather and organize people, if not specifically for mission, at least to a degree that will enable mission to be carried out. Robert Hefner (1993:19) using Max Weber's insights states, "The real force of the world religions lies in their linkage of...strict transcendental imperatives to *institutions* [italics mine] for the propagation and control of religious knowledge and identity over time and space."

Most of the world religions have organized, but they vary considerably in how they have organized and particularly in the extent to which they have been motivated and able to send out missionaries or carriers of their religions. These variations not only may be seen between religions, but also within religions, and they reveal that the organization of religions is necessary if they are to spread. Effective organizations require effective leadership, which in turn requires an adequate belief system. In discussing the importance of leadership in organizations, Stark (1996:139) notes:

> That doctrines can directly cause ineffective leadership is widely evident in contemporary New Age and "metaphysical" groups. If everyone is a "student" and everyone's ideas and insights are equally valid, then no-one can say what must be done or who is to do what, when. The result is the existence of virtual non-organizations–mere affinity or discussion groups incapable of action (Wagner 1983.) In similar fashion, the early Christian Gnostics could not sustain effective organizations because their fundamental doctrines prevented them from ever being anything more than a loose network of individual adepts, each pursuing secret knowledge through private, personal means (Pagels 1979). In contrast, from the start Christianity had doctrines appropriate for an effective structure of authority, since Christ himself was believed to have selected his successors as head of the church.

I will discuss more of Christianity later. However, in my theory regarding the three successfully spreading religions, gathering and organizing is a necessary religious activity along with the important belief and moral guidance and energy discussed in the previous two chapters for spreading to take place. In fact, the better religions are able to bring people together and connect them to one another under effective leadership, the better they are able to spread.

Humans cannot live without some organization. All societies have organization or they would have no continuity at all. I am speaking of the bringing together of people, beyond the primary connections that they have through kinship. Primary relationships of the family and larger kin networks of clans and tribes are largely involuntary organizations. As societies grew and became more complex, people were brought together under the political leadership of ruling groups with kings and emperors. The kingdoms and empires that developed encompassed people in organizations in which the ruled (often conquered peoples) had largely involuntary membership. Religions associated with the rulers and pervasive among the people continued the pattern of socialization into involuntary identification with the common religion. As the three spreading religions entered new societies they interrupted or broke into the typical pattern of involuntary religious identification. The first chapter revealed that a religion was most effective in spreading if access to God and salvation was available through a central elevated human figure. Such a figure is able to bring people together on a voluntary basis of loyalty that transcends all other human relationships. The three religions that spread most widely have all been able to form voluntary organizations under leaders based on a common belief and loyalty. Such organizations were necessary for the spread of their faiths. Thus the initial proposition guiding the analysis in this chapter is:

3.1 *Religions with voluntary organizations to which people make personal commitments are necessary for religions to spread, while religions with involuntary and/ or transient followers will not ordinarily spread.*

One of the characteristics of early civilizations was the presence of an organization of religious specialists who presided at various worship centers over religious practices for the people at large. Bellah (1969 [1964]:71-73) classified this type of religion as "archaic religion." Regarding organization of archaic religions, he states, "The cult centers provide facilities for sacrifice and worship to an *essentially transient clientele* [my italics] which is not itself organized as a collectivity, even though the priesthood itself may be rather tightly organized." This type of religion was pervasive in most traditional societies so that identification with it was primarily by descent or was involuntary and largely unconscious. While there may well have been organization among religious specialists, people at large were socialized into the religion as members of their families or simply their social groups.

Identification by descent with a religion has continued to be a major tendency in all religions, including the three religions that spread. This has become the case particularly as single religions obtained government sponsorship or special recognition (often as "the majority religion") in order to become pervasive and monopolistic in whole societies. The lack of voluntary organizations under effective leaders has been a handicap for spreading even for the three spreading religions. When this is the case, membership is primarily through descent. For example, the organization of Christianity on a territorial basis instead of a voluntary basis, whether in Eastern Orthodoxy, Roman Catholicism, or Protestantism, has been associated with a lessening of mission activity. This will be discussed further in the next chapter that considers the alliance of religion with government control of particular territories.

The two mother religions (Hinduism and Judaism) of the three widely spreading religions (Buddhism from Hinduism and Christianity and Islam from Judaism) are both religions to which people belong primarily by descent and socialization by families. However, Judaism's concept of personal faith in God, who established a covenant with ancient Israel, provided a basis for change from membership by birth to membership by choice. This meant that religions could change from the older pattern of membership through childhood socialization to membership through joining voluntary religious organizations, especially in its daughter religion of Christianity. Then over time the alliances made by Christianity with governments beginning in the fourth century, to be discussed in the next chapter, reversed the pattern of voluntary organizations under strong local leadership that was predominant in the first three hundred years. For Christianity, after this period, the voluntary principle atrophied except in the orders and various religious movements, both inside and outside of the Church. The voluntary religious body was revived in Medieval religious innovative ("heretical") movements and with the sixteenth century Reformation. The Pietistic Movement of the eighteenth century further stimulated voluntary religious organizations, which became the major basis for religious organization in North America.

Historically, Buddhism, Christianity, and Islam became religions that were identified with particular societies and to which people belonged primarily by descent and socialization. They became and to some extent still are cultural identity markers for members of these societies. In spite of this, the three religions have in varying degrees and in various places encouraged voluntary and life-time commitments that involved participation in organizations to a greater extent than other religions, even though they have often been little different from other religions in maintaining nominal and involuntary memberships. It is the characteristic of continuous organizational participation and activity by believers that was necessary for religions to spread widely.

A special feature of the three spreading religions has been their ability to draw people to very emotionally energizing gatherings that were open to all individuals. Collins (2004) has drawn special attention to the importance in all of social life of "interaction ritual chains." Such social interactions are able to provide the emotional energy that appears to be a universal need and certainly a necessary ingredient for human life to be at all satisfying. Although human interaction through expression of ritual or symbolic solidarity exists in all societies, the three spreading religions have been able to spread because any individual may join them, at least in principle, to find and maintain the emotional energy that humans want. The worship services of the spreading religions have provided unusually effective "rites of intensification" because they offer symbols of the immanent Divine through which people can renew their emotional energy. These symbols enable people to affirm their solidarity both with the Divine and one another. Each one of the three religions has also had periods and places where their "interactions rituals" failed to attract people or even came to an end because of emotional satiation or dissatisfaction with the rituals or symbols offered. In spite of these failures, the ritual assemblies providing emotional energy have been maintained to the present (Collins 2004:149).

A number of propositions could be made related to "interaction rituals" and "emotional energy," a very important part of social and individual life that is only beginning to be understood. This area of sociological theory will be considered again in the two chapters on micro social factors, but here I propose:

3.2 *Religions are able to spread widely because they organize open gatherings in which people can interact around important symbols of the divine that provide solidarity and emotional energy for life.*

Another proposition related to religious organization, which is a necessary condition for religions to spread, is:

3.3 *Religions spread only when there are carriers to take the religions to new people in new areas.*

Carriers may be unintentional carriers, but most often they are intentional carriers known as "missionaries" usually sent by groups of believers. Without people to carry a religion it cannot be expected to spread, and, in fact, the spreading religions have specifically sent out missionaries, which included many who actively propagated the faith. This proposition is very similar to the proposition given by Stark (1996:140): "Religious movements will grow to the extent that they can generate a highly motivated, volunteer, religious labor force, including many willing to proselytize." This certainly is true for the successful movements belonging to the spreading religions.

Lewis Rambo (1993:66-86) introduces a useful discussion of missionaries under the term "advocate." He discusses missionaries primarily as individuals, but it is clear that missionaries are based in groups. As he (1993:68) says, in comparing growth by childbirth with growth by mission, "Mission, however, is the intentional *effort of a group* [italics mine] to proselytize and incorporate new members, which in some cases requires that the new member repudiate old allegiances and affirm an exclusive membership." Of course, missionary activity varies considerably between and within religions, as Rambo (1993:79) points out.

Even though it is not recognized by many scholars of religion, the modern Christian missionary movement has become larger and more diverse in the last fifty years than ever before, but other religions, particularly Islam, Buddhism, and to some extent, Hinduism, have increased their missionary efforts also. The theoretical view of this chapter is that religious voluntary organizations and their representatives are necessary, though not sufficient for religions to spread. The presence of missionaries alone does not guarantee the spread of religions. That was one of my points in my book, *The Lopsided Spread of Christianity* (2002). However, for religions to spread at all, there must be people available to carry them, and such people are found in voluntary religious groups made up of people who are members through personal commitment. Missionaries may be formally sent out or go informally on their own, but having some carriers is a necessary cause for the spread of a religion, although (contrary to some thought) there is not a necessary correlation between the number of missionaries and the number of new accessions to a religion. I observed this in the case of the aboriginal Christian movement in Taiwan, as well as in other Asian countries where very few if any missionaries were involved in the conversion of large numbers of people. On the other hand, sometimes large numbers of missionaries labor with few people responding. Then, in some cases there is a delayed response to missionaries, as in China where foreign missionaries were very active for well over a century without a large response, but where "official" foreign missionaries have been virtually absent for more than five decades. There are, nevertheless, numerous indigenous missionaries. Now a large movement to Christianity is underway. Thus the sending of at least some missionaries does serve as an indicator of probable eventual spread of a religion given the right beliefs and behaviors, already discussed, and the right social conditions, to be considered later.

BUDDHIST GATHERING AND ORGANIZATION

One sees the "archaic" type of religious organization or at least the remnants of it, in which the specialists organize, but followers or clients are transient, most clearly today in the old civilizations of Asia. Hinduism, Buddhism, Jainism, Confucianism, Taoism, and Shintoism represent these types of religions. Sikhism, a monotheistic religion, is an exception since its followers tend to follow their religion exclusively and be identified as coming from a particular area of India. The tendency for Hinduism as a whole in India is for people to maintain their general religious identity, but be transient participants at various religious temples and in various rituals.

In Asia, people often alternate worship of various divinities, but, except where they maintain a single religious identity as being Hindu in South Asia and Buddhist in Southeast Asia, they tend to maintain a single ethnic-cultural identity while shifting religious identities or claiming no religious identity at all. Although most of the Asian religions are similar in having transient clientele, Buddhism has shown the greatest propensity to have well organized groups of volunteer specialists in the form of orders or sanghas with varying numbers of lay followers. It is the scholar monks from the sanghas who functioned as missionaries throughout Asia and more recently in the Western world. It is important that becoming a monk is primarily a choice of the individual, unlike becoming a Brahman, which is by inheritance. It is this voluntary organization that was a primary source for missionaries in Buddhism, just as in Christianity from the fifth century to the present in the missionary orders of Roman Catholicism and the traveling monks of Eastern Orthodoxy and the Churches of the East. On the other hand, the arrival of Christianity in Asia in association with colonialism stimulated oppositional identification by people with traditional religions, including Buddhism. Bellah (1985 [1957]:51) states, "As a measure to combat Christianity the Tokugawa government required all Japanese to be registered members of some recognized Buddhist sect."

Other Asian religions had similar, but generally not as strong organizations as the Buddhist sanghas or the Buddhist sects that developed primarily in Mahayana. What became known as Hinduism spread in South Asia under the leadership of priestly brahmans who occupied the highest status and were the bearers of a religious literature in Sanskrit. Although conquest and political domination took place in northern India, the major means for the spread of Hindu beliefs and practices was through the peaceful acceptance of the social caste system associated with brahmans along with their epic religious literature. The Dravidian people to the south, who previously had occupied the north, left inscriptions in their own language at various sites. However, Sanskrit religious literature came to dominate South Asia so that the later Dravidian literature consisted primarily of themes originally presented in Sanskrit (Marr 1989 [1975]). Because Sanskrit became the "prestige language," its adoption by courts in the south and in Indianized Southeast Asia caused the spread of Hinduism in what became its "Great Tradition" with many of its elements drawn from the receiving societies, thus creating its many "Little Traditions." Keay (2000:132) notes, "[Sanskrit's] unexpected emergence as a language of contemporary record in the second century A D, and its subsequent acceptance as the medium of courtly and intellectual discourse throughout India, may be taken as a sure sign of brahmanical renaissance."

Alastair Lamb (1989 [1975]:446) discussing the various ways in which Indianization of Southeast Asia may have taken place primarily after the turn of the first millennium CE comments:

> Another mechanism can perhaps be detected in the deliberate borrowing by indigenous South-East Asian rulers of the techniques of Indian political organization, of which they learned either from merchants visiting their territories or from themselves visiting early entrepots...Since Indian political life was so inextricably bound up with the religious cosmology, one would expect that self-Indianization, as it were, would result in the establishment, at an

> official level, of an Indian-type religion in the charge of a brahmanical priestly caste, whose role would be comparable to that filled today by Western advisers in an under-developed nation.

Thus, it is not so much that Hinduism traditionally sent out missionaries, but that it was so embedded in a social system with scholar-priests at the apex, that it spread as Indian culture spread accompanied by its religious literature. In a rather similar way, Confucianism also spread to Korea, Japan, and Vietnam with Chinese culture, a major component of which is Chinese literature with its dominant Confucian thought. However, Chinese Confucian literati and their imitators in other countries, though at the top of the social scale and politically influential, did not carry religious thought to the same extent as Hindu brahmans. Instead, they helped to establish the system of "regulated religious pluralism" that is typical in the countries in which Chinese culture became influential. In the end the spread of Hinduism and Confucianism as primarily the spread of their respective cultures has proven more limited than the spread of Buddhism, even though Hinduism remained dominant in India with twice as many adherents as the more wide-spreading Buddhism. Confucianism re-established its dominance in East Asia after periods in which Buddhism was favored by rulers, but Buddhism drew the specific loyalty of many more people than Confucianism.

Let us consider the impact of Buddhist organizations on its spread. Both Buddhism and Jainism developed as religious innovative sects that were critical of the caste system of Brahmanism (Thapar 1969 [1960] ; Upadhye 1989 [1975]). As sectarian movements, membership was by choice rather than by descent, as with the brahmin priests. This sectarian characteristic remained with Buddhism and sets it apart from Hinduism. Mahavira, the reputed founder of Jainism and slightly older contemporary of Gautama Buddha, was already a member of a religious order or sect. The Jains and the Buddhists were both sramansas or recluses, who were antagonistic to the priestly Vedic religion of the brahmans. Jainism and Buddhism were organized in a very similar way into sanghas or orders of monks having lay followers. As sectarian groups, they were both more organized with egalitarian monks, who could be traveling teachers or missionaries, than were the brahman priests who developed the "Great Tradition" of Hinduism.

Jain ideas, especially ahismsa or universal love, has been very influential in Indian thought, including the thought of Mahatma Gandhi, and Jains were supported by prominent and wealthy people. Jainism, in fact, has been more influential in India over the long term than Buddhism. However, Buddhism, particularly its teaching of the dhamma (dharma in Sanskrit), gained the support of the Maurya Dynasty, who appointed officers to teach this primarily moral doctrine in their land and in other lands. It first took root in Sri Lanka where it gained the favor of the rulers. Sri Lanka was influential in the spread of Buddhism to the rest of Southeast Asia. Northern India was invaded by the Central Asian Kushans in the first century C. E., who accepted Buddhism and then aided in spreading it through Central Asia to China. Thus Buddhist organizations and missionary efforts were enhanced by the support of rulers. (Government support for religions will be considered in the next chapter.)

Regarding the sending out of Buddhist monk-missionaries, the best evidence we have is in the spread of Buddhism to China. Latourette (1956:165) writes:

> Buddhism was brought to China through numerous foreign missionaries. From the names that have come down to us we know that some were from

Cambodia, some from Ceylon and some from India, including South India, and that others, perhaps the larger proportion, were from what are now Northwest India and Afghanistan (where, it will be recalled, the Kushan kings, a Yueh Chih dynasty, had espoused it), and from regions in Central Asia to which the faith had spread from that center–Parthia, for example, and what is now the New Dominion [Xinjiang]. Some came to the South by way of the sea, and others to the North by overland routes.

Mahayana Buddhism formed a variety of sects with distinctive schools of thought in China and Japan. Some of the best examples are the Pure Land Sects, the Intuitive Sects, primarily Ch'an in China and Zen in Japan, the Rationalist Sects, primarily T'ien-T'ai in China and Tendai in Japan, the Mystery or True Word Sects, primarily Chen Yen in China and Shingon in Japan, and the Socio-political Sects, which have appeared primarily in Japan. The many sects of Mahayana Buddhism are an outgrowth of the sangha system in which committed and inspired individuals are able to develop innovative religious thought and attract members to their organizations.

Collins (1999) is interested in how religious organizations, particularly monastic orders, contributed to the development of capitalism. He (1999:201,220) states that "In China the most successful movements were the missionary-oriented Amidaists and later the Ch'an (Zen) sect, which broke with the ritualistic sects of the capital cities and set up rural monasteries using manual labor from novice monks." However, it was in Japan that Buddhist organizations became the strongest:

> The original Japanese society of kin-based clans was organized in the sixth and seventh centuries into a

> centralized state, primarily by establishing Buddhism as a state religion. The original Buddhist temples were modeled on organizational lineages imported form China and Korea, at just the time when T'ang dynasty Buddhism was wealthiest and most powerful. In Japan it grew even more dominant than in China, since the rival power of Confucian bureaucracy that eventually undercut Buddhism failed to develop in Japan...The major Buddhist temples became the leading landholders and centers of the largest extractive networks.

In recent times Buddhist lay people have established organizations to meet various changes in modern societies, and to some extent have modeled these organizations on Christian service organizations. One of the best examples of this is the Young Men's Buddhist Association developed in the late nineteenth century in Sri Lanka from where it spread to India, Burma, and other countries (Gard 1962). In Japan, especially, Buddhism has produced organizations based on Buddhist teachings that also functioned as political action groups. Soka Gakkai is probably the best known of such organizations. It expects exclusive loyalty, which is an exception to the typical pattern of nonexclusive religious practice in Japan.

Sikhism seemed to have the potential to form orders like Buddhism. It was founded in the fifteenth century after the entrance of Islam to South Asia and in many ways resembles Islam in its organization more than traditional Asian religions. Although it became a strong religious community within India, at the same time it became a distinct social group. Sikhism, however, did not break out of the caste system, as Buddhism was able to do. The Sikhs became identified with certain Indian castes, the leaders with the mercantile Khatri castes and their followers with the rural Jats (McLeod 1989 [1975]). Nevertheless, all Sikhs can join the Khalsa brotherhood and observe its codes and adopt its external insignia.

In many respects, what happened to Sikhism, is similar to what happened to Christianity and Zoroastrianism in India. Christianity was introduced at least by the second century and perhaps in the latter part of the first century. It maintained a Syrian and Persian connection that was represented in its ecclesiastical language and its traditions (Moffett 1992:266-7; Philip 1998:91-109). Although much larger than Sikhism and not considered "native," Christianity was early given a caste or at least a guild status and thus categorized as a "special people." Zoroastrianism was introduced to India primarily by the relocation of Iranians there. Even more than Christians, Zoroastrians are identified as a special people, namely as the Parsees, because of their ethnic origins. Thus, the identification of religions with distinct social groups having memberships by descent (as opposed to being voluntary associations) tends to hinder their spread. This is a circular movement since religions that don't spread tend to become mainly descent groups.

Of the three religions that spread widely, Buddhism was the least well organized and has the least emphasis on regular and large gatherings of lay followers. However, among the religions of Asia with which it primarily competed, Buddhism was usually better organized on the level of religious specialists (the sangha) than any of the others. Primarily, Buddhism had the necessary belief for a missionary religion, discussed in Chapter 1, in which a single or at least primary ideal human mediating figure offers access to the Divine and to salvation. At the same time, the spread of Buddhism was hindered because it incorporated popular religions, which emphasize transient participation in rituals and community festivals. Popular religions strengthen community social groups and local identities, but do not encourage voluntary commitments to organizations and to missions.

CHRISTIAN GATHERING AND ORGANIZATION

As in the case of many religious leaders, Jesus gathered followers around him. Furthermore, more than in any other religion, missionary training and a clear missionary mandate were given to the followers. In its early period for some three hundred years Christianity did not have orders of monks as in Buddhism or in later Christianity. Instead, it established open voluntary fellowships of ordinary individuals and households. Early Christians thought of themselves as "followers" of the Way and had a sense of being connected to one another as part of a common movement, which today could be called a "missionary religious movement" (Bird 2002:225,245n). Jewish congregationalism was an important model for forming the loose connection of Christian congregations, although the element of choice or voluntary association became increasingly more important for Christians than for Jews as Gentiles joined the movement. The rite of baptism, used from the beginning, became an important means of forming a Christian identity, as were the regular weekly gatherings with joint worship and celebrations of a sacred common meal (Horrell 2002:320). These regular meetings functioned as very effective "rites of intensification" in which common faith and values were continually reasserted and strengthened, creating emotional and moral energy.

From its beginning Christianity contained the clearest mandate to spread of all religions (Matthew 28:19,20; Acts 1:8). However, external conditions also had an important influence on the spread (or lack of spread) of Christianity, as witness the persecution in Jerusalem that scattered many of the Christians (Acts 8:1) or the special receptivity of people of lower social status (I Corinthians 1:26-31), but also of urbanized artisans and merchants together with women (Acts 16:11-

15; Stark 1997 [1996]). External conditions affecting the spread of religions will be considered in succeeding chapters. Nevertheless, the mixed groups of believers in Antioch were soon to show that the missionary mandate was taken seriously by formally sending out a missionary team led by Paul and Barnabas (Acts 13:2,3). Wherever Paul went he was careful to set up organized congregations with local leaders (Acts 14:21-23; 20:17) and also continually encourage them to be faithful as witnessed by his letters. Christians were encouraged to meet regularly (Hebrews 10:25).

Numerous loosely connected congregations developed in the Roman Empire as a result of the witness of traveling preachers or simply believers who witnessed to their faith as they moved throughout the empire. In its first three hundred years various "denominations" developed within Christianity made up of people who had different interpretations or simply emphases of the faith and lived in different areas. In fact, considerable diversity is shown within the New Testament itself, among the earliest Jewish followers, and then between Jewish and Gentile Christianities. Some of the latter showed leanings toward (or actual participation in) what came to be called "Gnosticism" (Colossians 2:16-23; I John 4:1-6). Significantly, the missionary Paul welcomed a certain amount of competition and diversity, as long as Christ was preached (Philippians 1:15-18), although he strongly opposed those who sought to impose legalistic requirements (see Letter to the Galatians).

Groups that came to be regarded as deviant, sometimes after long periods, were the Gnostics, the Marcionites, the Montanists, the Donatists, the Novatians, and the Arians. The Gnostics and the Marcionites, who had similarities in the basic changes they encouraged in their interpretation of the Scriptures and the nature of Jesus (particularly denying his humanity) and also in practicing asceticism, were strongly opposed by other Christians. They became unimportant in the Christian movement, except as they helped to crystallize orthodox Christian thought and its organization in opposition to them. Irenaeus (ca 140-202) is an example of one who worked intensely against the Gnostics. According to our theory, one of the reasons the Gnostics became unimportant is that they deemphasized the humanity of Jesus Christ and at the same time did not form strong organizations requiring personal commitments from members.

The other movements mentioned (Montanists and Donatists) were primarily movements against laxity among Christians and many of their leaders. The goal of greater "spirituality" was also present among the Gnostics and the Marcionites. To the present, churches have been periodically divided by efforts to purify them and create more "spiritual" bodies that are less "conformed to the world," for example the Medieval Cathars and Waldensians (quite different from each other in other respects). In Colossians 2:16-23, usually thought of as directed against people leaning toward Gnosticism, Paul argues against external asceticism or an outward show of piety. This passage, as well as the passages against judging others, shows that the tendency to make judgments on the scale of religious purity and orthodoxy began early in Christian organizations. Montantists and Donatists also had regional and ethnic influences in their origins, both of which today would probably have become denominations. The potentially largest denomination was Arianism that grew out of the famous struggle over the understanding of the nature of Jesus Christ and of the Trinity. Arianism placed Christ at a subordinate, though still elevated, position in relation to God the Father by rejecting the term, homoousios ('of one being') to describe the relationship. Most of the Goths, who invaded the Roman Empire and destroyed Rome in 410, had become Arian Christians.

A major change took place in Christian organizations in the fourth century with the alliance made between the government of the Roman Empire and Christian leaders. Other than Monophysitism and Nestorianism that came to exist largely outside of Roman governmental control, Christian leaders were able to have paganism and the unapproved versions of Christianity, already mentioned, suppressed by force. The various Christian groups also used violence and coercion during the doctrinal struggles surrounding the church councils and later in the iconoclastic controversy (Jenkins 2010). Monophysites and Nestorians to the east were both cut off from the Orthodox Church. The Western Roman Catholic and Eastern Orthodox Churches divided officially in 1054 accepting the principle that a single version of Christianity should be hegemonic in a particular area. In the West, particularly where Roman political power collapsed, Christianity adopted the hierarchical organization of the Roman Empire. Because of the single dominant state in the East, the Orthodox Church did not develop the hierarchical structure and organizational unity of the Western Church. National or "autocephalous" churches were able to develop in the East.

The single Church with multiple states in the West provided a basis for the sacred-secular distinction, originally made within the church that would become so important in Western European history. Added to that was the historical development of more or less autonomous bodies. Beginning with the monasteries, but soon in other aspects of life, such as universities, guilds, and towns, autonomous organizations developed that gave Western Europeans experience in forming corporate bodies. Opposition religious movements, such as the Cathars, Waldensians, Lollards, and Hussites, established effective organizations, spreading organizational skills (Kaelber 1998). The experiences in forming autonomous organizations provided a basis for the organization of Protestant voluntarily based congregations, as well as for the later institutionalization of science (Huff 1993).

Contrary to much opinion, I argue that the development of the hierarchical organizational structure of Christianity, that matched and to some extent replaced the hierarchical structure of the Roman Empire, did not add to the ability of Christianity to spread. Rather, the centralization of power, the monopolization of religious expression, and the shift to an emphasis on membership by descent instead of by choice all brought about a decrease in missions and a slowing of growth. The characteristic that Christianity had in its first three hundred years of being primarily a set of voluntary organizations was greatly weakened. The evidence from before the fourth century in the Roman Empire and before the adoption of Christianity by the many rulers and the establishment of state churches under "little Constantines" in Europe is that Christianity spread most effectively as a loose and noncentrally organized body. When it developed its state allied hierarchical structure Christian growth ebbed. The voluntary orders or organizations of religious specialists did the work of spreading Christianity in Europe, in some respects like the spreading of Buddhism, and also Islam, as we shall see. The constant spawning of orders, which competed with one another, did the most to sustain the vitality and growth to the present of the Roman Catholic Church and its missionary efforts (Finke and Wittberg 2000).

In addition to spreading throughout the Empire before the fourth century, Christianity spread beyond its borders to the east in Syria, Arabia, Armenia, Georgia, Persia, Central Asia, India, and China, carried primarily by missionary monks. It spread to the north among the Goths in its Arian version as already mentioned. As noted, Christianity spread throughout Europe most often by traveling individual monks or small groups of monks, led by strong missionaries, such as Martin of

Tours, Patrick, Columba, Ethelbert, Willibrord, Winfrith (Boniface), and the wandering (peregrine) Irish monks. It is true that the Pope sent Augustine to England from Rome, but this was to bring the gospel to England a second or even a third time among people already being reached by Celtic missionaries. The Christianization of Europe by around 1000 CE was carried out primarily by missionaries sent across borders from within Europe rather than from Rome. However, the voluntary basis of church membership was largely lost except among the orders. The church continued to grow in political power as leaders accepted Christianity, while missionary effort declined. Christianity entered a period in which it ebbed rather than flowed after 1000 up to about 1500. The Roman Catholic Church had become primarily a territorial church with Christianity an ascribed cultural identity, rather than a personal choice to participate in a voluntary body of believers and witnesses. The Orthodox Church, with a similar type of membership, and the Church in the East (Nestorian and Monophysite) were largely stymied by Islam in further expansion to the east. There were individual exceptions to the general lack of missionary effort, for example, Raymond Lull who urged missionary outreach to the Mongols and made three missionary trips to North Africa where he was stoned to death in 1315 or 1316 (Latourette 1953:404). Also, Franciscans and Dominicans carried out missions to North Africa, the Middle East, and as far as China.

After 1500 the spread of Christianity resumed with the age of exploration and colonization. The formation of Protestant congregations and the Reformation within the Roman Catholic Church brought a new focus on Jesus Christ and voluntary commitment to his cause. Roman Catholic orders, the Franciscans, Dominicans, and the Jesuits, began to carry out missions to distant lands along with the explorers from Portugal and Spain, who had a sense of mission for Christianity and usually carried monks with them. Protestants, except for the Radical Reformers, adopted the pattern of the monopolistic state church, which hindered the development of missions. Among major Protestant groups it was only after the voluntary association or congregational approach within Protestantism asserted itself, combining with a new emphasis on experiential or Pietistic faith in the seventeenth and eighteenth centuries, that the modern missionary movement got underway.

Beginning in the eighteenth century with European small evangelical groups, by the turn of the nineteenth century missionary societies were formed and the modern missionary movement that has continued to the present began to grow. The voluntarily organized missionary societies, organizations with high lay participation, made the vast modern spread of Christianity possible. In addition to obtaining missionaries from their ranks, they raised voluntary contributions from the new middle class that prospered from the industrial revolution. The mobilization of these resources made the modern missionary movement a reality. And the movement hasn't stopped, but continues to grow.

Church members formed mission societies dedicated to the cause of spreading Christianity. By the middle of the nineteenth century, whole denominations formed themselves into mission societies with mission boards focusing on efforts to carry Christianity to foreign countries, as well as carry out domestic missions. Organizationally speaking, mission societies and churches with mission boards, along with the missionary orders, such as the Maryknolls, the Society of the Divine Word, and the Jesuits, have proven to be the most efficient way of spreading Christianity. This is a form of specialization and competition that has become characteristic of economic and political organizations in modern societies.

Recent variations within Christianity in the sending out of

missionaries give added support to Proposition 3.1 at the first of the chapter. That is, voluntary independent associations continually increased their participation in missions over against long-established churches. In the last half century there has been a shift in the kinds of mission organizations sending out missionaries, with conservative and independent (para-church) agencies sending out more missionaries than the older mainline churches. There has also been a change in the kinds of missionaries going out in both new and old churches from life-term to short-term, with many part-time missionaries also going out from local congregations or on their own. Stark (2001:93) writes, "There is a substantial (but unknown) number of self-appointed American missionaries serving abroad who do not show up in the published statistics."

In spite of the fact that mainline churches have fallen behind independent and conservative churches in sending out missionaries, they are continuing to send out missionaries and provide support for churches, projects, and institutions in many parts of the world. They have actually increased the number of countries in which they have representative workers. When all the varied kinds of missionaries are included, Stark (2001:94) estimates that there are about 185,000 American Protestant missionaries abroad, not including tens of thousands of Mormons and Jehovah's Witnesses. If Roman Catholic missionaries are added the total comes close to 400,000.

Along with this enormous increase of people from North America serving as missionaries, it is important to take into account the internationalizing of Christian missionary service. This refers to the sending out of missionaries from numerous Christian bases all over the world. The Christian churches outside of the West are not as wealthy as the Western churches, some being quite poor, but nevertheless these churches are sending out missionaries. Korea may be the leader of non-

Western churches in sending out some 15,000 or more missionaries to foreign countries. Christian groups in Latin America, India, Africa, and other lands are also sending out missionaries, often primarily to people of other ethnic groups in their own or neighboring countries, but many missionaries are also going with the out migration from these lands.

ISLAMIC GATHERING AND ORGANIZATION

The most recent of the world religions to spread widely is Islam, which began spreading in the seventh century when Christianity still had much of Europe in which to spread. Islam, of course, originated among the Arab people, who carried it widely in their great revitalization movement and ethnic expansion of the seventh and eighth centuries. To a great extent, the organization of Islam as a religion took on a tribal character from its founding, with natural leaders and followers forming a community known as the umma. In the umma there was no clear distinction between political and religious leadership, as in the areas where Christianity was predominant. (Similarly, Christianity took on the organizational characteristics of the society in which it first spread, namely the Roman Empire.) Islamic leadership could be charismatic or traditional or with elements of both (Weber 1967 [1946]:297), while the followers remained connected through their loyalty to God and to one another.

Regarding the sense of belonging on an equal basis to a community created by Islam, Hourani (1991:147) states:

> Those who accepted Islam formed a community (*umma*). 'You are the best *umma* brought forth for mankind, bidding unto good, rejecting what is disapproved, believing in God': these words of the Qur'an express something important about the

adherents of Islam. By striving to understand and obey God's commandments, men and women created a right relationship with God, but also with each other. As the Prophet said in his 'pilgrimage of farewell': 'know that every Muslim is a Muslim's brother, and that the Muslims are brethren.'

Although membership in Islam was informal and nonbureaucratic (not rational-legal) it was marked and directed clearly and simply by the specific activities required in the "Five Pillars." The first of these acts or rituals is the shahada or testimony that "there is no god but God, and Muhammad is the Prophet of God." The second is the daily prayers in which the shahada is repeated, a ritual washing with various motions (bowing, kneeling, prostrating) performed, and prayers repeated. The third Pillar is the making of gifts (zakat) for the needy, which included liberating slaves. The fourth and fifth Pillars are sawn or fasting once a year during Ramadan and the Hajj or the pilgrimage to Mecca, to be made at least once in a lifetime. The five pillars emphasize the crucial element of choice and commitment in Islam, which carries it beyond being simply a religion with membership by descent. They also provided clear marks of identity for Muslims. The five pillars made it possible for Islam to break out of being a means primarily of ethnic identity for Arabs to become a worldwide community composed of people from many ethnic groups and nations.

Islam adopted both the authoritarian and egalitarian system that existed among the Arab tribes and this system became typical of Islamic organizations. This type of organization was acceptable to many other tribal peoples, especially the leaders, as the pattern to which they were already accustomed, but with a new uniting religion creating group loyalty based in the transcendent all powerful, but compassionate God. A series of multiple strong leaders exercised religious and political leadership over various peoples, each group united by a common faith and connected to other groups through a common faith. However, leaders and their peoples were often in competition and periodic conflict with each other and were periodically challenged and replaced by other members of the umma. Thus, after the first century and a half of Islamic history, Arab power declined as it became divided among numerous kingdoms and sultanates. In fact, problems with succession and authority developed soon after Muhammad's death and have plagued Arab kingdoms to the present. This helps to account for why Islam did not become elaborately hierarchical or centrally organized as Western Christianity. However, it did tend to become pervasive in societies, although this took some time where large Christian populations continued in the Middle East, at least until the Crusades and in some cases to the present, as in Egypt, where there are over 10 million Christians.

Muslims have carried the importance of the community for Muslim identity and for creating a sense of responsibility throughout the world. Esposito (2010:40) states, "Being a Muslim gives one a community identity and responsibility. Muslims of every sex, race, and ethnic or national background are members of a transnational, worldwide community of believers (ummah), responsible for creating a just society on earth."

Regarding the religious organization of Islam, Lewis (1993:263) states:

> As a building, a place of public worship, the Muslim equivalent of the church is the mosque; as an institution, a corporate body with its own hierarchy and laws, there is no church in Islam. For the same reason, there is no priesthood in the true sense of the term, and therefore no prelates or hierarchy, no councils or synods, to

> define orthodoxy and thus condemn heterodoxy. The ulema, the professional men of religion in the Islamic world, may perhaps be called a clergy in the sociological but certainly not in the theological sense. They receive no ordination; they have no parishes; nor do they perform any sacraments. There is no priestly mediation between the worshiper and his God, and in early Islam there was no constituted ecclesiastical authority of any kind.

Lewis goes on to say that classical Islam has no laity because it has no concept of something separate or separable from religious authority expressed by such words as lay, temporal, or secular. However, we can say that at least Islam has "religious specialists." These are the scholars of the scriptures (the Qu'ran or Koran) and the written traditions (hadith), who are known as ulema ('ulama) collectively. Also, Lewis (1993:263) notes, "From late medieval times, something like a parish clergy emerged, ministering to the needs of ordinary people in cities and villages, but these were usually separate from and mistrusted by the ulema and owed much more to mystical than to dogmatic Islam." Thus, it can be said that Islam, like Christianity, in principle is organized as a whole to spread and any believer can bring others to the faith. Moreover, Muslims, not having the formally organized clergy system of most of Christianity, are prepared even more in principle to spread their faith as individual believers. Nevertheless, in most areas where it has spread, Islam has produced functioning clergy, namely the people who have chosen to prepare themselves to know the faith more than others and are prepared to explain it.

Even in the nineteenth century, Thomas Arnold argued against the prevalent view that Islam spread primarily by the sword. However, in his actual treatment of the spread of Islam, he reports that preaching was often preceded, accompanied, or followed by an element of compulsion. This was largely due to the fact that the religion of Islam so closely allied or fused itself with governments. Nevertheless, Arnold (2006 [1896]:3) emphasizes:

> The spread of this faith over so vast a portion of the globe is due to various causes, social, political and religious: but among these, one of the most powerful factors at work in the production of this stupendous result, has been the unremitted labours of Muslim missionaries, who, with the Prophet himself as their great ensample, have spent themselves for the conversion of unbelievers.

Arnold (2006 [1896]:408-09) points out that Muslim missionary work has not been nearly as well organized as in Christianity. The very lack of a priestly class, "set apart for the work of propagating the faith" means that there is a "feeling of responsibility resting on the individual believer." The result is that ordinary Muslims from every walk of life, but especially traders, have been effective in spreading their faith. At the same time, there remain the scholars and teachers in the mosques and schools who inspire ordinary Muslims to share the knowledge of their faith with others.

To give an example of organized Islamic mission work, Sanneh (1996:12-18), in discussing the spread of Islam to West Africa, describes the work of "clerics" and a "clerical missionary center" that were instrumental in converting kings, who then peacefully led their people into Islam. This is very similar to the way Christianity spread to European kingdoms, although some Christian rulers used coercion to persuade their subjects as in Norway and Germany. One particular group in West Africa was the "Serakhulle clerics" better known as

"Jahanke," who "established a missionary career based on scrupulous abjuration of war and of politics (al-harb wa al-siyasah), including chieftaincy office for themselves" (Sanneh 1996:18). Although force was used at times, for example by the Fulani reformer, Shehu (Shaykh 'Uthman b. Fudi, 1754-1817), the broad pattern of Islamization was by peaceful means through "cleric" scholars, who were members of "clergy groups."

Basically, even if there is a large population that is only aware of inheriting their faith rather than choosing it (just as in Christianity), Islam has a core (many cores) of committed people who have chosen to be scholars or mystics or both (some of whom later became saints) and are prepared to teach the faith to others. In addition, as Hourani (1991:152) points out: "From the beginning there have been some followers of the prophets for whom external observances were of no worth unless they expressed a sincerity of intention, a desire to obey God's commands from a sense of His greatness and the littleness of man, and unless they were regarded as the elementary forms of a moral discipline which should extend to the whole of life."

When Islam is considered in all of its institutional variations, it appears that the Sufis were both often the best organized and the most active in missions, which supports our theory about the positive relationship of the central figure, moral energy, and organization with the spread of religions. Ernst (2003:167) writes that the Sufis had a notion of a "mystical spiritual community" traced back to the "People of the Bench," the "first example of organized spiritual life based on a community that shared everything." Ernst (2003:178-180) compared the institutional formation of Sufi orders to the more centrally organized Christian monastic orders, but noted that "the major impact of the Sufi orders in terms of religion was the popularization of the spiritual practices of the Sufis on a mass scale." In the nineteenth century, "with the overthrow of traditional elites by European conquest, Sufi orders in some regions remained the only surviving Islamic social structures, and they furnished the principle leadership for anticolonial struggles in places such as Algeria, Libya, the Caucasus, and China." Coming to the present, Ernst (2003:181) points out that "Sufi orders are surviving despite the restrictions of modern governments and the opposition of fundamentalists." They "preserve the influence of saints of the past and make possible a more direct personal access to God and the prophet through spiritual discipline."

Other scholars have recognized the importance of the Sufis as missionaries. Van der Veer (1994:34), speaking of the spread of Islam to South Asia through the Sufis, states;

> When I speak of Sufis I do not refer to something vague as "Islamic mystics," but to brotherhoods (tariqat) of people initiated by a vow of spiritual allegiance (bai'at) to a saint (pir) who claims to belong on a spiritual lineage going back to the founder of the brotherhood and ultimately to the Prophet himself. Most brotherhoods were founded outside of South Asia in places like Baghdad, but some, such as the Chishti brotherhood, are almost exclusively South Asian.

Thus, the search for the path by which the true believer would be able to draw near to God led to the formation of the Sufis, who have been leaders in the spread of the faith. In addition, throughout its history Islam has continuously generated groups of highly dedicated people. In the modern era a number of groups have been generated in reaction to secularization in Islamic governments and to the intrusion of the West in Muslin lands. It is not my purpose here to analyze the forces that generated the modern movements within Islam. It is simply to point out that Islam contains within it the capacity of forming groups based on strong voluntary commitments. Just as Roman Catholicism was kept vital by the continuous formation of competing orders, so Islam has been kept vital by competing schools, such as the jurists and the Sufis, each with its various subschools. Gunn (2003) reports on the various kinds of Islamic expressions currently vying with one another to be the major shapers of Islamic identity in Central Asia: Sunni Islam of the Hanafi school, Sufism, Shi'ism, "popular Islam," and Islamism.

The da'wa in Islam based on Muhammad being sent "as a universal (Messenger) to men" (Saba', 34:28) places an obligation on Muslims to share their faith with all people. Nevertheless, Islam did not have as clear a missionary mandate from its founder as Christianity. Historically, it is not known to have specifically sent out missionaries on the scale of Christianity. However, Islam clearly meets the necessary criteria for spreading of having organizations that offer people the opportunity to choose to make a commitment to the truths it teaches. Its lack of a hierarchical structure and sharp distinction between clergy and lay people, along with its varied organizational and intellectual expressions, has been an advantage rather than a disadvantage to it in spreading its message. Like Christianity, Islam gathers believers in regular weekly meetings that serve as powerful "rites of intensification" and producers of emotional energy. In addition, going beyond the formal observances in most of Christianity, Islam calls on its followers to follow a discipline of regular prayer, praying five times a day. Its greatest disadvantage in spreading, just as in Christianity, has been when religious membership has been primarily by descent, not by choice. In the end, it has been dedicated people in voluntary organizations that have been the major carriers of Islam to new societies. However, the major growth of Islam in the past was from the conversion of whole peoples, beginning with their leaders (as Christianity spread in Europe), such as the Turks, North Africans, Sub-Saharan Africans, some in the Balkans, Mongols, and Indonesians, who saw in Islam a means of uniting their people under God. In addition, Islam has spread among people in the West, primarily by immigration, but also by conversion of individuals. In the United States, conversions have been primarily among the African American minority, which has felt disaffected from the dominant Christian community. This matter will be considered again in Chapter 5 on Intersocietal Relations.

CONCLUSION

Religions consist of both beliefs and practices. The three religions that have spread more widely than other religions, Buddhism, Christianity, and Islam, had distinctive beliefs and practices that made it possible for them to spread and were necessary for them to spread. In the first chapter we considered their crucial belief in a mediating figure. In the second chapter we considered the moral guidance and energy these religions carried that made them attractive. This chapter focused on the gathering and organizing abilities of these religious that enabled them to spread. Specifically, these religions gathered people in emotionally energizing meetings that meet regularly and formed organizations that would propagate their faiths. The religions have been the most effective when the gatherings and organizations were based on voluntary religious commitment. These kinds of organization were able to send out missionaries and they gave people an opportunity to choose and commit themselves to new religious identities as part of a new community of believers.

Christianity has carried the principle of efficient organization further than any other religion by its development of organizations with constitutions, officers, regular meetings, membership records, and what can be easily recognized as bureaucratic structures. It has incorporated rational-legal principles of organization more than any other religion.

In fact, the very rational-legal organization of Christianity in some of its branches has threatened the "movement spirit" that is so important for its missionary activity and its spread. The earliest threat to the active spread of Christianity was when it adopted the pattern of the state church beginning in the fourth century. This tended to reduce the voluntary spirit in the church, as Christianity became primarily a cultural marker of identity. However, religious orders and later, congregations and mission societies, kept alive the principle of the voluntary religious body and continued to provide missionaries to carry the faith worldwide. It was the organization of local congregations and missionary societies that revived the voluntary religious body among the laity in the eighteenth and especially the nineteenth century. From the earliest days Christians sent out missionaries, but the number of missionaries greatly increased in the nineteenth century and has continued to grow with increasing local and part-time involvement. As a result, Christianity has become the largest world religion with over two billion people who identify themselves as Christians.

Part II A
MACRO SECULAR SOCIAL FACTORS

CHAPTER 4

INTERNAL SOCIAL CONDITIONS IN RECEIVING SOCIETIES AND THE SPREAD OF RELIGIONS

TRANSITION TO THE NEXT FOUR CHAPTERS

Buddhism, Christianity, and Islam needed to have certain distinctive beliefs and practices in order to spread more widely than any other religions. The necessary belief was in a central elevated human being who was able to be a means for all people to gain access to the Divine and salvation. The necessary practices were providing moral guidance and energy and gathering and organizing people in a body to which they could choose to commit themselves, and that could then be a base for sending out missionaries.

Although such belief, morality, and gathering and organizing abilities are necessary for religions to spread, they are not sufficient for this to happen because there are certain secular social factors external to religions that have the capacity to block or facilitate their spread. These social factors are not able to cause the religions to spread without the necessary internal religious causes already considered. In the next four chapters (Parts II A and II B) we consider four categories of secular social factors and how they affect the spread of religions, facilitating or blocking them. The first two categories of secular social factors (Part II A) are on the macro level: (1) internal social conditions in receiving societies and (2) intersocietal relationships. The next two categories of secular social factors (Part II B) are on the micro level: (3) social relationships and (4) motivations. The study cannot treat all the specific factors within the categories, but attempts to isolate some of the most important ones.

OPPORTUNITIES FOR RELIGIOUS CHOICES

The first secular social factor in receiving societies to consider is the opportunities available in societies for making choices. I make the general proposition:

4.1 *In order for a religion to spread successfully people in a receiving society must have the opportunity to choose to be identified with a new religion.*

Rambo (1993:60) in his study of conversion discusses "structural availability" or "the freedom of a person or persons to move from previous emotional, intellectual, and religions institutions, commitments, and obligations into new options." He is looking primarily at current societies, but in the present study the condition to be considered is for societies over approximately the last two thousand years. To understand the opportunities people have had over the last two millennia and across various societies to choose new religions means understanding the structures of societies and how they change. In particular, we need to understand how societies are held together and what the place of religion may be in this integration. The opportunity to choose a new religion is an important part of the total opportunity structure in a society. In every society authority and power are exercised by certain people and in certain ways that either allow, or prevent particular kinds of choices, including religious choices, to be made by people at various levels in societies. Rulers have an interest in societies being held together under their rule. If people in authority fear that the choice of a new religion threatens the unity of their society, especially if another religion (the traditional religion) has been used to strengthen unity and establish identities, they will seek to limit choices for a new religion in various ways, including by force. They are also likely to emphasize the importance of maintaining traditional beliefs and practices. On the other hand, they may not feel threatened by a new religion under certain circumstances and may even see it as an opportunity to enhance their rule and to create new unity and identity for their people. This is particularly true where no alliance has been made between the political and religious leaders.

It is true that freedom of religion is very much a modern concept. Even more, it has become a modern ideal or normative goal for many societies. However, freedom of religion can only be attained when a particular religion is not considered the key integrating force in a society by those with authority and power. This is why freedom of religion has been linked historically with the secularization process, understood as the separation of religion from government and other common public institutions, not necessarily the decline of religion. However, since the religions being considered spread over the last two thousand years (before the modern secularization process), I will consider why relative freedom of religion existed in the past for some groups.

In most traditional societies in which religions are embedded and pervasive, although a particular religion may not be officially recognized or established, most members of the societies are socialized into the common religion and the opportunity to know and choose new religions is very limited. Believing and practicing the religion is taken for granted as a function of being a member of a given group or society. Thus the religion becomes a marker for ethnic or national identity. Although in traditional societies, most of which are hierarchical in structure, people usually do not feel free to choose any religion other than the one commonly followed by those around them and into which they have been socialized, there are some important exceptions to this pattern. However, the exceptions are based not so much on the freedom of ordinary members of the society, but the freedom of leaders to choose new religions.

DIFFERENCES IN OPPORTUNITIES FOR CHOICES IN SMALL AND LARGE SOCIETIES

One of the important conditions in which people are able to know and to choose new religions is provided in small societies, such as tribal groups, not to most of the people, but to the leaders. Most small societies are quite homogeneous in their religious beliefs and practices. However, small societies are usually in contact with a variety of other societies, which follow other, though often similar, religions. In this sense most small societies exist in a "pluralistic religious field." If leaders see an advantage to a new religion that they have encountered or that is introduced to their group, *since the religion of their own society has no official status*, they feel free to lead their society into accepting the new religion. This is exactly what may be seen as happening repeatedly in the spread of Buddhism, Christianity, and Islam, as they spread to relatively small pre-literate societies without officially established religions. The question of perception of advantage or benefit will be considered later, but here, the point to be made is that the leaders of such small societies generally have the freedom to choose to bring about change, even if most members do not have the opportunity to make a choice to change religions unless such a choice has been made previously by a leader. Thus a second proposition that grows out of the first is:

4.2 *Religions spread more easily to relatively small pre-literate societies without official religions than to large complex societies with established literate religions that have strong links to governments.*

In large societies of the traditional type the opportunity structure is not likely to provide for many choices to be made by most people, surprisingly, including religious choices by the rulers. In such societies there are usually well-organized religious specialists and a strong religious tradition having its own literature. In most of these cases there is an official relationship between the governmental leaders and the organized religion in which the governing leadership is legitimated and the social order is considered grounded in the natural order with links to the cosmos. Leaders are considered divine or semi-divine, existing at the peak of the social order and connecting to the transcendent cosmos. These are van Leeuwen's (1964:165-71) "ontocratic" societies, which are unified with the cosmos through the leaders. A pyramidal structure or sacred mountain is often built, physically and metaphorically, in such societies. The structure symbolizes the pyramidal structure of the society with the few at the top who are connected to the transcendent cosmos and considered divine or semi-divine. In contrast, a major reason for the condition of freedom to choose by the leaders of small societies is that there is not yet an officially established religion limiting the freedom of the leaders.

"Small" and "large" are relative terms, but in general the small societies referred to here did (do) not have a highly organized state structure and do not have a religion with a literary tradition that has developed an ideology supporting the social and political order. Early small societies usually followed a primal religion. A primal religion is very similar to what Bellah (1969 [1964]:70,71) identifies as "primitive religion." Its two main features are "the high degree to which the mythical world is related to the detailed features of the actual world" and "fluidity of its organization." People in such societies are generally animistic in belief, namely believing that everything in nature contains conscious spirits, and religion does not exist as a separate social structure but is fused with society. In such societies, differentiation within religion and society are along lines of age, sex, and kinship. Primal religions typically do not have organized, only individual, religious specialists, for example, shamans, who carry out worship rites for individuals at special sacred sites. However, primal religions do not suddenly come to an end as civilizations develop. Instead, animistic beliefs are often preserved in popular religion in societies as they become larger and more complex. This may be observed in the traditional civilizations of the world, particularly in Asia, where large portions of populations follow animistic beliefs. Religions with a high animistic content may even be made into an official state religion as in Shintoism in Japan. Individual religious specialists may begin to organize in the period before a society becomes literate, as in the case of the Celtic Druids.

The fact remains that as societies become more complex and religions better organized and with literature, the state usually forms an alliance with the religion. It is not so much the sophistication of a religion that makes it difficult for a new religion to be received, but rather the embeddedness of the religion in the society and its alliance with the political order. The earlier freedom in which the leaders were able to choose new religions from a "pluralistic field" is lost as governments become allied to particular religions. However, there are special times in large societies when the alliances between religions and governments are weakened and a relative religious diversity comes into existence. It may be a time of unrest, turmoil, and transition when the old alliance is questioned and a new alliance has not yet been established between the rulers and a particular religion. An extension of this condition is when an empire has been newly constructed that incorporates a diverse group of societies, each having their own religion. The rulers tend to have great power and religious ideas and practices are relatively free to flow throughout such an empire. An additional proposition then is:

4.3 *New religions may spread in large societies where a particular religion has not yet been made monopolistic and thus where there is relative religious diversity.*

The matter of government influence on the spread of religions will be considered later in the chapter. However, I will first review the spread of the three religions to relatively small societies and also to large societies in which relative freedom of religion existed. This relative freedom is due to the lack of a strong alliance of the government with an official religion thereby allowing a certain amount of religious diversity. Some of these large societies did not need religion to integrate them and maintain order because of the extensive power of the rulers.

BUDDHISM

Buddhism spread and became most thoroughly embedded in societies over the centuries in the area to the southeast of India where numerous relatively small pre-literate or proto-literate societies existed that were open to the more advanced culture of India and sometimes China. Theravada Buddhism, after a period of competition in the courts with Hinduism, achieved official status where there had been no official religion previously.

In the northwestern part of India, Buddhism was accepted by the invading tribal people known as the Yeh Chih or Kushans in the first century CE. Subsequently, Mahayana Buddhism spread to Central Asian tribes, then on to China, and from there to Korea, Japan, and Vietnam. There were special conditions of unrest and change existing after the fall of the Han Dynasty in 220 CE in China that created opportunities and incentives for people to choose a new religion. China had not been a small, pre-literate society, but the largest and most complex society in East Asia. The native religions, Confucianism and Taoism, were organized and had literary traditions. Furthermore, Confucianism had gained official or quasi-official status as the religion of most government officials. However, the state of dislocation and turmoil caused by the invasions from the north influenced many people, including many literati, to migrate south. Thus at the time of the spread of Buddhism in China, the country was divided into warring kingdoms, with those in the north under the rule of invading tribal peoples. The new rulers, who were of Turkish origin with connections to Central Asia, often tended to favor Buddhism with which they were familiar. However, in southern China, there was also a movement toward Buddhism among the Chinese literati who had been displaced by invasions from the north (Zurcher 1959; Ch'en 1973 [1964]).

Buddhism also gained an entrance to Korea and Japan with ascendant rulers seeking ways to unify their kingdoms, a pattern observed in the spread of Christianity during the same period in Europe. It appears that the "axial age" (Jaspers 1949), which was in the first millennium B.C.E, was followed by the "diffusion age," although the "diffusion age" proved to be longer, even extending to the present. In East Asia, especially in China, a pattern of "quasi-secularism" developed which had some similarities to the Roman Empire and even to later Western Europe where full-blown secularism eventually developed. Thus in China, Korea, Japan, and Vietnam, Buddhism remained one religion among others, favored at certain periods, but not favored and even suppressed at other periods (although not dislodged from official sponsorship in Japan until the late nineteenth century). Strong governments basically adopted Confucianism or Neo-Confucianism (after 1000 CE) and created cults of the rulers, under which a variety of local religions were tolerated. This was different from the lands of Southeast Asia, where Buddhism in its Theravada form made strong alliances with the governments.

Buddhism failed to spread in India in which there was a well-organized religion with a literary tradition that had a close relationship with the rulers, as well as being well embedded in the society. It also failed to spread to Zoroastrian Iran to the West, which had a well-organized and literary state religion. Furthermore, as already stated, Buddhism was only partly successful in East Asia, compared to Southeast Asia, although it became hegemonic in the smaller societies of Tibet and Mongolia. In East Asia, Buddhism gained its greatest influence in Japan, where it was made the official religion through which rulers registered the population. However, in most of East Asia, revived Confucianism replaced official Buddhism. Eventually even in Japan, the ideology-religion of Shintoism replaced Buddhism as the national religion during the Restoration of the authority of the Emperor after 1868. However, after the disestablishment of State Shinto in 1945, Buddhism in its various versions remained stronger than in other East Asian countries.

CHRISTIANITY

In its first three hundred years Christianity spread throughout the Roman Empire. It also spread successfully beyond the borders of the Empire, at first eastward and southward and then northward to Syria, Arabia, Armenia, Georgia, Ethiopia, and Central Asia (Montgomery 2002). This is typical of what was to take place more commonly in

Christian history in which Christianity spread primarily to small societies. Even the westward spread of Christianity across the Roman Empire was to a series of small societies. That is, the Empire was newly constructed and made up of numerous small societies with their own religious traditions. It was held together by a strong government that tolerated relative religious diversity. In fact, the Empire was awash with religions, including Christianity. A previous example of relative toleration of religious diversity may be seen in the Persian Achaemenid Empire established by Cyrus the Great, who is remembered gratefully in the Bible as God's anointed one or "messiah" for allowing the Jews to return to Jerusalem and rebuild the Temple (Isaiah 45:1). Other examples of religiously tolerant empires are those founded by nomadic peoples: the Parthians, the Arabs under the Omayyads, and the Mongols. In the cases of these empires, a single religion was not yet considered necessary for the legitimization of power and for integration of the empire. Initially, at least, the secular power of these empires was overwhelming, thus allowing them to be relatively tolerant of religious diversity.

In contrast to the Roman Empire, the large societies or empires to the East, Sasanid Persia, India (South Asia), and China, at the time of the introduction of Christianity, all had governments allied in some way with traditional religions or at least not open to the influence of foreign religions. These large societies sought to regulate, limit, or confine new religions. Christianity was not able to spread successfully in them because of the lack of the kind of relative religious freedom and tolerated diversity that existed in the Roman Empire. This caused the lopsided spread of Christianity that has left its mark to the present (Montgomery 2002).

In the following periods of the expansion of Christianity to Europe and later to other parts of the world, the pattern of spreading to smaller societies with less complex and nonestablished religions became the norm. Christianity has spread around the world in a similar pattern in three great movements. The first great movement was its spread throughout the Roman Empire, from a conquered people to other conquered peoples under conditions of relatively tolerated religious diversity. The second great spread of Christianity was northward to the western and eastern European tribal peoples that took place from the fourth through the eleventh centuries (according to Proposition 4.2). Much of this spread was due to the traveling monks who carried the new religion to the kings and leaders of the tribes, who then often became "little Constantines." After an ebb in the expansion of Christianity for almost 500 years, the third great spread of Christianity took place after 1500 to small societies in the Americas, Africa, and the Pacific Islands, and also to numerous minority groups in Asia (again, according to Proposition 4.2). In this same period, Christianity failed to penetrate significantly the old civilizations of Asia, as well as the areas of Muslim domination, where societies and religions were well organized, with literary traditions, and with close relationships to governments. We are presently in a fourth period of expansion by Christianity to an increasingly religiously diverse world in which freedom of religion is increasingly recognized at least in principle.

ISLAM

Islam's spread from the Middle East in all directions is rather well known. What is generally not recognized is that it failed to spread to many areas even though it ruled these areas for many centuries. These areas were the Iberian Peninsula, Sicily, Greece, the Balkans (except among an oppressed minority religious group–the Bogomiles), and much of India. These are areas where major world religions, Christianity and Hinduism, had already become an aspect of the cultural identity of populations and where religions had established official relationships with rulers. Like Christianity, Islam's greatest successes were with tribal peoples or small societies: the Turks, North Africans, Central Asians, Sub-Saharan Africans, and Southeast Asians (Malaysians, Indonesians, and people in the southern Philippine Islands). Large Christian populations continued to exist in the Middle East, for example in Syria and Egypt, for many centuries, even to the recent out migration of Christians. Islamic hegemony in Anatolia and much of ancient Armenia came with the forced migration of Christian populations from these areas.

The apparent exception to Islam spreading to small societies with primal religions was the conversion to Islam of Persia or Iran, which was a relatively large nation with a state religion, Zoroastrianism that had a literary tradition. Persia had successfully prevented Christianity from spreading. Actually, the Persian Empire incorporated a variety of ethnic groups, some of which were recently tribal, hostile to the central government, and closely related to tribal peoples in Central Asia that were receptive to Islam. In addition, the rather brittle official relationship between Zoroastrianism and the government was broken by Islam, which was more egalitarian than the rigid hierarchical state religion of Zoroastrianism. Previous religious movements, Mithraism, Mazdakism, and Manichaeanism had been crushed by the government, which certainly did not endear Zoroastrianism to the people and showed their lack of loyalty to it as a state religion. Perhaps most important in spreading Islam, Persians were incorporated into positions of influence within Islam, becoming upwardly mobile within the new political-religious order. This was so especially in the powerful government of the Abbasids in Baghdad, in contrast to the initial Omayyads. In addition, an important factor to be noted in the next chapter on intersocietal relationships, Islam reduced the threat from the traditional enemy of Persia, Constantinople, and later contributed to a revival of Iranian culture and literature.

GOVERNMENTS AND THE SPREAD OF RELIGIONS

Let us consider more carefully the relationships established between Buddhism, Christianity, and Islam with governments and how this facilitated their spread and also blocked the spread of other religions. I have attributed the propensity of these religions to spread among small societies to the fact that even though members of small societies were typically socialized into more or less homogeneous religious traditions, the leaders of small societies were generally free to choose a new religion. This is because they were not committed to an alliance with a single religion and they perceived an advantage for their rule in the new religions. We saw that a condition of relative religious toleration existed in some large societies such as the recently constructed empires of the Achaemenid Persians, the Romans, the Parthians, the Omayyad Arabs, and the Mongols. The relative religiously pluralistic condition of the Roman Empire and of Post-Han Dynasty China allowed for the spread of Christianity and Buddhism respectively. The Parthians and the Omayyad Arabs tolerated Christianity and the Mongols even welcomed it for a period so that Christianity was favored and used (for example, through Christian scribes and emissaries) by the Mongols.

However, conditions that allowed for the freedom of rulers to choose new religions were lost when the rulers and their governments eventually made alliances with particular religions. Thus, in certain cases, the alliance between a religion and a government facilitated the spread of a favored religion, but after the spread of the favored religion, the spread of other religions was blocked. This leads to the proposition:

4.4 *The spread of new religions can be greatly accelerated*

> *or blocked by governmental power, depending on whether governments seek or approve of a new religion or already have an established alliance with a religion.*

After pointing out that religious specialists are among the first full-time specialists to emerge in societies, Stark and Bainbridge (1996 [1987]:94,95) state, "Once religious specialists have emerged in a society, they will tend to combine in organizations seeking a religious monopoly," and "In socially complex and cosmopolitan societies, a religious organization can achieve an effective monopoly only through an alliance with the state." On the one hand, by an alliance with governments, religions gain the monopoly they seek, which provides them the security of not having any competition. On the other hand, through the same alliance governments gain a means of strengthening their rule by obtaining religious legitimization and a unifying common ideology for the people.

Thus religions and governments appear to be drawn to each other, but at the same time they may be considered very dangerous to each other, at least over the long term. N. J. Demerath (2001) uses the metaphor of the moth and the flame to great effect in demonstrating both the mutual attraction and the danger that religions and governments are to each other. Each one may be either the moth or the flame. It is not difficult to understand the attraction that governments and religions have for each other in the light of the realities of power and authority in societies. Weber (1967 [1946]:334; cf. 159,177) is very clear in recognizing that "the state is an association that claims the monopoly of the *legitimate use of violence*, and cannot be defined in any other manner" (italics his). Governments do not want to have to rely on the continuous use of coercion or even the threat of coercion, as important as the latter may be. This is why authority, which is the recognition of the right to use power, is so important for governments.

John Scott (2001:20) points out, "Domination through command rests on the idea of the *right* to give orders and a corresponding *obligation* to obey" (italics his). Drawing on L. Althusser (1971) Scott goes on to identify the importance of "ideological apparatuses" for establishing the legitimacy or authority of governments. The ideological realm, of course, is an area that is highly relevant to religions.

Transcendent or Divine authority is the highest level of authority that humans can recognize. This means that governments can augment their authority if they can obtain an affirmation of this authority from those who have access to the Divine. Traditionally, it is the religious specialists who claim to speak for the Divine and therefore it is to the advantage of governments to gain support from the religious specialists. At the same time, it is to the advantage of religious specialists, especially as they organize and gain a variety of assets, to have protection and support from governments. Thus it can be seen why those with political power and religious leaders have tended to make alliances of one kind or another, but also why tensions and conflicts develop between governments and religions.

When we return to the first millennium BCE, we see that most rulers in major cultural areas had some established religious rites, which confirmed Divine approval to their rule. These cults of the rulers were practiced even though at the same time the people at large, while assenting to the official religion of the rulers, continued to worship a variety of local divinities. The hierarchical structure of most societies was matched by a similar hierarchical structure in religions with a division between elite and popular religions. This pattern of a distinction between elite and popular religions continued and became an important characteristic of all the world religions, as already seen in the first chapter. The interest in this chapter is how people might have the freedom to choose new religions given the need of the elite to maintain their positions of authority. At this point, I will review how the choices of government leaders facilitated or blocked the spread of new religions.

BUDDHISM, SOME OTHER ASIAN RELIGIONS, AND GOVERNMENTS

Spiro (1982 [1970]:379) writes:

> In classical Buddhist political thought, there is an intimate relation between the state (especially the king and the court) and the Buddhist church. The king (for normatively and actually, Buddhist political theory presupposes a monarchial government) is the protector of Buddhism, which means of course that Buddhism is the state religion. Obversely, Buddhist ideology is the reservoir from which the monarch derives charismatic authority... It is not surprising, then, that there should have been a symbiotic relationship between the monastic order (the embodiment of the Buddhist church) and the government (the embodiment of the state), in both theory and practice. This relationship is as old as the Asokan period in Indian (Buddhist) history.

At the time of the Maurya Dynasty, which came to power at the end of the fourth century BCE, it is probably too early to speak of Buddhism as a distinct religion, although it was clearly a sectarian movement in the developing "Great Tradition" of Hinduism. However, Buddhist teachings, in particular the principles of the dhamma/darma were officially favored by the Emperor Asoka. It can be said that he gave Buddhism its strongest initial impetus to spread when he sent out "teachers of the dhamma." He saw these teachings, which emphasized toleration, nonviolence, and social welfare, as useful for ruling a large area incorporating diverse peoples (Thapar 1969 [1960]: 308-09).

Actually, the idea of dhamma, which applied indiscriminately to all individuals, was threatening to the more particularistic conception of the varna-asrama-dharma, laws or duties applying to particular caste levels and particular stages of life taught by the Brahmans. This conflict of ideologies would be played out later in the ultimate inability of Hinduism and Buddhism to exist alongside each other either in South Asia or Southeast Asia. In other words, Buddhism was in basic conflict with a caste system.

In general, however, Buddhist and Hindu religious ideas were spread to South and Southeast Asia in the diffusion of Indian culture or a process of Indianization. Caste-based Hinduism gradually asserted itself over against egalitarian Buddhism in India. This took place beginning after the collapse of the Maurya dynasty, gained impetus under the Gupta rulers in the fourth to the sixth centuries, and continued into later centuries until Buddhism virtually disappeared from India by 1200 (Stark 2001:47; Sharot 2001:131). Hinduism did not have a centralized authority, but located authority "in caste custom, guild, religious tradition, the teaching and example of the sage, and the village council, as well as in provincial and central governments" (Drekmeier 1962:293). In the end, it was the diffuse caste system with brahmans at the top more than specific governmental edicts that prevented the spread of the Buddhist noncaste system in South Asia.

Sharot (2001:129) explains the relationship of brahmans to governments:

> Brahmans provided rulers with religious legitimation, but they retained a detachment from political power; they rarely sought to influence state goals, and they did not attempt to use their position to create hierocracy. Rulers were not presumed to be heads of anything

resembling a state church; individual temples became large landowners and amassed considerable riches, but they were amorphous in structure; they did not unite in encompassing organizations, and they did not incorporate the vast majority of the population.

Given the relationship of brahmans to governments, it is understandable that Hinduism did not outlaw Buddhism directly as a state church would deal with a heretical sectarian movement. Rather there was a process of gradual exclusion. Keay (2000:146-47) describes an early stage of the process that took place under the Guptas of the fourth and fifth centuries:

> As between the orthodox and the heterodox sects ecumenism was still the norm. The Guptas, although identifying themselves with Lord Vishnu and performing Vedic sacrifices, encouraged endowments to both Buddhist and brahman establishments with even-handed munificence. Yet the physical separation of the two communities, as implied in Fa Hian's [Chinese Buddhist pilgrim] account, may be significant. Buddhist monasteries were usually located outside the main centers of population and influence, near enough for collecting alms and instructing the laity but far enough for tranquility and seclusion. The 'brahmacharis', on the other hand, technically brahman students but here implying the whole Brahman educational establishment, were located within the city and close to the court.

Not only was Buddhism sidelined by the brahmans, it also was dealt a strong blow by the destruction of numerous establishments by invasions. "Where Fa Hian in the fifth century had found packed viharas and towering stupas, Hsuan Tsang, another Chinese visitor but in the mid-seventh century, found only devastation" (Keay 2000:158). The devastation had been the work of invading Huns. However, the continued presence of Buddhism in India is witnessed by the fact of the destruction of the Buddhist monastery-university of Odantapuri in Bihar by the Muslim Khalijis in the 1220s. Toward the end of the same century a Buddhist center in southern India was destroyed (Keay 2000:244,254).

While Hinduism was gradually replacing Buddhism in South Asia, Buddhism was gradually replacing Hinduism in much of Southeast Asia. Initially, both Hinduism and Buddhism were introduced to the area. J. D. Legge (1964:36) describes how Hinduism could be initially appealing to the leaders of the rudimentary kingdoms that existed on Java and Sumatra:

> Central to the Hindu-Javanese political system was the Brahmanic concept of the god-king, whose magical powers underlay the whole system of authority. The terrestrial order was regarded as a reflection of the cosmic order. The king in the terrestrial order was the counterpart of God and indeed was God. Below the ruler, though Indonesia did not assimilate the caste system of India, society was graded and rank was again supported by supernatural sanctions.

Both Hinduism and Buddhism also undoubtedly had great appeal because of their literature and scholarship. Mochtar Lubis (1990:35, 36) reports the evidence found in an inscription in the Pallava script of Sanskrit on a stone in Kalimantan (Borneo) that this writing was introduced to Indonesia around 400 CE. Fa-hsien (or Fa-Hian), who also had visited India, saw only brahmans when he landed in Java in 414 CE due to storms. However, a Chinese scholar was in Java from

664 to 665 CE to translate Buddhist texts with a Javanese scholar (Lubis 1990:36-37). The kingdom of Sriwijaya on the southeast coast of Sumatra (near present Pelembang) became a center for Buddhist learning of both Mahayana and Hinayana (Theravada) types by the eighth century. Sriwijaya continued to be a center of power for some five hundred years and a rival to the Javanese Hindu kingdoms.

Unlike Sriwijaya, which was a trading-based kingdom, Mataram on Java was an agrarian based kingdom, a distinction that continues to this day in Indonesia. Mataram Hindu Shaivite temple remains date from the first part of the eighth century. However, in the latter part of the century, both Sumatran and Javanese kingdoms appear to have come under the control of a single dynasty, the Sailendras ("Lords of the Mountain"). The greatest of the Mahayana Buddhist monuments, Borobudur, near the present city of Jogjakarta, dates from around 772 CE (van Niel 1963:273). Late in the ninth century, the Sailendra Empire appears to have been divided between Sumatran and Javanese states, with Sailendras continuing as rulers of Sriwijaya and remaining loyal to Buddhism. The Javanese claimed to have revived the Mataram kingdom and to have returned to Shivaite Hinduism. It seems clear, however, that many, if not most, people successfully combined ideas and practices of both Hinduism and Buddhism. As a matter of fact, after 1000, when Sumatran domination was thrown off (again), the strong kingdom in East Java blended Buddhism and Hindu Shivaism into a form of Tantric syncretism, the cult of Shiva-Buddha, to be the official religion. At the same time, many people adhered to Shivaism, blended with traditional animistic religion, a type of Hinduism still prevalent in Indonesia (van Niel 1963:274).

What determined the eventual ascendancy of either Hinduism or Buddhism, mostly Hinduism in South Asia (including Nepal) and parts of Indonesia and mostly Buddhism in Southeast Asia, with the exception of Malaysia and Indonesia (where Islam became prevalent)? The decision of political leadership was certainly important, but it is also true that Hindu and Buddhist ideas and practices could co-exist and selected features of both could be followed in the popular religions of the people. Nevertheless, most rulers would eventually come to favor one or the other. Of the two, Hinduism came to be favored in India (South Asia) primarily because the total social system that it encompassed with brahmans at the top was established first. Although courts in Southeast Asia may have favored Hinduism, the social caste system was not possible to be absorbed by the populations, many of whom had already accepted many features of more egalitarian Buddhism. Even in southern India, the caste system of Hinduism has been less rigid than in the north. Ultimately, the rulers in the Southeast Asian mainland found that Theravada Buddhism made a suitable official religion. The entrance of Islam to Malaysia and Indonesia largely replacing Hinduism and Buddhism will be considered later.

Turning to the spread of Buddhism northward and eastward, as already noted, the Kushan invaders accepted Buddhism (a simpler society accepting the literate religion of the conquered people) and then facilitated the spread of Buddhism into Central Asia from which it spread further to China and neighboring lands. As already noted, the relationship of the governments to religions in East Asia was somewhat distinct from what it was in the lands where Hinduism (India and Nepal), Theravada Buddhism (Southeast Asia, except for Vietnam), and Vajrayana Buddhism (Tibet and Mongolia) became allied with governments. Tibetan and Mongolian rulers accepted Buddhism as a national religion, but in China, Korea, and Japan, although in certain periods Buddhism was favored by governments, sooner or later (in the case of Japan, as late as the latter part of the nineteenth century) the governments reduced any special status given to Buddhism and recognized it only as one religion among others. This has probably aided Buddhism as a popular religion more than it has injured it.

I will limit my comments regarding East Asia since I have already noted that China set the pattern in which a strong government with an imperial religious cult tolerated a variety of local religions, as long as they did not threaten the order and unity of the realm. Heterodox sects or foreign religions could threaten this order and unity. The relative religious diversity in China resembled (resembles) somewhat the pre-Christian Roman Empire in allowing a variety of religious beliefs and practices. In contrast, South and Southeast Asia, where Hinduism and Buddhism respectively were monopolistic, were not as religiously diverse as East Asia. This is primarily because of the stronger central governments in East Asia. Strong quasi-secular Chinese governments generally have perceived religions as a potential source of disorder and threat to authority. Instead Chinese governments sought to maintain an "idealized national identity" over a relatively homogeneous ethnic population (Ng-Quinn 1993). This meant that an emphasis was put on Chinese ethnic-cultural identity (the Han people), infused by Confucian ideology, while seeking to control heterodox sects and foreign religions.

Korea, Vietnam, and Japan, at least partly through the influence of Confucian thought, had similar patterns of strong governments that gave a priority to national ethno-cultural identity of smaller and already more homogeneous populations than China. The establishment of a strong government with an attendant ideology supporting the authority of the rulers and national unity allowed for some variety in religious expression, especially when the religious beliefs and practices were of a local origin with a high primal religious content. Buddhism with its ability to incorporate local religions could survive well in these conditions, but only alongside other religions.

There were some variations over time in each land. Although Buddhism was favored in China by the powerful T'ang Dynasty and in Korea by the Silla Dynasty, later in both lands Confucianism became the dominant ideology and Buddhism was restricted. Vietnam also came under the influence of Confucian ideology, but Mahayana Buddhism was accepted broadly in the population. In Japan, however, the Confucian bureaucracy that undercut Buddhism in China and Korea failed to develop, although Confucian ideology of deference for authority was employed by emperors and governments (Collins 1999:220; Sharot 2001:161). In Japan Buddhism was regarded as useful for nation building, somewhat as in Southeast Asia, where Theravada Buddhism was made official. Maria Toyoda and Aiji Tanaka (2002:273-74) state:

> The elite took concrete steps to foster syncretism between the new religion and the existing system of Shinto worship, in order to facilitate the spread of Buddhism... [W]hile Shinto stresses ready acceptance of and harmony with the physical world, Buddhism views the world as the transient source of suffering, and the physical as something which believers strive to overcome. Yet there was the essential element of tolerance present in both religions that allowed the relationship between them to provide the ideological foundation for pursuing future nationalistic goals.

The Meiji government made Shinto the official state religion in 1889, replacing the position held by Buddhism during the Tokugawa period (1603-1868). "The traditional Shinto emphasis of unity was translated during the Meiji period into an emphasis on the homogeneity of the Japanese people; who were different from the outsiders on Japan's threshold" (Toyada and Tanaka 2002:276). Thus, official state Shinto came to function somewhat like Confucianism. It failed to gain a mass following, but provided a means of creating unity under the emperor. Once an ethnic-cultural unity was established, it was possible for the people to combine various beliefs and practices, as long as they were not threatening or challenging the unity of the people. Thus, in the end, in the Far East (China, Korea, Japan, and Vietnam) governments remained strong with the Confucian emphasis on deference toward authority and with an additional emphasis on national unity. In the nations of Southeast Asia and Japan, Buddhism was able to remain especially strong among the people, as well as establish official relationships with governments. Although Buddhism remained influential among the people in China also, China maintained a general religious diversity in which a set of domestic religions and their popular religious expressions were tolerated.

South Asia (India) was generally not characterized by strong central governments with a semi-secular political ideology like Confucianism. Rather, the governments were part of an encompassing socio-religious system. From the time of the introduction of Christianity to India, possibly as early as the first century, the Hindu socio-religious system dominated by brahmans was able to keep Christianity isolated. Christians were thought of as belonging to a particular guild or caste, making them a distinct people. After 1500, in reaction to colonialism and the new Christian missionary wave, Hinduism became increasingly identified with nationalism.

Since independence after World War II the issue of conversion has become a special source of controversy in which Indian national and state governments have become involved in the name of "freedom of religion." Sebastian C. H. Kim (2005 [2003]) describes the development of this controversy from colonial times and the attempts to control conversion through legislation together with the Hindu views that justified this legislation. He then focuses on the debates over conversion from both the Hindu and Christian perspectives. Although after much debate at the national level, particularly over the right to propagate religion, the national government accepted the concept of a "secular India" as promoted by Jawaharlal Nehru and other leaders and included the right to propagate one's religion, as well as to practice it. However, the debate "opened deep wounds of suspicion and resentment in the majority Hindus" (Kim 2005 [2003]:56) and stimulated the long-lasting debate in India over "conversion." The debate brought out the clear identification by Hindus of their religion with being Indian. Furthermore, it prompted legislative action in several states that distinguished freedom of religion from the individual right to convert to another religion. To give examples of legislation and subsequent Supreme Court action, the state of Orissa in 1967 and then Madhya Pradesh the next year passed "Freedom of Religion" laws. John Webster (2003:2) writes:

> In 1977 the Supreme Court upheld the constitutionality of these laws, arguing that the right to propagate religion (guaranteed in the constitution) and the right to convert were not the same as the latter impinges upon the freedom of conscience of the one whose conversion is being sought. Since then three other states have enacted similar laws: Arunachal Pradesh (1978), Tamil Nadu (2002), and Gujarat (2003).

In a very perceptive discussion Webster (2003:3) points to three features of these laws that deserve attention:

> First, the underlying assumption is that conversion is something one person does to another person rather than something one chooses for oneself. Thus

conversion is seen as the work of the evangelist rather than the choice of the convert. "Freedom of Religion" as defined in these acts is not the freedom to choose whatever religion you wish for your own reasons, but freedom from outside interference with the religious beliefs and practices you already have...

Secondly, these acts increase the penalties if the person converted is a Dalit, a Tribal, or a woman. The paternalistic assumption behind this appears to be that such people are more easily led astray because they are poor, "simple," and ignorant, unlike, e.g., high caste men...

Thirdly, the law is entirely silent about those who use force, fraud or inducement in order to prevent conversion. Apparently, that is socially and legally acceptable behavior because the government itself indulges in it; not only do the police stand by as silent witnesses to it but the government itself engages in it when using religious as well as caste criteria in granting or withholding affirmative action benefits and protections to Dalits.

As Kim (2005 [2003]:180-200) points out in his thorough discussion of the debates over conversion in India, the religious meaning of conversion is still an important issue for clarification, but this is not directly relevant here. A religious perspective includes theological concepts regarding the work of God in the human heart and mind, which is not available for sociological examination. In the analysis of this book, only a minimal empirical meaning of conversion is useful. In a minimal view, conversion may be viewed simply as a change in religious identity or it may be simply the acceptance of a religious identity when previously there was no clear consciousness of a religious identity.

This brief review of the relationships of governments to Buddhism and its mother religion, Hinduism, clearly shows that governments can facilitate the spread of one religion and block the spread of other religions both directly and indirectly. Not until recent times has freedom of religion become a worldwide political norm (although what it means is not agreed upon), but rulers of various societies, particularly traditional societies, still tend to approve certain religions and to limit other religions. This is especially the case in the many nations in which pervasive religions have become part of the ethno-cultural identity of the people and where this identity is perceived as threatened from the outside (considered in the next chapter). In South and Southeast Asia it was primarily Hinduism and Buddhism respectively that provided the rulers unifying religious umbrellas under which the people at large followed a variety of local religious practices, but maintained single religious identities. In East Asia, primarily China, Korea, Japan, and Vietnam, the ideology of Confucianism (with the special injection of Shintoism in Japan) provided unifying umbrellas that made ethno-cultural identities, not particular religions, central to societies. Within these societies rulers tolerated a variety of religions, including Buddhism. In Japan especially, rulers tolerated a variety of Buddhist sects and Buddhism remained a major part of the ethno-cultural identity.

CHRISTIANITY AND GOVERNMENTS

Christianity in the Roman Empire followed a similar route in the fourth century as taken by Zoroastrianism in Persia in the third century by being established as a state religion. Christianity provided a unifying ideology for the Roman Empire just as Zoroastrianism did for Persia.

Western historians and Christians generally are so accustomed to viewing the "winning of the Roman Empire to Christianity" positively that it takes a major reorientation to view it negatively. H. A. Drake (2000) in his *Constantine and the Bishops, The Politics of Intolerance* has thrown considerable light on the official Christianization of the Empire by viewing it politically rather than theologically. Drake (2000:16) makes clear that the condition of early civilizations in which there was no conceptual category for the separation of church and state was still in effect in the age of Constantine. In short, the state was regarded as a religious institution and religion an arm of the government. (This is still an issue in some Christian and Islamic countries where "separation of religion and state" is considered as placing a limitation on God, rather than protecting religion and state from each other.) Before Constantine, the sacredness of the Roman rulers was guaranteed by the Imperial Cult that maintained the rituals supporting the Imperial rule. At the same time, although the Imperial Cult demanded the homage of all people at specific times, it tolerated the worship of local deities, as Christianity later did not. Specifically, Rome tolerated the westward movement of eastern religions, which came to include Christianity, and the reception of these religions in the capital.

The Imperial government had been reorganized by Diocletian (245-313 – resigned in 305), who was proclaimed emperor by the army in 284 after a period of war and anarchy. He established a system of absolutism that was continued by his successors. Constantine I (272?-337), who was proclaimed emperor by his own and his father's troops in 306, had to deal with rivals to power. Finally, in 324 he defeated Licinius and became the sole ruler of the empire. Politically, Constantine had the task of maintaining imperial power and establishing unity in the empire. He thought the Christian Church provided one of the best means of accomplishing these political goals. Christianity had spread throughout the empire under an imperial system that tolerated local religions as long as proper worship was given to the emperor. This arrangement led to periodic persecution of Christians, but rarely, if ever, was it systematically applied over the empire. Christianity became the only Empire-wide organized network besides the government and the military. At the beginning of the fourth century, in which Christianity won legitimization (313), Christians probably made up between fifteen and 20 percent of the population. However, Constantine gave both legal authority and financial resources to the bishops. He called the Council of Nicaea in 325 to create unity in the newly legitimated church because of disunion over doctrine. After the rule of the Emperor Julian (361-363), who tried to restore paganism, Emperor Theodosius (Emperor 375-395) added to the monopolistic power of Christianity by having other religions made illegal. Thus a Christian monopoly in the empire was established officially. Drake (2000:465-466) writes of the whole process:

> In the case of the Roman Empire, the continuities that underlie the shift from pagan to Christian emperors were the twin demands of legitimacy and patronage. As had emperors in the first century, so emperors in the fourth sought to make their subjects, and particularly the armies, believe that they ruled in accordance with some principle greater than armed might, to make them, in Xenophon's useful phrase, "all willing to be his subjects." In addition to willing subjects, fourth-century emperors continued to need willing subordinates, governors and civic elites, to carry out the imperial will. In return, these subordinates received patronage in all its manifold forms, from

> the basic promise of resources and fiscal gain to the more intangible guarantees of access and preferment, all adding up to a comfortable sense of protected interest. At this level, what the change from paganism to Christianity, symbolized in the confrontation between Ambrose and Theodosius, represents is the arrival of a new player in an age-old game. Access and influence, patronage and prestige–these are the constants in the game of empire.

In the confrontation between Ambrose and Theodosius, it is worth noting that Ambrose appealed to Theodosius, not demanded as portrayed by Christian historians and artists that Theodosius do penance for sanctioning the massacre of several thousand people in Thessalonica.

Drake (2000:466) concludes that although Constantine had adopted a tradition with the teaching that people should return hate with love and that belief cannot be coerced, the century saw an escalating use of coercion by a Christian government. Constantine's inclusive public policy that would tolerate various religions but "would avoid those aspects of state cult, such as blood sacrifice, which had previously restricted Christian participation in government," eventually failed. The reason for the failure was that the new center of legitimacy and patronage acquired by Christian bishops favored coercion on behalf of an exclusionist faith.

From Drake's account, therefore, it appears that religious monopoly arises from two sources. One source is found in the desire and need of those with political power to obtain all the support possible for the legitimacy of their rule, hence reducing the need for the exercise of rule through raw power alone, without attendant authority. However, power attracts power, and for religious authorities the acceptance of the aid of governmental coercion that goes beyond mere protection, but extends at some level to the coercion of belief, seems to be an irresistible temptation. The temptation may be as simple and subtle as seeking privilege for one's beliefs over other beliefs. It appears that in the fourth century Christianity fell for the temptation Jesus rejected in the wilderness to accept the allegiance of people based on the display or exercise of power or privileged position.

By first making Christianity legal and then making it illegal not to be Christian, the government enabled Christianity to grow rapidly so that the great majority of the population became at least nominally Christian (Stark 1997 [1996]; MacMullen 1997). The problem, of course, is that Christianity became highly coercive and church leaders often used force against those that disagreed with them, as brought out clearly by Jenkins (2011) in his book, *Jesus Wars*. The pattern of the alliance of Christianity with governments continued in Europe for many centuries and in many respects is still in effect. At least the historic effects of the pattern are certainly still evident. After the fourth century, Christianity continued its spread northward in an ambiguous fashion, combining the peaceful methods of the first three centuries with the coercion adopted in the fourth century. Initially, the peaceful method of missions was dominant. This was aided greatly by the decline of the power of Rome after the alliance of Christianity with the government in the fourth century. Rome was actually dominated by the tribal or former tribal kingdoms instead of being dominant over them. Rome was overrun by Goths in 410 CE, most of whom were Arian Christians. The same year, Rome also began withdrawing its troops, many already of tribal origin, from the new power centers in the north.

The decline of Roman power meant that the Christian religion was not associated with Roman coercive power as it spread among the various peoples, but rather with the advanced culture of the Mediterranean basin, which was much desired by the mostly illiterate peoples. The spread of Christianity to Ireland in the fifth century and the subsequent activity of Irish and English missionaries in Europe are examples of the peaceful spread of Christianity. However, as tribal kings were converted, for example Clovis in 496, they typically became "little Constantines." Charlemagne, in fact, aspired to perpetuate Constantine's rule and the Roman Empire with his "Holy Roman Empire," which continued in idealized, but unattained form for many centuries up to and including the rule of the Hapsburgs of Austria. Charlemagne established the rivalry of Western Europe with "Rome continued" in Constantinople. Charlemagne and the Scandinavian kings did not hesitate to use force in spreading Christianity among their peoples, although they recognized the need to request missionaries from Britain who would gain the hearing of the people.

In its first 300 years in its home base around the Mediterranean Basin, Christianity began the formation of denominations that eventually resulted among other things in the separation of the Orthodox and Roman Catholic forms of Christianity. Also, Nestorian and Monophysite Christianties broke off and were later to be made into religious minorities by governments in the large societies of Persia, India, and China and by the ascendancy of Islam in a large area. The transfer of the capital of the Roman Empire to Constantinople in the fourth century CE, just in the period when Christianity was being made the official religion, together with the barbarian invasions, created conditions that isolated the church in the West from the protection of the Empire. However, many of the forms and functions of the governmental patterns of the old Roman Empire were adopted by the Western Church. Church leaders were often the major negotiators with invading barbarians. Gradually, the Roman Catholic Church became the major alternative source of power to the numerous kingdoms that developed in Europe and a major arbiter to disputes over succession and territory.

In contrast to the Roman Catholic Church, the Orthodox Church was in the shadow of the Imperial government of Constantinople. Furthermore, the Imperial government in Constantinople and the Orthodox Church came under continual pressure from outside forces, either invading pagan barbarians or the forces of Islam. Even Western Christianity, especially during the Crusades, was a threat to Constantinople, sacking the city in 1204. Originally, Christianity in the Eastern Empire was both larger and more diffused in various centers than the Christianity based in Rome. However, as Christianity spread among the European tribes and the Christians in the East came under increasing pressures from Islam, the Christianity of the West became stronger over the centuries. Nevertheless, Orthodox Christianity spread northward geographically, extending the division between Orthodoxy and Roman Catholicism that became official in 1054.

Both major branches of Christianity, Orthodox and Roman Catholic, continued the "Constantinian compromise" of accepting the use of coercive power to support, protect, and advance themselves. Christianity to the east remained a minority (sometimes large) in the various Islamic societies, although it found favor during the Mongol domination in the thirteenth and fourteenth centuries because of prominent Christians among the Mongols. Major differences appeared between Roman and Orthodox Christianities due to the different forms of relationships to governmental coercive power. In Eastern Orthodoxy, Christianity had to be more subservient to governmental power due to strong central governments and the unity required because of outside pressures. Christianity came to place more emphasis on mysticism and became less of an activist in the East than in the West. It also was able to establish "autocephalous" or independent churches among various peoples. In contrast, in the West, Christianity grew in power as it mediated between the various governments and legitimated selected rulers. However, the development of numerous centers of power, and eventually nationalistic movements created a basis for challenges to the power of the Roman Catholic Church.

Following the distinction that was established between religious and secular powers, Western Europeans in the Middle Ages developed the concept of the corporation resulting from (and resulting in) the establishment of distinct authorities in monasteries, guilds, towns, and universities. The legal theory of the corporate body brought about great changes in political experience such as constitutional government and political and legal representation and legislation (Berman 1983; Huff 1993). Within kingdoms there was also an ongoing struggle between central rulers and feudal nobility. The many power centers and independent authorities and the struggles between them gave Western Europe a dynamism that was lacking in Eastern Europe, as well as in other societies in the world. Although monotheism provided governments a basis for increasing autocratic power, the "hidden card" in monotheism of the possible withdrawal of God's approval, contributed to the development of resistance to religious and political authority. This eventually was to result in the fostering of self-government and the creation of new religious bodies.

Growth in the power of Christianity over against secular powers reached its climax in the thirteenth century. Religious innovations such as those expressed by the Albigensians (Cathars), the Waldensians, Millenarian movements, the Lollards, and the Hussites were either eliminated or suppressed. The Roman Catholic Church established the Inquisition against heretics and mounted the Crusades to reclaim the Holy Land from Islam, as well as to eliminate the Cathars in what is now southern France. Some religious innovations were co-opted as orders, such as the Franciscans, the Dominicans, and the Jesuits. In spite of or, as I am arguing, because of its association with political power, Christian missions to the world actually seemed to be on the decline in the world in the period between 1000 and 1500. Latourette (1939:1), the great historian of the expansion of Christianity, wrote:

> In the fifteenth century and in the first half of the sixteenth century Christianity faced a major crisis. It was now fifteen hundred years old. The first flush of enthusiasm, characteristic of a new religion, was presumably long past. A younger rival, Islam, was continuing to supplant it in wide regions and was threatening its remaining strongholds. Cultures that professed other faiths, now surpassed in area, population, and power those which called themselves Christian. No longer, as in the fourth, fifth, and sixth centuries, was Christianity the faith of the richest and most important unit of mankind. Even in the lands where it was still officially the religion of the community, Christianity was in jeopardy. The culture–that of "Medieval" Europe–which had grown up under its aegis and of which it was an integral part, was passing. A new order was coming into being. Much of that new order was indifferent or even antagonistic to Christianity or sought to control it for its own purposes. In Western Europe, where Christianity had seemed more vigorous, decay had fastened itself on the Church. Ecclesiastical leaders disregarded Christian ethics in their program and practices and used their positions to advance their private interests in the promotion of art, the accumulation of wealth, and the acquisition of political power for themselves and their families.

Thus the association of religions with coercive power may give religions certain advantages in their initial spread and maintenance within given areas of governmental control, but there are certain evident long-range disadvantages and costs to religions and the societies in which they exist. The costs are stated in the proposition:

4.5 *The association of religions with coercive power leads to covert and overt resistance from within and outside of religions..*

The dilemma faced by religions is that ultimately religious authority is discredited by reliance on coercive power, rather than Divine authority alone. Also, religions that rely on the coercive power of governments lose spiritual vitality because of the loss of voluntarism that is important for their ability to spread. The imposed religion becomes pervasive in the society, but also merely nominal as people passively accept religious identity without religious commitment. The voluntary character essential to vital religion discussed in the last chapter is lost. In addition, there is a deadly kind of covert resistance. One of the best evidences of this is what happened to Christianity in Europe between 1000 and 1500 when Christianity largely ceased spreading. The releasing of missionary energy took place primarily after the separation of governmental power from religions. The new missionary energy found expression in missionary orders, such as the Franciscans and Jesuits, and in minority Christian groups in Europe. These were seen in the Radical Reformation (Anabaptists, Mennonites, Moravians) and were then given expression in the Pietistic Movement in Germany and England and the subsequent organization of missionary societies in the nineteenth century.

The alliance of Christianity with coercive power not only created the covert resistance of nominal religion or outward compliance without inward conviction, it also created overt resistance that played out over many centuries. The Orthodox Church did not have the political power that was exercised from Rome. Hence it did not produce the overt resistance that was seen in the West eventuating in the Reformation. However, it could be argued that the lack of revolutions in Eastern Europe as compared to Western Europe prepared the East for the cataclysm of the atheistic Communist revolution in the twentieth century. The numerous opposition movements to the Roman Catholic Church leading up to the Protestant Reformation have already been mentioned. However, the Protestant churches themselves that had been created by opposition, both religious and nationalistic to the dominant religion, continued many of the same policies of alliance with coercive power. The Protestant churches became state churches in Europe and their influence was limited by the boundaries of the state. Even following the Protestant Reformation, the wars of religion were basically conflicts between governments over whether Roman Catholicism or Protestantism would be the legitimate and legitimizing religion. Thus the Reformation in terms of church-state relations perpetuated the pattern going back to the fourth century.

Eastern Orthodoxy, Roman Catholicism, and Protestantism were all aided by governments initially in their spread. Once these versions of Christianity were recognized by particular governments, they were able to block the spread of the other versions of Christianity. To this day, religious diversity moves against tradition in Europe where the concept of Christendom (territorial Christianity) is deeply embedded. If Christianity is "privileged" by being mentioned as foundational in a future European Union constitution, will there be courage to mention the negative influences of the alliance of Christianity with coercion? And the most serious consequence of this alliance is yet to be mentioned.

The most serious consequence of imposed religion was the antireligious movement that was generated as an element of the Enlightenment (not the whole Enlightenment) in Europe, especially in France. The much discussed secularization movement (Casanova 1994; Swatos and Christiano 1999; Dobbelaere 1999; Stark 1999; Voye 1999; Beyer 1999; Lambert 1999; Bruce 2002), regardless of how it may be defined, was certainly not simply a movement against religion. Secularization was (is) part of the process of differentiation of power and functions in societies, but it is aimed specifically at the removal of religion from its official privileged association with the state and other public institutions. This process was welcomed and encouraged by many Christian leaders and denominations, especially minority or dissenting religious groups. In North America, where a variety of Christian groups settled in the same area, secularization actually became a movement led by religious people. However, the antireligious part of the secularization movement adopted the general ideology of secularism and produced a variety of secular ideologies that were able to obtain political power. The most extreme forms of these ideologies may be seen in Fascism and Marxism or Communism. I will deal specifically with the subject of the spread of irreligion in Chapter 9. Here I am simply noting that according to Proposition 4.5 the alliance between Christianity and coercive power did much to spawn antireligious secularism that has spread in the world. A second serious modern consequence of the association of Christianity with governmental power came after 1500 as Christianity spread to non-Western lands. The alliance between Christianity and the coercive power of imperialism and colonialism created considerable overt and covert resistance to Christianity. This will be considered in some detail in the next chapter.

With the emphasis on maintaining ethno-cultural unity and

identity with traditional religions, governments in Asia were able to block the spread of Christianity. Christianity (because of its exclusivity) was not able to absorb or accommodate local religions as Buddhism did. In the seventh and eighth centuries Nestorian Christian missionaries were tolerated and even encouraged to some extent by the powerful T'ang Dynasty (618-907), except during the reign of the Empress Wu Hou (690-705). The Mongol Yuan Dynasty (1279-1368) especially fostered Christianity and there were Christians among them, including their scribes, some tribal groups, and some individuals, for example, wives, of high rank. However, after both the T'ang and the Yuan dynasties, Christianity was eliminated largely because of its foreign associations. Later, under the early Ching Dynasty (1644-1911) Christianity was welcomed in the court because of the scientific achievements of the Jesuit missionaries. However, restrictions were then placed on it because of the conflict between the Emperor and the Pope over the incorporation of Confucian rites within Christianity--the "rites controversy," which extended from 1628 to 1742 (Latourette 1956:318,319). In the nineteenth century, due to the Opium War (1839-1842), subsequent conflicts, and the "unequal treaties" forced on China, the Chinese government lost the ability to block the entrance of Christian missionaries, but Christianity was clearly associated with the "foreign devils" and rejected by a large majority of the population.

ISLAM AND GOVERNMENTS

In Islamic culture, governments were fused with religion from the beginning, a pattern similar to surrounding societies. Muhammad himself had been a statesman and military leader, as well as a prophet. The first four successors to Muhammad (the rashidun or the "rightly guided") saw their responsibility as uniting all of the Arab tribes within Islam, which means "submission." Force was used, particularly under the first successor, Abu Bakr, to bring the recalcitrant tribes into the umma or community. The Omayyads, who ruled from 661 to 749 from Damascus and continued to rule in Spain to 1031, saw Islam primarily as a uniting religion for only the Arab people. They therefore were not inclined to use force to convert non-Arabs. However, the Abbasid revolution, which moved the government to Baghdad in 762, only some 130 years after the death of Muhammad, changed to a conversion policy. Pressure to convert was exerted primarily through taxing non-Muslims. Non-Arab Muslims became prominent in the Abbasid government and military. In addition, restrictions were placed on non-Muslims. The dhimmi system, adopted from the Persian melet system, kept foreign religions as minorities who were responsible for their own communities. In addition, at different times minority religious populations were removed from certain areas. All of these government policies aided the spread of Islam and at the same time hindered the spread of other religions.

Arab armies carried the faith of Islam eastward to the Atlantic and westward to Central Asia and India. However, in a development not recognized by many in the West to this day, Arab power began a precipitous decline with the establishment of the Abbasids in Baghdad The tradition of tribal rule combined with a lack of a clear line of political and religious succession provided a basis for authoritarianism combined with divisiveness that led to the establishment of numerous scattered sultanates. (This tendency is still seen in the divisiveness noncohesiveness of Islamic countries, since Islam carries forward many tribal characteristics found in Arab and other earlier populations.) The close relationship of religion and government meant that religious and political disputes affected (affect) one another. The Sunni-Shia dispute over succession became a basis for much political unrest to be exploited by different factions that has continued to the present.

Internal Social Conditions in Receiving Societies 187

This is in accordance with the view in this chapter that religion does not benefit by association with coercive power, but rather benefits by separation from political power. The same applies to the state associated with religious authority. Significantly, as Arab power declined with the ascendance of Iranian and Turkish political and military leaders, Islamic religious and cultural civilization flowered in its new center at Baghdad, the opposite of what might be expected. Various Islamic kingdoms developed under a variety of local rulers. At the same time, various religious innovations were created within Islam and numerous sectarian divisions took place. These innovations, along with the decentralization of Islamic power, actually aided in the spread of Islam.

In spite of the pressures brought by Islamic governments on non-Muslims, coercion was not successful in a number of areas in bringing about the conversion of the populations as already mentioned (namely in Spain, Sicily, Greece, the Balkans, and most of India). Furthermore, most important for showing the advantage of separating coercive power from religion, the conversions of many groups of people to Islam was not associated with Muslim conquest, but rather with the ascendance in power of these groups, for example, the Turks, many Mongols, many Africans, and many Southeast Asians.

The Crusaders established themselves in the Middle East as a result of Pope Urban II's call in 1095 to retake the Holy Land, but they were forced to abandon Jerusalem for the second and last time in 1244 just before the Mongol onslaught in the Middle East. Earlier the Crusaders had been defeated by Saladin (Jerusalem had been retaken by Saladin in 1187), and Europe had lost its enthusiasm for a war against Islam. The Abbasid caliphate dragged on in Baghdad until overthrown in 1258 by the Mongols, who remained, ruling from Iran, until their power was broken in 1303. The last of the Mongol rulers in Iran accepted the faith of Islam, as had the Mongols to the north. The Ottoman Turks replaced the Seljuk Turks so that by 1326 Othman's dominions stretched from the eastern Black Sea to the Bosphorus and included most of Anatolia. Persia remained under separate and competing rule. The Ottoman Turks eventually established their rule over the whole Middle East, North Africa, and the Balkan Peninsula, taking Constantinople in 1453 and becoming the last great Muslim power in the Middle East before their decline in the nineteenth century and major losses in the twentieth century. In addition to the Middle East, North Africa, and West Africa, Muslim rulers established themselves in India, Central Asia, and Indonesia.

Islam's association with the coercive power of governments has been a means of giving legitimacy to a great variety of rulers, but it has not established external or formal unity to the religion of Islam. The many Islamic rulers gave Islam their support and protection and welcomed its advanced culture of learning in science and literature. The strength of Islam has grown more from its culture and from the economic advantage of trade in the Muslim world than from any coercion used on its behalf. Although coercion has blocked the spread of other religions, particularly Christianity. The diffuseness and variety within Islam, which does not have a central organization, has turned out to be a major source of strength. The early decline of Arab power did not prevent the enhancement of the Arab language and culture within Islam among the many non-Arab peoples. A major disadvantage to Islam of its close relationship with governments has been that religious reform becomes confused with political change and vice versa. Religious leaders have to be concerned with maintaining political influence just as political leaders also need to maintain control over religions.

CONCLUSION

This chapter has been the first to examine specifically secular social factors that have affected the spread of religions, particularly those belonging to the internal conditions of societies to which new religions have been introduced. The theory has made the opportunity for choice of religions as a key independent social condition variable in determining whether religions that otherwise have the capability of spreading (primarily Buddhism, Christianity, and Islam) are able to spread to a receiving society. Even the spread of antireligious ideologies needed opportunities given in societies to develop, beginning in Western Europe.

The opportunity for rulers to choose new religions helps to account for the common phenomenon in which many relatively small societies with primal religions have received the three spreading religions. These societies are usually homogeneous religiously and most people are socialized into their traditional religions. Thus they do not have what is commonly known today as religious diversity and formalized religious freedom. However, the leaders are not committed to or have an alliance with any well-organized religion with a literary tradition that has a developed ideological support for the established order. The small societies are usually in contact with other societies and are in a position to choose a religion (or parts of a religion) that they perceive as beneficial to them. Thus they exist in a larger religiously pluralistic field. Buddhism, Christianity, and Islam were all able to spread to numerous small societies where leaders had relative freedom of choice because their social structures had not formally adopted a particular religion as an integrating and legitimating ideology.

As societies became more complex, with some important exceptions, governments formed alliances with religions which limited choices of both the rulers, and consequently, of the people at large. The

Roman Empire, as a newly organized empire, was among the exceptions since there existed in the Empire relative freedom of religious choice among diverse religions. In this culturally diverse setting with relative tolerance for religious diversity Christianity was able to spread. This form of ancient religious pluralism seems to have existed in situations where the government had overwhelming power or in periods of transition. Ancient and modern Far Eastern nations (primarily China, Korea, and Vietnam) have some parallels to the "Roman Empire pluralism," (by tolerating a variety of religious practices). Like Rome, they usually had strong governments. However, these governments, especially in China, have been at great pains to maintain national unity by clearly distinguishing orthodox from heterodox and "foreign" influences. A kind of ethno-cultural identity was established which tolerated a variety of local religions, but successfully resisted the introduction of Christianity as a foreign religion in the modern era. Japan especially forcefully resisted the introduction of the foreign religion of Christianity and established Buddhism as the official unifying religion. In South Asia (India) Hinduism was fused with the social system so that when foreign religions were introduced, they were made into distinct and separate social units. This is similar to what was done in Persia with the melet system, which was later adopted by Islam and known as the dhimmi system.

What took place in the major societies of Asia and the Middle East to keep out foreign religions by limiting choices was not unique to these societies. Christianity itself made alliances with governments that had the effect of limiting the spread of other religions, as well as of internal religious innovations. As with the other major societies of the world, religion became part of the social structure with the function of providing an integrating or unifying ideology. By becoming monopolistic, the world religions have become a primary means for granting religious identity to various populations, as part of an ethno-cultural identity.

Although the alliance of religions with governmental coercion gave an advantage to religions in spreading within the areas of governmental control and blocking the spread of other religions, there have been certain costs to religions, which have become increasingly apparent in the modern age. One of the major costs, especially apparent in both Christianity and Islam, is that political resistance and religious resistance became closely related so that any attempt at religious innovation leads to political disruption. In Christianity particularly, resistance to religious coercion generated a movement to separate organized religion from governments and other public institutions. This secularization process has been supported by religious people, who wanted freedom of religion, but also by antireligious people, who wanted freedom from religion. The movement for democracy and freedom of many kinds, including religious freedom, has accompanied secularization. These have resulted in a worldwide movement to establish freedom of religious choice legally. However, there is resistance in societies in which there have been (are) monopolistic religions. Such religions have been major identity granting and integrating forces and many of the leaders and ordinary adherents are reluctant to encourage a change in the social structure that would take away these traditional functions and "privileges." A coming struggle in societies where religious choice is now absent or limited will be over how to define the place of religions in the social structure in a way that does not limit religious choices. The demand for individual freedom of choice in all aspects of life, including religion, is likely to increase. (This will be considered in detail in Chapter 9.) Before religious freedom can be established in societies, it is necessary to recognize one thing: that religion is too important, as both a potential source of good and of evil, to be allowed to be either interfered with or externally imposed. To separate religion from coercive power is not to demean it, but to exalt it. Such separation recognizes that taking political power from religious organizations is to keep them and protect them from the misuse of power and to elevate the inherent rewards of religion.

CHAPTER 5

INTERSOCIETAL RELATIONSHIPS AND THE SPREAD OF RELIGIONS

FRIEND OR FOE?

The last chapter considered how the spread of religions is affected by the internal social conditions of receiving societies. We saw that social structures that either hinder or facilitate the making of religious choices were a crucial factor. This led to the special consideration of how governments and religions affect each other. The last chapter and the previous ones unavoidably made some references to intersocietal relations, but in this chapter we consider specifically how such relations affected the spread of Buddhism, Christianity, and Islam.

When a religion spreads from one society to another, an intersocietal relationship is created. However, the relationships established through spreading religions are rarely the only relationships between societies. Most often there have been earlier, as well as other simultaneous relationships, such as relationships established through exploration, trading, or military invasion and control. Some intersocietal relationships are sporadic and relatively rare with little threat in one direction or the other, but other relationships are frequent and involve some level of threat or domination in one direction or the other. There may be equality or inequality in all of these relationships. Typically, there are simultaneous multi-relationships in which a society is dominant in some and dominated in others or unthreatened in some and threatened in others. It is almost certain that the quality of intersocietal relationships between societies will change over time. The theory of this book is that the spread of religions is affected not only by the internal characteristics of religions (Chapters 1, 2, and 3) and the internal conditions existing within receiving societies (Chapter 4), but also by the quality of the relationships between societies (present chapter). It is important to know if a spreading religion is associated with a friend or foe of the receiving society.

The analysis of this chapter is guided by two related propositions:

> **5.1** *Domination or threat from a sending society of a religion toward a receiving society creates resistance to the spreading religion, which may result in rejection or, if pressure is extreme, acceptance with significant change of the spreading religion.*
>
> **5.2** *When there is no domination or threat from a sending society, but rather from another nearby society (or societies), then a receiving society may be receptive to the spreading religion, particularly if the new religion is an aid in resisting other dominating or threatening societies.*

I will review briefly the intersocietal relationships that existed at the times Buddhism, Christianity, and Islam spread to see how their spread was affected. This was the type of influence, namely domination and resistance to domination, to which I (Montgomery 1991, 1996) initially gave major attention. I make use of some additional data here.

BUDDHISM AND INTERSOCIETAL RELATIONSHIPS

Sectarian resistance to Brahmanism, as seen in the rise of Jainism and Buddhism, is consistent with the expression of religious innovation as a form of resistance to a dominant group. The resistance expressed in religious innovations may often arise from members of elite groups, who are none-the-less from marginal groups in a larger society. Gautama Buddha was a prince of a small kingdom existing among other kingdoms and his new religious order drew many people from upper castes, who were not brahmans.

Buddhism gained its greatest recognition in India during the Mauryan period when imperial control was extended over many small kingdoms and republics. However, Buddhism remained a religion of the rulers attempting to establish a moral order for ruling over diverse peoples. In the long run, Buddhism failed to win over the peoples of South Asia (India), who continued to follow their popular religions and live within the established caste system under the leadership of the high caste brahman priests. However, the people of Sri Lanka were very receptive to Buddhism, which came to them from somewhat distant and nonthreatening Northern India. Furthermore, Buddhism clearly contributed to establishing the Sinhalese as a distinct ethnic group from nearby and competing Tamil kingdoms in South India, a distinction that continues to this day.

Invading groups often accept religions from those they have invaded, the dominant from the dominated, who are naturally nonthreatening, but are often more advanced culturally. The invading Kushans received Buddhism from the people they conquered. The invading Burmese likewise accepted Buddhism from the conquered Mons, the Mons having already received Buddhism from India and especially Sri Lanka across the sea from which no threat came. The pattern of conquerors receiving a religion from a conquered people was repeated often in the spread of all three religions.

It is now clear from historical studies that Hinduism spread throughout South Asia primarily in a process of peaceful acceptance of Hindu culture, not through conquest. In fact, both Hinduism and Buddhism spread throughout Southeast Asia peacefully in a process of Indianization. There were conflicts between Buddhist and Hindu kingdoms in Indonesia in which the religion in one and then the other kingdom was dominant, but neither religion was able to eliminate or completely absorb the other. At times both religions were tolerated and regulated in the same kingdoms. If domination is a feature of an intersocietal relationship, as in the case of the Kushans over the Indians and the Burmese over the Mons, then it can be seen that a religion is quite likely to spread from the dominated (invaded) to the dominant (invading) society, not the other way around.

Many centuries later during a period of conflict between Buddhist Thailand and the kingdom of Malacca, the ruler of Malacca turned to the outside religion of Islam for help and was successful in driving off the Buddhist Thais. To the northwest of South Asia, Hindu India and Zoroastrian Iran were in a relationship over many centuries in which neither society dominated the other. Instead both societies were invaded and briefly dominated by Greece (Alexander the Great), but most invasions came from Central Asia (from which the Aryans of both societies had originally come). Eventually both Iran and India were invaded by Arab and Central Asian Moslems, who were followed by Western colonial powers. In these latter cases, Iran and Central Asia accepted Islam, but India resisted both Islam and Western Christianity.

Returning to the spread of Buddhism from Central Asia to China and then on to Korea and Japan, there seems to be little if any association of Buddhism with outside threat so the major factors affecting the spread of Buddhism seem to be internal religious factors of Buddhism and internal social factors in the receiving societies, dealt with in previous chapters. Buddhism traveled a two-way intersocietal trade route. There were periods when China was invaded from Central and Northern Asia, but also times when China extended its domination over Central Asia. For much of the first half of the first millennium CE China was divided into warring kingdoms. At times China dominated Korea, especially northern Korea, but Korea was also divided into competing kingdoms. Japan was not successfully dominated from the outside even though there were attempts by the Chinese and Mongols to invade it. In all the complicated history of East Asia, Buddhism does not seem to have been imposed by domination or outside threat. Instead, as in Southeast Asia (and in the spread of Christianity and Islam) the rulers of certain ascendant societies seemed very receptive to Buddhism as a unifying religion. This would be various kingdoms in China in the first millennium, including the northern Turkish-ruled kingdoms and the later powerful Tang Dynasty of China, the Koguryo, Packche, and Silla Kingdoms of Korea (especially the Silla Kingdom), the Kingdom of the Soga Dynasty of Japan, the Tibetan Kingdom, and the Mongol Kingdom. In most of these societies, Buddhism appears to be like an imported item that was freely chosen, usually by leaders or elites because of the perceived benefits or advantages of having a literate world religion. However, once chosen, Buddhism (also like Christianity and Islam) was able to gain favors from governments so that in many societies, particularly in Southeast Asia, Tibet, Mongolia, and Japan, Buddhism was able to become pervasive and part of the identity to which people were socialized. They thereby were discouraged from accepting any new religion introduced from the outside. On the other hand, as already seen, in major societies in the Far East (China, Korea, Vietnam, and eventually Japan), Buddhism became one religious identity alongside other religious identities, which could be held simultaneously with one another.

In the case of the modern spread of Buddhism to the West, there has been no association with outside domination or threat. Instead, Buddhism appeals to many intellectuals as a means of opposing the authority or possible domination of Christianity.

CHRISTIANITY AND INTERSOCIETAL RELATIONSHIPS

For the first three hundred years, the carriers of Christianity were not associated with any dominating power, but rather with being from one of many small kingdoms that were overrun and incorporated into the Roman Empire. Thus there was little to detract from consideration of the intrinsic message of the religion. Outside the eastern edge of the Roman Empire various societies, Syria, Iran (Persia), Armenia, Georgia, and a number of Arabian tribes, received carriers of Christianity from small or smaller societies, who were not in any sense representing Roman power. In fact, the Roman Empire was still under pagan rule. Resistance to Christianity would come later when Constantinople became a dominating or threatening power.

Greeks, who were under Roman rule, accepted Christianity from people who came from the east, not from Rome. Romans and other Latin speakers received many religions from the eastern part of the Empire, which had been conquered, for example, the worship of Osiris from Egypt and mystery religions from Greece. They also received Mithraism and later Manichaeanism from Iran further east. Christianity was among the many religions flowing around the Empire. Thus, before Constantine in the fourth century, there was no sense in which Christianity was associated with outside political-military domination. Before the fourth century CE, however, pagan Roman power extended beyond its borders and came into conflict with peoples to the east,

Arabs and Iranians, and peoples to the north, the "barbarian" tribal peoples. Some, such as the Celts of Gaul and Britain, had been brought into the Empire, but many Germans and Irish and Scottish Celts had remained outside the Empire. Goths, on the northeastern edge of the Empire, accepted Christianity, but a different version (Arianism) from that of their enemies in Rome.

The lack of association of Christianity with outside political domination changed with first the toleration and then the official sponsorship of Christianity by Rome in the fourth century, discussed in the previous chapter. From this period on, Christianity became associated with Roman power. However, it is very significant that Roman power, at least in the West, entered a period of decline in the period when Christianity had its greatest expansion in the north. In 410 CE Roman armies (already including many tribal people) were withdrawn from Britain. In the same year Rome fell to Goths. The center of power in the Empire had already shifted to Constantinople. The previous chapter noted how much the change in government policy toward Christianity accelerated its growth within the Empire, which was limited at first primarily to the Mediterranean Basin. Christianity grew throughout the fourth century from its approximately 15 percent level at the beginning of the century to a large majority by the end of the century. However, this was clearly growth under coercion and there were costs to pay as already seen.

The eventual cost of resistance in the form of irreligion, mentioned in the last chapter, will be discussed further in Chapter 9. However, the immediate cost was the inclusion of other religions, particularly on the popular level. MacMullen (1997) has detailed how paganism survived, in spite of the legal actions taken against it. Furthermore, much of it survived within Christianity! However, due to the collapse of Roman power, the coercion exercised within the Empire generally was not able to be applied externally from Rome or even Constantinople as Christianity spread northward. This was primarily because many of the tribal peoples were outside the area of Roman control and furthermore, what power Rome had was greatly weakened. Even the Empire that continued with its base in Constantinople did not extend its power northward in a consistent fashion, but was under continuing pressure from Slav, Alan, and Bulgar invaders. Constantinople also had ongoing conflicts with societies to the east and south. These did have a negative effect on the spread of Christianity to Persia and laid the groundwork for the spread of Islam in areas to the east and south dominated and persecuted by Constantinople and its official Orthodox Church.

Ulfilias (c. 311-380), the major missionary to the Goths was Gothic himself or had been raised as a prisoner of the Goths. He translated part or all of the scriptures to Gothic. He was also an Arian Christian and Arian Christianity subsequently spread among the Visigoths, the Ostrogoths, the Gepidae, and the Vandals, all of whom were soon pressing in on the Western Empire, which had become officially Roman Catholic. This is an example of a receiving society that accepts the religion of the enemy, but follows another version of it. If there had been freedom of religion in the modern sense, Arianism may have become a major denomination.

In Gaul, Martin of Tours (c. 316-390), is remembered as an effective missionary. He was especially energetic and outgoing. Both he and his father served in the Roman army. Martin became a bishop and an exponent of monasticism. He along with other bishops did much to bring about the conversion of people in the countryside of Gaul. Significantly, at this time for people in Gaul the major threat was from German barbarians, who steadily increased in numbers leading up to the major German invasions that began early in the fifth century. In short, Rome was a friend, not a foe, and an ally against invaders.

Christian Rome represented advanced culture, but not a military threat in Gaul. The invading tribes, for example the Burgundians, accepted the Christianity of the people among whom they settled, first Roman Catholicism, then Arianism (due to the influence of the Visigoths), and then Roman Catholicism again through contact with the powerful Franks, who had by then been converted (Latourette 1937: 206). The major outside threat of this period for the Gauls and the newly arrived Germans was the Huns, led by Attila (c 406-453). This drew the later arriving Germans (Franks) toward Christianity of the earlier Goths and the native Gallo-Romans. Attila was finally defeated in 451 in Gaul by a combined Roman and Gothic army. Although he later threatened Rome, which Pope Leo I begged him to spare, he died suddenly in 453, after which his empire collapsed. The Franks under Clovis (c 466-511) established the Frankish kingdom over much of Christian Gaul, creating the foundation for the future nation of France. Clovis accepted the faith of those he ruled and of his Christian wife. He was baptized in 496 and was followed into Christianity by most of his warriors.

The fifth century, the century in which Roman power crumbled, was not only an important century for the conversion of the Frankish invaders of Gaul, who would give the name "France," to the area, but it was also the era when Christian British Celts, particularly a man named "Patrick" (c. 389-461), would take Christianity to the Irish Celts, the people the Romans called "Scots." There remained many peoples in northern, central, and eastern Europe, who were yet to accept Christianity. However, the general pattern of Christianity spreading from the invaded to the invading groups continued from the earliest invaders by the Goths and Franks to the last great wave of invasions by the Vikings.

The Irish contributed numerous wandering monks (peregrine) to the spread of Christianity to Scotland (Picts), England (Anglo-Saxons), and the Continent. They were joined by missionary monks from the Anglo-Saxons, who themselves had earlier invaded England, but had received missionaries from Ireland and later from Rome (Augustine in 597). The major exception to the movement of Christianity between societies upward from the dominated to the dominant was the effort of western Germans (Franks) to convert the eastern Germans (Saxons). This followed the pattern of conversion by rulers using force on those they conquered and ruled.

Because of the conversion of the invading Franks in Gaul and the Anglo-Saxons in Britain, Christianity recovered most of the ground it had lost in Gaul and Britain by the end of the seventh century. In the eighth century missionaries carried Christianity to the Low Countries and in the ninth century to the Germans. However, the Franks used force in backing the missionaries, especially in the conversion of the Saxon Germans. In the tenth, eleventh, and twelfth centuries the Scandinavians (Vikings) were converted, not so much by outside force, but by force exerted by their own leaders, who had adopted the new faith. The missionary help they requested was not from their Frankish enemies, but from the English "from whom they had nothing to fear politically and with which they had close relations through their own conquests" (Latourette 1938:79). The Franks themselves had requested missionaries from England to convert the people of the Low Country and the Saxons. The Franks recognized the hostility of these people for themselves as opposed to their German cousins now settled in England. The Frisians, especially, in the Low Country were resistant to Christianity because they feared domination by the powerful Franks to the south. Willibrord (c. 658-739) of England was the major missionary to the Frisians, who by the time of his death saw at least the conversion of the southern part of the Low Countries, but the Frisians continued their resistance for several more decades.

Another Anglo-Saxon missionary, Winfrith or Boniface (675-754), who had helped Willibrord in the Low Countries, was the major missionary to the Germans. Before Boniface, Christianity had already been accepted in much of Switzerland, southern Germany, and western Austria. Frankish influence and Irish missionaries had brought Christianity to Bavaria and Thuringia. Boniface, however, was an especially effective missionary, particularly in the Hesse area, not only winning many to Christianity, but in renewing and reorganizing Christians throughout Germany and even in the Frankish realm. He did this according to the administrative system that had been developed in the Roman Empire and continued in the Roman Catholic Church. At the end of his life he returned to Frisia, where he had started and where there were still numerous pagans, and met his end as a martyr (Latourette 1938:92-98).

At the death of Boniface there were still numerous unconverted Frisians, as well as the main body of Saxons and Slavs. A number of missionaries continued his work, but the work was completed under Charlemagne, who came to the throne in 768 and ruled until 814. Missionaries were often backed with force, for example in putting down a combined revolt of the Frisians and Saxons. The Saxons, whose lands extended eastward, continued their resistance to the Franks and to Christianity. However, after several vigorously suppressed revolts, by 776 the Saxons were incorporated into Charlemagne's realm as Christians. Charlemagne's kingdom was the European replacement for the Roman Empire with a "Second Constantine" as Emperor. In addition to many resistant Saxons, there were also the Wends, a Slavic people among the Saxons, who continued to resist Christianity for centuries because of its association with coercion. Slavic subgroups are still recognizable minorities in Germany.

The Scandinavian invaders of Normandy, Great Britain, and Ireland eventually accepted the faith of those among whom they settled in the already familiar pattern. In the case of the kingdoms in Norway, Denmark, and Sweden, it was a matter primarily of rulers accepting the new faith and requiring or naturally obtaining compliance from their followers, again a familiar pattern. Force was often used by leaders on ordinary tribal members and Christianity became the state religion, the pattern that was to last to the present day. In Norway especially, Olaf Tryggvason (c. 963-c 1000) followed by Olaf Haraldsson (c. 994–1030), used force in making Norway a Christian land. As in other lands, enforcing Christianity was a method of bringing local nobles, who followed the old religion, in line with the king, thus creating a more unified nation. The Norwegian rulers used primarily missionaries from England, rather than from nearer Germany, which posed a threat to them, to help them convert their people.

I have not tried to cover each of the tribes or kingdoms of Western Europe, but enough to show that Christianity was not initially introduced from the outside by force in most of the societies. Instead, typically after Christianity was freely accepted by strong rulers, they used coercion to unite their people, often including rival leaders, under a state that they had made stronger. Thus, Christianity spread in Europe primarily from the dominated societies to the dominant societies, but it remained and spread in each society in association with dominating government power, in the pattern of Constantine and the Roman Empire of the fourth century. The receiving societies were not dominated from the outside by sending societies, but more from the inside by their own converted rulers.

Turning to Eastern Europe, Christianity moved northward from Constantinople in much the same manner as it did from Rome. That is,

Christianity was spread peacefully against the primarily dominating pressure from the invading barbarians. The Slavs pressed in after the Goths in the sixth and seventh centuries, erasing much of the previous Christianity. Subsequently, the Slavs were converted by missionary effort rather than by force. Even though the political-military power in Constantinople was much greater than in contemporary Rome, the empire was not extended northward to any great extent. The barbarians were held at bay and Byzantine influence extended over the Balkans, but Constantinople was generally not able to force Christianity on the invading peoples. Most ominous for the future of Christianity to the east was the hostility that developed between Christian Constantinople and Christians in Egypt and Syria. These Christians were later to welcome a more tolerant Muslim rule.

The missionary, Severius, worked along the Danube in the latter part of the fifth century. However, the most notable missionary work to the Slavs was carried out by the brothers, Constantine or Cyril and Methodius, who were from Thessalonica and had some familiarity with the Slavic languages. In 862 the brothers were sent to Ratislav, the Slavic prince of Moravia, who had requested Christian teachers (Deanesly 1981 [1925]:76). Central European societies developed relationships in three major directions: toward the west (the Frankish kingdom and Roman Catholicism), toward the south (Constantinople and Orthodoxy) and toward the east (the eastern Slavs, still pre-Christian). Ratislav, for example, had earlier received missionaries from the Franks. The Franks were closer and more threatening than Constantinople. Furthermore, the Frankish missionaries used Latin, whereas Cyril and Methodius worked to translate the liturgy and the scriptures into Slavic. The pope approved the use of Slavic in Moravia, but a later pope withdrew approval. However, Slavic was used in Bulgaria, Serbia, Croatia, and later Russia, and its use became permanent. After Cyril died, Methodius continued his missionary work, but at one time was confined in a monastery in Germany. After he was released and returned to Moravia, the Moravians drove out the German priests and welcomed Methodius as their Archbishop. It is also true that the Moravians were at this time victorious against the German arms (Latourette 1938:164). The Czechs (Bohemians) accepted Christianity not from the Germans, but from the more recently converted fellow Slavs of Moravia. Nevertheless, German help in conflict with Moravia drew the rulers toward Western Christianity at the end of the ninth century. The people converted more slowly to Western Christianity during the next century (Latourette 1938:166-68).

The invading Turkish Bulgars threatened Constantinople in the second half of the seventh century coming to the very walls of the city, but were eventually defeated and converted. The Bulgarians assimilated to the dominated Christian Slavs, who had invaded the area earlier, in a similar pattern to the Franks in Gaul. A Bulgarian bishop was consecrated by the Patriarch Ignatius in 870. A Christian Slavonic literature developed in Bulgaria and spread to the rest of the Slavonic world. Simeon, son of the strong king, Boris, expanded the territory of Bulgaria, took the title of Emperor, and had the Bulgarian bishops declare the Bulgarian Church autocephalous or self-governing within the Orthodox family, and appointed a Patriarch. When Simeon died in 927 the formal conversion of the Bulgarians is said to have been completed (Latourette 1938:246).

In the early tenth century, the non-Christian Magyars moved into the area (now Hungary) and destroyed the Moravian state to their north. They made numerous raids in which they wrecked havoc in churches to the north, west, and south and were not finally defeated until 955 by Otto I of Saxony. The Magyars or Hungarians continued to have strong leaders who converted to Christianity of the Western type, unlike the

Orthodoxy of the surrounding Slaves. They united their people and land through Christianity in the early eleventh century in the familiar pattern of the conversion of tribal people.

Latourette (1938:175) states that the conversion of the Poles followed a similar pattern to that of other kingdoms, "like Norway and Hungary, where the growth of the monarchy appears to have been closely associated with the process of conversion to Christianity." Even though the rulers promoted Christianity among their people as a means of unification, there was considerable resistance and occasional revivals of paganism. This was especially true of the Wends and Obodrites, Slavic peoples, who were along the Elbe to the northwest of the Poles. The domination and tyranny of the Christian Germans had much to do with the continuing strong opposition to Christianity of these Slavic peoples. Even when their leaders were converted the people were often slow to follow.

Constantinople and Rome competed for the loyalty of the Serbs. In 1077 Rome "accorded the royal dignity to Serbia's ruler on the condition that the Pope be acknowledged the overlord of the land" (Latourette 1938:247). However, by the early part of the twelfth century Christianity became thoroughly established among the people in Serbia under Greek Orthodox auspices. Then, sfter the capture of Constantinople by the Crusaders in 1204, Stephen, the ruler of Serbia, looked to Rome and was crowned with his Venetian Roman Catholic queen by the Papal Legate. However, his brother, Sava, a monk in the Orthodox Church, became aware of the danger of Romanization and led the resistance of clergy to the process. He obtained from Constantinople (Emperor, Patriarch, and Holy Synod), the right of the bishops of Serbia to elect and consecrate their own Archbishop, thereby making the Serbian Church autocephalous or independent (Latourette 1938:247-48). It is apparent that Orthodox Christianity was able to maintain its position in Serbia to a great extent because of the perceived outside threat of domination from the Latin West of Rome and Venice on the one hand and the nonthreatening relationship to Constantinople on the other hand.

Orthodox Christianity from Constantinople spread to tribal peoples north of the Black and Caspian Seas, although among the Khazars, many of whose rulers accepted Judaism, Christianity had limited success. The greatest success in the north was with the kingdom based in Kiev. Igor (913-945), the king, was a non-Christian, but his wife, Olga, was a Christian, again, a familiar occurrence in the Christianization process. Her son, Vladimir was baptized and allied himself and his kingdom with the Orthodox Christian Faith in 988. In the succeeding centuries that were marked by pressure from outside societies to the east, particularly in the period of domination by the Mongols, the Orthodox Church "became the one expression of Russian unity" (Latourette 1938:258). It is notable that Orthodox Christianity also spread northward among people who were under great pressure from the Mongols.

To the east of Constantinople, Christianity encountered societies that were more culturally advanced than the tribal societies to the north. Before the official adoption of Christianity in the fourth century by the Roman rulers, it had already begun to spread to Syrians, Arabians, Persians, Armenians, and Georgians. Edessa in Syria (now in Turkey), capital of Osrhoene, and Armenia, under pressure from both pre-Christian Rome and Persia, had accepted Christianity before Constantine. The Christianity of the East, however, like the Christianity that first spread among the Goths, showed a tendency to be different "denominationally" from the Christianity of Rome and Constantinople. Monophysite (Jacobite and Coptic) and Nestorian communities represented ancient nationalities and resistance to domination by the

Christianity to the west (Deanesly 1981:6; Latourette 1938:1).

The intersocietal conflict between Constantinople and Persia in particular resulted in tremendous difficulties for the Christians living under Persian rule and greatly hindered the spread of Christianity among the Persians. Christianity made considerable headway in Persia until Rome became officially Christian. Moffett (1992:137) notes, "When Rome became Christian, its old enemy Persia turned anti-Christian." This is one of the clearest early examples of the negative effect of conflicting intersocietal relationships on the spread (failure to spread) of Christianity.

The dramatic rise and spread of Islam beginning in the seventh century helped to reinforce the line of hostility between the west and east that had existed from the time of Alexander and especially the succeeding Roman Empire. The spread of Islam in the Middle East and North Africa was in no small measure due to the welcome of the people, including the non-Orthodox Christians, to the armies that liberated them from the heavy hand of Constantinople (Carmichael 1967:61-78). This will be considered further in looking at the spread of Islam. The point here is that Christianity had difficulty spreading further where there was fear of domination from Christian power centers. On the other hand, Christianity did spread to some areas where there was not any perceived threat from Christian power, but rather from nearer powers. This would include the spread of Christianity to Central Asian tribes, some of whom later became part of the Mongol Empire. The result was that Christians were prominent among the Mongols (wives of Khans, scribes, and military leaders) and the Mongol rulers often tended to tolerate or even favor Christians. Given more time, it is conceivable that the Mongol Empire might have followed the path of the European tribes and accepted Christianity. On the other hand, the spread of Christianity in China was hindered by its association with the Mongol conquerors so that when the Mongol Empire collapsed, Christianity was rejected with it.

Another example of Christianity spreading to where there was not a perceived threat from Christian power, but rather from nearby non-Christian powers, is the case of Abyssinia or Ethiopia. The major threat to this isolated kingdom was from nearby non-Christians and later from Islam, not from far away Constantinople.

After 1500 Christianity entered its third great period of expansion (after expanding in the Roman Empire and Europe). Western nations entered the era of exploration, imperialism, and colonialism, with which Christianity thereby became associated. New areas of the world were made available for carriers of the faith. This era only came to an end soon after the middle of the twentieth century and the devastating World Wars. Beginning in the sixteenth century Christianity was associated with conquest and domination in Latin America and the Philippines, although there were some exceptions to domination. Portugal, much smaller and with less wealth than Spain, began the Western expansion with exploration on the African coastline and the west coast of India in a much less overwhelming way. Andrew Walls (2002:92) notes that "the unintended result was the invention of the missionary movement–the establishment of a body of people whose task was to commend, convince, illustrate, and persuade, but who were unable to coerce." One of the best examples of this noncoercive approach was the conversion of the kingdom of Soyo at the mouth of the Congo River that was clearly independent of any Portuguese control.

The spread of Christianity in Asia and the Pacific Islands after 1500 had some important variations supporting the theory that association of a religion with threat of outside domination hinders its spread, but when domination is not associated primarily with the introduced religion, but comes from another, usually nearby power center, there may be receptivity to the new religion, particularly if the new religion is an aid in resistance to domination (Propositions 5.1 and 5.2). Regarding the major civilizations of Asia, the internal conditions of monopolistic religions discussed in the previous chapter were already in place and had already limited the spread of new religions, especially Christianity and Islam, before the civilizations began to experience Western intrusion. That is, by 1500 these ancient societies already had in place social systems that included well organized religions with literate traditions with which political authorities had alliances and broad populations identified themselves. Regarding the effect of intersocietal relationships on the spread of religions, the subject of this chapter, the power of the Western nations only gradually became apparent. The first to feel Western power were the Americas and the societies at the edges of Asia.

The Portuguese took Ormuz, at the entrance to the Persian Gulf, and Malacca, in Malaysia, in 1498 in order to dominate trade in the Indian Ocean and to the Far East. Cochin, on the southwest coast of India became their first major headquarters, but by 1530, Goa had succeeded to that position. Probably the first large scale conversions in India were the low-caste pearl-fishing Parayas, who lived north and east of Cape Comorin (Latourette 1939:253). Even though the Portuguese were primarily interested in establishing trading posts, not in acquiring territory, they used coercion when possible to spread Christianity, for example, forbidding the practice of Hinduism in their small domains (Latourette 1939:255).

Adding to the association of coercion with Christianity, in the sixteenth century, the Iberian powers, followed by the other European powers, began the slave trade that would extend for over three centuries. Nevertheless, the interior of Africa remained free from

European intrusion until the nineteenth century. Although there was exploration and intrusion, the height of the colonial era did not come to Africa until as late as 1880. This is surprising to many people because European colonies had already been established much earlier in the Americas and in Asia. The missionary movement that began at the end of the eighteenth century in concert with the antislavery movement initiated the conversion of the interior of Africa. In particular, freed slaves from the "receptive" community in Sierra Leone (established in 1792) and their descendents were very important for the spread of Christianity in West Africa.

While the colonization of Africa was largely delayed until the nineteenth century, the conquest of Latin American went forward from the explorations and invasions of the sixteenth century. The Christianization of Latin America after 1500 provides one of the clearest cases of the spread of Christianity in association with conquest. It has provided many people with their major image of the spread of Christianity when actually it was quite different from most other cases of its spread, for example, in the Roman Empire during the first three hundred years and in Europe to most of the tribes. In Latin America there were numerous small societies, which, as we saw in the previous chapter, are normally open to an outside world religion if introduced peacefully. However, the Spanish brought down two empires, the Aztec and the Inca, and extended their rule over as many tribes as possible, employing forceful tactics and enslaving laborers. It is worth noting that aiding the Spanish in their conquests was the fact that many of the tribes were as hostile or more hostile to each than they were to the Spanish, a typical condition aiding the conquest of tribal peoples.

The best feature of the Christianization of Latin America (and the Philippines) was the existence of strong defenders of the indigenous Americans among the Spanish. They had as their major weapon the official positions of Spanish kings and the Pope who affirmed the humanity of the Native Americans. The most influential theologian in Spain in the first half of the sixteenth century, the Dominican, Francisco de Vitoria, stated "that Indians could be converted, that Christians had the duty to spread the Gospel, and that no one should be forced to accept Christianity" (Latourette 1939:90). There were also defenders of the Indians on the scene, the most famous being Bartolome de Las Casas. However, in practice, those who wielded the sword and exploited the native workers were also on the scene and had a dominant influence in what was happening to the people. The overall effect was that Christianity was imposed rather than offered as a free choice. Just as there was resistance to coercive Christianity in Europe, so resistance to the new faith developed in Latin America and the Philippines. In some cases the resistance was overt, when groups were sufficiently isolated to escape the presence of the invaders, but typically the kind of resistance that developed in Latin America has been covert.

The major form of covert resistance used in Latin America and the Philippines was to bring features of the pre-Christian religions into Christianity to form what has been called "Christo-paganism." (Something like this also happened in the Christianization of the Roman Empire and Europe.) In the twentieth century, Roman Catholic leaders have been divided over the efforts to purify the faith and bring about spiritual renewal to the vast numbers of poor people of Latin America. The base community movement has been promoted by some church leaders, but especially by clergy who are close to the people. However, the more highly placed leaders, including the Pope, have not supported the movement. Also, many of the people for whom the base communities were intended did not follow the movement. In the meantime, in the last half century especially, the Pentecostal and

Evangelical Christian movement has provided an alternative way for numerous people to the dominant form of Roman Catholic Christianity.

Christianity was imposed in a similar way in the Philippines. The Spanish occupied the Philippines beginning in 1542 very much as an extension of their conquests in the Americas. The Philippines contained numerous small societies and did not have in place the kind of conditions found in the major civilizations that would enable them to resist the new religion. Individual leaders had the freedom to choose a new religion, but at the same time, Christianity was associated with overpowering force, even if it was not usually directly applied. Leading chiefs had previously had contacts with Muslim traders from the south. In all of Asia, the conversion of the Philippines was most similar to the conversion of the European tribes and Latin America. "Tact, the show of arms, and the efforts of missionaries, with very small contingents of troops and very slight bloodshed, brought about, in an amazingly brief period, the political and religious submission of the non-Moslem peoples of the lowlands" (Latourette 1939:312).

Spanish colonizers systematically brought indigenous people together into new fixed settlements, thereby breaking up their traditional culture. They also introduced a feudalistic land owning system and production mode. However, the Filipinos had defenders, as in Latin America, in some of the friars who sought to win converts by example instead of by force and were critical of social injustices and colonial oppression. Nevertheless, covert resistance developed within Christianity. Kathy Nadeau (2002:84) comments:

> However, the indigenous Filipinos interpreted Christianity in terms of traditional Southeast Asian cultural practices and beliefs. Many articulated the language of Christianity as a means of expressing their own values, ideals, and

hopes for liberation from their colonial oppressors. In effect, Filipinos developed their own version of folk Catholicism to contest and eventually transform Spanish rule. This folk Catholicism was largely an indigenous resistance to Spanish Christian colonialism.

Japan appeared to be following the same track as the Philippines with large numbers of conversions, but with less show of force by the Portuguese who were seeking trade. By the end of the sixteenth century there were probably several hundred thousand Christians. Japan did have a more strongly established religious tradition than the Philippines, but, in addition, the rising new leadership recognized a threat associated with Christianity. Japanese were aware through their trade contacts that Christianity had accompanied conquest in the islands to the south and these forces were not only competitors in Asia, but a threat to Japan itself. Near the end of the sixteenth century periodic persecutions of Christians began, and in 1614 a decree against Christianity contained the words that Christians "wanted to change the government of the country and obtain possession of the land" (Latourette 1939:131). Severe persecutions followed over a number of decades so that by the middle of the century, Christianity became a "hidden religion." Some two hundred years later in 1859, Japan was forced open by Admiral Perry. Within less than ten years the Emperor Mutsuhito (Meiji) began his reign that lasted until 1912. He initiated a nationalistic movement (the Meiji Restoration) in which Japan sought to become equal economically and militarily to Western nations. Shinto was made the national religion and Japan increased its cultural insularity in the face of the worldwide dominance of Western culture. Japan offers a sharp contrast to its neighbor Korea.

Korea like other Asian societies was highly resistant to efforts to introduce Christianity in the nineteenth century, but after Korean forces were defeated by the Japanese in 1876 and especially after the annexation by Japan in 1910, Koreans became increasingly open to Western missionaries and their message. Japan forced Japanese language and religion on Korea, but Korean Christians stood against these efforts. Similar Christian messengers went with the same message to Japan and Korea in the same period of time–providing for a simulated "controlled experiment." The major difference or independent variable (making Korea the "experimental group") was the difference in intersocietal relationships. Japan was dominated or threatened from the same direction as those who came from the outside with the Christian message. In contrast, Korea was dominated by its neighbor Japan while the message came from a source that offered no threat to Korean identity. So to become a Christian in Japan became a subtraction to being Japanese whereas to become a Christian in Korea strengthened one's Korean national identity (Kane and Park 2009). This will be discussed further in Chapter 7, but here the comparison of Japan and Korea supports Propositions 5.1 and 5.2 above.

Turning to the islands that became Indonesia, the Dutch replaced the Portuguese as the major Western colonial power in the area. They took Malacca (in Malaysia) from the Portuguese in 1640 and extended their influence across the many islands of Indonesia, leaving the Portuguese only in Timor. The people who proved to be most responsive to Christianity, giving Indonesia the largest number of Christians in Asia apart from the Philippines and most recently China, were minority tribal groups and peoples in the outlying islands. The Ambonese are an example. They were dominated by the Islamic kingdom of Ternate who brought Islam to some villages. However, many Ambonese were converted by Roman Catholic Portuguese and Protestant Dutch missionaries and educated in mission schools so that they were able to serve in the colonial government throughout

Indonesia. Strong Christian communities also came to exist among the minority Batak people of Sumatra and the Toradja of Sulawesi (Celebes). Again, Propositions 5.1 and 5.2 are supported.

The pattern of minority groups accepting Christianity can be seen throughout much of Asia providing the best examples of dominated people resisting the religion of those who dominate them and accepting a religion from another source that offers no threat, but rather assistance to maintaining their distinctive identity (Proposition 5.2). This is particularly evident on mainland Southeast Asia in Myanmar (formerly Burma), which was annexed by Great Britain in 1895 after three wars that began in 1824. A number of tribal groups, Karens, Chins, Kachins, Lahus, and Was, the latter similar to tribes across the border in India, turned to Christianity in the nineteenth and twentieth centuries. Although not as numerous as in Myanmar, a similar kind of trend can be seen among minority tribal people in the other Southeast Asian lands of Thailand, Laos, Cambodia, Vietnam, Malaysia, Indonesia, and Taiwan. (In Taiwan where I worked from 1956 to 1972, some 40 percent of the Presbyterian Church membership, the largest Protestant church on the Island, come from the less than 2 percent aboriginal population.)

Turning to the two largest civilizations in Asia, India and China, the majority populations have been rather resistant to the Christianity that came to them in association with Western intrusion. Regarding the Christian missionary effort in South Asia up to 1944, Latourette (1945:314) wrote, "It had won comparatively few from the religions of the majority, Hinduism and Islam. These two faiths remained dominant and apparently were not seriously shaken, either by Christianity or by any other force." Nevertheless, there was considerable receptivity to Christianity from low castes, untouchables, and tribal peoples, all dominated by the surrounding majority society. Apart from the tribal groups in northeast India, the highest proportion of Christians in the population is found in southern India, the area that is at the greatest distance from centers of brahman power. Regarding the openness of dominated groups in India to Westernizing influences found within Christianity, Susan Billington Harper (1995:15) writes:

> The mass movements to Christianity must be understood as part of–indeed, as a catalyzing agent in–this broader effort to reject caste traditions and to adopt new, more respectable forms of social identity... Far from being a weak concession to domineering missionaries, Westernization represented a symbolic challenge by long suppressed lower classes to an oppressive indigenous social order. In this context, indigenization along the lines expected by Western orientalizing individuals [who desired Indian Christians to be "more Indian"] would have been viewed as just another form of indigenous oppression.

At the same time, while dominated classes and tribal groups often have been relatively receptive to Christianity, Hinduism has been stirred to lead a nationalistic movement that is highly resistant to outside religions, as seen in the previous chapter.

In the other major civilization in Asia, China, no real military threat from the West was perceived by the Chinese until the nineteenth century when force was used to open China to trade. In addition to the political-military threat (the Opium War and the period of "unequal treaties"), the cultural threat from the West was felt by the leaders of a system that had endured for centuries and had been separated by a great distance from the West. Following the Nestorian Christians of the Tang and Yuan Dynastic periods, who left no Christian community, China received Jesuit missionaries in the late sixteenth century and gave them a warm reception at the court where their scientific learning was highly respected. The Jesuits were joined by Dominicans and Franciscans who worked in various parts of China and had considerable success in spite of periodic persecutions and the upheaval of the Manchu conquest in 1644. However, a major setback occurred when the Chinese (Manchu) Emperor turned against Christianity because of conflict between the views of the Emperor and the Vatican. In 1706 the Emperor Kang Xi ordered the Papal Legate, Tournon, to leave Beijing and banished other Christians because the Vatican they represented did not agree with his opinion favoring the Jesuit's approach in the famous Rites Controversy. For our purposes the content of the controversy is not so important as the fact that the foreign religion was put in the position or put itself in the position of questioning the authority of the local highest political authority. The result of this conflict was that Christianity received increased limitations.

The nineteenth and first half of the twentieth centuries saw an enormous missionary effort in China during the period when Western powers were able to establish dominance over China. In spite of this great effort, the response to Christianity in actual numbers of converts was a very small proportion of the population. However, in accordance with our theory, China showed itself receptive to Marxist ideology that came from the outside, but became associated with the assertion of Chinese nationalism against dominating powers. Then, also, according to our theory, after a period from 1950 in which Western nations were excluded from China and local Christianity was able to disassociate itself from Western domination, China has become highly receptive to Christianity. By the turn of the twenty first century, along with a general revival of all religions, an unprecedented movement toward Christianity became evident.

Africa has similarities, but important distinctions from other cases of the spread of Christianity. Christianity was not imposed as early in Africa as in Latin America and the Philippines. Walls (2002:96) notes, "Outside some special situations such as the Cape and Sierra Leone, missionaries could operate only on terms laid down by African powers." This was very similar to the situations during the spread of Christianity among many of the European kingdoms. However, once European powers began establishing colonies in the latter part of the nineteenth century in Africa, all of this changed. Walls (2002:97) states:

> Colonial rule changed the basis of missionary life. Missionaries ceased to live so directly on terms set by Africans. They could not now be removed except by their compatriots in governments, within whose framework they operated; they were part of the structure of power. The nature of their task changed... Western education became the most noticeable aspect of missions in Africa.

The two world wars of the twentieth century broke European power and brought an end to colonialism in Africa and elsewhere. In 1900 after four hundred years of contact and one hundred years of increasing missionary effort only approximately 9.2 percent of the population of Africa was Christian. After de-colonization in the 1950s and 60s, in 1970 the proportion of Christians had risen to 40.6 percent (Barrett 1982:782). However, this includes North Africa, which is mostly Muslim. In Sub-Saharan Africa, high proportions of the populations of many countries are Christian. For example, in the Congo (formerly Zaire) the proportion of Christians in 2000 was 91.3 percent, in Kenya 76.7 percent, in Uganda 87.0 percent, and in South Africa 78.8 percent (Barrett and Johnson 2001). The greatest growth of Christianity in Sub-Saharan Africa took place after the collapse of European colonial power. Now it is not considered unrealistic for a leading missiologist to state, "At the end of the twentieth century Africa was appearing as the Christian heartland" (Walls 1976; 2002:118).

In the meantime, in the Americas one of the most dramatic cases of accepting a religion under conditions of duress, but then introducing changes to it (Proposition 5.1) is the case of Christianity spreading to the African slaves and their descendents. Here Christianity was clearly associated with domination and discrimination of the most extreme forms. Nevertheless, African Americans accepted Christianity, but then through it created distinctive expressions that emphasized their distinctive identity. More than that, in North America particularly, because of conditions brought about through struggle and through governmental action (antislavery movement, emancipation, and civil rights movement) they elevated themselves in a long struggle largely through Christian leadership and in the process created an expression of Christianity that has had a worldwide influence. In the Caribbean and in Latin America, except for former British colonies, African American Christianity has incorporated more popular religion with African roots than in North America. The older version of Christianity, Roman Catholicism, has shown a greater propensity to incorporate popular religion than the newer version, Protestantism, which has been dominant in the British colonies and in North America. In North America, Protestantism perpetuated racism and segregation, now much of it related to residential segregation. On the other hand, Pentecostalism has broken new ground in inter-racial relations, as well as religious expression.

ISLAM AND INTERSOCIETAL RELATIONSHIPS

The influence of intersocietal relationships on the spread of Islam has already been seen in the case where domination or threat from

Constantinople and the West facilitated the acceptance of Islamic rule and eventually Islamic faith in the Middle East and North Africa. Lapidus (2005 [1888]:34) notes:

> The reasons for the relatively rapid success of the Arab-Muslim conquests are not hard to find. The Byzantine and Sasanian empires were both militarily exhausted by several decades of warfare prior to the Arab-Muslim invasions. The Christian populations– the Copts in Egypt, the Monophysites in Syria, and the Nestorians in Iraq–all had long histories of troubled relations with their Byzantine and Sasanian overlords. Their disaffection was important in the cases where Christian-Arab border tribes and military auxiliaries joined the conquerors and where fortified cities capitulated.

On the other hand, where Islam became a ruling power for many centuries it was resisted by local populations with well established religions. Such resistance was seen in Iberia, southern France, Sicily, Italy, Greece, the Balkans, and India. An important exception to this resistance was in the receptivity to Islam found among the oppressed minority of Bogomiles in the Balkans. In other words, as we have been saying, oppressed people may welcome a religion that is associated with liberating forces.

Persia is a special case. Although conquered by Islamic armies, unlike the conquered areas which successfully resisted Islam, Persia eventually converted to Islam. This is not a problem for most studies since the spread of religion by conquest is taken for granted, but we have seen that religions usually do not spread through conquest. The spread of Islam to Persia seems to be an exception to the rule. However, there are a number of conditions which make it look less like an exception.

Zoroastrianism was the established state religion of Persia, although it had moved away from its earlier and clearer monotheism. It had also become a rigid religion in a highly stratified society that suppressed other religions and religious innovations. In terms of intersocietal relationships, Islam had not been a long-time threat to Persia, but came from the area previously dominated by Persia. Instead, the Byzantine Empire based in Constantinople was the long time enemy of Persia. The Islamic armies defeated and drove back the armies of Constantinople just prior to the invasion of Persia. Islamic society was egalitarian in a tribal fashion and from the beginning was divided into various groups who struggled for power based on various claims to the right of succession to leadership. Persia contained ethnic minorities, especially toward the northeast in Khurasan. Many of these Persian peasant and tribal minorities joined the Arab army as mawali (clients of the Arabs) and participated in the overthrow of Omayyad power based in Damascus.

Thus following the conquest, Arab Islamic society proved to be very porous, especially leading up to and after the Abbasid revolution. It allowed Persians and Turks access to power in the government and the military. Within a very short time after the Arab conquests in the name of Islam, a paradox was introduced: Yes, Islam had been introduced to Persia in association with force, but Arab power became divided almost immediately between different factions and began to dissipate entirely in little over a century so that power within Islam became locally administered. With the installation of the Abbasids in Baghdad in 762, Persian viziers began running the government and Persian governors administering the provinces. Most of the Abbasid caliphs were at least half Persian or Turkish (Nutting 1964:136-37). It was quite possible for Persians and later Turks to be upwardly mobile within the government and within Islam.

Arabic remained the sacred language of the Qu'ran and theology, but this represented religious thought, not political and military power. The mixed Arab, Persian, and Turkish population of Khurasan in northeastern Persia led in the conversion of Persians to the new faith. It was an area that had become important with the overthrow of the Omayyads in Damascus. Eventually, the Persian language was revived under Islam. Later the Shi'a branch of Islam, a traditional opposition group to the dominant Sunni, became the primary faith of Persia. All of these influences show that Islam instead of being forced "from above" on Persia came to be associated with the elevation of dissident elements within Persia and the affirmation of Persian identity. These are some of the major reasons that it is not accurate to think of Persia being converted simply or primarily by force.

It is even clearer that Islam was not spread to the Turks and later the Mongols by force. Rather, these were peoples who conquered Islamic lands and accepted the religion of those they dominated politically and militarily in the familiar pattern. This, of course, is similar to the case of the conquering barbarians of Europe accepting Christianity and the conquering Burmese of Myanmar and Kushans of India accepting Buddhism.

Intersocietal relationships were also important in the spread of Islam to Malaysia and Indonesia. With the rise of Mongol power Arab trading increased in the Indian Ocean to India and Southeast Asia. Malacca in Malyasia, originally a small fishing village, developed into a major trading center between India and the Spice Islands. The Malaccan ruler, Paramesvara, converted to Islam and also defeated an army from Buddhist Siam that had exerted pressure from the north. After a little more than a century under Islamic rule, Malacca fell to the Portuguese in 1511. However, Ache, on the tip of Sarawak, already converted to Islam, was able to keep out the Portuguese. Legge

(1964:45) writes that "the challenge of the Portuguese was a factor in encouraging the subsequent consolidation of Islam throughout the archipelago." Islamic traders had already carried their faith to the coastal cities where many became local rulers. Some of them had been little more than pirates, but found legitimacy in Islam as a means of challenging the older upper classes and introducing principles for ruling through Islam. The port cities were often in conflict with the inner agriculturally based cities of Java, which had been primarily Hindu, but later became Islamic.

The Achenese actually assisted the Dutch to overthrow the Portuguese in Malacca in 1640. However, the coming of the Dutch had the overall effect of increasing the strength of Islam among the people of the archipelago. One of the great advantages that the strict followers of Islam had was that they became the focal point of resistance to the Dutch colonizers. In the nineteenth and twentieth centuries, it was those who attacked religious laxity, for example, followers of the late eighteenth century Wahhabi movement from Arabia that led the opposition to Dutch authority. These efforts led to the Diponegoro challenge to the Dutch in 1825 and the Padri War in west Sumatra in the 1820s and 1830s. Also, the santri Muslims of Ache resisted longer than any other group. The resistance of Islam to the Dutch helped to spread Islam throughout the islands. Nevertheless, certain marginal areas, particularly Bali, remain Hindu, and other outlying areas, already mentioned, have large Christian populations.

A review of the spread of Islam would not be complete without mentioning the particular appeal Islam has had for African Americans. This is an example of acceptance of a religion that comes from a distance and is associated with no threat, which at the same time is able to support a people against domination and oppression from a surrounding society (Proposition 5.2). One of the major appeals of Islam to African Americans is that it has successfully resisted European Christianity and even conquered and ruled large numbers of white Christians.

CONCLUSION

The review of the spread of religions and intersocietal relationships is consistent with the previous chapter in showing that the spread of religions is not basically aided in the long run by an association with coercion. Just as the association with coercion creates resistance to religions within societies, so it creates resistance as religions seek to spread across borders. At the same time, an old or new religion may find acceptance and support in a population if it aids a population in resistance to outside pressures. I (1991, 1996, 1999, 2002) have previously noted the relationship of the spread of religion with providing aid to resistance to outside threat or intrusion. Steve Bruce (2002: 31, 34) similarly has discussed this phenomenon as "cultural defense." When an alien religion or rampant secularism challenges a nation, "religion often provides resources for the defense of a national, local, ethnic or status-group culture." Bruce quotes David Martin (1978: 107): "An indissoluble union of church and nation arises in those situations where the church has been the sole available vehicle of nationality against foreign domination: Greece, Poland, Belgium, Ireland, Croatia. In such countries bishops have spoken for nations and in Cyprus one actually led in the independence struggle." In Greece and Serbia it was Orthodox Christianity that provided a defense and in the other countries it was Roman Catholicism. However, far beyond Bruce's examples, religions have spread to many groups around the world when they aided those groups to defend themselves against outside groups by maintaining distinctive identities.

Islamic countries have experienced reformist movements in Islam, often from conservative Islamists, in opposition to domination from Western nations. Certainly, revived Hinduism and Buddhism have been a means of opposing foreign colonial and religious intrusion. In Japan, Shintoism was used to assert Japanese distinctive identity against intruding Western power. Religions are an important part of culture and over time become a means of group or national identity. This may be one of the most difficult obstacles for spreading religions, namely when they are labeled as "foreign" and conversion to them is considered as disloyalty to the ethnic group or nation. This will be considered again in Chapter 7.

On the other hand, Buddhism, Christianity, and Islam have spread most effectively when they have been perceived not as imposed religions, but as religions that brought benefits and enhanced people's identities. Sometimes this perception was conveyed to people in spite of the association of the introduced religion with domination and coercive power. However, the perception of enhancement has been especially present when the spreading religion supported the people of a new or developing nation or ethnic group against outside domination. Such perceptions have been evident in the cases of Christianity in Korea, the South Pacific, and in numerous minority groups in Asia and in the cases of Islam in Central Asia, Indonesia, and Africa.

The two sets of macro social factors (conditions in receiving societies and the quality of intersocietal relationships) affect the individual perceptions and choices of people as they come to know new religions introduced from the outside. In the next two chapters, we turn specifically to the micro or individual level to see how the spread of religions is affected by micro or individual experiences and motivations.

PART II B

MICRO SECULAR SOCIAL FACTORS

CHAPTER 6

SOCIAL RELATIONSHIPS AND THE SPREAD OF RELIGIONS

TRANSITION TO THE NEXT TWO CHAPTERS

In this chapter and the next, the focus shifts from how whole societies (macro level) are related to the spread of religions to how individuals (micro level) are related to the spread of religions. The two levels are interacting, as we have already seen. It is possible to discern a meso level, which in this study is the religions themselves, dealt with in the first three chapters. This is because religious beliefs, morals, and organizations are shared by groups. The different levels simply provide a means of approaching the subject from different angles. First, we saw that the spread of religions required certain characteristics in the religions themselves so that they would be prone to spread (Chapters 1, 2, and 3). Then, we considered that the spread of religions is a social process that is affected by the conditions of whole societies, particularly the social conditions in receiving societies (Chapter 4) and the relationships between societies (Chapter 5). Finally, the social process of the spread of religions takes place through multiple individuals and there are important ways in which these individuals participate in social processes of religious change as agents. One way is through the social relationships that all people have, to be considered in this chapter (Chapter 6). Another way is through the perceptions and motivations that all people experience and that guide their decisions, to be considered in the next chapter.(Chapter 7).

In studies of current societies, we have more direct access to individuals than to large-scale social processes. The opposite is true of historical studies. Thus, macro social factors are relatively evident in historic events and changes, but the relationships, perceptions, and motives of many individuals from the past are not known. In the previous chapters I made reference to a few well-known individuals, but little is known about numerous ordinary individuals that enabled the religions to spread. This means that the social relationships and views of large numbers of individuals in the past have to be inferred from relatively few cases and from what is known about individuals from current studies.

BEING A PERSON

Being a person cannot be separated from social relationships. Christian Smith (2010:328) in his consideration of what constitutes a person makes it clear that "patterns of social relations emerge" from the interaction of persons and "these patterns of social relations are durable, historically continuous, and capable of exerting influence on other entities, including those from which they emerged." I follow Smith (2010:332) in viewing human social life with its numerous social structures from the micro to the macro levels as rooted in the natural capacities and incapacities of persons to "construct patterned social meanings, interactions, institutions, and structures," which then act upon them. This does not mean that humans are purely passive receivers of influence from what they construct. The chapter on conditions in receiving societies (Chapter 4) has already shown that social structures can hinder or facilitate how an outside religion is received, but that chapter and particularly the next chapter (Chapter 6) showed that persons could change inherited or traditional social structures. In this chapter we consider "micro social structures" created by persons as they seek to develop stable personal relationships. Again, because of the tensions and uncertainties that are part of human life, these personal relationships may be hindrances or facilitating influences in the spread of religions. But the relationships themselves are so important that there existence is considered "natural" until they are lost or changed.

WHO DO YOU KNOW AND TRUST?

The fact that religious identities along with a broad range of views and opinions are transmitted to individuals from one generation to the next through close social relationships in the socialization process is well known. In fact, it is so much a part of how life is experienced that this fact is simply taken for granted by most people. We know from observing traditional societies, which are less individualistic than modern industrialized societies, that the socialization process is especially effective in transmitting viewpoints as well as social identities. In traditional societies the socialization process involves more people in informal relationships from outside the immediate family than in modern industrial societies with numerous formal educational systems and organizations.

We are accustomed to thinking that only in modern times have social relationships outside the biological family or kin group (secondary relationships as opposed to primary relationships) become important. Actually in modern societies the immediate family has gained importance as a socializing unit in contrast to the extended family and the larger community. Nevertheless, in ancient times, just as today, social relationships were complex. There were numerous crosscutting relationships beyond the immediate family. The anthropologist, Alexander Alland (1980:407), states:

> Societies organized according to descent groups have a set of vertical divisions. But cross-cutting horizontal divisions may also exist. Because they cut across loyalties based on descent, these divisions can serve to unify rather than further divide a social system. Among the organizing principles that can function in this way are *ritual interdependence, religious leadership, territorial affiliation, the elder-younger distinction, castes, and secret societies* (italics his).

The fact that "ritual interdependence," (for example, in community religious festivals), is strong in most traditional societies and explains why new religions introduced from the outside have often been opposed by the group. However, if there has been a disruption in society and leaders are receptive, the new religion may be readily accepted and disseminated relatively quickly through established relationships. This is seen in the numerous conversions of tribal groups, already noted; but also the resistance to new religions of traditional societies which seek to maintain their unity based on their traditional religions.

Thus, in the past, but even now, most people obtain their religious views and sense of their various identities along with other general normative viewpoints and aspects of social identities not only from their parents, but also from the extended family and the community that surrounds them and with which their parents and they have many social relationships. Religions in traditional societies are primarily transmitted from one generation to another (vertical transmission) through the social relationships of families and communities, especially community leaders, who can be called "opinion leaders." In contrast, the spread of new religions is a horizontal transmission that has to break into the vertical transmission process. It is clear that this can be quite difficult when the forces supporting vertical transmission are very strong, as in most small and large traditional societies with well-established religions that form the social identities of individuals. Nevertheless, in the spread of religions this is exactly what happens. This chapter seeks to clarify how this has happened for the three religions that spread most widely.

In Chapter 3, I referred to the work of Collins (2004) showing the importance of both formal and informal "interaction ritual" (IR) chains, based in social relationships. They provide the emotional energy (EE) that is important for maintaining social solidarity, as well as individual lives on a satisfactory level. All societies have interaction rituals of varying kinds and with varying strengths for producing emotional energy. (There will be further discussion of emotional energy in the next chapter.) The spreading religions were able to spread because they introduced new interaction rituals in social relationships that were able to provide emotional energy successfully. Chapter 1 introduced the power of the symbols of the beliefs of the spreading religions for creating the interaction rituals that produce emotional energy. Chapter 2 proposed that needed moral energy was produced in the interaction rituals of the spreading religions. Chapter 3 proposed that the spreading religions were adept at creating emotional energy in their gatherings and organizations. However, as pointed out in Chapters 4 and 5, the spreading religions have not always been successful in replacing existing religions with new interaction rituals that would replace the established ones. In fact, due to the various macro factors discussed, people often held to familiar interaction rituals and thereby blocked the spread of new religions. Nevertheless, in other cases, new religions were able to spread through social relationships to create new interaction ritual chains. This was especially true in small societies when leaders accepted the new religion or even in large societies in periods of social change and where there was religious diversity.

The key factors in social relationships and the interactions by which they are maintained are trust and respect and the desire to maintain relationships with others who provide important emotional and material support. This applies whether people live in modern societies with numerous secular relationships or in traditional societies where the community is united through a religio-cultural identity and numerous common religious rituals and festivals. In the following Proposition I express the two possibilities for the effect of social relationships in modern or traditional societies on the spread of religions:

6.1 *Social relationships can facilitate or block the spread of religions depending on the influence of those who are known and trusted and provide important emotional and material support.*

Stark and others working with him (Lofland and Stark, 1965; Stark and Bainbridge (1996 [1987]); Stark (1997 [1996]); Stark and Finke (2000; Stark 2001) have shown the importance of social networks in the spread of religions. The term "social networks" incorporates both the primary and secondary or crosscutting relationships already discussed. Networks are also created and maintained by the interaction rituals that are so important in maintaining the emotional energy needed for satisfactory living. By using the term "networks," the emphasis is placed on a stable and ongoing relationship in which there is "trust and intimacy." As Stark (2001:51) states concerning the importance of social networks for religious conversion:

> Conversions are based on social networks, on bonds of trust and intimacy between those who believe and those who come to accept their beliefs. Converts are

made through direct, person-to-person influences–
people adopt a new faith as a matter of aligning their
religiousness with that of their friends, relatives, and
associates who have preceded them into the faith.

At the same time as social networks provide a means for religions to spread, it is also true that "friends, relatives, and associates" may help to block the acceptance of a new religion. In discussing "structural availability" for conversions Rambo (1993:60) notes, "The various networks that shape our lives–family, job, friendship, religious organizations, and so forth–are often powerful in discouraging or even preventing change and development, however desirable that change may be to the individual." He goes on to illustrate:

For example, a practical concern may be the amount of discretionary time a person has available. If a religious group requires communal living or full-time education and proselytizing, joining such a group would simply not seem practicable for many middle-class, married, employed people. People who could respond to such a group would be those who are generally single or unemployed, or who for some reason have enough free time and energy to pursue the new option.

Rambo adds that this is why proselytizing strategies, for example, by The Church of Jesus Christ of Latter-Day Saints (Mormons) seeks out whole families. This can also be noticed from New Testament times. The Apostle Paul (Acts 16:14.15; 31-34) responded to Lydia's eagerness to listen with the result that she and her household were baptized. Paul also responded to the Philippian jailer's question as to how to be saved by saying that in believing in the Lord Jesus he and his household could be saved. Subsequently, the entire family was baptized. In these cases, both Lydia and the Philippian jailer were the "opinion leaders" for their larger households, and probably Lydia, a business woman, for an even wider network.

Proposition 6.1 attributes the spread or the blocking of the spread of religions to the influence of trusted people who could be called "opinion leaders." These become especially important when societies and ordinary relationships are disrupted. As we survey history, we can see that community unity around accepted leaders and a common religion was broken at various times allowing new religions to spread through reconstituted social networks and "interaction rituals." The conquest by the Roman Empire of diverse peoples with diverse religions was one of those times. After the fall of the Han Dynasty (221 BCE–220 CE) in China, when numerous new kingdoms were established under foreign rulers, was another such time, as was the period of Arab conquests. In these periods social relationships were disrupted and reconstituted. Likewise, the colonial era, when numerous societies were invaded and dominated from the outside, was another era when social relationships were disrupted. Industrialization in the modern era has also been highly disruptive to social relationships as people moved from rural areas to new industrial areas. Thus whether in the Roman Empire, ancient China, the ancient Middle East, or in many modern societies (including China) families, kin groups, and communities have been broken up, become scattered, or undertaken stressful migrations. Of course modern wars and revolutions also have had a major disrupting effect. However, social relationships that are disrupted or broken are then either restored or replaced in some fashion. They may be maintained in stressful conditions or they may be reconstituted as soon as possible, given the opportunity. Thus, when social relationships are disrupted, there is a special opportunity for a new religion to facilitate the reconstitution of relationships.

However, this is not the only possibility. There may be a reversion to or reassertion of relationships within the traditional religion and culture. An additional Proposition is:

6.2 *When social relationships have been disrupted, a new religion may spread by facilitating the establishment of new relationships or a new religion may be resisted by the strengthening of former relationships.*

This proposition begs the question regarding what determines whether a new religion becomes part of the reconstitution of relationships or whether a new religion is rejected and a former religion or no religion (or an antireligious ideology, as in the last two centuries) becomes the means of reestablishing relationships. The question can only be answered by taking into consideration what caused the disruption of relationships. This was considered in the Chapters 4 and 5. If the spreading religion was associated with the disrupting force, then it is likely that it will be rejected. People may turn away from religion or seek a revived traditional religion. However, if the disruption was caused by internal developments or outside forces not associated with a spreading religion, then a new religion that is introduced at this time may find acceptance as a means of reconstituting relationships.

Both the direction from which the religion comes and the timing for its introduction are crucial. Many times outside religions are introduced in periods of relative social stability, when social networks have not been disrupted. In these situations a new religion may appear to be a cause in itself for disrupting social relationships. Other things being equal, it is expected that caste members are likely to resist a new religion that breaks up the social relationships based on caste membership (unless they are at the bottom or outside of the caste system); family members are likely to resist a religion that objects to family ancestor worship or polygamy; and members of a community are likely to resist a religion that opposes the traditional community religious festivals that express community solidarity and provide emotional energy.

Even in these situations, opinion leaders may decide that a new religion offers an improvement to the traditional practices that are both sustained by and sustain current social relationships. The traditional "interaction rituals" may have lost their power to renew emotional energy. In these situations, new religions are likely to be accepted by opinion leaders and then transmitted both horizontally and vertically. As already seen in Chapter 4, leaders of small societies with single religions may decide that a new religion is advantageous to the whole group. Subordinate members of such societies or groups are usually willing to follow the example of the leaders. Thus the small group theory (receptivity of small groups) of Chapter 4 is closely related to the social relationship theory of this chapter. Also, intersocietal relationships, discussed in Chapter 5, that destabilize societies may cause leaders to choose a new religion or reaffirm an old religion depending on which is perceived as contributing the most to maintaining relationships. This answer to the question regarding acceptance or rejection of the new religion demonstrates (again) that the micro level of individual social relationships is influenced by the macro levels of both social conditions in receiving societies (Chapter 4) and intersocietal relationships (Chapter 5).

Before turning to consider how social relationships affected each of the spreading religions, there is a special feature of the new social relationships established by the three religions that is related to their moral and social force and sets them apart from other religions. They establish fellowships that are egalitarian, universal, and worldwide. They have greatly affected the globalization process, even though their influence has often been ignored by scholars. In other words, the spreading religions have given common values and perspectives to large sections of the world's population, as well as shared networks and institutions. Although this feature may often be overlooked by those on the outside of these religions, members of these religions are usually very conscious of their global connections and, in fact, enjoy great satisfaction and benefits in these relationships. In short, the universal character of these religions has lead to the establishment of international relationships across ethnic and national boundaries, and this activity is increasing with modern globalization. A third Proposition for this chapter is:

6.3 *Spreading religions have a universal appeal that leads to the establishment of global social networks that both aid and are aided by globalization.*

BUDDHISM AND SOCIAL RELATIONSHIPS

The spread of Buddhism has to be considered first in the light of its nonspread in its homeland of South Asia where Hinduism blocked its spread. Hinduism is a religion with a very strong social relationship component. It can even be described as a socio-religious system. However, the popular religious content of Hinduism and its identification with a particular hierarchical (caste) social system, has helped to prevent the spread of Hinduism through the establishment of strong social networks in non-Indian populations. An exception to the tendency for Hinduism to be ethnic-bound is when groups are established around particular gurus or religious leaders. .

Even though the consciousness of Hinduism as a distinctive religion did not develop until the first millennium CE, essential parts of its social system had been introduced with the Aryan migrations of a thousand years earlier. The three pillars of an Aryanized society is defined, according to Keay (2000:28) "as one in which primacy is accorded to a particular language (Sanskrit), to an authoritative priesthood (brahmans) and to a hierarchical social structure (caste)." Keay points out that it is not necessary to think of the process of Aryanization as the result of conquest or mass migration, but rather as a gradual acculturation to which the indigenous people contributed much from their own culture. Thus, "Ayranization" itself may be a misnomer for the hybrid culture that was produced. For our purposes, we are interested primarily in the "three pillars" which show how what became Hinduism had a long period in which it became embedded in and identified with the distinctive social relationships of the society of South Asia.

Jainism and Buddhism both appeared as sectarian movements in the middle of the first millennium BCE, which challenged the socio-religious system under brahman leadership. This is a reason for the development of the Jain and Buddhist orders of monks that were stronger than any similar organization of priests or recluses in Hinduism and were necessary in order to replace the established social relationships. Nevertheless, the eventual elimination of Buddhism from India by Hinduism can be seen as the blocking of the egalitarianism of Buddhism, which would cause members of the numerous castes to lose the social networks supplied by the caste system. Added to the power of the caste system to establish and maintain social relationships between groups of people, the numerous local religions incorporated into Hinduism included numerous community rites and festivals that fostered strong local social networks. These reinforced the social relationships existing within Hinduism, but also kept Hinduism from becoming a global religion to the extent that egalitarian Buddhism has become a global religion.

Whether one accepts Keay's (2000:147) following view of Hinduism or not, it can hardly be denied that its power to resist other religions lies in the numerous social relationships that make up its socio-religious system:

> Hinduism as a religion with specific doctrines and practices was still unrecognizable [at the time of the Gupta rulers of the fourth and fifth centuries CE]. Arguably it still is. The criteria of orthodoxy lay–and lie–in conduct rather than belief. Deference and support to brahmans, acceptance of one's caste, public participation in traditional rituals, festivals and pilgrimages, and the propitiation of familial or local deities remained of the essence.

In addition to Buddhism, other religions, Christianity, Islam, and Sikhism, later challenged the social networks of the caste system, but encountered the same difficulty as Buddhism. Significantly, tribals and those of the lowest castes or untouchables (also known as Dalits) have turned to Buddhism, Islam, and Christianity. These people who were at the lowest level of the socio-religious system, have had little to loose in their old social relationships and much to gain in the new social relationships offered in the more egalitarian religions. For example, the majority of India's twenty five million Christians are from Dalit or tribal background.

Turning to the spread of Buddhism outside of South Asia, it was able to spread to numerous societies where the social networks of the Hindu caste system had not been established. The sangha proved to be especially effective in creating a center of new social relationships in both Southeast and East Asia. Members of the sangha often had kinship relationships with people in the local communities. In addition, Buddhism did what Hinduism had done in incorporating and fostering local religions with their numerous ties to local social networks, while at the same time introducing the universal figure of Buddha. Incorporating local popular religions is equivalent to supporting rather than disrupting local social networks and is a testimony to the strength of these networks.

In China Buddhism made its greatest early gains during a period of foreign invasions and great social unrest when many social relationships were broken. This was the period between the fall of the Han Dynasty (220 CE) and the beginning of the Sui Dynasty (589 CE). Latourette (1956:164) comments regarding the Chinese converts to Buddhism, many of whom migrated south to escape the invasions: "[D]isheartened by the chaos in society, [they] welcomed the refuge from the world which Buddhist monasteries and Buddhist philosophy seemed to afford." At the same time, in the North, "were non-Chinese peoples, some of whom had contacts with that Central Asia where Buddhism was now so strong, and upon most of whom the esteem for native Chinese culture rested more lightly than upon the pure Chinese." The social networks of the Turkish rulers were already under Buddhist influence. In the case of the "gentry Buddhists" in the south, the new social relationships surrounding the sanghas replaced those that had been broken by the social upheaval. In the north, a similar process was taking place, but in addition, the new rulers had previous relationships with Buddhists in Central Asia.

Ch'en (1973 [1964]:153-58) gives an example of how Buddhism became important in establishing new social relationships. He uses research from Zenryu Tsukamoto (1942). Tsukamoto tells how the Buddhist monk, T'an-yao, who was elevated to the position of chief of monks in the period of time when the Northern Wei rulers were favorably disposed toward Buddhism, established the "Sangha and Buddha households." In 467 CE the ruler of the Northern Wei reduced to slavery and resettled near the capital the leading families of a particular area in Shantung. T'an-yao, as chief of monks who was interested in the spread of Buddhism, persuaded the ruler to let him set up "Buddha Households" who would farm the land. They had the responsibility of paying the local sangha office a certain amount of grain, but could live on the rest of their crops. The local sanghas kept the grain to distribute in time of famine. It happened that this was a period of famine so that these institutions preserved the lives of many. The Northern Wei emperor granted amnesty to those in the Buddha Households who were considered criminals. The result was that Buddhism was strengthened in this time through the many social relationships that existed between the general population and the monks in the sanghas and also within the many "Buddha Households." A census at this time (477 CE) showed that there were 6,478 temples and 77,258 monks and nuns in the entire country, but by the end of the dynasty some thirty years later there were 30,000 temples and 2,000,000 monks and nuns. Later, some of the emperors felt that Buddhism was antagonistic to traditional family values and at times aggressively broke up Buddhist monasteries and forced monks and nuns to undertake productive work. It is also generally true, that the societies dominated by Confucian values with their emphasis on the centrality of the family (China, Korea, Japan, and Vietnam) have placed less emphasis on the value of celibacy than in Southeast Asia, where monkish Theravada Buddhism has been dominant.

Even though Buddhism was able to spread through numerous social networks, within the societies of East Asia there existed other overlapping social networks that supported Confucian, Taoist, and a variety of other religious beliefs and practices. Ancestor worship, especially, was supported by strong family and clan ties. Buddhism, therefore, became a kind of additional religious layer to the many religious layers in China and other East Asian societies. On the other hand, in Southeast Asia, where Buddhism did not have to contend with already well-established literate religions, it was able to spread by being accepted by ruling courts and, at the same time, incorporating popular religions with their local social networks.

The global networks established by Buddhism (Proposition 6.3) have already been seen in the international character of the Buddhist missionaries that spread Buddhism. Latourette (1956:165) noted that Buddhist missionaries from many different lands traveled to the Far East. The international or universalistic drive can also be seen in the famous Buddhist pilgrims who traveled to Southeast Asia and to India building global networks. Fa-hsien traveled from the Far East to India from 405 to 411 and returned by way of Indonesia. Hsuan-tsang traveled to India from 630 to 643. These and other pilgrims left valuable records of what they observed, but are also early evidence of the global character of Buddhism and its ability to establish global networks. This has been reinforced in the last two centuries as Buddhism has spread to the West.

CHRISTIANITY AND SOCIAL RELATIONSHIPS

From the beginning Christianity was maintained within a social group with many crosscutting social relationships. John the Baptist was the first cousin of Jesus. Among the disciples of Jesus were at least two sets of brothers, and there were sisters among his close followers. The family of Jesus himself very early indicated their concern for him, although apparently not joining his followers initially. However, after his death, his brother, James, not one of "the twelve," became the leader of the "mother church" in Jerusalem. A strong evidence of Christianity spreading through social networks is in how Paul maintained contact with numerous individuals in the various churches. At the end of his letter to the church in Rome, to which he had never been, he greets some thirty five people, a number of whom were his relatives or people who could be called "relatives" because of special relationships. Former social relations were transformed into a new community of social relationships in the church.

In his ground-breaking study of the spread of Christianity in the Roman Empire (sociologists have greatly neglected the study of the spread of Christianity or of any religion), Stark (1997 [1996]:61-71;111-15) makes the spread of Christianity through social networks one of his major hypotheses for its success. He uses two kinds of supporting data in particular. One is evidence, much of it archeological, that there were numerous Jewish Christians into the third century and perhaps later, showing that there were close social relationships between the two communities. This was particularly true for the Jewish Christians and their Hellenized Jewish relatives from which many converts to Christianity came. The other evidence is from the numerous marriages between Christian women and Gentile men that converted many men and resulted in the creation of many Christian families.

When we turn to the conversion of the European tribes, the tribal units consisted very much of extended families that formed clans and groups of clans. It is notable that the conversion of tribal leaders often came about through their marriage to Christian women. One of the significant close social relationships that may be observed in the growing Christianity is how many of the church leaders and missionaries were close friends and often related to one another. Latourette (1938:93-94) reports on the ability of Boniface (Winfrith) to enlist enthusiastic support for his missionary work from many helpers, a number of whom were his own relatives. He kept up a lively correspondence with his friends and supporters, many of them in his native England.

In later centuries social networks were very important in the spread of various religious movements within Christianity. In a study of Cathars (Albigensians) and Waldensians in the Medieval period, Kaelber shows how both groups used social networks to spread their faith. Regarding the Cathars, Kaelber (1998:215) states:

> Previously itinerate Cathar perfects took up stable residence and set up a network of shops through which to spread their faith. As the organization of Catharism, with its increasing social and cultural influence, consolidated in a widespread network of houses of heretics in the late twelfth and early thirteenth centuries, a new method for recruiting future Cathar perfects and followers gained in importance. Young people from surrounding communities, taken in as apprentices by Cathar perfects, went through what could be called, in more modern terms, a dual-apprenticeship program. Initially neither heretics nor weavers, they were instructed in religious matters as future perfects and taught the skills of an artisan. Journeymen, too, were employed and exposed to Cathar religion...The Cathars could also establish ties to the families, friends, and peers of the youths and journeymen, and thereby further strengthen their influence in the villages and hamlets in southern France.

The Waldensian movement was carried throughout much of Europe by tradespersons following the trade routes and sustained in numerous households in family lineages. In comparing the Waldensians to the Cathars, Kaelber (1998:223) comments, "Similarly, the Waldensians, while always guided by an austere code of conduct, were strongest when able to establish textual communities in schools and community houses, in which their heretical views were transmitted and from which they could rally against what they perceived as deviations from the true apostolic life prescribed in the Gospels."

Stark and colleague scholars have done more than other sociologists to expose the importance of social networks in the spread of religions. Stark and Finke (2000:125,126) question the common reference of religious scholars to "mass conversions." In regard to the growth of Christianity in the Roman Empire they point out, as Stark (1997 [1996]) had earlier, that a growth that was equivalent to the Mormon Church growth could account for the commonly agreed upon number of Christians about the year 300, which is between five and seven million. Building on earlier work (Stark and Lofland 1965; Lofland 1966) in which conversions to the Unification Church were studied, Stark and Finke (2000:127-35) look in detail at the early conversion to the Mormon Church. Most of the conversions were made through familiar social networks. They conclude:

> Even today, when there are more than ten million Mormons worldwide, networks are the basis of conversion, as revealed in records kept by a Mormon mission president in 1981-82. When Mormon missionaries make cold calls, when they knock on the doors of strangers, this leads to a conversion once out of a thousand calls–and never immediately, only after a series of contacts as a friendship is established. However, when missionaries make their first contact with a person in the home of a Mormon friend or relative of that person, this results in conversion 50 percent of the time. (Stark and Bainbridge 1985). What is really going on in such instances is that the missionaries offer religious instruction to persons

whose network ties already have inclined them to join. This pattern is not peculiar to Mormons; it is how all successful movements spread.

I was an observer of a large movement to Christianity of aboriginal people in Taiwan. There are some ten aboriginal language groups of varying sizes. Much of the movement had taken place before we arrived in 1956. The Amis language group with which I worked had approximately 100 villages. In every village the people had constructed a thatched roof church, but there was not a single Amis ordained minister–only lay leaders. The movement had actually begun during the 1930s under Japanese rule, primarily in the Taroko and Amis tribes. After the end of the war in 1945 growth took place in these and all the other tribal groups. However, instead of being a "mass movement," most people who came to the church told stories of contact through family members and friends. Furthermore, a common occurrence was for villages to divide by extended family groups in which certain families joined the Presbyterian Church and other families joined the Roman Catholic Church. In some cases a third group of families would be in the True Jesus Church, an indigenous Chinese church.

I made another observation regarding leadership in churches. There may be systematic studies of this phenomenon, but I have not seen them. This phenomenon has already been noted for Biblical times, as well as in the case of the missionary, Boniface. I noticed both in Taiwan, where I was a missionary for some sixteen years, as well as in my own country, the frequency in which church ministers and lay church leaders are closely related to one another either as parents to children and grandchildren or as siblings and cousins. This has not prevented, however, frequent "new blood" from gaining places of leadership.

One of the most powerful effects of Christianity that was evident from its earliest days has been its ability to transcend all borders in establishing relationships (Proposition 6.3). This universalistic principle is often expressed in the Bible, for example, when the Apostle Paul states to the Roman Christians, "Your faith is proclaimed throughout the world (cosmos)" (Romans 1:8) and of himself, "I am a debtor both to Greeks and barbarians..." (Romans 1:14). A basic consciousness of many Christians, so basic that it is often taken for granted by other Christians and ignored by people who are not familiar with Christianity, is that there are numerous relationships within Christianity that are global in extent. In the past, it was primarily church leaders and missionaries who were aware of these relationships, but now numerous local Christian fellowships undertake projects in other countries and in the process establish relationships with Christians in other lands. In addition to the innumerable personal relationships among individuals and small groups, there are the thousands of relationships established through denominational, interdenominational, and nondenominational bodies. These international relationships within Christianity both result from and contribute to the spread of Christianity.

ISLAM AND SOCIAL RELATIONSHIPS

The origin of Islam was very much a family, clan, and tribal affair and in many ways Islam still carries these characteristics. I am indebted to Nutting (1964) for the following details about the family followers of Muhammad. The dominant Qoreish tribe of Mecca was founded by Qosiy, the ancestor of Muhammad, and of every caliph of Islam for six hundred years after Muhammad. By the time of Muhammad the Qoreish tribe was divided between two main clans, the leading Omayyads and the Hashemites, of which Muhammad was a member. (Hashem, the grandson of Qosiy is the forebear of al-Abbas, founder of the Abbasids and the Hashemites of today, including Hussein of

Jordon.) Muhammad's father died a few months before his birth and, after a childhood in the desert, he was given to the care of his grandfather and then his uncle, Abu Talib, a Hashemite. Muhammad married the rich widow, Khadija, who became one of his early converts, as did his cousin, Ali al-Husayn (son of Abu Talib), who married his daughter, Fatima. Abu Bakr, Muhammad's closest friend, who became his successor, and Othman Ibn Affan, an Omayyad, who also married one of Muhammad's daughters, were among his early followers.

Muhammad was forced out of Mecca by the Omayyads and for a time found refuge among Christians in Abyssinia. The Omayyads also turned on the Hashemites, but the Hashemites remained loyal to Muhammad. An uncle, Abu Lahab sided with the Omayyads and ordered his son to divorce Muhammad's daughter, Rukayya, who then married one of the few Omayyad converts, Othman, later to become a leading Omayyad successor to Muhammad. Another prominent Omayyad, Omar Ibn Khattab, also became a convert after the death of Khadija and Abu Talib.

In 622 Muhammad left on his Hijrah for Medina (Yathrib) where he became both the temporal ruler and military leader, as well as the spiritual guide. After a see-saw struggle with the Qoreish in Mecca, another major convert from the Omayyads was made, Khalid Ibn Walid, who became Muhammad's great military leader. Muhammad soon married Khalid's aunt and then the daughter of his arch-enemy, Abu Sufyan, the Omayyad chief of the Qoreish army. Finally, in 630, Muhammad entered Mecca unopposed and granted clemency to Abu Sufyan and all the people of Mecca so long as they admitted "that there was no other God but God." After Muhammad's death in 632, Abu Bakr, Omar Ibn Khattab, Othman Ibn Affan, and Ali Al-Husayn (together "The Rightly Guided"), all of them related to him by marriage, succeeded him in turn up to 661.

Clearly, family and tribal connections were influential in establishing the leadership of Islam. However, struggles over leadership among the related leaders created blood feuds and conflicts that have continually plagued Islam to the present. Muhammad, the son of Abu Bakr, killed Othman. The tensions between the Omayyads and the Hashemites became a blood feud. Muawiya, the able son of Muhammad's former enemy, Abu Sufyan, took leadership of the Omayyads. For a time, Muawiya ruled in Syria and Ali in Iraq, but eventually Muawiya gained power and Ali was murdered by a Kharijite ("outsider"), who refused to accept Ali or the Omayyad caliphs, Muawiya and Amr in Egypt. Hassan (Hussein), Ali's son, was supported only by the people in Kufa, in southern Iraq. He was allowed to retire to Medina where eight years later he was poisoned by one of his wives. However, Ali and Hassan were recognized as saints by the Shia ("Partisans"), who became a major branch of Islam.

The above discussion shows how early Islamic leadership followed family connections within two branches of one particular tribe that was based in Mecca. The leaders were able to unite other Arab tribes behind them, at times using ruthless force. However, loyalty was assured through the enormous success of the Arab forces and their allies, which brought in great wealth and prestige to all participants.

Islam could not have spread without its distinctive beliefs, moral guidance and energy, and gathering and organization abilities already discussed in Chapters 1 through 3. These gave leaders a means of uniting people under a single moral-social-political order. However, this chapter shows that when leaders accepted Islam, their social relationships also served as a means of gaining followers. It was a contributing cause for the spread of Islam, particularly among tribal people, but social relationships based in other major religions also blocked the spread of Islam, as in Spain, Sicily, Greece, the Balkans,

India, China, and the Philippines.

Islam spread among Syrians, Persian, Turks, Central Asians, Africans, Malays, and Indonesians so that today Islam is the majority religion in over fifty countries. More recently Islam spread by immigration, but also by conversion, to Europe and the Americas. This is ample evidence that in addition to building on the social relationships of tribes, clans, and families, Islam also has the ability to establish a global religion with social networks that transcend ethnic and national boundaries (Proposition 6.3). These international networks both result from and aid the continuing spread of Islam.

CONCLUSION

Human beings live in and almost by social relationships. It is totally accurate to say that human beings are social animals with numerous social ties and continue to be so even in modern supposedly impersonal societies. The assumptions in classic sociology, for example, by Ferdinand Toennies' (1957 [1887]) *Gemeinschaft and Gesellschaft* that communal societies are being replaced by modern associational societies is sometimes misunderstood or exaggerated to mean that people in modern urban societies have few social ties (Hirst 2003). The fact is that social networks continue to be extremely important. It is not surprising, therefore, that when religions spread, both in the past and more recently, that they should spread through social relationships that are important to individuals. Once religions have spread (horizontal transmission), a new way of transmission is added, which is through the vertical social relationship in families. This is the first and strongest relationship that individuals can have. It is the primary family relationship that sustains children and youth and is remembered throughout their lives. Two studies making use of the National Study of Youth and Religion provide clear evidence of the strong influence of family ties in religion (Smith with Denton 2005; Smith with Snell 2009). Nevertheless, religious innovations or new religious movements continue to require adult social networks based on trusted relationships through which to spread.

It is not surprising that valued social relationships have the potential to block or facilitate the spread of religions. If a new religion threatens to break up valued relationships in families and among friends, then it will likely be resisted. Sometimes, however, social relationships are broken due to social chaos, rapid social change, or migration. Modern societies are characterized by individualism and the continual establishment of new relationships. In these cases a new religion may well spread in a population as social relationships are reconstituted through the new religion. It is well known, however, that migrants often carry their religions with them and create strong networks in their new lands through their traditional religion. However, many international and rural-to-urban migrants reconstitute social relationships in new religious groups.

One of the important characteristics of modern societies is that populations have become increasingly mobile as they seek improved living conditions. This results in increasing numbers of individuals who are thrown on their own resources in establishing new social relationships. This means that there are increasing opportunities for new religions to attract adherents through creating new social relationships for them.

CHAPTER 7

MOTIVATIONS AND THE SPREAD OF RELIGIONS

WHAT DO I WANT?

The final section of the theoretical framework has to do with the motivations of individuals, particularly motivations based on perceptions regarding the contribution of religions to their lives and to what they think of themselves or their self-concept. This is the most difficult section of the framework to develop because of the inner or psychological nature of perceptions and the motives that arise from them, as well as guide them. A number of elaborations and distinct paths of theoretical development can undoubtedly be made within this section of the framework. It is often necessary to infer the perceptions and motives of people who lived in the past and in far away places and therefore a certain amount of reasonable speculation based on current studies and informal observations is necessary. However, care must be taken because it is easy to produce circular or tautological propositions about inner states of mind. For example, receptivity to an outside religion and a high view of the contribution of the religion to life are very similar, if not identical, states of mind. Nevertheless, intuitively it is difficult to avoid the view that religions spread because people recognize them as in some way enhancing their lives and hence what they think of themselves. At the same time, religions fail to spread when people feel that a new religion would subtract or detract from their lives and what they think of themselves. This will be restated as guiding propositions below.

Before proceeding, I must bring together two streams of thought related to motivation that seem in opposition to one another, both of which have influenced me: (1) rational choice theory applied to religion, particularly as expressed by Stark and others and (2) a social theory based on believing, moral personhood as expressed by Smith (2003). He (2010) has recently presented his views as based in critical realistic personalism. Smith (2003b:151) states, "Finally, recognizing that we humans are believers at our core means that we will never really understand human social life if we do not pay close attention to the content and function of the beliefs that humans together hold and build their lives on." This is certainly the view of this book. Although Smith (2003b:156) is critical of rational choice theory when it makes human choice revolve "exclusively around calculated exchanges to maximize benefits," it is significant that Stark (2001, 2003) makes a special point (unlike most social scientists) to emphasize the influence of belief content in his writings, as I have also done. It may be "grotesquely hilarious" to claim that choosing a life of service, as done by Mother Teresa, is "a self-interested choice to maximize benefits ('given her particular preference structure')" (Smith 2003b:157-58), yet there are still many people in various forms of service, including Mother Theresa when she was alive, who find such satisfaction in what they are doing that they would not do anything else.

Clearly the language of rewards and even supposedly self-interested choices is extremely ambiguous so that the same terms can be considered either selfish or other directed. This same ambiguity, for example, applies to such terms as "pride" and "self-esteem," which can be understood either negatively (perceiving the self as superior to others) or positively (a form of self-respect and healthy self-regard or self-love). For me, the two streams of rational choice theory and social theory based on believing and moral personhood (along with personhood found in emerging capacities) come together in persons who live in socio-cultural systems of moral orders that influence their motives and choices and at the same time seek to make choices that benefit the self at a deep or intrinsic level. The choice to benefit the self and build a sense of self-esteem may be based on extremely selfish and prideful motives, or in extreme contrast, the choice to benefit the self may actually encompass motives to embrace others in uplifting service and to perceive the self in healthy self-love and respect. Individuals are constantly pushed and pulled in both directions (self-centered or other directed and inordinate pride or self-respect) by both internal drives and the influence of the religious, moral, and cultural systems in which they live.

Turning to the various motives that are important for the spread of religions, Rambo (1993:63-65) discusses the complex question of motivations to convert to a religion, referring to the work of several scholars. Seymour Epstein (1985) postulates four basic motivations for human beings, which vary among different people and individuals at different times and circumstances: "the need to experience pleasure and avoid pain; the need for a conceptual system; the need to enhance self-esteem; and the need to maintain relationships." The desire to experience pleasure and avoid pain is certainly an important motivation for much ordinary behavior, but it can be overridden by the motive to fulfill moral obligation, as Smith (2003b) makes clear, and by the motive to express gratitude for Divine favor, as I would add. Furthermore, to make the motive to experience pleasure and avoid paid relatively useless for predicting religious behavior, a way of pain and suffering actually may be chosen in order to achieve joy, if not pleasure, at a very deep and intrinsic level (Note Hebrews 12:1,2). Thus the simple formula for explaining behavior as motivated by the desire to experience pleasure and avoid pain can hardly account for much behavior, especially religious behavior that is based on belief in God and transcendent values.

Regarding Epstein's second motive, the importance of the belief content discussed in Chapter 1 relates to the need of people for a meaningful conceptual system. The motive to have such a system certainly helps to account for why people have responded positively to the belief systems of the three religions that have spread widely. They offer belief systems that connect the individual to transcendent reality and give meaning to life. The fourth and last motive is the desire to maintain relationships. This is dealt with in Chapters 3 and 6. That is, Chapter 3 emphasized that the spreading religions offer the opportunity to people everywhere to live in ongoing interaction with others. And Chapter 6 points out that the three religions spread when they were able to link people through social networks and their ongoing interactions.

The remaining motive (third motive) mentioned by Epstein, which is the need to enhance self-esteem is a focus of the present chapter. This means that in one way or another, Epstein's four basic motivations are covered in this book. However, other important motivations have been identified. Rambo also mentions two other areas of life that are related to motives. One is James Beckford's (1978, 1983) emphasis on power in religion, "ranging from the power to heal and the power to be successful to the power to gain control over one's life and the power over death." I will not be dealing specifically with motivation for gaining some kind of power through religion. However, let us recognize that the motivation to gain the spiritual power offered in religion is probably closely related to the desire for self-esteem. Without any power, it is difficult to have much self-esteem. Religions give spiritual power, which includes the power to be a whole person having self-respect and a purpose in life. Spiritual power also includes the power to influence others. The offer of spiritual power is especially appealing to those with very little external material power in societies, and such power certainly adds to self-esteem.

Closely related to the motive to obtain spiritual power is the motivation mentioned by Rambo that is found in Walter Conn's (1986a, 1986b, 1987) stress on the yearning for transcendence. The necessary condition for the spreading religions of offering a means of access to God and salvation that was addressed in Chapter 1 certainly supports the view that there is a universal yearning for transcendence, and one could add, the power (Beckford 1978, 1983) that goes with having such a connection. Clearly, as Rambo (1993:65) says, "motivations to convert are multiple, complex, interactive, and cumulative." My focus here on the enhancement of the self-concept is not meant to exclude other motives since motives tend to be linked and interactive, as this discussion shows. Thus I recognize that the desire for self-respect based on a sense of whole personhood both incorporates and is incorporated by the other motives mentioned. For example, a sense of personal power (Beckford 1978, 1983) and a sense of connection to the transcendent (Conn 1986a, 1986b, 1987) both contribute greatly to a sense of self-esteem and self-respect. Clearly there is a great deal of fluidity among the motives that aid the spread of religions with many motives contributing to other motives. However, the problem of tautology or circular reasoning in identifying these motives remains. This may also be seen as reverse causation.

Probably the best way to overcoming the tautology problem is to take into account change over time or time sequence in cause and effect. Even then perceptions and motives may have to be inferred in part or in whole. For example, in relation to spreading religions, a particular sequence often observed is: (1) Certain people are in a subservient position in which they are conscious of being considered in some sense inferior to others and may well feel that way about themselves; (2) A new religion is introduced to them and they respond positively to it; (3) After acceptance of the new religious identity people are able to elevate themselves, in their own minds if not objectively, and in some sense or to some degree lose their consciousness of being inferior. When this sequence is observed repeatedly, then it seems likely that the desire for self-esteem or a positive self-conception is a key cause for acceptance of a new religion.

I observed such change in Taiwan where the majority of Taiwanese aboriginals became Christians over a ten to fifteen year period. It was not a "mass" movement in the sense that everyone became Christian at once, but the Christian message was passed primarily through social relationships while being proclaimed in churches. The people worshipped in churches built by their own hands and later improved them by building concrete structures to withstand typhoons, as well as probably to compare favorably to the buildings used by the majority society. The aboriginals worshipped and received the Scriptures in their own languages and many of them organized themselves through electing their own leaders in congregations and larger church bodies. They took pride in the fact that their language was capable of being written and could be used to express the word of God. A disorganized people that were looked down upon by others became a people who could respect themselves and gain the respect of others. I saw this same pattern of change in minority peoples repeated in other societies, particularly in Asia where majority societies were non-Christian. However, I also realized that Christianity was rejected in many cases around the world, even by people in subservient positions, for example among many aboriginals in my own homeland (U.S.A.). It seemed clear that people in these situations did not have a perception that Christianity was an enhancement or a means of lifting their lives, but rather that in some way it, or at least the people and culture associated with it, denigrated aspects of their lives that they valued. I should note, however, that even though there was micro-level motivation involved, the motivations would not have developed without macro-level social effects.

Some time after making these initial observations I found help in understanding the acceptance and rejection of the same Christian message by different populations. The help came from social identity theorists and then from rational choice theorists. The concept of social identity was first developed by Henri Tajfel (1972, 1974, 1981), who died in 1984. However, social psychologists, primarily in Europe, but now also in North America, have continued to use the concept of social identity to advance various theories of group processes. John Turner, a former colleague of Tajfel, and Rina Onorato (1999:18) define social identity: "'Social identity' was conceptualized as that aspect of a person's self-concept based on their group memberships; it was a person's definition of self in terms of some social group membership with the associated value connotations and emotional significance (e.g. a self-definition as 'us women' or 'we Americans')." Since people have many group memberships in addition to their religious memberships, religion provides only one aspect of social identity. When religions spread, the religious aspect of social identity changes while many other aspects, for example, ethnicity, nationality, gender, and occupation usually remain the same. The question for those encountering a new religion is whether any of these other aspects of social identity will be enhanced or in some way denigrated by the change in religious identity.

The self concept, of course, is larger than the combination of social identities since it includes concepts of the self based on personal characteristics. The unique aspects of religious experience would relate particularly to the idiosyncratic or personal parts of identities. Turner and Onorato (1999:22) describe the difference between personal and social identities:

> Personal identity refers to the self-categories that define the individual as a unique person in terms of their individual differences from other (ingroup) persons. Social identity refers to social categorizations of self and others, self-categories that define people in terms of their shared similarities with members of certain social categories in contrast to other social categories. Social identity is the social categorical self (e.g. us versus them, ingroup versus outgroup, us women, men, Whites, Blacks). It is a more inclusive level of self-perception than is personal identity in the sense that the category scientist is more inclusive than biologist.

Thus, social identity theory has been elaborated by the addition of self-categorization theory. In self-categorization theory, personal and social identities are considered as different levels of inclusiveness of self-categorization. The choices that people make in self-categorization, whether to use an aspect or aspects of social identity or an aspect or aspects of personal identity or to use different levels of one or the other, depends upon the specific context. To give an example related to the spread of religions, when workers from different Christian denominations meet in their home country, they tend to be conscious of their distinctive denominational identities, but when they meet in another country where there are few Christians, they tend to be conscious of their common identity. Moffett (1992:209) noted that early Nestorian and Monophysite missionaries in Central Asia worked together even though they were clearly separated and even hostile to one another in Syria and Persia. To this day, foreign missionaries of different denominations away from home are usually more cooperative with one another than the different groups that sent them.

My particular interest is in change and resistance to change in religious self-categorization. In the case of the religions that have spread, people in many new locations accepted new religious identities. It is true that some people who accepted the religious identity of a spreading religion were not previously conscious of having a religious identity because of the pervasiveness or taken-for-granted nature of their traditional religion. Nevertheless, as religions spread to their societies they accepted a religious identity that was new to them. In some cases, where the new religious identity was rejected, people became conscious of their own traditional or native religion for the first time as they came in contact with the outside religion. This has been true in many traditional large and small societies.

From the earliest days of their studies, social identity theorists recognized that social identities had value connotations and emotional significance to people who carried them. Furthermore, from the earliest days they emphasized how much the motive to gain self-esteem or a positive self-evaluation affected a person's decision to change some aspect of social identity. Michael Hogg and Dominic Abrams (1993:x), who have done much to summarize social identity theory, state, "In its broadest formulation, social identity theorists explain intergroup relations and processes in terms of the interplay of the cognitive processes of social categorization and the motivational process of self-esteem." They recognize that the study of human motivation is fraught with difficulties and that there are other important motivations besides self-esteem. They (1993:173-90) suggest, for example, uncertainty reduction as the basic motivational assumption underlying the explanation of group processes and intergroup relations, with self-esteem as a derivative, or higher level, motivation. Uncertainty reduction is very similar to increasing or maintaining distinctiveness between groups, which often contributes to maintaining self-esteem. As some social identity theorists have said, "Indeed, possession of a distinctive identity may be even more important than having a positive identity" (Branscombe, Ellemers, Spears, and Doosje 1999:43). This may be a major motive for many minority groups threatened with extinction. Certainly the motive to reduce uncertainty is consistent with why a person who provides access to God, as presented by the three spreading religions, would be appealing to numerous people.

Whatever is specified as a key motivation, one of the propositions made by Tajfel (1981:255) struck me as expressing very well what I had observed in Taiwan and other places: "It can be assumed that an individual will tend to remain a member of a group and seek membership of new groups if these groups have some contribution to make to the positive aspects of his [sic] social identity; i.e. to those aspects of it from which he derives some satisfaction." (I object to any limitation implied by "his" because females specifically have found that Christianity made a contribution to their social identity as women.) Aboriginals and other minority groups in Asia, including Koreans as the "hermit nation," have generally been denigrated by nearby majority groups that dominated them. However, they came to perceive that a Christian identity enhanced their ethnic or national identities. On the other hand, the major Asian societies that had suffered intrusion from Western societies from which Christianity came to them, saw Christianity as a subtraction or denigration of their ethnic and national identities along with their religious identities. Maintaining traditional identities in opposition to foreign domination was more likely to enhance self-esteem.

In general, social identity theorists have not given much attention to religion, particularly change in religious identities, the subject of interest here. One possible exception that awaits application to religion is the study of conversion by Barbara David and Turner (1996). However, in their study "conversion" refers to change in viewpoint on a social issue, in this case conservation. On the other hand, rational choice theorists have given a great deal of attention to religion and I found that their perspectives were often consistent with the work of social identity theorists. For example, Stark and Bainbridge (1996 [1987]:138) make the proposition: "Every person seeks a positive self-evaluation." Thus choices are made to gain a positive self-evaluation. The rational choice approach has particularly emphasized that people make religious choices in order to gain rewarding social exchanges in social relationships, the topic discussed in the previous chapter. However, in general the perspective can also be applied to choosing religions that will be rewarding in terms of making any kind of positive contribution to the individual or to the group with which one is identified. In the case of a contribution to a group, it may be a leader or ruler who sees a new religion as adding to the prestige, power, and unity of the group, which, of course, contributes to the prestige of the leader. Could we not say this of Constantine and the many "little Constantines" of Europe? Individuals and leaders of groups may see new religions as giving them access to or help from new allies with power over against old rivals. Self-esteem may not be the only motive, but it seems to be at least indirectly related and often directly related to acceptance of a new religion.

Although Bruce (2003) does not refer to the social identity theorists, his view of cultural defense is consistent with what has been said here. He is interested in how secularism, not a religion, has spread, but he recognizes that religio-ethnic groups may retard its spread. A desire to maintain distinctiveness and a sense of worth is defended whenever possible and religion as a cultural marker has often been a means of defense, sometimes through rejection of an outside religion or irreligion (secularism) by using a traditional religion as a cultural defense.

International political analysts recognize that the motive to have self-esteem is a powerful force affecting international relations. In analyzing the situation in the Middle East where young Muslims have been willing to kill themselves in order to kill their enemies, both military and civilian, Thomas L. Friedman, writing on the Op Ed page in the September 18, 2002 New York Times, states:

> These undeterrables are young men who are full of rage, because they are raised with a view of Islam as the most perfect form of monotheism, but they look around their home countries and see widespread poverty, ignorance and repression. And they are humiliated by it, humiliated by the contrast with the West and how it makes them feel, and it is this humiliation–this poverty of dignity–that drives them to suicidal revenge. *The quest for dignity is a powerful force in human relations* [emphasis mine].

The question is, can we see the quest for dignity and enhancement of life, either spiritually or materially or in both ways, as a reason for the spread and nonspread of religions? I believe we can. The Proposition, then, that guides this analysis is:

> **7.1** *People will be receptive to or resist a new religion according to whether they perceive that it enhances or detracts from an aspect of their social identities which they value.*

Typical aspects of social identities that people value are ethnic, national, gender, occupational, or status identities. In the modern world being an intellectual also may be an aspect of social identity. For example, some people may find that in the United States, being a Buddhist enhances their identities as intellectuals or especially as psychological healers. They also may want to be religious, but at the same time be intellectuals who are free from the authority of the dominant Christian religion. Perhaps people may change religions to enhance an occupational identity, for example, people became Muslim in Indonesia to enhance being a merchant-trader or changed to Christian in America or China to enhance being considered a trustworthy business person.

In this chapter I have focused primarily on understanding why people are motivated to change religious identities because such change will necessarily take place when religions spread by propagation and recruitment, the type of spread being analyzed in this book. I am proposing that the perceived potential effect of change in religious identities on other valued identities will affect the motive to accept or reject a new religion. However, before leaving the discussion of motives, I recognize that it is possible to push further, perhaps much further, into human motivation related to conversion than done in the above discussion of various motives or in my focus on enhanced identity.

Assuming that emotions are closely related to motives, work on the sociology of emotions is highly relevant. Collins's (2004:146,172) writing on "interaction ritual chains," already referred to, makes a strong case that emotional energy (EE) is "the key to individual long-term motivation" and "the central payoff that persons are seeking." He states, "Emotional energy is the common denominator of all social comparisons and choices." The EE that all people seek is a product of both formal and informal "interaction ritual chains," which are an important part of almost all religions. As Collins (2004:372) states, "I have put the central formula as follows: human beings are emotional energy seekers, thereby linked to those interactions and their derivative symbols that give the greatest EE in the opportunities presented by each person's social networks." This shows an important linkage between motives (this chapter) and social relationships (previous chapter). Also, it is important to make clear that it is "emotional energy" and not just "emotion" that people seek. This is consistent with Durkheim's (1965 [1915]:464) insight that it is religion that gives people power to live: "The believer who has communicated with his god is not merely a man [sic] who sees new truths of which the unbeliever is ignorant; he is a man who is stronger." People need emotional energy in order to cope with life. Collins connection to Durkheim is clear in Durkheim's comment on the same page:

> From this point of view [the view from within religion] it is readily seen how that group of regularly repeated acts which form the cult get their importance. In fact, whoever has really practiced a religion knows very well that it is the cult which gives rise to these impressions of joy, of interior peace, of serenity, of enthusiasm which are, for the believer, an experimental proof of his belief.

In ordinary language people want power to live satisfactory or basically happy or (more deeply) joyous lives, and this comes through direct and bodily social interaction employing significant symbols. Building on the work of primarily Emile Durkheim (1965 [1915])—on religious ritual and social solidarity) and Irving Goffman (1967 —on symbolic interaction), Collins shows how humans need and use interaction to build emotional energy.

For Collins (2004:144) desire for emotional energy is consistent with rational choice theory except that "rational choice" becomes more of a metaphor than a literal reality. Many choices are made that are not technically or literally "rational" and yet are made to gain satisfaction that comes with emotional effervescence through worship and interpersonal interaction. Collins also shows, as this book contends, that the micro level motivation to gain emotional energy is affected by macro level factors that affect how people understand symbols. Some emotions, of course, are transient and relatively superficial, but the "interaction ritual chains" found in religions often touch emotions deeply. As Collins points out, further work must be done in the sociology of emotions, but as a general proposition I state:

7.2 *People will receive or resist a new religion according to whether they perceive that it heightens their emotional energy through ritual interactions.*

The world that is increasingly cosmopolitan, culturally pluralistic, and individualistic has probably started to shift from the narrower focus of Proposition 7.1 on enhancing social identities to the broader and more basic focus of Proposition 7.2 on individual emotion. There will be more discussion of this in Chapter 9 that looks to the future. At this point in history both propositions continue to be relevant in spreading religions. The motives to enhance social identity and gain emotional satisfaction are not mutually exclusive; rather overlapping, with the latter being the more basic. The former is more like a specific pathway to the latter in which change of religious identity takes place.

The desires to enhance an aspect of social identity and to have a happy life do not have to be either based in pride or be selfish. They have the potential of being either a desire for healthy self-respect and dignity or a desire for superiority over others based on pride. They also have the potential to be selfishly self-seeking or generous and kind to others. In the end, motivations in most people are mixed and shifting and certainly interrelated.

Before turning to each of the three religions, I want to add that this chapter does not discount the evidence provided in Chapter 1 that the motives people have for choosing a religion are affected by the content of its beliefs and its organization. That is, people are motivated to be in touch with God and others in the special ways offered by Buddhism, Christianity, and Islam. This motive may involve both fear and attraction, awe and love. However, this chapter recognizes that motives are usually not single, but that the three religions being considered at least attracted people because they enhanced self-esteem and gave people joy and satisfaction in their lives.

BUDDHISM AND MOTIVATIONS

The motives of ancient people will have to be largely inferred. However, if we consider the spread of Buddhism in Southeast Asia and Central Asia, we can see that it served to raise the self-esteem of the primarily animistic peoples. Buddhism carried a large body of literature with organized monk-scholars to these societies that lacked these elements found in more advanced societies. Although Theravada monks of Southeast Asia did not believe in any active intervention in life by Buddha, who had entered Nirvana, they did support a popular religion with images, relics of Buddha, and wats, where religious ceremonies were carried out. Included also were opportunities for interaction with priests who taught from the Scriptures and carried out the ceremonies. In short, Buddhism offered a sophisticated literate culture with impressive rituals and at the same time incorporated many of the features of the popular religion already followed by the people at large. The people could enjoy a raised level of culture and at the same time maintain their emotional energies through popular religious practices connected to local deities.

The Kushan invaders of Northwestern India clearly raised their level of culture and self-esteem by adopting the Buddhism of those they dominated. This could also be said of other Central Asians tribal peoples. Buddhism was late in arriving in Tibet and even later to Mongolia. Again, Buddhism represented a cultural advance as it was transformed into Lamaism and given civil authority. As in Southeast Asia, it adopted numerous features of popular religion.

In East Asia a tradition of literature and scholarship already existed in Confucianism, Taoism, and other schools of thought. However, Buddhism arrived at a time when the traditional scholarship was discredited during the period of turmoil following the fall of the Han Dynasty in 220 CE. It seemed to meet the religious needs of many literati with both its scholarly and mystical aspects. In the end, of course, Buddhism did not attain the pervasive influence in East Asia, with the exception of Japan, that it did in Southeast Asia. Japan, in fact, was somewhat similar to Southeast Asia in being animistic and not having the native scholarly traditions of China. After the arrival of Buddhism, the other scholarly traditions were revived, especially in China and Korea, and Buddhism had to take its place alongside other religions or, in some respects, as part of other religions. However, within the various schools of thought within Mahayana Buddhism, intellectuals were able to obtain recognition and leadership. While Buddhism was not the only religion to give self-esteem, it could take its place alongside Confucianism and Taoism.

In Japan, Buddhism accepted a variety of schools of thought from China such as Chan (Zen) and Pure Land (Jodo Shinshu) and has created numerous new schools of Buddhism. What is often forgotten, as Mullins (1998:7) points out, is that Japan up to the development of the nationalistic consciousness of the late nineteenth century was characterized by great diversity in local loyalties to the 270 political domains (bakuhan). This internal diversity also finds expression in the development of numerous independent religious schools of thought and practice. Since the late nineteenth century many indigenous Christian groups developed (Mullins 1998), but especially a large number of groups from the majority religion, Buddhism. New religions in Japan coming out of Mahayana Buddhism grew rapidly in Japan after World War II. Some, for example, Soka Gakkai and Rissho Koseikai, have been active politically. Intellectuals have developed theoretical approaches, going back to Nichiren, the thirteenth century Buddhist intellectual. Thus in Japan the various Buddhist schools have provided opportunities both for fulfilling emotional religious needs along with enhancing self-esteem as public spirited intellectuals.

The modern spread of Buddhism, along with other Eastern religions, in the West is of particular interest. Buddhism has not spread significantly among African Americans or other non-East Asian minority ethnic groups as Islam has done for reasons to be discussed shortly. Instead, Buddhism has spread most significantly among intellectuals, particularly those with training or interest in psychology (Benz 1976; Kapleau 1979). It could be said that among secularlized or antireligious intellectuals in the West, Christianity lost much of its ability to enhance the identity of being an "intellectual." As I argue in Chapter 4 (and will again in Chapter 8), this has much to do with the long imposition of Christianity through governmental authority and the presumed limitation of Christian doctrine on "free thinking." Among many intellectuals in the West, knowledge of and adherence to Buddhism appears as an enhancement of their identity as intellectuals, who have a deep understanding of the self and of such important goals as world peace. At the same time Buddhism is able to fulfill emotional religious needs.

In regard to Proposition 7.2, Buddhism does not match Christianity and Islam in the number, size, and regularity of "interaction rituals." It is not as well known for having weekly meetings, membership roles, or established annual observances. Nevertheless, Buddhism does have gatherings and carries out numerous rituals that are valued by its followers. In its period of spread in Asia, the primary communal ritual life of Buddhism was in its sanghas led by its monks, but the participation by lay followers has tended to be transient and limited to irregular occasions. Beginning primarily in the nineteenth century and continuing to the present, Buddhism has been highly influenced by Christianity, particularly in organizing service activities. There is little question but that Buddhism exists with two tiers: (1) those who renounce the world and become monk members of sanghas based in monasteries and (2) lay people, who participate in temple activities and rites led by monks. Lay organization has not been a major strength in Buddhism, with the exception primarily of Japan, where Buddhist lay organizations have been more active than in most lands. The lack of regular and intensive "interaction rituals" for the large majority of lay people helps to account for why Buddhism is not spreading as rapidly as Christianity and Islam.

CHRISTIANITY AND MOTIVATIONS

Christianity first spread from the margin of Jewish society to the center (Galilee to Jerusalem) and then from the margin of the Roman Empire to other societies on the margins and beyond and then to the center at Rome. Indigenous peoples all around the Mediterranean Basin received Christianity, finding that it enhanced their distinctive identities.

An early example is the Syrian people, long under outside domination and cultural influences, who found through Christianity a revitalization of their culture. A revealing statement about the Christian Syrian scholar, Tatian (ca. 110-180), is given by Moffett (1992:74):

> Tatian was emphatically and unashamedly Asian. "I am an Assyrian," he said proudly in his Address to the Greeks, the only one of his writings to survive in its entirety. The whole thrust of the work is a recapitulation of all the ways in which Asia (the whole non-Greek world, in fact, for he includes ancient North Africa) excels the West. Where did the Greeks learn their astronomy? he asks, From Babylon (in Asia). Their alphabet? From the Phenicians (also Asia). Their poetry and music? From Phyrgia (Asia Minor). Their postal system: From Persia. "In every way the East excels," said Tatian (to summarize and paraphrase his argument), "and most of all in its religion, the Christian religion, which comes from Asia and which is far older and truer than all the philosophies and crude religious myths of the Greeks."

Tatian, was thoroughly familiar with Greek and Roman cultures, having been trained under Justin Martyr in Rome. He translated the New Testament to Syriac, probably the first translation to a non-Greek language, back from Greek to a language very much like that of its original speakers! Later, as noted by Tabitha Petran (1972), Christianity was very much behind an "Aramaic renaissance." What happened to Tatian and among the Syrians was repeated all around the Mediterranean basin in many other societies: Egypt, Anatolia, Greece, North Africa, Spain, Armenia, Georgia, Ethiopia, and in Rome itself. In North Africa, however, there was a problematic development of domination of the indigenous people by the Christian Latin colonists. The Punic and other indigenous groups, such as the Berbers, expressed themselves in the opposition Donatist Christian movement. However, representatives of Latin Christianity suppressed this movement. Later, Christian Constantinople dominated the area. These exclusions and dominations prepared the way for viewing Arabs as liberators and for the acceptance of Islam by indigenous (non-Latin) peoples. Nevertheless Christianity was perceived by people in most areas to the east and north of the Mediterranean basin as enhancing, not suppressing, their distinctive identities.

Translation of the Scriptures and otherwise use of indigenous languages seems to be one of the major means by which people came to the perception of the affirming power of Christianity for distinctive groups. We have already seen the example of Tatian. Another example is seen in the work of Ulfilias, mentioned earlier, who was raised among the Goths, and who translated the Bible into the Gothic language. This, with his missionary work, led to the fact that the Goths who invaded the Roman Empire, destroying Rome in 410, were primarily Arian Christians. The translation work of the brothers, Cyril and Methodius, into the Slavic language had a great effect on Slavic groups. In some respects, then, the spread of Christianity to the European tribes and to other tribal groups (e.g. Arab and Central Asian tribes) can be compared to the spread of Buddhism in Southeast Asia and probably to Japan. In these cases, the spreading religion represented a new learning and a more advanced culture with a literate base.

One distinctive group identified by Stark (1995; 1997 [1996]:95-128) as having perceived the enhancing power of Christianity was women. The granting of higher status to women was accompanied by several practical outcomes such as the decrease in female infanticide and abortion, higher birth rates, and the marriage of Christian women to the oversupply of pagan men. Anthropologists have noticed that the tendency for women to be attracted to the Christian faith is also a modern phenomenon. The anthropologist, H. G. Barnett (1953:48) commented, "It is noticeable that wherever Christian morality has been accepted in place of one embodying double ethical standards, female acceptors have outnumbered male." Of course, one of the secondary effects of the acceptance of Christianity in traditional societies where the elevation of the status of women has taken place has also been an increase in the divorce rate. This is one of the many complex effects accompanying what some from a traditionalist or conservative perspective call "too much freedom" among Christians.

Returning to the theme of ethnic and nationality enhancement, the missiologist Sanneh (1991a) points especially to the importance of the translation of the Bible for enhancing national-ethnic identities. He (1991a, 1991b) argues that the translation of the Scriptures into numerous African languages was a major stimulus to the development of nationalism in that continent, even if this was an unintended effect.

On the other hand, one of the most distinctive characteristics of the spread of Christianity in Asia since 1500 has been the general rejection of Christianity by the major societies, many of which began to assert their national independence against Western domination and their cultural distinctiveness from Western culture. At the same time, Christianity found acceptance among numerous minority ethnic groups located in or on the edge of the major societies. Clearly, Christianity was generally not perceived as enhancing national and ethnic identities in the major societies, but on the other hand was perceived by many minority ethnic groups as enhancing their distinctive ethnicities and in many cases as lifting their social statuses.

One of the first areas to be entered by missionaries from the newly organized missionary societies just before the turn of the nineteenth century was the Pacific Islands. Although Western explorers and traders were also entering the islands in this period, missionaries were not usually accompanied by force. They usually went unescorted to tribal leaders very much as missionaries went to the leaders of their tribal European ancestors. Furthermore, most of the island people learned to distinguish the missionaries as those interested in their welfare from the traders, who were primarily interested in exploiting them for profit. Because of the way in which Christianity came to the islands, it was perceived as contributing positively to island life and identity rather than as being a negative force. Today, most of the islands have majorities of their populations that are Christians. Exceptions are worth noting, one of the most notable being the Australian aboriginals, who were in a land being colonized, primarily by people from Great Britain. In this land where aboriginals were compared unfavorably with the white colonists, Christianity has generally not been perceived as contributing positively to aboriginal identity. In New Zealand, where Europeans also settled in large numbers and there was fighting against the aboriginals (Maoris), missionaries took the side of the indigenous people, helping to establish their rights as British citizens and as having possession of their own lands (Oliver 1961:139; Latourette 1943:181-82). This contributed to a large majority of the Maoris becoming Christians.

In North America, the perception of denigration by the whites greatly hindered the spread of Christianity among the aboriginals. The response to Christianity has been more mixed in North America than I observed in many parts of Asia. This is a complex story that requires more attention than I can give here. I will simply note that there were efforts made by some missionaries and others to show love and respect for Native Americans so that some groups were receptive to Christianity. Some Christian villages became known as "praying villages," although later some of these villages were attacked by whites. In spite of the "Trail of Tears" many Cherokees became Christians, in large part because of the attempts of the missionaries to defend them and then to suffer with them, going with them to Oklahoma on the "Trail of Tears."

The Korean-Japanese case has already been discussed briefly in Chapter 5, which was concerned primarily about intersocietal relationships. There was a very positive response to missionaries from Western lands that did not dominate Korea during and after a period when Korea was dominated by its neighbor Japan. Japan sought to "Japanize" the Koreans by the imposition of the Japanese language and even the national religion of Shintoism. Korean Christians were among the leaders in opposition to these efforts of the colonizers. Missionaries also supported Koreans in their efforts toward independence. Thus, Christianity became associated with Korean nationalism, as the sociologists David Martin (1990:138) and Danielle Kane and Jung Mee Park (2011) have noted. Having Christian identity, instead of being a subtraction to being Korean, was perceived as an enhancement of Korea identity.

The response in Japan has been notably different from in Korea. Although in the latter part of the nineteenth century and in the twentieth century people came to Japan from the same lands with the same message as those who went to Korea, Christianity was perceived quite differently. Christianity was associated with an intrusion and threat from the West that dated from the early seventeenth century and occurred again in the middle of the nineteenth century. Thus, instead of providing an enhancement for being Japanese, becoming a Christian in Japan is more likely to be perceived as subtracting from Japanese identity. However, once outside of Japanese society, the social pressures against Christianity are reduced. Significantly, while less than 3 percent of Japanese are counted as Christians, 43 percent of Japanese Americans claim a Christian identity, and only 24 percent identify as Buddhists (Lien and Carnes 2004: 50). Social relationships, discussed in the previous chapter, are probably also a contributing factor in the difference in proportions of Japanese who are Christians in Japan and America. Further study is needed.

The case of the largest society in Asia, China, is extremely important as an example of how an outside religion that was long associated with subtracting from Chinese identity can change in the perceptions of many people into being a potentially positive contributor to Chinese social identity. The size and diversity within Chinese society as opposed to the relative homogeneity of Japanese and Korean cultures may be a factor in producing cultural change in attitude toward foreign religions. That is, China has dealt with a variety of foreigners over many centuries and also incorporates many minority groups. However, after the industrialization of the West, China was humiliated by Western powers and Japan in the nineteenth and twentieth centuries. After the triumph of Communism in 1950 a change took place in which Western missionaries were excluded from China, thus breaking the long association of Christianity with outside intrusion and domination. The acceptance of Marxism by many Chinese demonstrated that a foreign ideology (quasi-religion) could be perceived by many Chinese as contributing positively to Chinese nationalism and being Chinese. "China has stood up," Mao Zedong declared in 1950 to the thousands gathered for the celebration of the Communist victory. Since then, Marxism has lost much of its luster (certainly as an economic system) while Christianity as a spiritual force for moral living has gained increasing attention and acceptance. Chinese intellectuals, unlike many intellectuals in the West, perceive Christianity as compatible with science and modern education, even as contributing to modernization. At least, for many Chinese, Christianity has become recognized as a world religion, not simply a Western religion, and as belonging as much to the Chinese people as to anyone else. Of course, as in so many cases, translation and distribution of the Bible has helped greatly in this perception. Certainly to read the Bible is to realize that you are not in America or any other Western or modern society.

Prior to recent decades, people in Japan and China were not the only people to which Christianity was introduced, who perceived that their identities were being threatened. India has been a major society in which the traditional religion has been used to assert Indian identity against other religions, most notably Christianity and Islam. Although Christianity has been present in India for close to two thousand years, Western colonialism stimulated nationalism and exacerbated anti-Christian views. The recent legal efforts to prevent conversions were discussed in Chapter 4. The term "Hindutva" was coined in 1923 by the atheist scholar, Vinayak Savarkar and has become an umbrella concept for Hindu nationalist groups. Specifically, the Hindu nationalist Bharatiya Janata Party (BJP) has had an increasingly larger influence on the national political scene (Demerath 2001:122-23).

Latin America is an important case where a separate Native American identity has been preserved through accepting, but changing the Christianity that was brought with force. In recent years scholars have noted that Native Americans have affirmed their ethnic identities through revivals of their pre-Christian religions (Parker Gumucio 2002; Garma 2002). Thus for many Native Americans, Christianity, at least in its Western version, is perceived as a detraction from their Native American identity and the traditional religion as an enhancement of that identity.

Regarding the spread of Christianity due to the emotional energy provided people by it (Proposition 7.2), Christianity from its beginning has been characterized by regularly repeated worship services combined with close fellowship and service, all related to a rich variety of symbols expressing the very basic elements of salvation and life. The power of such vital interactions to attract people is brought out in many places, for example in Acts 2:42-47. This passage serves as a model (the "marks of the church") for such "interaction rituals" and the emotional energy they generate. Of course, worship services have not always been vital in Christian history, but regular worship on "the first day of the week" has been a near universal mark of Christianity. Although worship services became more formally ritualistic under state churches, the attractive power of regular worship services as "rites of intensification" continued. Great music was produced, beginning with Byzantine and Gregorian singing coming up through classical oratorios and modern spiritual and gospel songs. Also, major annual festival celebrations such as Christmas and Easter were institutionalized, which attracted masses of people.

An example of the power of worship is in the traditional story of how a delegation from Vladimir, ruler of Kiev, was highly impressed by the worship service in St. Sophia in Constantinople. This led to the subsequent acceptance of Orthodox Christianity in the northern country in 988. In areas where Christianity has recently had explosive growth, as in Africa and China, it is commonplace for people to note the emotional impact of worship services. In all areas of Christianity, including in the West, where Christianity has a longer history, churches that are growing are those with "vital" worship services.

ISLAM AND MOTIVATIONS

Islam was associated with a major revitalization of Arab society and assertion of Arab ethnic identity. Muslim leaders were the leaders of the Arab ethnic break-out from their homeland and the Arab triumphs in a series of conflicts. The former disorganized and oppressed Arab tribes defeated the two great empires that had previously dominated the area, the Byzantine and Persian Empires. The initial successors to Muhammad (the four "Rightly Guided Ones") and the succeeding Omayyad rulers in the first period of Muslim conquest and rule (632-750) were much more ethnically oriented than the Abbasid rulers that followed. Arabs were expected to be followers of Islam, but other religions were tolerated as long as they paid their taxes and showed proper deference. Islam became associated with the elevation of a tribal people, the Arabs, from a lowly position of people on the edge of civilization to a position of strength and leadership and the source of a flowering civilization. Islam had clearly enhanced Arab identity and came to enhance other ethnic identities.

The mixing of Arabs with local inhabitants, particularly with Syrian, Persians, and Turks, together with the universalistic and egalitarian tenants of Islam brought about different approaches and perceptions with the establishment of Abbasid rule in Baghdad. It became evident to local people that they could be upwardly mobile within Islam. Social identity theorists (Hogg and Abrams 1990 [1988]:26-29) theorize that if subordinate people are allowed to be upwardly mobile and gain acceptance in the dominant group, then they will not develop strong and united resistance to the dominant group. In this way non-Arabs were able to join Arabs in the enhancement of their local identities through the universal brotherhood of Islam.

At the same time as former enemies or at least outsiders were able to rise to positions of power within Islam, Arab power began to disintegrate and Islam became associated with a variety of scattered centers of power. Nutting (1964: 136-37) describes the dual process of a flowering civilization and disintegrating power:

> Paradoxically, the cause of this inner collapse [of Arab power] was the very same factor that had contributed most to the Abbasid golden age–the predominance of foreign influence on Arab thought and action and the abandonment of that Arab racial supremacy which Omar had sought to maintain. The process of racial dilution had been going on since the great conquests of the Omayyad era...Thus even in Omayyad times the idea of an Arab military aristocracy became less and less a reality. Now all pretensions to Arab supremacy were cast aside. Even in the matter of the succession of the caliphate the Abbasids set no store by Arab blood. Not only were Haroun and al-Mamoun half Persian, but of the thirty-seven caliphs who followed Abul Abbas, thirty-four were born of Persian or Turkish slave mothers and only Abul Abbas himself, Haroun's father and his son al-Amin were of legitimate Arab parentage. Greek and Persian cultural influence dominated the social, cultural and political life of Baghdad, and Arab influence took a back seat. With Persian viziers running the government and Persian governors administering the provinces, the caliph's bodyguard and the imperial army became filled with Khurasanis [north eastern Persians]...

Only the Arabic language held its own for the five hundred years during which the Abbasid caliphate dragged on. From being a language of poetry in the pre-Islamic days and of religion in the time of Mohammad, it became the medium for expressing the ideas of science and philosophy and the language of diplomacy from central Asia to Spain.

Although Islam continued to be fused with political power, quite early this political power became diffused to a variety of local power centers, and in these various centers of power it became possible for local people to be upwardly mobile within Islam. Arab identity became more associated with a spiritual language of religious revelation and morality and with advanced culture and trade than with political power. Islamic identity came to have particular appeal to the leaders of tribal and nomadic trading cultures as a means of enhancing their groups–North Africans, Turks, Mongols, Indonesians, and Africans on the southern fringes of the Sahara.

The traders of Indonesia were a kind of sea-going nomadic people who found Islam supporting their aspirations to establish local dominions in the port cities. Legge (1964:47) describes the appeal of Islam in the port cities:

> In the cosmopolitan ports of the Indies, where people from many different parts of the world clustered in their separate quarters, preserved their separate identities, and met on a common footing only in the market place, a faith which made no distinction of race or class could cut across communal divisions and help to establish a new social unity. In light of these features, the connection between Islam and commerce seems a natural one, and it has led one observer to ascribe to Islam in Indonesia a role not unlike that ascribed by Weber to Protestantism in Europe–the role of handmaiden to a commercial class. "For Hinduism's attempt to sacralize a political community built around inequalities in military power, Islam substituted an attempt to sacralize a commercial community, built around commonalities in economic motivation" [Clifford Geertz 1956:91]. Such a thesis helps to explain the fact that the original strongholds of the faith–the

areas where indigenous traders have continued to play a leading role–have remained among the most devoutly Moslem areas of Indonesia today.

It is also important that Islam spread in the archipelago at the same time as first Portuguese and then Dutch traders were establishing themselves. By leading in the resistance to the foreigners, Islam became more strongly associated with Malaysian and Indonesian identities

In North America in the twentieth century and up to the present Islam has gained many converts among African Americans. This is an additional example of how a new religious identity is chosen by members of a dominated group that enhances ethnic identity. Upward mobility in the dominant White society was blocked and so a way of resistance was preferred. In spite of the attempt of part of the movement to incorporate the strong egalitarian theme in Islam that embraces all peoples, the Black Muslim movement has also preserved an anti-White interpretation of history that appeals to oppressed African Americans (Mamiya 1988; Lee 1988). Islam became a means of enhancing African American identity. It is also true that African American Christianity continues the large movement independent of White Christianity that expresses and enhances a distinctive identity of a people who have been long oppressed and discriminated against. This demonstrates that there can be different paths in asserting distinctive identities.

Regarding the spread of Islam due to the desire for emotional energy created by "interactions rituals" (Proposition 7.2), the mosque with its regular worship services is at the center of Islamic communities and provides the key to their solidarity. The sight of row upon row of people bowed in worship and the hearing of familiar and often repeated phrases that express faith and allegiance to God serve as powerful forces in sustaining and continually renewing Islamic communities. In addition to the regular Friday worship services, Islam has important annual religious observances, especially Ramadan, and the symbolically important once-in-a-lifetime pilgrimage to Mecca with the masses of fellow pilgrims. In reviewing the history of the spread of Islam, including the recent migrations to Europe and North America, it is clear that Islam has constantly produced emotional energy for its followers through numerous "interaction rituals."

CONCLUSION

Religions cannot spread unless people are motivated to become followers of the spreading religions. As difficult as it is to understand motives, the desire for self-esteem and for emotional energy appear to be highly important in determining choices. It is difficult to imagine that anyone would be attracted to a religion that they perceive as denigrating them or as subtracting from some valued aspects of social identity, such as ethnic, national, or gender identity. In contrast, many lands people perceived that Buddhism, Christianity, and Islam would elevate them in some way and make a positive contribution to how they viewed themselves.

When the spread of these religions is reviewed we see that they contributed to advancement of culture in developing literature and learning and increasing the influence and often the power of societies. A flowering of culture ensued whether it was in ancient Buddhist Southeast Asia, Christian Syria, Constantinople, and Europe, and Muslim Baghdad and Central Asia, to give a few examples. Distinctive peoples were formed who could survive and prosper and, in many cases, successfully defend themselves and defeat their enemies, at least for a period of time. However, whatever may have happened on a societal level, on the individual level people of low or marginal status obtained positive self-evaluations through the spreading the three religions. This is seen especially with women, tribal people, and oppressed minorities.

At the same time, Buddhism, Christianity, and Islam failed to spread where they were perceived as detracting from self-esteem or were perceived as threatening or detracting from the distinctive identities of people. Some of the best evidence for this is the resistance of populations to Christianity associated with colonialism and the resistance to Islam in some of the lands under Islamic rule for long periods. Unfortunately, Muslim and Christian populations continue to be in conflict with one another in certain places, particularly in Africa, Indonesia, and the Philippines because each feels in some way threatened by the other. Opposite effects from the same religion in different areas and periods are possible because of historical circumstances. For example, Christianity is not perceived as enhancing identities by many people in much of the Western world (particularly where secularism is strong in Europe and among Western intellectuals generally), while in many other parts of the world, Christianity is perceived as enhancing personal and social identities, including intellectual identities.

In addition to spreading when they were perceived as enhancing self-esteem (and failing to spread when they were perceived as subtracting from self-esteem), the spreading religions attracted numerous people because they were able to meet the need for emotional energy through "interaction rituals" based on the rich symbolism they offered. At these times disrupted and unstable social conditions could make established religions seem inadequate in providing the emotional energy and confidence needed to cope with life. At the same time, when people perceived that sufficient emotional energy was being supplied by their own established religious rituals with which they were familiar, new religions could be blocked from spreading. Nevertheless, Christianity and Islam especially created worship services for large numbers of people that built solidarity and strong emotional satisfaction around the important symbols related to their beliefs and thus attracted additional large numbers of people.

It is clear by now that all of the social factors discussed are interacting. Social conditions in receiving societies (Chapter 4), intersocietal and intergroup relationships (Chapter 5), and individual social relationships (Chapter 6) are all related to how people perceive the religions introduced to them from the outside and how they perceive these religions may enhance or detract from their identities and their emotional needs. In addition, the content of the religions themselves (Chapters 1 through 3) have a direct effect on how people perceive the attractiveness of a religion. In fact, the distinctive contents of the spreading religions are necessary for the religions to spread. However, as the analysis of the book has shown, social factors either facilitate or block the effect of the content of religions on individuals. Social factors are constantly changing and these changes have been particularly noticeable in the last few centuries and even the last decades. Changing conditions affecting the spread of religions will be considered in Chapter 9 that looks to the future. Before looking to the future, however, an important development in the modern world should be considered: the growth and spread of irreligion. This will be discussed in the next chapter.

PART III

ADDITIONAL APPLICATIONS OF THE ANALYSIS

CHAPTER 8

THE SPREAD OF IRRELIGION

A NEW PHENOMENON

The major focus of this book has been on the spread of religions, primarily the three religions that have spread across numerous socio-cultural borders, namely Buddhism, Christianity, and Islam. Surprisingly, irreligion appeared on a larger scale than ever before in the area in which Christianity was foundational in the development of Western Civilization. This, of course, was Western Europe to which Christianity spread following its initial spread in the Mediterranean Basin. I think it is appropriate therefore to give additional attention to the historically new phenomenon of large-scale irreligion, not simply individual irreligion, which has probably always existed. Irreligion has not only become a major phenomenon in the West, where it originated as a movement (set of movements), but it has spread all over the world. As an example of the spread of irreligion outside of the West, Jennifer Hecht (2004:434) has noted that the May Fourth Movement of 1919 in China included considerable antireligious rhetoric influenced by Western thought, and also that "Mao Zedong read Voltaire, Diderot, Montesquieu, and d'Holbach in his youth and took on philosophical materialism."

The modern movement or set of movements of irreligion is a new phenomenon in the sense of having a widespread influence, movement characteristics, and open opposition to religion. Irreligion is not just a lack of belief but is rather an opposite or alternative belief and practice from religious belief and practice, as will be seen. This is why irreligion takes on religious characteristics. Irreligion is probably as old as religion, even though both "religion" and "irreligion" were unknown concepts in ancient societies, at least until the beginning of the first millennium of the Common Era. In fact, Christians were called "atheists" because they opposed worship of the Emperor and the state gods. Although Hecht (2004:270) has written on the history of doubt beginning with ancient doubters and reports on individual doubters up to the modern age, she recognizes that "the nineteenth century was easily the best-documented moment of widespread doubt in human history: there were more doubters writing and speaking where they could be heard than ever before, and many more had come to hear them."

Another historian, Alister McGrath (2004), who distinguishes eras and major changes in history in his study of atheism, identifies the French Revolution of 1789 as introducing the "Dawn of the Golden Age" of atheism. Although the project to abolish Christianity during the French Revolution failed, people felt that "the unthinkable had happened" and "seeds were planted, mental horizons were extended, and hopes for change were ignited" (McGrath 2004:47). Significantly, irreligion rode this wave of hope for change and new freedom of thought, even though it did not constitute it. However, the predominantly Christian culture of Europe was to be permanently changed so that irreligion for the first time became a major public option for most people of Europe, especially intellectuals. Furthermore, irreligion spread to North America and then to much of the world. My purpose here is to examine this spread using the same theoretical framework that I applied to examining the spread of religions. Before beginning the historical analysis through the theoretical framework, I will review the basic difficulty of definitions and some of the current inconclusive data related to irreligion. These two sections contribute to our understanding of why irreligion as such is a rather neglected subject.

DEFINITIONS AND FIGURES

There is relatively little study of irreligion as a distinct phenomenon in the social sciences. Colin Campbell (1972 [1971]) sought to initiate a sociology of irreligion as part of the already recognized subdiscipline of sociology of religion. Instead, sociologists of religion seem to have become preoccupied with debating secularism and the process of secularization, which are related, but not equivalent to irreligion. Campbell (1972 [1971]:9) states:

> [I]t appears that irreligion [in contrast to religion] was assumed to be self-explanatory; as the natural state of mature civilized men [sic] (and of not a few early sociologists) it hardly required any discussion, let alone explanation. Paradoxically, therefore, it may be because sociology has its origins in an irreligious epoch that irreligion itself has not become a subject for study in sociology.

Campbell (1972 [1971]:28) views irreligion as a response to religion and defines it as "the rejection of available religious traditions." This rejection might be expressed openly or it might be expressed simply by indifference. Thus, the term "irreligion" may be applied simply to a life of non participation in any religious practice. However, many of the "nonpracticing" people "believe without belonging" or, as I would say, "believe without attending." They borrow and construct various combinations of beliefs, or waver between belief and unbelief (Davie 1994; Davie, Heelas, and Woodhead 2003). They have also made private religion or spirituality a popular modern option, even though the forming of religious communities is an integral part of most religions, especially Christianity. In short, many people in Europe and the United States who report not attending church worship, which is the major expression of organized Christianity, may well be turning to some other form of religion. The nonparticipants or nonpracticing are not at the core or leadership of irreligion, but rather it is those who openly reject religion, which has meant primarily rejection of Christianity, the dominant religion in Western lands. The open rejection of Christianity has been led primarily by intellectuals, but in Europe, not so much in North America, nonintellectuals and working people have been drawn into irreligious movements. Paul Froese and Stevan Pfaff (2005:404) describe, for example, how in Germany "[b]y 1912 half a million people belonged to socialist cultural associations and clubs and many more took part in socialist festivals and cultural events." However, they note that even though the Social Democratic Party leaders saw the promotion of atheism as part of their struggle against the regime, the large majority of Germans continued to have their children baptized and confirmed.

Just as there are many religions and many components of religions, so there are many irreligions or forms of irreligiosity. I am focusing on the kind of irreligion in which people deny belief in God. These people are convinced atheists or agnostics or they are simply unsure enough about God not to want to affirm belief in God, having a kind of weak or mild agnosticism. In general, these people are waiting for evidence of God's existence before believing. They are implicitly or explicitly saying to God, "Prove yourself to me; give me a sign that you exist." These are the leaders of the irreligion movement. Of course, from ancient times believers have struggled with the apparent absence of God, but often came through to faith, for example as in Psalm 10,

Psalm 73, and many other Psalms of the Bible.

Both religion and irreligion are complex realities because of their mixed objective and subjective nature, or mixed mental, emotional, and behavioral aspects. While religions are fairly identifiable, irreligion is more difficult to observe because of its typical lack of strong organizations, with the exception of its modern political expression in political party movements and Communism. However, from the nineteenth century to the present there have been a variety of associations, especially in Europe, but also in the United States advocating secularism, rationalism, "free thought," naturalism, humanism, or even atheism, but the numbers of members of these groups have been relatively small. I recently counted twenty nine organizations in America and eighty seven in the world listed on www.infidels.org that could be describes as at least partially atheistic. These overlapping organizations need to be studied since many members are not necessarily irreligious but rather simply hold to broadly humanistic values.

Antireligious thought was stronger in the general public in America in the first half of the nineteenth century than later. Since that time it has been maintained primarily among intellectuals, often academicians and writers. In a recent study of people who became atheists in the United States (Jesse Smith 2011), it is evident that the large majority became so in an academic setting, but the numbers remain very small being only 2 percent of the population. Even in Great Britain the agnostic movement that was strong in the nineteenth century lost much influence in the early twentieth century (Lightman 1987). Speaking of the relative weakness of the antireligious "free thought" movement in America in the first part of the nineteenth century, Campbell (1972 [1971]:59,61) states:

> [T]he secularists in America had to contend with a phenomenon almost unknown to their British counterparts of this period–a vigorous Christian anti-clerical movement. In fact, during the 1820s the Christian anti-clericals had more periodicals in circulation than the free-thinkers–a fact which made it that much more harder for the real infidels to mobilize support and which may account for their excessive crudity of approach...Thus, ironically enough, it was the same conditions which appeared to favor the growth of secularism in America [religious freedom and lack of a state church] which in fact worked against a strong and influential movement.

Later, in the secular revolution of the late nineteenth and twentieth centuries analyzed by Smith et al (2003a), antireligious (mostly anti-Christian) intellectuals obtained the help of Christian liberals to oppose the domination and restrictions of conservative Christians. The two groups working together secularized the field of education and a range of other professional fields. However, subsequently, especially in the last few decades, religion has reasserted its influence in the United States. Thus there is great variety in how the movements of irreligion spread and affected Europe, North America, and the rest of the world.

We can gain some understanding of the irreligion phenomenon by considering some data. To take a particular case in Europe, in Great Britain atheists, agnostics, and others, willing to say they don't believe in God, probably make up just under 30 percent of the population, even though convinced atheists are probably less than 10 percent (Gill, Hadaway, Marler 1998:508-09; Bruce 2002:138,193). The just under 30 percent figure for unbelief correlates with the 71 percent figure that report belief in God in 1998, probably about 15 percent less than in the United States. However, 56 percent report never attending church

(Davie 2000:9, 10), some 35 percent more than in the United States in which about 20 percent report never attending church.

To show the variety within Europe, from the recent past, percentages in a group of European countries reporting never attending church are: France – 59, Great Britain – 56, Belgium – 52, Netherlands – 47, Portugal – 47, West Germany – 41, Spain – 38, Italy – 19, Northern Ireland – 18, and Ireland – 5. Another set of figures (incorporating Scandinavian nations) showing percentages of those who do not report believing in God are: Sweden – 55, France – 43, Netherlands – 39, West Germany – 37, Belgium – 37, Denmark – 36, Norway – 35, Great Britain – 29, Finland – 24, Portugal – 20, Spain – 19, Italy – 17, Iceland -15, Northern Ireland – 5, Ireland – 4 (Davie 2000: 9,10; adapted from Ashford and Timms 1992:40,46).

These two sets of figures show first, those who are the most apathetic toward Christianity, and second, those who are the most unsure about belief in God. Figures for 1998 or 2000 for Europe show a slight increase for most countries in those reporting that they do not believe in God, except for Italy, Spain, and Portugal, where slight increases report believing in God (Pollack 2003).

I have not taken up the situation in Eastern Europe, which is quite complicated, but should be considered briefly. Only in the Czech Republic, East Germany, and possibly Estonia does a majority of the population not affirm "belief in God." In every other European country 'atheists' remain below 20 percent of the population, although there is another approximately 10 percent not affirming belief in God. The most important fact for religious views is that Eastern Europe was under the domination of officially atheistic regimes. Detlef Pollack (2003), in his examination of religiousness throughout Europe, found that although there was an upswing in religiousness in Eastern Europe after the breakup of Communism, the religious revival could not compensate for losses that the churches had suffered under Communist rule, particularly in East Germany, the Czech Republic, Estonia, Slovenia, Hungary, Bulgaria and Slovakia. This effect of Communist rule was confirmed in a study by Sinisa Zrinscak (2004). After the fall of the Communist regime that actively promoted atheism there were an especially high number of atheists in East Germany (25.4 percent). In short, the active promotion of atheism by Communist governments was able to increase irreligion, particularly in the generation under Communist rule. On the other hand, Froese (2008) in *The Plot to Kill God* has described the failure of the Soviet regime's vigorous antireligious policies to eliminate religion from the general population. In short, Communism was able to increase the proportion of the irreligious in the population, but certainly failed to eliminate religion and may have increased its strength among those who held to religion. In contrast to the other countries under Communist rule, Poland, like Ireland and possibly Iceland, is similar to the United States and unlike most other European nations in the large proportion of the population who believe in God.

The figures indicating the strength of irreligion in the United States are quite different from most of Europe with exceptions such as Ireland, Poland, and Italy. In the United States over the last approximately two decades, according to the General Social Survey, over 80 percent of the population report belief in God with some 20 percent doubting all or some of the time. In other words, 60 and 65 percent report having a firm faith in God. Only 7 percent or less of the respondents report beliefs that could be considered atheistic or agnostic. About 20 percent of the population report never attending church and another 25 percent report seldom attending, but those reporting that they attend church has inched up slightly to about 43 percent (Gallup 2011). A recent study of teenagers–National Survey of Youth and Religion (Smith and Denton

2005:41)–shows figures that are consistent with those of the General Social Survey. Approximately 84 percent of teenagers believe in God. Only 3 percent affirm that they do not believe in God and another 12 percent are unsure of their belief about God.

There is strong evidence to support the view that the irreligion movement has been an elite movement based primarily among intellectuals, some of whom have had high profiles and major influence. The United States provides an interesting case study in how irreligion has appealed to some intellectuals and aspiring intellectuals, but not necessarily to all intellectuals, and seems to have had little effect in the general population. The Carnegie Commission Survey of 60,028 American Academics in 1969 has been cited as showing that among scientists, those in the natural or "hard" sciences are the most religious, in fact differing very little from the general population (Finke and Stark 2000:52-55; Stark 2003:192-97). However, the case is quite different with other intellectuals. Wuthnow (1985:190-91) brings together data on the religiousness of academicians:

> [T]he Carnegie data on faculty members showed that 49 percent in the social sciences were indifferent or opposed to religion, compared with 46 in the humanities, 41 percent in the biological sciences and only 37 percent in the physical sciences (Steinberg 1974). Another study of faculty members showed similar patterns: 41 percent of social scientists did not believe in God, compared with 36 percent of those in the humanities and 20 percent in the natural sciences; similarly, 48 percent, 45 percent, and 34 percent, respectively, said they never attended church (Thalheimer 1973). Several studies of graduate students and a host of undergraduate surveys also

reveal these patterns (see, for example, Feldman and Newcomb 1970).

Elaine Ecklund and her colleagues (2010, 2011a, 2011b, 2011c) have conducted a number of studies of the beliefs of academic scientists from the natural and social sciences. About 60.4 percent of the scientists from the 21 elite universities surveyed in a 2005 to 2007 study reported beliefs about God that are consistent with an atheist or agnostic orientation, almost ten times the proportion in the general population (2011c: 731). However, irreligious people are more likely to enter the sciences and to come from families where they were not socialized into a religion. Of course, in nonelite schools that include many Christian schools there are higher proportions of religious scientists. Surprisingly, Ecklund and Elizabeth Long (2011b) found that "the majority of scientists at top universities consider themselves 'spiritual'." Furthermore, many scientists are willing to negotiate the boundaries with religion, recognizing a mutual influence (2011a). Some scientists, especially with religious spouses, recognize the need for religious and moral socialization of their children (2011c).

The overall data from many studies support the view that Europe, where the irreligion movement had its origin, has been affected to a greater extent than the United States. While some 7 to up to 20 percent of the U.S. population report not believing or having some trouble believing in God, in various parts of Europe two, three, or even four times as high a proportion of populations are nonbelievers in God. In addition, the indications are that irreligion is most appealing to intellectuals or aspiring intellectuals in the United States, who may subsequently serve as leaders of the movement. However, even within the United States there is considerable geographical diversity in the distribution of "no faith" (Kosmin and Keysar 2006).

Only with historical analysis can the distinctions between Europe and the United States, as well as distinctions within both be understood. This leads to the approach I will take in the rest of the chapter. An important study by Froese (2005) called "Secular Czechs and Devout Slovaks: Explaining Religious Differences" points both to how large differences can be within Europe and also to the importance of historical analysis in understanding these differences. The histories of the Czech Republic and Slovakia are complex. Froese traces the secularization of the Czech Republic to the nationalistic struggle that took on an anti-Roman Catholic flavor, even though many Roman Catholics supported it. In contrast, in Slovakia the Roman Catholic Church was associated with the support of nationalism, very much as in Poland. In another study Froese and Steven Pfaff (2005) brought out the importance of understanding historical factors in their study of atheism in East Germany.

In the remainder of the chapter, I specifically use the same theoretical framework that I used in the previous seven chapters to analyze the causes for the spread of religions. The first three parts of the theoretical framework refer to the internal characteristics of irreligion that contribute to its spread: (1) belief (2) morality, and (3) organizational characteristics. The last four parts of the framework refer to two macro and two micro external social factors influencing the spread of irreligion: (4) internal social conditions in receiving societies, (5) intersocietal conditions, (6) social networks, and (7) motivations. It will be impossible to cover many of the historical details of the modern irreligion movement, but my purpose is to demonstrate that the theoretical framework used for analyzing the spread of religions can be useful for understanding the spread of irreligion. It is my contention that the spread of a phenomenon reveals a great deal about the phenomenon itself, as well as about human life in general.

THE BELIEFS OF IRRELIGION

To understand the spread of irreligion it is most useful to recognize that it is not simply the lack of belief in God, but rather the replacement of one kind of belief with another kind of belief. The beliefs of irreligion have made it attractive to many people and greatly aided its spread. The central beliefs of modern irreligion began to emerge in the seventeenth century, but received their earliest strong expression in the eighteenth century French Enlightenment, which was more antiorganized religion or antichurch than simply irreligious. In many respects the modern irreligion movements are based on an exaggeration of or making absolute selected ideas taken from previous movements that had been religiously inspired. This can be seen by tracing the historical roots of what later became the ideology (beliefs) of the irreligion movements.

In the sixteenth century the Protestant Reformation successfully challenged the over-arching authority of a single Church and also emphasized the importance of individual faith. This greatly increased the spirit of freedom and individualism in Western culture. There had been a number of such challenges prior to the Reformation, but they were suppressed. The challenge to traditional religious authority prepared the way for the institutionalization of science in England and France in the seventeenth century. In this movement, religious people used the "new learning" gained from "experimentation" to challenge the traditional Aristotelian thought approved by the Church. Francis Bacon (1561-1626) (1952 [1605]:12), the ideologue of the "new learning," wrote concerning the traditional intellectuals:

> This kind of degenerate learning did chiefly reign amongst the schoolmen: who having sharp and strong wits, and abundance of leisure, and small variety of reading, but their wits being shut up on the cells of a few authors (chiefly Aristotle their dictator) as their

> persons were shut up in the cells of monasteries and colleges, and knowing little history, either nature or time, did out of no great quantity of matter and infinite agitation of wit spin out unto us those laborious webs of learning which are extant in their books.

This is not the place to review in detail the causes for the institutionalization of science in the century preceding the Enlightenment, but it was clearly not irreligion. Stark (2003:147; 2005) gives considerable evidence that Christianity was responsible for the emergence of the scientific movement, even though there were also other contributing social causes. Many of the scientists in the formative era of modern science in the seventeenth century were devout Christians. At the very least it is clear that Christianity was highly compatible with modern science from the beginning. However, the questioning and skeptical spirit of early scientists toward traditional knowledge, which had been dominated by religious authorities, stimulated people to challenge the authority of the established church and its supporting governments through the perspective provided by science. This took place particularly in France in the eighteenth century, after the institutionalization of science in the previous century and where the church was particularly authoritarian. Science gave the irreligious, who were primarily opposed to the authoritarian church, a powerful weapon to use against authoritarianism. Later, Communism, as a political expression of irreligion that developed in the nineteenth century in the West, but only successfully overthrew governments outside of the West, adopted "scientific materialism" as its official ideology. Thus for irreligious people and many people influenced by them, it came to be assumed that to be "scientific" was to be irreligious. Science had become the concrete, immanent god of irreligion, the "incarnation" of "Reason" ("logos") to which it appealed for its authority. This opposition to authorized traditional thought helped to establish the value of skepticism and questioning in scientific studies, but this attitude affected all intellectual endeavors. Thus a foundation for "free thinking" was established. "Free thinker" was coined by John Locke (1632-1704) in speaking of John Toland (1670-1721), a famous skeptic (Hecht 2004:335).

In addition to the scientific movement, the movement toward democracy prepared the ground for irreligion movements by introducing the concept of the right to freedom for individuals. The movement toward democracy was expressed in a number of ways: (1) the growth of participatory organizations in the Church that could carry off successful revolutions in England (Walzer 1965) and the Netherlands; (2) the growth of Parliamentary power in the Netherlands and England that resisted autocracy in Church and government; and (3) the growth of emphasis on individual rights by thinkers, in particular John Locke.

Thus, it is extremely important to note (and contrary to the thought of many people) that the Enlightenment that climaxed in the French Revolution did not create the scientific and democratic movements, but rather followed them and employed the thought associated with them to oppose governmental and religious authoritarianism. The antireligion emphasis of the French Enlightenment did not encompass the whole eighteenth century Enlightenment as it appeared in various European countries and in North America, but it became a major component of the movement leading up to the French Revolution and the irreligion movements that came from it and expanded in the nineteenth century. Commitment to "Reason," of which science was considered a major expression (incarnation), was made the initial unifying ideological aim of the Enlightenment and its antireligious leaders in France. The Rationalism of the Enlightenment that built on reason and science, however, was followed by the Romantic movement that built on the autonomous individual. Individualism had long been a trend in Western culture. Although not an atheist, Rene Descartes (1596-1650), had much earlier given expression to the Western focus on the individual with his famous sentence, "I think therefore I am."

Thus, science and the autonomous individual became the immanent and concrete objects of belief for the modern movements of irreligion. It was as though these beliefs became twin conceptual "incarnations" or "idols" inspiring the commitment, and emotional loyalty of the irreligious, who sometimes emphasized one and sometimes the other. However, both beliefs owe their origin and basic foundation to religion so that they could be call distorted extensions of beliefs found in religion. Christianity accepts the importance of the individual and of scientific reasoning, but does not recognize that the self is absolute or solely sufficient apart from God; nor does it recognize scientific knowledge as encompassing all knowledge. As with the autonomous individual, instead of regarding science as a tool or instrument, people in irreligion movements regarded science as providing complete knowledge. It became an ideology (idol) that drew the commitment of intellectuals. I refer to this as "scientism," which has been thoroughly discussed by Stenmark (2001). I agree with him that scientism is a form of intellectual expansionism (imperialism) in which science is thought of as accounting for all reality and the only source for true knowledge. There are other usages of the term, scientism, but this much is sufficient to understand the basic nature of scientism in which science becomes a substitute for God. Science becomes more than simply a tool and a means to knowledge and service. Science was very closely linked to Reason and Rationality so as to be almost interchangeable in many people's minds.

Support for our view of the two major beliefs of irreligion is found in Smith's (2003a:33,34) study of the secularization movement in the United States. Building on comments from Edward Shils (1972:18), Smith states:

> Those intellectuals most responsible for the historical secularization of American public life came largely from the first two traditions [out of four: scientism, romanticism, apocalypticism, and populism]–they were scientific intellectuals and romantic intellectuals. The former were mostly academics and scientists, situated within the scientism tradition…The romantic intellectuals, on the other hand, were mostly journalists, independent writers, and other artists. At first glance, scientists and romantic artists might seem very unlike, even quite opposed to each other– and in some ways they definitely are. But in relation to the nineteenth-century Protestant establishment, scientism and romanticism were united on some crucial commitments. They shared a dedication to the ultimacy of individual experience, and a deep antagonism toward external authority and traditional conventions.

Smith (2003a:44,45) later notes that the intellectuals' love of autonomy provided them a basis for opposing religious authorities that are beyond and above oneself such as God, but also Scriptures, bishops, church teachings, moral commands, and clergy in general. Of course, whether positivist scientists or bohemian rebels, all humans "live, move, and have their being within historical traditions entailing real dependence on authority, verbal testimony, and the binding power of collective narratives." Irreligious "devotees predictably react against other traditions more explicit about dependence and authority."

It is significant that Smith uses religious terms such as "devotees" to refer to those who elevate the autonomous individual, which fits with the view that irreligion can function and spread as a religion carried by its "devotee missionaries." I would add that the themes of "apocalyticism" or "populism," which also had their influence in the United States in religion and politics, did receive emphasis in European irreligion movements and especially in the non-Western world, many parts of which were longing for radical change. These concepts coming from the Bible fit well with the call for justice issued by movements in which many irreligious people were active. This leads to the consideration of the morality emphasized in irreligion movements that has attracted people to them.

THE MORALITY OF IRRELIGION

The irreligion movements not only proclaimed their beliefs in science and the autonomous individual, but they attracted many people primarily by developing a strong moral thrust. The connection of the scientific movement to democracy has already been mentioned. This moralistic emphasis found expression in France, the birthplace of the irreligion movements, in the ideals of the French Revolution related to human rights and to a new humanity. These ideals were further articulated in the philosophical developments of the nineteenth century, particularly in Marxism and socialism. The religious goal of justice for all was co-opted and became especially appealing wherever there was lack of justice. Needless to say, the emphasis on justice had special appeal because of the failure of dominant Christian churches to include justice concerns in their messages.

The fact that there are two main "gods" of irreligion, science and the autonomous individual, together with the added moral idealism of human freedom, justice, and equality for all, points to why irreligion is not limited to the strict followers of scientism, and individual autonomy, but extends to people in the humanities, such as philosophers, writers, poets, and journalists, as well as activists for social justice. Irreligion movements can thus include a variety of people with a variety of concerns and values, some of which come in conflict with each other. For a scientist to support his or her irreligion, it may be sufficient simply to say (as said by some well known scientists), "There is no evidence for God." For people who prefer to draw on the romantic tradition, it may be more appealing to say something like, "I am the master of my fate, I am the captain of my soul" (From "Invictus" by William Ernest Henley 1849-1903). For secularized social activists, the call for "liberte, equalite, and fraternite" or some version of it has special power and appeal, even though these ideals have religious roots.

As irreligious ideology relied on its version of "expansionist science" and the autonomous individual, together with the cause of human justice, it was able to appeal to people in the world that were awed by the power of science and technology, desired greater individual freedom, and longed for relief from oppression. In fact, the idealization (idolization) of science, the autonomous self, and a utopian society, central elements in the belief and moral system of irreligion, gave it great power to spread because of the awakened desire for all of these things in Western societies and later, even more, in the rest of the world. It is this aspect of irreligion of shared values with a broad population, particularly those seeking to be liberal and progressive, rather than any strong organization that made it possible for irreligion to spread in Western countries. It was outside of the West, unless Russia be considered Western, that the political organizations of irreligious movements in the form of Communist parties were able to gain dominance in a number of societies.

The moralistic thrust of the irreligion movements is an elaboration of the value of the autonomous individual, even though this value came in conflict with the value of rationalism and science. This idealistic moral goal (with many expressions) adopted by the irreligion movement, envisioned the creation of a fulfilled and authentic new humanity. This goal built on the idealism that can be traced back to Medieval "Chiliasm" or Millennial Movements (Mannheim 1936:211,227; Cohn 1961). This source, in fact, was pointed out by Engels, Marx's colleague. In addition, the ideal of the new free individual was built on the previous religious views and religious struggle for freedom in the sixteenth and seventeenth centuries. The ideal of a new society created by people freed from autocracy and religious domination inspired many of the eighteenth century French Enlightenment leaders. It found a more subjective expression in Germany, particularly in nineteenth century German philosophy, and was made central in Marxian revolutionary thought. Jose Casanova (1994:34,35) points to the contributions of the German atheists, Nietzsche and Feuerbach, to the elevation of an idealized humanity that takes the place of God. It is this aspect of the irreligion movement that enabled it to gain the most recruits from liberals and progressives, who wanted (want) to overcome injustices in societies. In many respects, in the end it was the moral goals of freedom, justice, and equality held by irreligious intellectuals, not simply the elevation of science and the autonomous individual, that gained them the most followers and allies and spread their influence to a larger public. This corresponds to the emphasis on compassion and egalitarianism found in the religions that spread. It fact, these emphases in the irreligion movements, just as in millennial movements, were outgrowths of themes found in the Bible. However, when the moral guidance and energy of irreligion movements, characteristics found in the spreading religions, are considered, the irreligion movements reveal certain weaknesses that are also seen in religions. They showed the same tendency toward top down guidance that results in weakening moral energy. These weaknesses have kept irreligion movements from growing and have even caused their retreat, as in the Soviet Union and China. This ineffectiveness of irreligion movements is shown particularly in their failures in gathering and organizing people and, when organizing effectively, in creating oppressive regimes.

In a recent study of atheist identity in America, Jesse Smith (2011) supports the view that atheists perceive the moral superiority of atheism, particularly as morally superior to conservative religion with its politically conservative ideas. Clearly, a move toward irreligion was seen not as a move away from morality, but toward higher morality.

THE ORGANIZATION OF IRRELIGION

Regular gathering and organization is not as significant a part of most irreligion movements as it is of religions, at least of the religions that spread. It has been noted that organization has never been the strong suit of irreligious people because skepticism is not conducive to organized life in which mutual trust is necessary. Steven Shapen (1994:20) comments, "Mary Douglas's (1986:78) observation that radical skepticism is incompatible with 'the commitment to ordering and organizing' people is, therefore, a moral expansion of Wittgenstein's (1976:Pt II, v) dictum that 'doubting has an end.'" Belief impels action to relate to others as unbelief does not. However, as pointed out, irreligion has beliefs and a moral thrust that has impelled strong actions of a particular type, primarily social and political action. Thus skeptics were able to organize certain kinds of opposition movements, particularly when they were against oppressive authoritarian rule in church and state. Over time, movements of irreligious people have been most successful when they have focused on the positive ethical goal of human justice and sought the support of religious and generally idealistic people.

Before the birth pangs of the irreligion movements during the eighteenth century French Enlightenment, there was a period in which Europeans gained experience in organization, including organizations for reform and for revolution. The irreligion movements built on this earlier experience. I have already mentioned in Chapter 4 the long history in Europe of forming autonomous organizations, going back to the forming of monasteries, towns, guilds, universities, orders, and Medieval religious movements, which were followed by the Reformation, the scientific movement, and the democratic movement.

In the seventeenth century, Italy, France, and England became the first centers for informally organized intellectuals and scientists carrying on investigations that questioned traditionally authorized knowledge of the world. However, religious authorities in Italy blocked the efforts there to organize a scientific society (Ornstein, 1975 [1913]). In France, during the period of relative tolerance in the seventeenth century under the Edict of Nantes, intellectuals began networking in salon gatherings. In England under the Puritans, the "invisible college" held meetings, and "the new learning" of the "experimenters" and the "natural philosophers" was promoted by intellectuals, mostly devout Christians. The networking (and competition) between England and France resulted in the establishment of scientific societies–the Royal Academy in 1662 and the Academie de Sciences in 1666 respectively. All of this took place before the rise of strong antireligious rhetoric that was to come in the following century. However, preparing the ground for the antireligious intellectuals to come in France was the fact that the French scientific society was sponsored by an authoritarian government allied with the established Church. This was in contrast to the independently organized Royal Academy (which represented an "amateur" and voluntaristic approach to science) and the growing power of Parliament versus the king in England. Most fatal to the encouragement of diversity in France and the development of a moderate approach to change was the revoking of the Edict of Nantes in 1685 under Louis XIV. France then entered a period of increasing authoritarianism and corresponding resistance that led to the French Revolution. Charles Taylor (1989:335) in discussing the "radical Enlightenment" states:

> In France, the struggle against religion, in particular Catholic Christianity, takes on over-whelming importance, at times threatening to crowd out other crucial aspirations. It was essential to show its falseness, its misanthropy, its destructiveness. It was important to prove again and again what Bayle had first asserted, that an atheist can be a virtuous person, but this merges into the attempt to demonstrate that religion must make you bad.

Collins (1999:164) comments:

> In France, secularization was the subject of a lengthy series of battles that resulted in swings between clerical and anticlerical dominance. For this reason, it was in France that the issue of secularism was debated in most explicit and intense form, but the actual transformation to a modern base of cultural production occurred relatively late.

Thus, in seventeenth century France, the meetings of intellectuals took on a spirit of strong resistance to traditional religious authority. The intellectual resisters were primarily writers (not scientists) and they organized the project of producing the great French Encylopedie. For them, it could be said, "Reason is to philosophe what grace is to the Christian" (Brinton 1967:520). Thus the irreligion movement took its earliest shape as a loose network of the popularizers or philosophes of the French Enlightenment, such as Voltaire (1694-1778), Diderot (1713-1784), d'Alembert (1717-1783), Condercet (1743-1794), Holbach (1723-1789), and Beccaria (1738-1794) (Brinton 1967:519). These and other intellectuals (and aspiring intellectuals) were in informal contact with one another. The fact that the French antireligious movement was by the "popularizers" rather than so much by scientists themselves shows the ideological nature of their movement and of their faith in and devotion to science. All the philosophes were critical of religion, not necessarily nonbelievers, but some, such as La Mettrei (1709-1751), Holbach, and Helvetius (1715-1771), were atheists. The nonatheists were also rather vehemently against the established religion, which was particularly authoritarian. Diderot maintained that "men will never be free till the last king is strangled with the entrails of the last priest." However, the resistance of the philosophes provoked strong attempts to suppress the irreligion movement. Voltaire was twice arrested and had to flee to England and the Netherlands. Louis XIV ordered the project of the Encyclopedie halted, but Diderot managed to complete the work in secret and deliver the volumes to the thousands of subscribers whose patronage made the project possible.

The French Revolution, which failed in establishing democracy, used many of the ideas of the earlier intellectuals of the antireligion movement. Symbolic of the importance of the antireligious intellectuals was that Voltaire's body and his portrait, along with Rousseau's, was paraded in the streets of Paris as "fathers of the Revolution." The Revolution was both antigovernment and antireligious, the latter shown by the fact that Christianity was briefly abolished during the period of turmoil. Hecht (2003:368-369) notes that three self-proclaimed atheists, Pierre Chaumette, Josephe Fouche, and Jacques Hebert, began an atheist campaign in 1793 that involved heavy taxes, stripping churches, and establishing the cult of the goddess of Reason. However, in March 1794 Robespierre had them and their major followers "killed by the cartload" and repudiated their atheism saying that people needed to believe there was a God and an afterlife. He also celebrated a deist God in a "Festival of the Supreme Being." France subsequently continued the struggle between an authoritative traditional religion and some kind of alternative religion, even a kind of religious state.

The revolutions that came in Europe beginning with the French Revolution showed that antireligious activists could provide an ideology for political oppositional organizations, even though the subsequent revolutions failed to establish new regimes—except for the Russian Revolution in the next century. France continued throughout the nineteenth century with numerous political crises and changes in religious policies before finally establishing a secular government in 1906. McGrath (2004:261) has noted:

> Without doubt, atheism was seen as a liberator in France in the 1790s, in Germany in the 1840s, and in Russia during the 1910s, to mention just a few especially important moments in recent Western history. But at other times and places, atheism has been seen as socially and intellectually repressive—for example, throughout Europe after the Second World War.

The irreligion movements in Europe had both the radical and moderate approaches to change represented by Communism and Socialism respectively. However, Socialism included many religious people and "Christian Socialist" parties. Thus in Europe irreligious people found that they could have the most influence in societies where they were free to organize around common political goals with liberal and progressive religious people. Many people in free and nonoppressive societies shared values with the irreligious, specifically the values of science, freedom, and universal justice. This is seen in the socialist, as opposed to the Communist, organizations in Europe, such as the Fabian Society in England, the Social Democratic Party in Germany, and various other coalitions formed by socialist parties.

In contrast to socialist parties, the Communist party, in which atheism was made official, proved to be effective militarily in overthrowing governments and establishing irreligious regimes only outside of Western Europe. In Western Europe Communist parties were most successful where there had been authoritarian religious structures of the Roman Catholic Church, as in Italy, Spain, and France, but they were not able to achieve lasting power. There was marginal success in Germany, but there, as in both Italy and Spain, authoritarian Fascist governments that claimed allegiance to religion suppressed the Communist movements. Communist parties were revived after World War II in Western Europe, but were not able to gain control of the governments. Communist parties were only able to come to power outside of Western Europe, in Russia, and certain countries in Asia (China, North Korea, Vietnam, and Laos) and Latin America, most notably Cuba. Of course, Communism came to control the parts of Europe that came under the domination of the Soviet Union.

In the United States, irreligion movements had practically no success as a Communist organization, and only slightly in connection with socialism in the labor union movement. In general, the most successful approach in irreligion movements in the United States was for irreligious and antireligious intellectuals to establish themselves in the educational world and in various professions, which they then led in secularizing. However, this was done in cooperation with others who shared the value of intellectual freedom and scientific investigation. In a secular environment irreligious and innovative (or unorthodox) religious people could be assured of freedom of thought. From the initial secularized academic base they were able to carry out a secularizing program in a variety of fields. This effort has been analyzed most clearly in *The Secular Revolution*, edited by Smith (2003a), which will be referred to again in the following discussion of social factors affecting the spread of irreligion. Social factors have already been introduced in the discussion of the belief, morals, and organizational characteristics of the irreligion movements originating in Europe, but the following sections will seek to look at these factors in a more systematic way.

Authoritarian and oppressive irreligious organizations, as in the case of similar religious organizations, have in the long run proved to be to the disadvantage of the spread of irreligion and may be a major reason for "the twilight of atheism" (McGrath 2004). Irreligious organizations in the form of Communist parties aided in the spread of irreligion primarily outside of Europe and North America and in areas of Europe which they came to dominate, for example East Germany (Pollack 2003, Zrinscak 2004, Froese and Pfaff 2005).

SOCIAL CONDITIONS IN RECEIVING SOCIETIES

Turning now from the internal characteristics or content of irreligion in its various movements, irreligion movements could not have developed and spread from Europe without certain external social conditions that made them a possible option. A basic condition was the existence of freedom to make choices concerning religion and irreligion. Stark and

Finke (2000:13) note, "What was unusual during the "Enlightenment" was the public expression of atheism–that it was possible to form and sustain an antireligious movement." They add that this was not because irreligion has been so unusual in human history. It was rather evident during the Greco-Roman period. This brings them to the point: "What was unusual about this period in Greco-Roman history was also unusual about the era of the 'Enlightenment,' not the existence of irreligiousness, but the freedom to express it in public."

Major movements that changed European society before the Enlightenment have already been mentioned. These movements brought: increased individual and group autonomy, an emphasis on religious and philosophical individualism, national independence, democratic practices, and the modern scientific movement. In addition they also created conditions that I have not stressed up to now: the industrial revolution with the resulting great expansion of urbanization and the lifting of standards of living, including the general increase in educational levels. Justin Barrett (2004:118) in his discussion of theism and atheism points out that the "unnatural" mode of thought that is expressed in atheism has been able "to emerge and spread only among the more privileged members of the developed nations of the world–in Europe and North America particularly." People who do not want to believe are best able to divorce themselves from the natural conditions that support theism when they are in the humanly constructed and somewhat artificial world brought in by the industrial and technological revolution of the last two centuries. Academics are especially able to divorce themselves from ordinary life and to find mutual support for atheistic arguments. This is consistent with the findings of Bainbridge (2005), who found a tendency for atheists to be social isolates. On a less extreme level, irreligion is associated with individualism that was made possible by both norms of freedom and of economic security.

The raising of standards of living due to the industrial revolution leads to a consideration of the theory on religiosity put forward by Pippa Norris and Ronald Inglehart (2006 [2004]:4). They state:

> This book develops a revised version of secularization theory that emphasizes the extent to which people have a sense of existential security–that is, the feeling that survival is secure enough that it can be taken for granted…We believe that the importance of religiosity persists most strongly among vulnerable populations, especially those living in poorer nations, facing personal survival-threatening risks.

Norris and Inglehart only apply their theory to the recent spread of secularization, which they define as "a systematic erosion of religious practices, values, and belief." There are other definitions of secularization, which are more neutral and useful. They do not make secularization necessarily a negative influence on beliefs, but rather a process of removing religious authority from government and from public institutions. If the separation of religion and government is part of the secularization process, then secularization contributed to the growth of religiosity in the United States. Regardless of what I regard as the confusion by Norris and Inglehart of "secularization" and "secularism," if we simply focus on the growth and spread of irreligion, as in this chapter, it is worth considering the theory of Norris and Inglehart about the relation of security and vulnerability to irreligion. The advance of political and individual freedoms and the lifting of economic standards took place together in Europe and both conditions gave people greater opportunities to make choices for or against religion.

The greatest problem for Norris and Inglehart is that the United

States is both an advanced industrial nation and also highly religious, especially compared to Europe. Norris and Inglehart (2006 [2004] :106-110) deal with this by emphasizing the insecurity of life in the United States as compared to Europe, where social security programs are more prevalent. The observation that wealth and the security it brings is damaging to faith is familiar to most people, especially Christians. For example, Jesus speaks of the danger of wealth (Mark 10:23), James strongly criticizes the rich for their over confidence (James 5:1), and the Magificat celebrates the rejection by God of the rich and powerful (Luke 1:46-55). It certainly seems to be consistent with both Biblical and ordinary norms that those who are "existentially secure" and do not need to be concerned about their physical or earthly survival are less likely to feel the need for Divine aid, hence are less likely to be religious.

According to the understanding of popular and elite religion in Chapter 2, popular religion is very much based on the felt need of most people for help in dealing with life's difficulties and basic survival. The elite, who tend to be more secularized, are more likely to be concerned about the survival of their power than personal survival. What the last few centuries in the West (Europe and North America) have done for many people is to remove basic concerns about subsistence. A large middle class has been created for whom life is relatively secure. Of course, Norris and Inglehart (2006 [2004]: 108) point out that "[m]any American families, even in the professional middle classes, face risks of unemployment, the dangers of sudden ill health without adequate private medical insurance, vulnerability to become a victim of crime, and the problems of paying for long-term care of the elderly." They then note that even in the very religious United States, the least well-off income group is more likely to pray daily and consider religion very important than the highest income group (66 percent to 47 percent). Of course, this leaves almost half the highest income group quite religious and only two-thirds of the poorest income group very religious. The search for relevant data and the debate over the data and how it is used will continue (See Smith 2006). For my purposes here it can be recognized that increased economic security along with increased individual freedom gave more people than ever before the opportunity to choose to be irreligious. The implications of this for the future will be discussed in Chapter 9.

As important as the social and economic conditions were that allowed freedom of religious (and antireligious) choices for the development of irreligion movements, they were especially stimulated when freedom of choice encountered authoritarian religion. This is what has contributed most to the lingering effect of irreligion movements seen in the higher level of secularism that exists in Europe than in America. England and France both experienced an increase in freedom in the seventeenth century, but France reversed the movement toward freedom and in the next century experienced a very oppressive state allied with a very authoritarian Church. With greater democracy England learned a greater measure of toleration for its dissenters than France. Also, while England and Germany experienced forms of the Pietistic Movement in the eighteenth century that brought vitality and diversity to religious life, France had earlier suppressed the religious reforms of Jansenism, which had been defended by the scientist-theologian Blaise Pascal (1623-1662). Added to this, the revocation of the Edict of Nantes in 1685 led to renewed suppression of Protestant dissent so that by the eighteenth century France contained a single authoritarian Church that blocked reform from within and without.

What about other countries with authoritarian religion that did not have outbreaks of irreligion as early or on the scale of France? France shared with Spain, Italy, and Austria, which ruled wide areas, including what is now the Czech Republic and Slovakia, the social condition of the authoritarian Roman Catholic Church allied with autocratic governments. However, these nations did not experience as early as France did the advances in freedom and in intellectual and scientific networking. The greatest potential intellectual innovation existed earlier in Italy that led the rest of Europe in intellectual development during the Renaissance. However, as already noted, scientific advancement was blocked and religious diversity was never countenanced.

France initiated the antireligious thought and activity that climaxed in the Revolution of 1789, but the movement spread rapidly throughout Europe in the nineteenth century and has continued to the present. Although less authoritarian than the Roman Catholic Church, the major Protestant churches accepted the principle of the state church, which tended to be authoritarian. For example, people were executed for atheism in Protestant Switzerland and Scotland. Even in America, witches were burned and Quakers were executed, tortured, and banished in the seventeenth century! This happened in a part of the country, New England, which later reacted against authoritarian religion and became the most religiously liberal area in the nation.

When Europe is considered today, the primarily Protestant countries along with the primarily Roman Catholic countries of France, Belgium, and the Czech Republic are the countries with the highest proportions of people who never attend church and don't believe in God, as seen in the data presented earlier. These are the countries in which there has been a single dominant religion and, at the same time, more opportunities to make religious choices. In contrast, in the other European countries where the Roman Catholic or Greek Orthodox Churches are dominant there has not existed as much freedom of religious choice and people have been more likely to affirm belief in

God. At the same time, the religiousness and relative lack of irreligion, except in its most extreme form, Communism, of Southern European countries and especially Poland, Greece, and the Balkans are cases that cannot be understood without also taking into account historical intersocietal relations to be discussed in the next section.

The high level of nonbelief in Protestant countries compared to Roman Catholic countries (except for France and Belgium) may be understood by considering several factors. The Protestant Reformation did not change the practice of relating churches closely with governments. In fact, the Thirty Years' War ending with the Peace of Westphalia in 1648 largely determined the monopolistic religious territories that have remained to this day. At the same time, there was a greater measure of diversity and freedom of choice about church participation in northern Europe than in most Roman Catholic countries. Thus the alliances of governments with the Roman Catholic Church in the south were more effective in blocking both dissent and irreligion, than were the alliances of religion and governments in northern Europe. The latter were more like France in having both established churches and higher levels of freedom of religious choice than the Roman Catholic nations in the south.

Spain is a case in point. The alliance of nation and religious faith in Spain spared it the civil wars experienced in early modern France and England, which brought some measure of freedom to both lands. Later there were three civil wars in Spain–the First Carlist War (1833-40), the Second Carlist War (1870-76), and the Spanish Civil War (1936-39), all of which strengthened authoritarianism. They "all started as antimodern counterrevolutions and were sanctified by an embattled Catholic church as religious crusades against godless liberalism or atheistic communism" (Casanova 1994:77). Casanova goes on to note David Martin's (1978:6) characterization of "the French (Latin) pattern" of secularization:

> Such revolutionary explosions become endemic, and religion as such is frequently a political issue. Coherent and massive secularism confronts coherent and massive religiosity....One ethos confronts an alternative ethos, particularly where the elite culture of the secular Enlightenment acquires a mass component and achieves a historicized ideology i.e. Marxism.

The effect of social structure on the irreligion movement cannot be complete without comparing the European Protestant countries with the United States, which has had a dominant American (not European) Protestant religious pattern of voluntary association in congregations and denominations as opposed to the traditional European pattern of state related monopolistic churches. The data on belief in God and church attendance show that irreligion movements have had much less influence in the United States on both the elite and popular level than in Protestant Europe. There is as much freedom to choose irreligion in the United States as in Protestant Europe, but in the United States there is greater opportunity for voluntary religious participation and religious innovation as opposed to being assigned a religious identity. It is as though secularization released the large nominally religious population in Protestant countries of Europe from their church obligations, but in the United States secularization stimulated religious opposition to religious monopolies and encouraged religious voluntary activity.

Thus, the social condition factor in the spread of irreligion means considering both the presence of opportunity for choice for or against religion and the presence of a dominant religion allied to the government. These factors are interrelated and the combination of both freedom and a monopolistic religion seems most favorable for the spread of irreligion. The irreligion movement requires some opportunity for choice that will not be blocked by a very authoritarian regime. An authoritarian regime that is allied with a dominant religion may simply block the spread of irreligion. However, if the irreligion movement is successful in overthrowing the regime in a revolution or by conquest (as in Eastern and Central Europe, Asia, and Cuba), it may institute a very authoritarian irreligious regime that will suppress religion and spread irreligion. Irreligion became associated with coercive power, just as previously religion sought or accepted such an association. The spread of religion or irreligion, depending on the association with the government, could be limited, but the effects of such control may linger for long periods as seen in Europe that was under state churches or Communist governments.

If there is considerable freedom of choice, but also an existing "established" religion with little religious variety, then the irreligion movement is likely to gain considerable influence in the society at large. This has been seen primarily in the "bridge" country of France and in Northern Europe, but may be more evident in the future in Southern Europe, particularly Spain. If there is considerable freedom of choice and a variety of voluntarily based religions, then irreligion is likely to have little impact in the population at large, however influential it may be among intellectuals. This is the situation in the United States.

On the macro level, in addition to social condition factors in host societies, it is also important to consider how intersocietal factors may affect the spread of irreligion.

INTERSOCIETAL RELATIONSHIPS

International competition in Europe after 1500 was exacerbated by the religious competition between Protestantism and Roman Catholicism. Religious wars took place within nations–between Roman Catholics and Protestants in France and Germany, primarily in the sixteenth century, and between different Protestant groups in England in the seventeenth century. Also in the seventeenth century, the highly destructive and cruel Thirty Years' War took place in Europe between nations over which territories would be under Roman Catholicism and Protestantism respectively. Following the settlement of religious territoriality in 1648 at the Peace of Westphalia, international competition continued, but primarily on the economic, political, and knowledge levels and not with religious justifications. Advancement of knowledge with science and technology became a major goal for nations. The competition between the nations meant that all of Europe opened up for intellectual and scientific development.

In the nineteenth century the "intellectual" became a recognized international authority in new knowledge needed by every land. Following the French lead in science in the eighteenth century, Germany began to lead in scientific and other intellectual work in the nineteenth century with the development of research universities. At the same time Germany produced the most outstanding antireligious philosophers and social scientists, for example, Ludwig Feuerbach (1804-1872), Friedrich Nietzsche (1844-1900), Karl Marx (1818-1883), and Sigmund Freud (1856-1939). Aspiring intellectuals from various lands, including the United States, crossed international boundaries to obtain the new knowledge being generated by German scholars, many of whom were anti-Christian and antireligious generally. The spread of irreligion between nations in association with the aspiration for intellectual advancement and the desire to compete in knowledge production proved to be the most effective means for irreligion movements to move between societies, at least in the West.

When irreligion became associated with political power, it proved ineffective in the West (except for those areas in Central and Eastern Europe that were conquered by Communist power), but it proved effective in gaining control of societies outside of the West that perceived themselves as oppressed from within and especially as threatened by outside powers. Thus, irreligion in the form of Communism was best able to spread when it became identified with nationalistic aims in opposition to outside domination. Communism in a number of instances, for example, in China, Vietnam, North Korea, and Cuba, was able to become identified with nationalistic resistance to outside domination from nations identified with Christianity. However, Communists in Russia and the other countries, as the revolutionaries previously in France, first directed their efforts against internal regimes, and later strengthened themselves by nationalistic struggles against outside powers. The case of Communism outside of the West is parallel to the way religions have been able to spread when they became associated with preserving and enhancing ethnic or national identities against outside threats.

When religions have been able to support resistance to outside forces, whether they represented another religion or irreligion, they have been able to limit acceptance of the outside culture, whether it was religious or irreligious. This seems to be the case especially with Poland and Ireland, but also much of Eastern Europe, Greece, and Southern Europe, as noted in the Conclusion in Chapter 5. The fact that the Roman Catholic Church has been a support to Poland and Ireland against outside aggression helps to explain the high level of loyalty to the Church and the relative lack of impact of the irreligion movement, as well as of other religions, at least so far. There is evidence of an increase in secularism in both countries in recent years. In the case of Poland, the outside intrusion was from the irreligious Communist Soviet Union (earlier from first, Protestant Germany and then, irreligious Nazi Germany), but in the case of Ireland, it was largely from the threat and oppression from Protestant Britain. The question remains as to whether the loyalty to the Church will be sustained at previous levels after the threats have been removed. We have already seen how historical intersocietal relationships affected Slovakia and the Czech Republic (Froese 2005). In Eastern and Southern Europe the domination or threat of domination from Islam also served to strengthen established Eastern Orthodoxy and Roman Catholicism and block irreligion.

Irreligion did not prove itself to be necessarily a great boon in the international competition in the natural sciences and technology, which from the beginning were supported by religious people. Communism also, even though espousing scientific materialism, did not prove itself to be more productive in the scientific field than non-Communism. If anything, scientific work under Communism proved to be less sophisticated than elsewhere. In the end, the desire for freedom of thought united many religious and irreligious intellectuals against the highly ideological antireligious authoritarianism and overt oppression of Communism, contributing to "the twilight of atheism" (McGrath 2004) as already noted.

SOCIAL NETWORKS

The section on organization above showed that the ability of irreligion movements to organize was rather weak or at least uneven. Irreligion movements included on the one hand revolutionary organizations, which proved to be very authoritarian and destructive to religion, to, on the other hand, loose networks of intellectuals, which have been most effective in spreading irreligion in democratic societies, primarily among the elite knowledge class. Just as with religion, the short-term effectiveness and long-term ineffectiveness of irreligion to spread in association with political power has been made evident by the return to religion of people in the nations of the former Soviet

Union and Eastern Europe. Even more revealing is that in continuing Communist countries outside of the West, such as China, Vietnam, and Cuba, religion is spreading. Only under the very oppressive rule of North Korea is religion highly stifled, as it was in earlier Communist countries. Thus, irreligion, just as religion, has proved most able to spread effectively through loose social networks, in this case primarily of intellectuals and professionals, not from the broader cross-section of population who are largely religious.

There have been few studies of the sources of atheism. However, as noted above, Bainbridge (2005) recently carried out a survey study, not of the amount or distribution of atheism in the United States population, but of possible sources of atheism. The survey data he used indicated that atheism was more common among people whose social obligations are weak. This is consistent with hostility to religion being most prevalent among those who are able to be socially isolated in academic settings. Thus, while irreligion has tended to be highly individualistic based to a great extent on its belief in the autonomous individual, it has been most successful in establishing social networks when it has been in an oppositional mode to religious authority in publicly operated institutions and other public arenas. Smith (2003a:1) introduces the analysis of how intellectuals led the "secular revolution" in America through networking:

> The rebel insurgency consisted of waves of *networks* [italics mine] of activists who were largely skeptical, freethinking, agnostic, atheist, or theologically liberal; who were well educated and socially located mainly in knowledge production occupations; and who generally espoused materialism, naturalism, positivism, and the privatization or extinction of religion.

Academia became and remains the major base for networking among intellectuals, but networking is also possible in a variety of professions, most of which are supplied with new recruits by academia. Religious and irreligious people are included in the networking. Smith's et al's (2003a) analysis shows how members of irreligion movements and other intellectuals opposed to religious domination tended to become prominent in particular fields. In academia, the social sciences and the humanities, not so much the natural sciences, became primary bases for networking. These fields through their professional organizations and publications were able to provide opportunities for networking among irreligious and antireligious intellectuals, but also with liberals and social activists who were sympathetic with the goals of obtaining freedom from religious domination or control and advancing human rights. In the area of literature, for example, the goal was to obtain freedom from censorship (Kemeny 2003:216-68). Smith (2003a:97-159) and Kraig Beyerlein (2003:160-96) examined the secularization of academia. Other areas in which networks of intellectuals, both irreligious and religious, were able to disestablish religious authority were science (Garroutte 2003:197-215), psychology (Meander 2003:269-309), the legal field (Sikkink 2003:310-54), education (Thomas, Peck, De Haan 2003:355-94), journalism (Flory 2003:395-433), and bio-ethics (Evans 2003:434-61).

Although individual members of these professional organizations are far from all being antireligious, the social networks in the secularized professions provide an ethos in which irreligion can be maintained and even thrive. For many, socialization into the social sciences, for example, is to consider religious motives irrelevant in drawing conclusions and religion as primarily if not only a dependent variable. Significantly, there are signs that this socialization of aspiring social scientists may be changing in some quarters with the "turn toward culture" (Wuthnow 1987, Alexander 2003; Collins 2004) and the "new paradigm" (Warner 1997; Lambert 1999) in sociology of religion. However, whatever social scientists and scholars from the humanities may promote among their students and colleagues, the evidence is that socialization into religious belief or nonbelief precedes socialization into academic fields. Wuthnow (1985) points this out, as will be noted in the next section. Thus, while networks of irreligious intellectuals are important for advancing the process of secularization, usually allied with colleagues who share values with them (considered "liberal" or "progressive"), the social networks in which irreligion first develops for most is probably found in families and local communities. Furthermore, socialization to irreligion may not be so much from ideologically irreligious parents and mentors as from parents and mentors with weak, vague, or "practical atheistic" religious views and life styles. This may be seen partly from the research in vital religious communities and the religion of teenagers, which shows that parents have the major influence in transmitting beliefs (Smith 1998; Smith with Denton 2005).

Even though the irreligion movement has been advanced by networks of intellectuals in the United States, it also has been blocked effectively by strong religious networks in groups and institutions so that irreligion seems to have had little impact in much of the general population and even among many intellectuals. However, where religious communities do not exist as strong vital groups forming "subcultural identities" (Smith 1998), individuals may live and work in secular or semi-secular networks where irreligion or at least a vague religion (for example, "Moralistic Therapeutic Deism"–Smith with Denton 2005) becomes an easy option.

The diversity of religions in the United States and the attendant "culture wars" (Hunter 1991), contributes to the secularization of the public sphere, where people want to avoid religious disagreements. However, the result has not been the triumph of irreligion in the general public. Many religious intellectuals joined irreligious intellectuals to resist religious domination because of the extreme differences among religious groups within the United States. An example is that most religious people do not trust other religious people to teach the Bible in a satisfactory way in the public schools. Nonliteralists do not want literalists teaching the Bible in public schools and likewise, literalists do not want those they consider "liberals" and "secular humanists" teaching their children. Also, each religious group does not want the morals and values of other groups imposed on them. Thus, the very diversity of views and behavior among religious people has contributed to the advancement of the influence of the secularization movement that in turn has provided a cover for irreligion movements. However, even this cover may not have contributed significantly to the spread of irreligion. It does seem to be true that some of the religious groups most favoring secularization of the public sphere, for example, Mainline Churches, Unitarians, and Reformed Jews, now seem the least able to form the "subcultural identities" that resist irreligion. However, in general the ability of religious people to organize and to network with others with common interests and to maintain their own institutions has served to mitigate to a great extent the influence of irreligious intellectuals on the general public in the United States. In short, irreligious networks appear to have been relatively ineffective in spreading irreligion, but rather to have functioned primarily to give it expression.

MOTIVES TO ENHANCE SOCIAL IDENTITIES

Irreligion movements made irreligion and antireligion a typical aspect of the social identities of many intellectuals in the nineteenth and twentieth centuries. In the first place, intellectuals became an identifiable group beginning in the nineteenth century. In regard to that century, McGrath (2004:49) comments:

> The emergence of the intellectual as a recognized social type is one of the most remarkable developments of recent centuries. Intellectuals became a secular priesthood, unfettered by the dogmas of the religious past, addressing a growing audience who were becoming increasingly impatient with the moral failures and cultural unsophistication of their clergy.

Note especially the term "secular priesthood" indicating that intellectuals had become rivals of the clergy. Intellectual specialists took their place alongside religious specialists, who had existed since the dawn of human history, or in many cases intellectuals replaced religious leadership as institutions secularized. To some extent the creation of intellectuals has taken place in all of the great civilizations, for example, in the case of the literati in China. However, in nineteenth century Europe, the added element of resistance to dominant religion with a long dominant intellectual clergy, both allied with the state, added a special element of competition for the secular intellectual. Although especially true for Europe, even in the United States learning was dominated by the clergy long into the nineteenth century, even longer than in much of Europe. This meant that many irreligious people would perceive becoming secular intellectuals as a way of challenging religious authority.

In his analysis of the secularization process in the U.S.A. Smith (2003a:37) writes concerning the rising intellectuals:

> Seeking to increase their own cultural authority and class autonomy–and to reinforce their own intellectual *identities* [italics mine]–these knowledge elites struggled to displace Protestantism's authority and to advance themselves as new alternative cultural authorities.

In spite of the reinforcement of intellectual identity through a secularizing program, it does not mean that people become irreligious in order to become intellectual. In fact, it is more likely to happen the other way–people become intellectual because they are irreligious. Being an intellectual is a way to challenge religious authority.

Irreligious identity was made increasingly acceptable in various professions, but more acceptable in some professions than others. This is seen in the data on academicians in the brief review of data in the second section of the chapter. An openly expressed irreligion is acceptable and is even rewarded among some intellectuals and especially in certain professions, such as the social sciences and in literature. Wuthnow (1985:191) discusses this phenomenon:

> [M]any of the studies done among students and aspiring scientists or academicians indicate that it is the irreligious who are selected into academic careers in the first place, not that the process of being socialized into academic life causes them to become less and less religious as time goes on...In short, the conflict between religion and academic careers does not seem to occur as part of the socialization into

> those careers, but prior to it...[T]hose majoring in the social sciences were most likely to have been raised in nonreligious families, humanities students were most likely to have defected from religion in which they were brought up, and natural science students were more likely to have retained their religious faith... The point is that people in the natural sciences not only have higher levels of religiosity later in life than do their counterparts in the social sciences and the humanities but are also less deterred by religiosity from embarking on these careers in the first place.

Thus, in considering the motives for becoming irreligious, the desire for self-esteem does not seem to have aided irreligion movements. It anything, the desire for self-esteem or to gain intellectual support for irreligion may draw the irreligious to become particular types of intellectuals, for example social scientists or writers. In other words, choosing to be irreligious, at least in the United States, does not seem to be made in order to enhance some other aspect of social identity, such as being an intellectual. However, it is possible that in some countries where political power is wielded by Communist Parties, that some might choose to be irreligious in order to gain status within the power structure. Then, what are the rewards that may motivate the irreligious? The answer to this question appears to show a basic weakness in irreligion movements.

The individual choice to be irreligious does not seem to offer the rewards that are ordinarily offered by the choice to be religious, at least by the choice to follow one of the religions that have spread. Religious rewards may well include extrinsic or outward rewards, such as social acceptance and respect or enhancement of ethnic or national identities. The extrinsic rewards of religion, in fact, are ridiculed by the irreligious, who perceive themselves as more intellectually honest. However, in the end the most important rewards offered by religions that are not offered equally by irreligion are the intrinsic rewards of peace, joy, and hope for the future in this life and the next.

What do people say when asked why they doubt or do not believe in God? The extent and basis of religious doubting was investigated and discussed by Smith (1998:154-72). In the first place, contrary to ordinary views, the majority who had attended college, in other words sought to advance in intellectual life, did not find that their experience caused them to doubt their religious beliefs. This supports the view that most beliefs for or against religion are already established before seeking advanced education. When people in the General Social Survey were asked about the problems that caused doubt about their religious faith, 65 percent said the "conflict of faith and science" never caused them doubts, whereas only 5 percent said that it often caused them doubts and 25 percent said it sometimes caused them doubts. The "conflict between faith and science" ranked after "evil in the world" and "personal suffering," but before the "feeling that life really has no meaning" as a source of doubts. One of the major idols of irreligion movements, science, seems not to be a major source for irreligion in the general population. However, the desire of people to have autonomy and be free of religious authority was also not given as a reason for why people doubt.

The "non-religious" (most of whom still believed in God) were specifically asked why they left the religions of their childhood. Of the answers given by 34 people only three seemed to reflect resistance to religious authority: "offended by churches" (7 people or 20.6 percent), "decided religion is false" (6 people or 17.6 percent), and "incompatible moral views" (1 person or 2.9 percent). Although this needs further study, resistance to religious authority, contrary to eighteenth century

France, does not seem to be a major rationale for most Americans who left their religion.

More recently Smith and Denton (2005:86-92) studied and discussed religiously disengaged teenagers. When those who had been raised in a religion were asked why they became nonreligious, the most common answer (32 percent) was some version of intellectual skepticism or disbelief. When the various answers are summarized, it was found that half of nonreligious teens left the faith in which they were raised for "seemingly significant emotional and intellectual reasons, and half drop out or lose their faith for what sound like rather unremarkable reasons," namely they seemed simply to have drifted away. In general, teens followed their parents so that those who were nonreligious tended to have parents who were nonreligious. This supports the view that the major immediate motive in America for being either religious or irreligious is to gain the approval and support of parents and other persons who are the main agents of socialization. It is worth noting, however, that the parents in religious and nonreligious groups identified by Smith and Denton (2005:36) had the following percentages of their teenagers who become nonreligious: Nonreligious–63, Other Religions [minority religions]–35, Indeterminate–32, Jewish–18, Mainline Protestant–17, Black Protestant–17, Latter Day Saints–13, Conservative Protestant–10, and Roman Catholic–10. The many implications of this study are important for those who want to understand teenagers and plan for their guidance in making religious choices, but in terms of understanding motives for choosing to be irreligious (the purpose of this section of the chapter), there does not seem to be any widespread desire to become irreligious because it offers a better option than religion to benefit oneself and others. In America and perhaps much of the world, the lesson may be that irreligion is not a particularly strong challenge to religion, but a kind of negative option for those who do not encounter vital religion. If this is the case, the greatest danger to religion, therefore, is not irreligion, but bad religion that fails to motivate its followers or motivates them in ways that are open to the criticism of irreligion.

CONCLUSION

This chapter was intended to demonstrate that irreligion spreads because of many of the same factors that cause religions to spread, including factors that show irreligion to be, not a lack of religion, but rather another form of religion. The use of the theoretical framework previously used to analyze the spread of religions showed that although the spread of irreligion is based on certain parallel characteristics and conditions to those associated with the spread of religions, that irreligion has certain distinct weaknesses. These weaknesses are best seen in societies where there is religious diversity and people are free to choose to be religions or irreligious.

The modern irreligion movements have been able to spread because they have the freedom to present the following set of beliefs with which to oppose authoritarian religion and to offer as a substitute for religion: (1) science provides a sufficient basis for knowledge and for life, (2) the individual is autonomous and should be free from outside authority, particularly religious authority. In addition, irreligion presents a morality in which it calls for the construction of a new and just society based on science and by individuals who are free from restrictive authorities, especially religious authorities. The social moral ideals associated with irreligion movements have been a means of attracting followers and allies in efforts to change societies. However, the basic fact is that irreligion was not able to emerge as a set of movements until there was sufficient freedom and the economic security for intellectuals to challenge authorities and form mutually supporting networks. These conditions were created in Western Europe after the Protestant Reformation and the subsequent advance of freedom and improved economic conditions in the following centuries.

Irreligion movements began as intellectual elite movements and have remained primarily as such. Justin Barrett (2004:118) notes, "Only privileged minorities enjoy atheism. If religion is the opiate of the masses, atheism is the luxury of the elite." This in itself is not a reason for failure because religious movements, like social movements in general, are usually led by intellectuals. However, irreligion was "tempted" to make the same kind of alliance with governmental power (namely in Communism) as made by religions (in established state religions), and with similar results–the creation of resistance. Nevertheless, irreligion allied with power, just as religion allied with power, seems to be able to exert influence that continues over time (as in East Germany), becoming related to personal identities and the domestic socialization process. It remains a question for investigation as to how long this influence over personal identities (from monopolistic irreligion, as well as monopolistic religion) will last when political power is lost and freedom of thought and belief established.

Inner conflicts in the beliefs of irreligion in scientific reason and the autonomous individual became apparent especially in the efforts to bring about the moral goal of a new humanity in a perfectly just society. In these efforts irreligion used oppressive methods. Irreligion in its political form, some might add also in personal interactions, demonstrated that it could be even more authoritarian and restrictive than religion. Irreligion gained its greatest successes through informal networking among intellectuals and social activists who shared similar moral values, values such as individual freedom, science, and social advancement. These values were created before the irreligion movement, but were co-opted and especially emphasized by it.

Through networking with others in societies with increasing freedoms, irreligion movements have been able to join with others to create secular space for themselves. However, by emphasizing resistance to authority, while at the same time threatening the freedom of others, irreligion movements have not proven themselves strong enough to compete with vital religions in a free environment. The greatest danger to religion turns out to be not irreligion, but the loss of vital religion that falls back on authoritarianism and is perceived as a greater threat to freedom than irreligion.

CHAPTER 9

LOOKING FORWARD

REVIEW OF THE BASIS FOR PREDICTION

This book has distinguished seven categories in which important causes may be found for the spread of religions, specifically for the spread of three religions that have been more successful in spreading than any of the other major religions. These three religions, namely Buddhism, Christianity, and Islam, to name them in historical order, were able to break out of identification with any single ethnic group or set of groups to a greater extent than other religions have been able to do.

It is true that Buddhism spread throughout most of Asia and was not in direct competition with the latter two for most of its history, but rather with other Asian religions. Also, there are about twice as many Hindus as Buddhists (970 million versus 474 million. Johnson, Barrett, and Crossing 2012). But the large majority of Hindus (93 percent) are in India, whereas Buddhists exist in a wide variety of nations (over 150) (Jaffarian 2003). Buddhism has also shown itself somewhat better able to spread in the West than Hinduism. There are more than twice as many Buddhists in America than Hindus. Because the spread of Buddhism has been primarily in Asia until the nineteenth century, the distinctive characteristics of Buddhism, therefore, should be compared primarily with other Asian religions. However, in certain respects,

Buddhism shares characteristics with the other two religions that have spread even more widely. The other two religions, Christianity and Islam, both drew heavily from their mother religion, Judaism, and Islam also from Christianity. Christianity and Islam often have been in contact, competition, and, unfortunately, conflict with one another.

The first three causes for the spread of these religions are found in their content, namely their beliefs, their morality, and the gathering and organization of their followers. These religious content causes were necessary, but not sufficient, for the spread of these religions. Without the distinctive universalistic beliefs and moralities, together with the organizational capacities identified, the three religions would not have spread to the extent that they did. They would have remained confined to limited areas or to particular ethnic groups as other religions. Even these spreading religions show the tendency to become identified with particular ethnic groups, but they were also able to break out of such confinements.

Even though the religious content factors are necessary for the religions to have spread, there are certain secular social causes, external to the religions that have affected their spread, in some cases facilitating, but in other cases blocking them. If we consider the religious content factors as primarily on the meso level of religious group life, the secular social factors are on the macro level of large scale social life (social conditions in receiving societies and intersocietal relationships) and the micro level of individual life (social relationships and motivations). Given the initial presence of the religions prone to spread because of their beliefs, moralities, and abilities to gather and organize, the macro and micro social causes are additional strong reasons for their spread. Any one the social secular factors may block or at least greatly hinder the spread of these religions. They may also facilitate their spread. For example, under the first macro secular social factor considered of conditions in receiving societies, governmental coercion can facilitate the spread of one religion and block the spread of another. But even after facilitating the spread of a religion, government alliance with religion can have negative effects on both. The analysis sought to distinguish what made the social secular factors have these different effects. It was seen that the four categories of secular social factors at the two levels (macro and micro) are distinguished for analytical reasons, but they are to a great extent interacting.

There are not any single sufficient factors or causes for religions to spread, even all of the factors together that I have identified may not be considered entirely sufficient. More factors may be added to or elaborated from those examined. I have given a set of categories of major factors or causes that can be elaborated or specified in further research, some of it social scientific, but some of it more normative or theological. The study raises some questions that are not answerable by the social sciences. For example, what does it say about human nature (not a direct subject for the social sciences) that people respond to the distinctive messages of Buddhism, Christianity, and Islam? What does it say about human nature that people accept these religions with no further evidence than the word of some strangers who come to them with a "message from God?" Basically, what are the implications of this study for those who carry such a message? I will delve into theological matters in the discussion of Missiological Implications in the Chapter 10.

For the sociological analysis of the major part of the book that uses the theoretical framework, I stated Propositions to express key elements of a social scientific theory for the spread of religions. By using propositions, I hope to stimulate discussion and further research and elaboration, both in social scientific and in religious and theological (missiological) studies belonging to the humanities. In the analysis, the Propositions were supported by comparative historical cases. The analysis in each of the seven categories of factors actually included a number of additional theoretical statements, but the Propositions seek to provide at least the main thrust of the argument. The Propositions are listed in Introduction B.

THE CHANGING IMPORTANCE OF THE DIFFERENT CAUSES

The purpose of theory is not only to explain why conditions and phenomena have occurred, but also to aid in predicting the future. While it is difficult, if not impossible, to predict specifically how religions will spread in the future, it is possible to throw light on how the various factors listed and discussed in the book might affect the spread of religions in the future. This is done by considering these factors in combination with trends in world history, many of which have already been identified. In other words, theory about religions should be placed in dynamic relationship with theories about historical changes. This needs to be done because the trends in world history will change the salience of the various causes in the future. I consider below some of the theories of changes identified by social scientists and how they will affect the various causes for religions to spread.

Social scientists use the term "modernization" to describe the changes of the last five centuries. It is not a single or nonreversible process. Collins (1999:155) has identified at least four processes that are part of modernization: bureaucratization, secularization, capitalist industrialization, and democratization. Each of these and other master dimensions of change are much debated and are often used in questionable ways. Rationalization, Weber's favorite term for master change in the West, has proven largely unsatisfactory because of its ambivalence in meaning. However, his work on historical change is highly useful in its contribution to understanding why and how the world has changed. In spite of the impossibility of describing any master process of change in the world and the great irregularity of changes, the fact remains that certain changes have taken place and are continuing to take place that will affect how each of the factors listed in the Propositions will affect the spread of religions.

I will attempt to set forth what I see as possible future developments within the various categories of the theoretical framework. However, instead of beginning with the religious content causes, I will begin with the secular social causes, starting with macro level social factors found in the social conditions of receiving societies (Chapter 4) and continue with the remaining secular social causes: intersocietal relationships (Chapter 5), social relationships (Chapter 6), and motivations (Chapter 7). Finally, I will turn to the religious content causes discussed in Chapters 1 through 3.

INCREASING OPPORTUNITIES FOR CHOICES

The internal social condition in receiving societies that is most relevant to the spread of religions is the possibility for making choices of religions. The fact is that several of the processes involved in modernization are contributing to making social conditions in many societies more favorable for freedom to choose to be identified with a variety of religions. One important reason for this is that democratic ideas and practices, which include freedom of religion, at least in principle, are spreading around the world.

Democracy, which provides for freedom to make political choices, is a complex reality and its development is not fully understood. Collins (1999:155-156) speaks of theories of democratization as being especially unsatisfactory and explains:

> Evolutionary modernization theories are a stumbling block here, for it is not at all clear that democracy is a specifically modern institution, except in the brute historical sense that the societies conventionally taken as exemplars of modernity–Britain and the United States–have been democracies. [He writes earlier, p. 113, of the neglect of democratic developments in the Netherlands.] The structural features of democracy do not follow from any of the classic unidimensional polarities of change (Gesellschaft, differentiation, rationalization). Historically, democratic structures of various kinds existed long before the other dimensions of modernity: collective assemblies in many hunting-and-gathering bands and in tribal societies; Greek city-states; collegial power-sharing bodies of notables, elective kingship, and independent judiciaries in medieval feudalism. The range of historical comparisons needed has been an obstacle to developing a full causal theory of democracy.

In Proposition 4.2 I referred to the fact that freedom of choice existed in small pre-literate societies, particularly with leaders, but this was often lost in later civilizations. There have been periods in which the opportunities for religious choices have actually decreased as they did in the fourth century when the relative pluralism of the Roman Empire was followed by the religious hegemony of monopolistic Christianity in the Mediterranean Basin and later in Western and Eastern Europe. Of course, freedom of religious choice is almost absent in many Muslim countries due to the fusing of religion with governments and the strong association of monopolistic Islam with national identity. At any rate, the ideals of democracy that recognize freedom of religion have found increasing acceptance globally, at least in principle, if not in practice. The increase in political freedom means a certain pressure is exerted toward the increase in freedom of religion. Freedom of religion is often affirmed in newly developed national constitutions. However, even when political freedoms do not exist in practice, there is a growing worldwide recognition that religion cannot be coerced and should be voluntary.

To complicate the picture, although China is not as institutionally democratic as India, a tradition of quasi-secularism in the government combined with the outright secularism of Communism contributed to conditions in which there is greater freedom in making religious choices than in India and some European countries. In India and in Eastern and Southern European countries the linking of nationalism to the traditional religion has created social conditions that make freedom to change religious identities difficult for many people, as seen in Chapter 4. Now, international and internal pressures are for the unlinking of nationalism and religion, but monopolistic religious influences continue forming cultural identities and thereby supporting "culturalism." "Culturalism" like nationalism can be associated with a defensiveness of one's own culture and hence of one's own cultural-religious identity.

Regarding the spread of democracy generally, the difficulty is that most people in many traditional societies have little experience in democratic organization and processes that include open disagreement and debate, and also protection of the rights of individuals to criticize leaders and those with power. Christianity with its mother religion, Judaism, has done more than other religions to give people experience in democratic processes, though much of this has come only in last two centuries. This is often their best gift to the societies in which they exist. There is also usually little experience in traditional societies with one of the most important elements in a democracy, an independent judiciary which can protect the rights of individuals without fear of reprisal. Without an independent judiciary there hardly can be the kind of debate that gives meaning to elections. The concept of the rights of individuals is often not robust in many traditional societies, at least the rights of freedom of thought and speech. Mere survival and economic security have a higher priority in many of these societies. A free press and the right of assembly are also important supports for democracy. Unless these democratic institutions become part of the experience of people, not simply the rhetoric of leaders, then elections, that most people think are the primary element of democracies (even though they are not), have little meaning. Elections are comparatively easy to stage compared to establishing the other important democratic institutions, for example, an independent judiciary and freedom of the press. In spite of all these difficulties and the time required to develop democratic institutions, the direction toward attaining the freedoms protected in democracies has been established for many nations. This bodes well for the increase in the ability of people to choose new religions or irreligion along with making other choices.

Along with the pressure toward the granting of individual rights in the political realm, economic developments (capitalist industrialization) in various parts of the world have given people a greater ability to support an independent life-style in which they can (must) make decisions for themselves. Worldwide industrialization continues to encourage, even require, greater individual autonomy. Norris and Inglehart (2006 [2004]) have drawn attention to the possible influence of increased economic security for decreasing religiosity. At the very least, increased "existential security" gives people the opportunity to avoid any appeal to a "power greater themselves." At the same time, there will be those, who with increased security, have time to contemplate and seek answers to the mysteries of life. They thus have the freedom to choose to be irreligious or to choose to identify with a religion that provides them answers to their questions.

Greater freedom and independency for individuals to make economic choices is accompanied by increased awareness of the varieties of cultures and religions in the world. through worldwide communication, travel, and migration. Perhaps even more important, as individuals and nuclear families move from villages, social ties that tied people to traditional religions and other "interaction ritual chains" (many with religious significance) are weakened or broken. These long-term technical and economic macro trends in numerous nations are likely to continue giving increased autonomy to individuals with opportunities to make choices regarding religions. The vertical transmission of religious identities from generation to generation will continue, but shift from extended to nuclear families, which become increasingly important for such transmission. At the same time, the horizontal transmission of religious identities is likely to increase because of increased freedom for individuals to move about and to make choices free of the influence of previous social ties. Nuclear families become more important in industrial societies in comparison to the larger group, such as the clan or village. At the same time, voluntary associations, such as many religious bodies, increase in industrializing societies.

One of the best illustrations of how new networks and interaction chains are established is the way in which both rural to urban migrants and international immigrants form new religious groups in their new settings. Migrants to urban areas in Latin America and immigrants to North America have greatly stimulated the growth of Pentecostalism and Evangelicalism in new settings (Bowen 1996; Guest 2003). Other religious groups, both traditional and new have also benefited from migration. In North America, mainline churches, as well as newer churches, have benefited greatly from immigrants from Asia, Africa, and Latin America. The spread of Buddhism and Islam has also been greatly aided by the establishment of new social networks by immigrants in new settings in North America and Europe (Kim 1981; Warner and Wittner 1998; Yang 1999).

Secularization is one part of the modernization process that is much debated since it seems to have opposite effects on or correlations with religion in different areas. That is, on the one hand, participation in state established religions has declined (Europe), but participation in voluntary religious associations has increased (United States). Nevertheless, as governments and powerful public institutions separate themselves from religions, then some of the hindrances of the past in making religious choices are removed, including choices to have no religion. Even in democratic societies, the existence of monopolistic or hegemonic religions in these societies offsets the development of freedom in making religious choices. This is due to the tendency for monopolistic religions to be closely identified with the cultures of nations and ethnic groups so that single religions become part of national or ethnic identities. As already noted, Japan, various Buddhist nations in Southeast Asia, almost all Muslim nations, and nations where Orthodoxy, Roman Catholicism, and Protestantism have been monopolistic are examples where social pressures (and some legal restrictions) exist against choosing new religious identities. To choose to identify with a nonmonopolistic religion means in some way to reject national or ethnic identity. Secularization separates religion from nationalism; it also separates religion from culture, although this is a more difficult task.

The rise of irreligion in Europe as a result of the introduction of freedom of choice and in reaction to authoritarian religion was discussed in Chapter 8. Europe has still not recovered from its long period of assigned or imposed rather than chosen religious identities. The evidence from the United States is that religion competes very well with irreligion where there is freedom of religion and there is no strong legacy of assigned religious identity against which to react. In other words, Chapter 8 showed that the introduction of freedom where it did not exist before gives irreligion an opportunity to grow and spread, but in a free environment with a long democratic experience irreligion does not compete well with essentially voluntary and vital religions.

LEVELING OF THE NATIONS AND INCREASING DIVERSITIES AND DISPARITIES AMONG PEOPLE

In regard to intersocietal relationships (Chapter 5), one of the most important changes taking place in the world is the general leveling or equalizing of the nations. This will greatly reduce the negative effects of intersocietal relationships on the spread of religions. Power relationships between peoples have always been important, but after 1500 there was an intensification of power distinctions among nation states and peoples brought on by the increasing contacts of the Western industrializing nations with ancient kingdoms, empires, and scattered peoples around the world. Industrialization in the West, which was preceded by a long period of development (Collins 1999: 167-169), created great contrasts and shifts in power between different areas. The forming of nation states facilitated power struggles and efforts to balance power within Europe. At the same time, the European nations competing with each other initiated a colonial era that gradually reached its climax in the late nineteenth and first half of the twentieth century. Ancient civilizations and smaller power centers and nation states that formed around the world eventually followed the European model and challenged European powers in the latter part of the twentieth century. (Japan had earlier mounted a major challenge by defeating the Russian navy in 1904.) However, the greatest destructive force affecting the European colonizing states was probably the two major conflicts of World Wars I and II that greatly weakened the European centers of power. Shortly after the middle of the twentieth century, colonialism, as it had been known, collapsed. Thus European expansion, which was followed eventually by the collapse of colonialism, greatly stimulated the growth of new nations and the assertion of sovereign powers. This has been accompanied by increasing consciousness of ethnic, national, and religious identities.

Collins (1999:70-109) presents a state-centered theory of ethnicity in which geopolitical relations between states are the switch that determines whether nations move toward "Balkanization" (multi-ethnic hostility) or "Americanization" (multi-ethnic harmony). Collins' argument is important for the future spread of religions based on the predictions of Propositions 5.1 and 5.2. Whether nations move toward multi-ethnic hostility or harmony bears directly on how religions may on the one hand become part of maintaining ethnic distinctiveness in a hostile atmosphere or on the other hand may play no part in ethnic relations so that ethnic groups may become open to new religions. If religions help to maintain ethnic distinctiveness, such ethnic groups become very hostile to new religions. If the connection between ethnicity and religion is broken, then there is greater freedom for new religions to spread.

There is not enough space here to review Collins' (1999) whole argument. In short, he first explains how ethnic groups are socially constructed using physical and linguistic distinctions and other markers such as family names and cultural or life-style differences. Religions have usually been a part of the cultural distinctiveness of ethnic groups. When ethnicity is oriented toward using the state as an instrument you have ethno-nationalism, which is the highest degree of ethnic mobilization. An option exists, however, to back away from creating a strong ethno-nationalist citizenship to creating a multicultural or tolerant citizenship in which there is a coalition of ethnic identities sharing in legitimacy.

Collins (1999) makes the geopolitical strength of the state a key to the power-prestige of dominant ethnic groups, which in turn determines the degree to which internal smaller groups assert their identities. "Balkanization" or ethnic separation is the result of a weak state. On the other hand, a geopolitical balance of power between strong nations fosters cosmopolitanism in which ethno-nationalism is devalued. An increased harmony between internal ethnic groups is possible, which means that there will be less emphasis on ethnic markers. One of these ethnic markers, of course, is religion. With less stress on religion as an ethnic marker there will be increased openness to new religions and the movement of religions between ethnic groups.

The leveling of the power of nation states or the movement toward a geopolitical balance of power that accompanied the collapse of colonialism has been very conducive to the spread of religions, a major example being the spread of Christianity in Africa. Christianity began its most rapid growth after the collapse of colonialism. At the same time, as states remain weak, ethno-religious groups remain defensive. If the leveling of the power of nation states continues into the future, ethno-religious groups will become less defensive. Regarding leveling of the power of nations, the case of the United States is an indicator of the general direction of change. Following World War II, the greatest world power of the day, the United States, was held to a stalemate in Korea. Then it was challenged successfully by a small nation, Vietnam, which was able to establish its independence and national unity. Of course, part of the reason for the stalemate in Korea and the defeat of the United States in Vietnam was the restraint place upon the United

States by its own and international norms against the mass killing of civilians (as had earlier taken place in World War II). These nations could have been defeated as Japan was defeated with atomic weapons, but the moral and political restraints were too strong.

The United States has found it increasingly necessary and useful to cooperate in numerous international relationships. It did succeed in overcoming the threat of the Soviet Union. At the writing of this book (Second Edition) the United States is still involved militarily in Afghanistan, although it has withdrawn from Iraq. It also maintains a military presence in various places, most notably in South Korea. The restraint against producing large scale collateral damage with civilian casualties is still in effect, making it very difficult to defeat even weak states. However, hostile state power is not the major problem. The use of terrorism as the weapon of those without the power of ordinary states, but with deeply held grievances has increased and has been extremely difficult to stop. Whatever the future may hold in detail, it seems clear that the ability of the United States or any powerful state that observes the restraints of internal and international moral norms to extend its power over other states is more limited than it has ever been, for example, as it was before and at the time of World War II. The need for states to seek coalitions with other states is likely to increase, not decrease, which points to the slow increase of the influence of the United Nations and regional coalitions of nations.

While the collapse of colonialism and imperial pretensions has greatly leveled the nations politically and militarily, globalization with highly increased interchanges of people, goods, and knowledge has highlighted and increased local diversities and disparities. Two kinds of diversity have appeared. One is cultural diversity as people hold on to and assert local cultures in opposition to intruding cultures. The other kind of diversity is less benign and consists of economic differences that industrial capitalism has exacerbated. These great disparities and inequities in wealth both within and among nations lead to considerable resentment and strained relationships. The challenge to all nations and the international system as a whole is to create and maintain the means of upward mobility that give hope to disadvantaged people that are easily oppressed by the privileged. Religions are also challenged to facilitate upward mobility through education and through promoting greater economic justice. Of course, establishing economic justice has caused controversy from the time of the Biblical prophets and requires modern prophets, many of whom find there strongest opposition from within religious communities. This is evidence of the great need for religious diversity within societies.

There is evidence that a leveling of the nations has begun technologically and economically, which is certainly linked to the leveling of political power. Thomas Friedman (2005) has written about this technological and economic leveling that will dominate the twenty first century as *The World is Flat*, which is similar to my "leveling of the nations." He focuses particularly on the large nations of China and India, whose economies are rapidly expanding and who have large bodies of trained engineers and technicians. These skilled people are already linked closely to the world economy, as well as contributing to the development of their own lands. Although there is still great disparity of wealth within these lands, the very size of their economies and their continuing rapid economic growth promises to make these nations leading forces in the world. One of the most dramatic developments in this worldwide linking of technologies and economies is the personal contacts between American customers and technicians located in India. In addition, trained scientists and technicians from Asian countries are employed by American companies, many with bases of operations in other parts of the world, including their countries of origin. Predictions regarding how nations will balance their power and be related to one another politically and economically are very difficult to make. However, the trend toward increasing interconnection, exchange, and cooperation among nations is clear. From a religious perspective this making the world small and flat will give individuals increasing opportunities to know the world and its religions and to make choices, including religious choices.

In the last section we saw that the macro level trends in internal social structures are in the direction of greater opportunities for individuals to make religious choices. In this section it is seen that the reduction in domination and threat in international relations and growing multi-culturalism within nations reduces the need to maintain group solidarity through assertion of distinctive religio-cultural identities. Although the consciousness of ethnic and national identities has continually increased, with the decrease in domination in international relations, there is less sense of threat to these identities than previously. Thus the macro level hindrance to the spread of religions of the association of intersocietal domination with their spread (Propositions 5.1 and 5.2) will become less important. This, combined with the reduction of the macro level hindrance of social structural limitations on choices (Propositions 4.1-4.6) throws greater weight to the micro level influences for the spread of religions (Propositions 6.1, 6.2, 6.3, 7.1, 7.2). The growth of individualism and increase in knowledge exchange are having striking effect in numerous nations. These micro level factors will have major effects on the spread of religions, though in changing ways. It is worth considering what these may be.

INCREASING INDIVIDUALISM IN SOCIAL RELATIONSHIPS AND IN MOTIVATIONS

The discussion in the previous sections shows that macro level factors (social conditions within societies and intersocietal relations) are changing and are sometimes chaotic. They will remain important, but micro factors working through individuals because of increasing individualism will increase in importance in their effect on spreading religions. New approaches in the social sciences will be developed to understand the thoughts and actions of individuals.

Charles Tilly (1984:29) brings together the concerns of Chapters 6 and 7 in an interesting way. He shows how identities or categories of individuals, discussed in Chapter 7, and social relationships or networks, discussed in Chapter 6, come together to form a single factor referred to as catnet:

> A population forms a catnet (category x network), finally, to the extent that both conditions–common characteristics and linking ties–apply. A catnet, thus described, comes close to the intuitive meaning of the word "group." Nuclear families, households, firms, voluntary associations, churches, states, armies, and parties, among other sets of persons, commonly meet the criteria for a catnet. Whether those entities we refer to indecisively as communities, institutions, classes, movements, ethnic groups, and neighborhoods, correspond to genuine catnets remains an empirical question: Some do, some don't. Societies, cultures, civilizations, peoples, publics, and masses, as analysts ordinarily use these words, almost never qualify as catnests. Indeed, in most cases the words do not even designate bounded populations, categories, or networks. The elementary units of categories, networks,

and catnets are not individual mental events, but relationships: relationships established by the sharing of social characteristics on the one hand and by the presence of social ties on the other.

Tilly (1984:30) goes on to stress the value of rational-action models over society driven irrationalism that has dominated explanations of social movements in the social sciences, noting that this doesn't mean that all collective action is "fundamentally calculated, willed, desirable, feasible, and efficacious." Rather, "We need only assume, provisionally, a coherent set of relationships among the interests, organization, shared beliefs, and actions of the actors." I understand this to mean that as societies move toward allowing greater freedom and movement, individual thoughts, feelings, and actions in small group relationships will become increasingly important in societies, including in religious decisions.

In the following trend analysis I have drawn much from Collins (2004). He now pushes the social sciences toward the development of a sociology of emotions. He (2004: 366) notes the historical movement toward individualism and the focus on the inner life: "The transition from religious inwardness to the modern introverted personality was set in motion with the Protestant Reformation." Then he (2004:368) describes the modern outcome:

> Secular rituals and their cult objects, as we have seen, range across mass entertainment and sport; technical equipment; hobby materials; texts and objects of art; substances for bodily ingestion; the shaping of the body itself. These markets give rise to the modern fan, the nerd, the hobbyist, the intellectual and the connoisseur, the addict, the exercise or weight-control fanatic – personality types scarcely found in medieval and ancient societies.

Ad hoc and voluntary gatherings have replaced the involuntary participation in community and household gatherings typical of traditional societies. However, in addition, oppositional groupings have formed, for example, religious and moral communities define themselves in contrast to groups they consider immoral or overly secularized. Also, "intellectuals, the technology-obsessed, alienated introverts, and various kinds of solitary cultists" define themselves in contrast to their opposites, as their opposites likewise distinguish themselves from the solitary. The modern "cult of the individual," beginning mainly after 1500, has accelerated since the middle of the twentieth century. However, this historical shift does not represent simply the creation of individuals, but rather is an historical product so that attention is drawn to the inner life of all people. Everyone gains "the standing of at least honorary introvert" (Collins 2004 372). The paradox is, as Collins discusses at great length in his analysis of modern life, the emotional energy (EE) that everyone seeks in the inner life is generated in ritual interaction, both informal and formal, with others. The catnets of Tilly (1984) will continue to be important for spreading and sustaining religions, but individuals will increasingly be concerned with how well the religious groups to which they belong are able to satisfy their inner needs.

Religions will increasingly be forced to acknowledge that their primary appeal must be based on the content of their faith and its inherent or intrinsic rewards. This will take place with the spread of secularization in the world that separates religion from authority in public life and places the provision of many services in secular institutions. Religion becomes basically personal and voluntary. Both Buddhism and Islam have been able to appeal to individuals in the West who are particularly aware of (and have experienced) the failures of Christianity. In the case of Islam, it has been particularly the complicity of Christianity with racism that has helped to turn people, primarily, but not solely, African Americans, from Christianity. Becoming Muslim has given them an enhanced sense of personal identity as belonging to an egalitarian spiritual family that successfully opposed Christianity. Buddhism has been especially appealing to intellectuals, many of whom do not like authoritarian Christianity and are looking for a religion that emphasizes inner spirituality. This attraction to the mainly intrinsic rewards of Buddhism and Islam, as well as of other religions and no religion, is likely to continue due to various failings of Christianity as the dominant religion.

Growing individualism does not mean that people always carefully calculate their decisions. At the same time people do make decisions and form networks that "make sense" to them because they find inner satisfaction through them. Religions that take seriously each individual's unique set of relationships and search for an emotionally satisfactory life are most likely to gain followers.

The attempt to look forward so far has shown that the micro level causes for the spread of religions are likely to increase in importance as the macro level causes become increasingly "made constant" through the spread of opportunities for freedom in making religious choices in societies and the leveling of national power and ethnic status. This brings us to the most significant prediction for religions. The shift toward the importance of micro level causes means increasing attention will be given to religious content in the spread of religions.

THE CONTENT OF RELIGIONS

After reviewing future changes in the social factors affecting the spread of religions, I turn to the factors that were considered first in the book: the beliefs, morality, and gathering and organization abilities of religions (Chapters 1 through 3). In many ways these are at the meso level of human experience, which will increasingly be approached from below (the micro level), while at the same time, the macro level of broad social changes will continue to be important. One thing appears clear: people will give increasing attention to the content of religions. The discussion above has already noted this fact. With more opportunities for individual choices and the creation of social networks with their own interaction chains, people will take more seriously than ever before the content of beliefs, both religious and irreligious. Even the increase in "existential security" (Norris and Inglehart (2006 [2004]), while setting people free from "foxhole religion" will give people more time to contemplate the meaning of life and the answers given by religions. The greater possibilities of making personal religious choices will be accompanied by an ever increasing free flow of information around the world, which will include information about religions.

The content of religions have conceptual and experiential parts. People will want to know not only the articulation or statement of beliefs of religions, but also the emotional and moral energies that are available through religious activity. What does it mean in one's life to be an actual follower or member of a religious group? This means that the second part or participatory or interaction aspect of religions will come especially under scrutiny. It will be crucial for religions, therefore, how well they are able to incorporate people so that they feel fully accepted and part of vital communities.

If this prediction is correct, there will an increasing discussion of the persons of Buddha, Jesus Christ, and Muhammad and of the meaning of what they said and did. This also means that the quality of life demonstrated by their followers and of the communities to which they belong will also come under scrutiny. Individuals within these religions will find themselves asking more than ever, "What do I really believe?" and "Am I getting from my faith what I should be getting from it?" Religions will be increasingly required to define themselves and what they have to offer, particularly as intrinsic rewards. The important implication for Christians of these predictions will be discussed in Chapter 10.

It will be the organized followers who will primarily carry on the discussions and do the proclamation of the message of each religion, as well as demonstrate the quality of life resulting from their faith and found in their religious communities. There are numerous diverse groups of followers of each of the religions and they disagree strongly among themselves. The diversity itself will add to the richness, some would say confusion, of the discussion. This leads to the consideration of the problem of conflict between and among religions that has become a major concern, even raising fears that conflicts fed by religions will lead to a "clash of civilizations" (Huntingdon 1996). Will increased attention to the content of religions lead to an increase of one of the great plagues of human existence, religiously based or fed conflicts? I believe it will not, but will address this fear next.

The shift to focus on belief content is just beginning. In Chapter 8 I reviewed the spread of irreligion as a significant phenomenon of the last two centuries beginning in Europe, but extending around the world. I necessarily simplified irreligion to contrast its spread to that of religions, but it is clear that both religion and irreligion have become very complex realities in modern societies. Just as there will be increasing focus on the belief and practice content of the various religions, so there will be more attention in the future to clarifying the range of beliefs and practices that are represented in the various irreligions of modern societies. It has become clear that irreligion is not so much nonbelief, but rather contains a range of different beliefs and moralities. These will gain increasing attention by scholars. One of the signs of this among sociologists has been the "turn to culture" in which they take seriously the drive among humans to find or create, live by, and transmit meaning in life.

Jeffrey Alexander (2003) is a leading sociologist who gives attention to the content of the beliefs people live by. He criticizes the materialistic philosophy represented by Marxism and the "radical historicism" of the Critical Social Theory coming out of Germany as unrealistic. He makes it clear that even in modern technologically based life, beliefs come into play. Contrary to those who reject the view that life rests on norms and posited meanings, he (2003:184) states: "The ideas that inform even the most modern societies are not cognitive repositories of verified facts; they are symbols that continue to be shaped by deep emotional impulses and molded by meaningful constraints."

It turns out that human beings, including scholars, live by beliefs that can be expressed in narratives as pointed out by Christian Smith (2003) in his book, *Moral, Believing Animals*. Smith (2010) gave a full expression of human capacities that included belief and moral formation in his (2010) book, *What is a Person?: Rethinking Humanity, Social Life, and the Moral Good from the Person Up*. He places belief content, especially of those who assume they have no beliefs, but live by "the facts," squarely in the center of his discussion. Smith (2003:54,55) says, "We are all necessarily trusting, believing animals, creatures who must and do place our faith in beliefs that *cannot themselves be verified except by means established by the presumed beliefs themselves* (italics his).

One of the areas where Smith puts into effect his view that life is based on beliefs is in his study of American teenagers. First of all, he (2005:181) notes that some teenagers like their parents are still accepting "cultural mentalities," namely beliefs, such as logical positivism and naïve empiricism that have been discredited in the academy for decades as philosophically untenable. In other words, there is a kind of "residual version of these old doctrines" of irreligion that remains in popular culture. Some people still enjoy being the "village atheist." As we move into the twenty first century, the presence and corrosive influence of these kinds of beliefs that are present in much of secularized aspects of society, for example in education, literature, and the media, will be increasingly revealed for what they are: beliefs that are in conflict with other beliefs.

However, it is not only that irreligion is represented by a variety of beliefs, but modern humans are creating new combinations of religious beliefs (Davie, Heelas, Woodhead 2003). Some of these new religions are organized and self-conscious and have long been studied by sociologists of religion. However, perhaps more interesting and significant for religious leaders to take seriously are the unorganized and informal belief systems that exist alongside and even within the religions that have their own traditional and long-held "official" beliefs. Smith and Denton (2005: 162, 163) identify such a set of religious beliefs Based on interviews with 267 teens in 45 states they describe the dominant "creed" of American teenagers as "Moralistic, Therapeutic Deism" that may be summarized:

> 1. A God exists who created and orders the world and watches over human life on earth.
> 2. God wants people to be good, nice, and fair to each other, as taught in the Bible and by most religions.
> 3. The central goal of life is to be happy and to feel good about oneself.
> 4. God does not need to be a particularly involved in one's life except when God is needed to resolve a problem.
> 5. Good people go to heaven when they die.

It is not that these beliefs are bad or wrong in themselves, but they are extremely vague and indicate little in depth in knowledge of Christianity or other religion. What is important to consider, however, is that the content of this teenager dominant religious creed is drawn from parents and mentors. It is not simply the creation of teenagers, but is based on what they have learned from believing parents who do not have a very clear grasp of the contents of classical Christianity.

This study provides a strong challenge to both religious bodies and parents to communicate their faith clearly. The increasing need for clarifying belief and moral content provides a major challenge to religious leaders together with religious parents, who have the task of teaching what cannot be taught through the secularized institutions of modern society. In addition, individuals cannot escape their responsibility to clarify their own deeply held beliefs and not be simply dependent on assenting to others.

RELIGIOUS CONFLICT

Given the history of religions, one of the major concerns about them is that the increasing religious diversity within societies being predicted here will lead to increased conflict in the world, especially with the shift to focus on the content of religions. Lester Kurtz (1995:211) in his sociological study of world religions states, "Few concerns of social life can lead as readily to conflict as the combination of religious differences with other forms of struggle." Of the three spreading religions, the greatest concern at present is conflict between followers of Christianity and Islam, both religions that call for an exclusive commitment.

At the present time there are some signs that seem to support the dire predictions of those, who see coming a general conflict between Christian and Islamic civilizations, although not between the actual religions. Samuel P. Huntington (1996) expresses this view:

> The underlying problem for the West is not Islamic fundamentalism. It is Islam, a different civilization whose people are convinced of the superiority of their culture and are obsessed with the inferiority of their power. The problem for Islam is not the CIA or the U.S. Department of Defense. It is the West, a different civilization whose people are convinced of the universality of their culture and believe that their superior, if declining, power imposes on them the obligation to extend that culture throughout the world. These are the basic ingredients that fuel conflict between Islam and the West.

In the first place, it is rapidly becoming clear (Walls 1996, Jenkins 2002; Sanneh 2003) that Christianity cannot be identified with the West, but rather with major areas of the non-Western world. Furthermore, both the West and the areas in which Islam predominates are divided into numerous national states that have often been in conflict with one another. Not only so, but Western and Islamic nations have often been in alliances with one another against alliances of other Western and Islamic nations. Consider the terrible wars in the twentieth century in which Western nations were pitted against each other and Islamic nations against each other with Western nations having alliances outside of the West and Islamic nations having alliances with non-Islamic nations.

Akbar Ahmed (2003:17) writes that the simplistic division of Islam versus the West is no longer valid, and adds:

> Besides, the traditional Muslim division of the world has collapsed: What Muslims once saw as the

> distinction between dar al-harb (house of war), land of anarchy and disbelief, and dar al-Islam (house of peace or Islam) in which they could practice their faith and flourish, is no longer valid. In the last decades of the 20th century the division became largely irrelevant. Muslims could freely practice their faith and flourish in the United States and elsewhere; meanwhile they were persecuted in Iraq. After September 2001, the distinction disappeared altogether. Muslims everywhere felt under siege. Nowhere was safe. No society was immune to the forces of chaos and anarchy. Violence was routine. The entire world had become dar al-harb.

Carl Ernst (2003:3-11) is another among those who seriously questions Huntington's division of civilizations and prediction of "an eventual death struggle" between the West and the Islamic world. There are more than fifty nations that have a majority Muslim population with "a bewildering diversity of languages, ethnic groups, and differing ideological and sectarian positions." Furthermore, the basic roots of so-called Western civilization, which include Middle Eastern and Greek influences, are shared with Islam. What is taking place now is that religious language, and I would add cultural language, is being used rhetorically as a vehicle for political opposition. When the complexities of the history of Islam are examined, even the term "Islam," like the terms "Hinduism," and "Buddhism," is seen to be a European product of the colonial encounter and of the Muslim response to it. (We should also be reminded that "Christianity" is not a Biblical term and that even "religion" is a socially constructed concept, at least partly like "race.")

Having said all of this about the unreality of a Western-Islamic divide, rhetoric and attitudes, especially since September 11, 2001, have made it seem real, which increases its danger. Osama bin Laden used the language of Islam selected for his purposes, against the West and found much popular support in the Islamic world. At the same time, Islamaphobia has become a rising tide in the United States and Europe. Some people, unfortunately, are using the rhetoric of Al Queda calling for an Islamic "caliphate" stretching from the Atlantic to Southeast Asia to raise fears. This phobia overlooks the fact that no such "empire" has ever existed and that Islam, since the eighth century, has existed in and supported a number of competing nations. It is becoming clearer that a set of radical groups with a loose affiliation, now usually called "Islamists" or Al Queda (better terms than "fundamentalists" which comes out of Christianity), have reacted with violence against the West, and, as noted, most significantly they have received broad support from Muslim populations, not because of their violence, but because of common grievances.

Western nations, particularly the United States, need to pay greater attention to what has stimulated the violent actions of relatively small groups, who nevertheless have attracted sympathy from many Muslims. Ahmed (2003:62) points to the extreme importance of honor and dignity in traditional societies and how many Muslims feel that their honor has been violated while the Western societies do not uphold the concept of honor that they take for granted. Many other feelings have been generated by the impact of Western culture so that, in short, Islam is in turmoil. In Ahmed's analysis (2003:46) the basic problem is that:

> Islamic societies–like other world cultures influenced by traditional religions – are reacting to the global transformations taking place. The reaction is a mixture of anger, incomprehension, and violent hatred. There is also an element of fascination with

Western modernity and therefore a seduction. The relationship between Islam and modernity is much more complex than the simplistic clash of civilizations theories would have us believe.

To understand the reaction to the modern world, Ahmed makes use of the early Muslim social scientist, Ibn Khaldun (1332-1406) (a true pioneer in the field), and his theory of asabiyya, which refers to group loyalty, social cohesion, or solidarity. Ahmed (2003:158) states: "By recognizing the argument of this book–that Muslim societies are in a state of turmoil as a consequence of the breakdown in social cohesion and the resulting sense of anomie–the West can help Muslims rebuild their sense of dignity and honor." The way forward will not be easy because of the complexity and plurality of modern societies. There are traditions of openness and toleration in Islam that can be drawn upon. Ahmed (2003:162-163) challenges those who believe in God to realize that "God certainly does not approve of sharing praise with rivals called 'tribe' or 'nation.'" He goes on, "By conflating God and the group, leaders of the community employ an effective strategy: The honor of the group can now be defended in the name of God. As a consequence we see the emergence of a frenetic, distorted and dangerous form of asabiyya–one I am calling hyper-asabiyya." Social scientists and theologians are both challenged to spread understanding of these issues of the misuse of religion to justify group action.

Islamic scholars, both theologians and others, have a task before them to save Islam from those who are actually distorting its traditions, particularly those traditions that predate the colonial period, at which time most Islamic lands came under outside domination. At the same time, Christian theologians and writers in general in the West, have an important task to help people understand the sources of anger and frustration in Muslim populations.

A major task for Christians is to look at themselves and understand how Christianity was subverted by its alliances with governments. There is no doubt that religions have provided a rationale or legitimization for conflict, just as they have provided legitimization for the force exercised by governments on their own people. In Christian history, the establishment of the state church in the fourth century imposed Christianity on populations for many centuries. Thus by adopting secular power to maintain and advance itself Christianity "fell" for the temptation its founder rejected. It distorted the doctrine of a noncoercive God exemplified in Jesus Christ by using force to establish conformity (Jenkins 2010). This distortion created an enormous impression on Westerners and non-Westerners that is partly responsible for anti-Christian and anti-religion secularism in the West and anti-Christianity from the old civilizations. Islam arose some 300 hundred years after the fourth century association of Christianity with coercive power. Would Islam have arisen if it had encountered a voluntarily based Christianity under a secular state instead of an imposed and persecuting Christianity allied with the state? Later, the association of Christianity with the Crusades and then the spread of Christianity with colonialism only strengthened the sense of Christian association with force and coercion. Continuing conflict within Christianity, as in Northern Ireland, between Christians and Muslims, as in Africa and Indonesia, and between Jews and Muslims, as in and around Israel, all contribute to the sense that religion engenders conflict.

What is most important in the theoretical perspective of this book, however, is that force has been much less important for the actual spread of religions than is conventionally thought. The secularization process, understood as the separation of religion from a position of power or domination (not influence) in public institutions, therefore, has been ultimately good for the spread of religions. It meant forsaking the notion that religion is something that can be forced on people. Both Christianity and Islam, the religions that have had the most association with force and conflict, both agree in principle that religion cannot be coerced. Jesus told his disciples if they were not welcomed to go on somewhere else (Mark 6:11). In the Qur'an (Surah 2: Verse 256) it says, "There is no compulsion in religion."

The secularization process in the sense of separating religion from governmental and other public institutional power will undoubtedly continue. This does not lead necessarily to a decrease in religion, at least religion both of the heart and of the voluntary association, especially where people are not reacting against monopolistic religion. However, the decrease of religious power may lead to the decrease of religion as simply a culture or social identity marker that is ascribed to people. This is because as the external constraints seen in the macro factors of Chapters 4 and 5 that favored particular religions are reduced, people have increased freedom of choice to examine the content of religions and to make their own choices of commitment and association. However, the decrease of religion as a culture or social identity marker provides an opportunity for religion to increase as a voluntary activity. The best evidence for this is what has taken place in the United States and is taking place in many non-Western countries with the growth of Christianity.

The fact is that religious pluralism is here to stay, even if there are setbacks at different times and places. Robert Wuthnow (2005:287) points out that religious pluralism means that religions with fundamentally different claims exist alongside each other. In the United States so far the response among religious people has been to become either "exclusivists" or "inclusivists." The former does not consider other religions worthy of understanding and the latter, which is highly relativistic, does not understand the significance of deep religious commitment. Wuthnow advocates a "reflective pluralism," which is briefly described in the next section.

DIALOGUE OR CONVERSION?

It is commonplace for those who want to avoid religious conflict to encourage dialogue between religions. Dialogue has its place because it is important for religious people to be familiar with the history and thought of other religions in a religiously diverse world, especially the perceptions religious groups have of each other. In addition, and perhaps most important, dialogue gives personal experience with the essential humanness of others. Dialogue, in which different religious perspectives are set forth, is better than debate, in which the two sides are trying "to score points" and be declared "winners." Dialogue corresponds to mutual education and should be associated with the study of the writings of and about the religions of others. At the same time, study of religions should not avoid the subject of popular religion and the way in which religions have influence the behavior of whole societies.

Having emphasized the importance of dialogue and mutual study, however, it is unrealistic and inappropriate to ask religions to give up the goal of conversion of others. Tolerance does not require declaring that all religions are alike. Convinced followers believe that they have a treasure in their religion to share and would be selfish not to share their treasure. Of course, there are ways of attempting to convert others that are not appropriate. This is an area where many people are too ready to place limits on religious people simply because they find attempts to convert others to be irritating or offensive. People may resent the efforts of others to convert them because of psychological reasons related to their own resistance to conversion and to participation in active religious life. Whatever the reason, as long as civil rights, and

I would add "civility," are observed, I have no objection to someone trying to convert me as long as they allow me the right to try to convert them. Governments can and should protect civil rights to privacy, but in a religiously diverse world, all people should have the right to have access to knowledge about any and all religions, as well as have the right to disseminate information about their religion. The world is moving in the direction of making access to knowledge about all religions a reality for all people. Freedom of thought and religion demand this.

Thus dialogue and the goal of conversion of others both have their place and are not necessarily mutually exclusive. However, it is important that the goals of dialogue and conversion be pursued in appropriate ways that are commonly called "civil." An approach that can be placed alongside dialogue and conversion will greatly aid not only in maintaining civility, but in actually advancing religious cooperation. Wuthnow (2005:287-292) advocates such an approach, which he calls "reflective pluralism," in response to the condition of religious diversity. A summary of the characteristics of such a response are: (1) Interest in the substantive aspects of pluralism, particularly a "focal issue" of another religion that is particularly puzzling; (2) Becoming a "studier" of other religions; (3) Consideration of how particular "views" are formed; (4) Emphasizing respect for the personal religious identity of people; (5) Showing a willingness to compromise, which is not giving up deeply held beliefs and values, but being willing to "move into social or emotional space in which differences are more common." I see as underlying "reflective pluralism" a willingness to consider not simply the explicit beliefs and practices of other religions, but even more the reasons why people believe and practice what they do and also why they tend to emphasize certain beliefs and practices. Many people are blind to how their views are socially conditioned and assume that they are "objective." Certainly the social sciences are useful for creating awareness of the social conditioning of all people, including oneself and one's religion (or no religion). Whatever one may think of Wuthnow's "reflective pluralism," the fact is that inter-religious cooperation is beginning to take place in the United States and other places, with some efforts failing and some succeeding. In the end, those that succeed are those that are self-critical and recognize "the sincerity and seriousness with which followers of other religions practice their faith" (Wuthnow 2005:305). Probably one of the best areas of inter-religious dialogue is in the area of morality. Given the mixed history of religions in this area, and the disagreements within religions, there is much that can be learned from each other.

CONCLUSION

A basic conclusion of this chapter is that the growth of individualism and of freedom to make religious choices around the world means that increasing attention will be given to the belief contents of religions and irreligion(s) together with the experiences they offer individuals as a source of meaning for their lives. This places great responsibility on religious bodies to proclaim and teach the content of their beliefs and morality. It also means that religious bodies must give great attention to the quality of organized group life they offer to people. In particular, does their religious group life offer the formal and informal "interaction rituals" that are deeply satisfying?

Although it is clear that social factors that facilitate or block the spread of religions will always be present, the focus on individual rights and freedoms reduces the hindering effect of macro social factors on the spread of religions. The macro factors of increasing opportunities for choices within societies, and increasing international equality, will facilitate people receiving new religions under conditions of the free international flow of information about religions. However, the persistence of governmental control of religions, the identification of culture with religion, and the continuation of international tension and conflict will continue to make the macro level social factors a negative force on the spread of religions. In the face of outside threat, autocratic governments will continue to limit freedom of religion. Traditional societies where monopolistic religions are identified with particular ethnic and cultural groups will continue to limit other religions to the best of their abilities. Religion as an ethno-cultural identity marker will continue to be an major obstacle to the spread of religions. This will be the case in lands where particular world religions make up the majority of the population. However, the increasing free flow of information in the world means that people will be able to compare various religious beliefs and the quality of life they offer. Even more important, the leveling of power among nations means the reduction of the ability of nations to threaten one another. Therefore the perception of outside threat to national and ethnic identities is reduced. Traditional religion thereby becomes less important as a support for ethnic identity. Religious leaders will have to give up their attempts to maintain followers on the basis of their religion as a cultural marker.

These directions of change will cause micro level factors affecting individuals to gain in relative importance over macro factors in the spread of religions. The social relations of individuals will increasingly be of two types: relations with close family members and relations in voluntary associations to which they belong. This will cause religious voluntary associations to become increasingly important, as well as with the families they are a part of.

With increased self-consciousness, individuals will give greater attention to the effects of religions and of irreligions on the self, particularly how self-esteem may be increased and how emotional needs for inner joy, peace, and satisfaction are attained. This means giving increased attention to the meaning of the rewards offered by religions; whether they are more intrinsic or extrinsic and whether they tend to be offered as earned rewards and obtained through some kind of exchange or whether they are offered as outcome rewards from a life under Divine grace. Likewise, irreligion will be increasingly challenged regarding what it offers in terms of meaning and purpose for life. The major division of people will not be between the religious and irreligious, but between people with different kinds of beliefs and moralities. Thus, individuals will be divided between those choosing extrinsic and tangible rewards and those choosing intrinsic and intangible rewards. Some will prefer to have a sense of having earned their spiritual status and others come to realize that everything comes as a gift of grace. Increasingly individuals will face religious choices along with the other choices of life. The growing emphasis on the rights and responsibilities of individuals means that people will want to know ever more clearly the religious options before them.

Religiously diversity within societies will increase, together with the push for public legitimacy characteristic of religious pluralism. This will challenge religious leaders and members to provide clear teaching, but to also gain understanding and respect for the members of other religions with which they will be in contact as never before. The recognition of adherents of other religions as human beings will be considered first. Even what it means to be human persons will gain increased attention. Religious tension and conflict may flare up in different parts of the world, but efforts to cooperate in certain social service and even religious goals are also likely to increase.

CHAPTER 10

IMPLICATIONS FOR MISSIONS

The purpose of this book is to present a sociological analysis of the spread of religions, an important historical phenomenon of the last two millennia, but a phenomenon rarely studied in the social sciences. The social sciences can only view religions and their spread as human phenomena. Missiologists, who seek to understand the work of God in human history, have the task of incorporating valid findings from the social sciences into their theological perspective. This study demonstrates that various social forces, including religions themselves, affect the spread of religions. Since mission planners want to participate in God's work in the world, they need to relate social scientific findings about the world to their mission planning.

In the following discussion, I will develop implications for mission planning based on the analysis in the chapters of the book. This chapter is meant to demonstrate some ways in which Christian missiologists can make use of social scientific work. None of the implications or applications discussed below are unique in missiological study and discussion, but the social scientific analysis helps to place an emphasis on certain activities which might otherwise be overlooked or not given due attention. Social scientific findings can enable missiologists to post guide signs, as well as warning signs, for mission work. The discussion is certainly not meant to be exhaustive. My major hope is the applications presented will stimulate discussion, study, and change in viewpoint where these topics have been neglected or not emphasized.

In each section, I state the Propositions that belong to each of the categories of the theoretical framework and guide the analysis in the related chapter. After dealing with the implications of the analysis in each of the seven categories, I will add a section on the implications of the spread of irreligion. Each section of the missiological implications also will take into account the projections of Chapter 9.

FOCUS ON JESUS CHRIST

1.1 *The three widely spreading religions build on the source of the widespread influence of popular religion, which is its immanent, accessible, and tangible means of contact with transcendent sources of power for help in coping with the difficulties of life.*

1.2 *The most powerful religious belief factor affecting the spread of religions is the presentation of a single human figure who becomes a means of access to the divine and to salvation through the offer of compassion.*

The findings that support these propositions were quite exciting to me. Proposition 1.1 does not deal directly with the spread of the three religions examined, but it does refer to a phenomenon that is very widespread in the human race and in all religions. This phenomenon points to an important reason for the spread of religions. A theological assertion related to popular religion is that worship of tangible objects and even their use as "worship aids" is a demonstration of the desire for direct contact with God. The phenomenon of popular religion (in contrast with elite religion) is also a reminder that the creation of elite religion in complex societies shows a tendency for those with power to use religion for the maintenance of order and the continuation of their rule. We saw that elite religion has little broad appeal, even if it may have broad influence in establishing monopolistic religions.

While popular religion helps to explain the powerful appeal of Jesus Christ, who is human and gives direct access to God, the analysis also showed that Christianity itself is not immune from producing both popular and elite religions. Christianity as elite religion focuses on institutional maintenance and has little missionary drive or appeal. A heavy or single emphasis on Jesus Christ as a judge, moral guide, or teacher is typical of elite Christianity, which does not emphasize missions.

The top down moralistic emphasis of elite religion is often combined with encouraging popular religion among ordinary believers. As popular religion developed within Christianity, it created a certain "popularity" for various objects and practices, but the spread of the Christian message about Jesus Christ was hindered. Popular Christianity both detracts attention from Christ and results from reduced attention to Christ as a personal Savior and Mediator. Popular Christianity tends to become a kind of "cultural religion" with various "observances." People obtain part of their cultural-social identities through popular religions. Popular Christianity gives a weak witness to people of other religious-cultural identities.

Proposition 1.1 leads to Proposition 1.2, which is the central belief content cause for the spread of religions. It is Proposition 1.2 that is consistent with the central theological assertion of the Christian faith: Because humans could not gain access to God, God came into the midst of human life to make it possible for humans to have direct access to God.

Like many social scientific theories, after their statement, they appear self-evident or obvious. The findings supporting this theory were exciting to me because they point so clearly to the power of the essential message of Christianity to be accepted by people worldwide. That message is Jesus Christ himself and what he did and is doing, not simply what he taught. There is some variation in what Christians emphasize about Jesus Christ, but there is basic agreement in the Christianity that has spread worldwide that Jesus Christ is not simply a human being, but is also Divine himself and accomplished an atonement for humans. This makes his position as Mediator especially powerful and effective. What Christians offer the world (or rather God offers through Christians) is Jesus Christ, who lived, died for our sins, rose again, continually intercedes for us, and lives with us forever. God in Jesus Christ and the Holy Spirit is even nearer to us than any possible immanent and tangible expression of the Divine since Christ is "closer to us than breathing and nearer than hands and feet." Besides Jesus Christ we need no other intercessor, since this is specifically what Christ does for us (Hebrews 4:14-16; 5:1-10; 7:25). The task in missions, therefore, is to present Jesus Christ who embodies in himself the immanent and the transcendent.

Having said this, the findings discussed under the various social factors either facilitating or blocking the spread of the message about Christ tell us very plainly that not everyone was or is ready to hear the name of Jesus Christ or perceive what was accomplished for us by him. However, aside from whatever natural human resistance to God exists, a great deal of resistance to the message about Jesus Christ is a direct consequence of Christian misrepresentation of Jesus Christ. What can Christians do to present Christ adequately?

Not only is Jesus Christ the message of Christian missions, the method of missions should come directly from Christ. Christ himself showed both directness and indirectness in the presentation of his message, along with both simplicity and deep meaning. He was clear, determined, persistent, and above all patient and enduring in what he had to do, but he was gentle, kind, and compassionate toward all people. He challenged people and could be confrontational, especially toward those who were proud or of high status, but he always sought to draw out faith rather than impose it, and in the end, after the resurrection, he showed himself only to those who loved him. When his followers thought of his method, they were reminded of the passage in Isaiah (42:1-4) that said of the servant of God:

> Here is my servant, whom I have chosen, my beloved, with whom my soul is well pleased. I will put my Spirit upon him, and he will proclaim justice to the Gentiles. He will not wrangle or cry aloud, nor will anyone hear his voice in the streets. He will not break a bruised reed or quench a smoldering wick until he brings justice to victory. And in his name will the Gentiles hope (Matthew 12:16-21).

Thus the strong missiological implication of the findings supporting the first two Propositions is that Christian missions should focus clearly on Jesus Christ and his unique life, death, resurrection, and living presence. But this should be done in the way that Jesus presented himself, which was to draw out faith, not to impose it. In addition to our words of witness, it is highly important that the life and work of Christians should be a witness to Jesus Christ and not nullify our words. When it comes to the need for dialogue or profession of faith, Christians have nothing better to do than to speak of Jesus Christ, all that he said and did and the meaning of it according to the apostolic witness of the New Testament. Christian parents especially have a responsibility to explain to their children who Christ is and what he did for them. The behavior of parents especially needs to conform to the pattern set by Jesus.

People of other religions and of no religion need to hear, and many of them want to hear, what it is that Christians find so unique and rewarding in Jesus Christ. When it comes to living, of course, Christians have nothing better to do and nothing they need to do more than to follow Jesus Christ through the power of the Spirit of God. All of this is simple to state, but very difficult, even humanly impossible to do without Divine aid. The sad truth, of course, as was seen in the historical comparisons in this book, is that the witness to Christ has been carried out very inadequately over the last 2000 years. In spite of many heroic and beautiful examples of good witnesses, there has been much to nullify these efforts.

Although the mandate to be "witnesses to Jesus Christ" is often taken for granted in mission work, this study serves as a reminder that the witness to Jesus Christ is the standard of all Christian mission work. There will always be failures to do this adequately by Christians, as we have seen, but there is a constant need to study and debate the means for such witness. Even when there has been failure to witness adequately or successfully in one place, even in one's home area, for example, in the cases of slavery, racial segregation, and oppression in the United States, there may be success and great receptivity in other places. Even in the midst of the oppression that was practiced in the United States, a genuine witness to Jesus Christ was effective among many of the oppressed. The mixed and impure witness to Jesus Christ has been seen throughout Christian history with a wide variety of results ranging from rejection to mixed or selective acceptance to wholesale acceptance.

Propositions 1.1 and 1.2 strongly imply that it is important for Christians to struggle to maintain a clear conception of Jesus Christ, his redeeming work together with his continuing presence and intercession. There is no substitute for Christ or any need for secondary or supplementary intercessors. It was seen that when a clear witness is not maintained, people will introduce numerous supplementary intermediaries to meet their needs for the immanent presence and aid of God, who otherwise may seem distant. People have introduced intermediaries when Jesus Christ somehow became distant in Christian thought and experience, for example, when perceived primarily as a judge. They have also held to native intermediaries when Christ was associated with an invading and dominating power. Since Christ is perceived and interpreted by each individual and group through their cultural lenses, a variety of elements from local cultures will inevitably be introduced into the religious practices of the local followers of Jesus Christ. However, the introduction of various immanent and tangible means of contacting God in addition to Jesus Christ is a kind misguided response to the human need for God and at the same time a form of resistance to God. It limits the universality and hinders the spread of the full appropriation of the gospel of Jesus Christ.

The natural tendency for humans to resist God's way in Christ (see, for example, Christ's word to Peter: "Get behind me, Satan!" Mark 8:31) indicates the need for continual correction of Christian viewpoints. This is pointed out clearly by David Smith's (2003:70-82) discussion of the Peter and Cornelius episode (Acts 10). Peter's experience in the Cornelius episode caused a radical break in his understanding of how the gospel crosses cultural boundaries. This was followed by the Jerusalem Council (Acts 15), which established the principle of "conversion" (acceptance of Christ within culture) as opposed to the principle of "proselytizing" (acceptance of Christ with required adoption of specified cultural-religious practices) (Smith 2003:127-30). Such terms may be defined in different ways, but it is essential to return repeatedly to the Bible to understand important theological distinctions. This is why Scripture translation and education is of crucial importance in mission work.

The struggle of the early followers of Christ to understand the implications of following him established the pattern for the struggle of Christians throughout history to the present to understand what it means to follow Christ. The Bible presents Jesus Christ as the Word of God, the living revelation of the truth of God. His followers called themselves "people of the Way." This means that there must be a continual interaction between followers of Christ and the Bible in order to understand and live ("walk") in the way of Jesus Christ, which can only be done as the Spirit of God interprets the Word and empowers those who seek to follow it.

Sanneh (1991a) has written of the historic association of the translation of the Bible with effective mission work. He (1991b, 2003) has even pointed out the partially unintended effect of the translated Bible in revitalizing whole societies and creating strong ethnic and national identities. This took place because translation elevated indigenous languages previously considered "backward" or "inferior." Furthermore, the lack of translations of and education in the Bible has greatly hindered the healthy growth of individual Christians and churches. The Bible with its strong statements against idolatry, but especially with its presentation of the possibilities of direct contact with God, has been a major hindrance to the development of popular religious expressions local deities. Having the Bible in indigenous languages has also been a major stimulus to missions.

The importance of relating the Bible as interpreted through Jesus Christ to all of mission work brings to mind the enormous responsibility placed on the Church and Christian families to interpret and teach the Bible. The secularization of public education (Smith et al 2003a) means that explaining the central and vital place of the Bible in the Christian life is left almost entirely to the Church and to Christian families. In fact modern individualistic society has actually raised the importance of family life for general socialization in life skills and support of the rising generation, in addition to transmitting the faith.

In spite of the nineteenth century Sunday School movement and the ongoing Christian education movement in the churches, there is a great lack of Biblical knowledge in the general Christian population in America. This is clearly shown by Smith and Denton (2005). Based on extensive interviews they (2005:162) describe the commonly accepted belief in God among teenagers and their parents in God as "Moral, Therapeutic Deism." In short, this is a belief in a God who watches over the world from a distance, who wants people to be good, who gives us a goal to be happy and feel good about ourselves, and who allows good people to go to heaven when they die. These beliefs have elements of truth, but the specifics about Jesus Christ, his death, resurrection, and living presence are left out. Also, there is little about a life of service and spreading the good news of God's love and justice in the world. Clearly, the Church has an enormous task of teaching as mandated by Jesus Christ in Matthew 28:20, namely, "…teaching them to obey everything that I have commanded you…"

Important aspects of the character of Jesus Christ expressed in Scripture often go against dominant influences and trends in most societies. This is why Christian communities are always in some sense "counter cultural" and need to maintain subcultural identities (Smith 1998). Stark (2001, 2003) has written of the long struggle in Western society in which Christianity was associated with intolerance and persecution of the Jews, as well as of others. At the same time Christianity continually produced "prophets" and dissenting minorities, who often instituted great changes. The Crusades, numerous wars, slavery, racial discrimination, the Holocaust, gender inequality, and ongoing poverty all bring to mind that Christianity has both participated in and also opposed numerous social evils. Alliance with governments and especially surrender to dominant cultural values made Christianity a participant in numerous social evils. The major means for Christians to correct the social evils of their societies has been through the interpretation and application of Scriptural truths, even though Christians disagreed over applications, such as to the issue of slavery.

Because of the centrality of translating and teaching Scripture, missions have promoted literacy, education, and democracy (Woodberry 2004, 2006). Without an emphasis on the Bible, these have been neglected and the witness to Jesus Christ greatly handicapped, for example, literacy and public education were neglected for long centuries, when the translation and teaching of the Bible was not emphasized. In the end, belief content is not so much a list of doctrines that is learned, as important as it is to have intellectual knowledge of Biblical truths, but an expression of what (who) is trusted by a committed will. It should never be forgotten that orthodoxy is of both heart and mind, and according to I Corinthians 13, the heart comes first. Knowledge will always be "through a glass darkly." The Medieval mystics, the Jansenites (with Blaise Pascal), the eighteenth century Pietists, and a host of believers before and since were right. What is essential for Christians is not simply understanding or being able to state the doctrines of the incarnation, the atonement, the Trinity, sin, salvation, the means of grace, the Bible as the word of God, the Church as the body of Christ, the sacraments, the Kingdom of God, and the present and coming apocalypse (revelation), as important as these and other doctrines are. What is essential is knowing God through Jesus Christ in the Biblical sense of "knowing," which is personal, direct, and unifying. This is the faith that spreads, being first caught and then taught. The Apostle Paul gave this faith classic expression when he spoke of giving up everything in order to know Christ, the power of his resurrection and the fellowship of his sufferings. He went on to say that this single goal was always before him and that he was in a life-long process of moving toward it (Philippians 3:7-14).

I must add something important, however, before leaving the subject of the focus on Jesus Christ. Coming into relationship with Christ has from the earliest days of Christianity meant coming into living relationship with the Trinitarian God, a relationship that is beyond full understanding, yet nevertheless real. In addition to Jesus Christ whom we call "My Lord and my God" with Thomas (John 20:28) there is God "the Father Almighty," who so loved the world that he sent Jesus Christ (John 3:16) and to whom Jesus taught us to pray to as "Our Father, who art in heaven…" And then there is the Holy Spirit, sent to us as comforter and guide, and the one who empowers us, primarily by pouring God's love into our hearts (Romans 5:5). This experience with the Triune God (and the doctrine developed from it) may not fit into the human mind, but God does not conform to human reason. While this faith in the Trinity, not in three Gods, is not based on human reason, it is reasonable and it gives richness to the experience with God who wants to be in personal relationship with human beings.

It is difficult to end this section because of its importance. I will close with the comments of two theologians. Michael J. Buckley, S.J. (1987:361) toward the end of his extensive study of atheism comments, "For the Christian, Jesus belongs to the intelligibility and to the truth of god. What god is, and even that god is, has its primordial evidence in the person and in the event that is Jesus Christ." Buckley goes on to quote Wofhart Pannenberg (1988:130), "Who and what God is becomes defined only by the Christ event…Jesus belongs to the definition of God." The mission of Christians can be nothing short of witnessing to

Jesus Christ as he stated, "You will be my witnesses in Jerusalem, in Judea and Samaria, and to the ends of the earth" (Acts 1:8).

DEMONSTRATE THE CARE AND COMPASSION OF GOD FOR EACH PERSON AND FOR THE WORLD

2.1 To spread widely religions must offer moral guidance and moral energy.

2.2 To spread widely religions must offer salvation equally to all individuals thus emphasizing egalitarianism.

2.3 To spread widely religions must emphasize compassion for all people.

One of the most powerful and attractive qualities of Jesus Christ is that "he went about doing good" (Acts 10:38). However, he made it very clear that he was not introducing any new morality. In spite of his beautiful teachings and sayings, he was not offering so much new moral guidance, but a new moral energy or power.

Given the findings of the study that are consistent with the basic theological perspective about Jesus Christ and moral energy, Christian mission work is not an essentially moralistic activity. It should not be the goal of the missionary to seek to function primarily as a moral guide. What the missionary offers is a source of moral energy in the message of New Life in Christ and the gift of the Holy Spirit. At the same time, people are watching the behavior of the missionaries to see how they may be different from others. This is why missionaries have to think about moral behavior and seek to conform to the pattern of Jesus Christ.

One of the most striking features of the activity of Jesus Christ is that he allowed himself to be constantly interrupted by individuals in need. This is not easy in any society, but it is especially difficult in modern societies with bureaucratic systems, schedules, and appointments. Bureaucratic systems are necessary for serving large numbers of people. Christian missions built numerous such systems over the last two centuries. Hospitals and schools were established in many lands that have served the needs of millions. Many of these systems were the earliest modern institutions to be built and subsequently became foundational to national medical and educational systems. Woodberry (2004, 2006) has shown the enormous impact of missions in the world through these efforts. The needs for large scale efforts still exist and there are innumerable ways in which they can be and should be met. Mission agencies and individual missionaries may well need to become involved in large scale projects and programs that serve large numbers of people. However, whether these take place or not, the missionary still has the basic task of seeking to live personally like Jesus Christ in caring about individuals, an impossible task, but one to which believers are called. One of the main reasons for Christian fellowship is to encourage one another in this extremely difficult task and to seek the power of the Holy Spirit together for Divine energy to follow Christ.

It is essential that mission agencies and missionaries represent to the world the care and compassion of God through Jesus Christ and the Holy Spirit for each individual equally. This is clearly what being "followers of Jesus Christ" means. This leads to the consideration of how moral progress has been made, sometimes very slowly and with many setbacks. It is important for Christians to recognize the need for pluralism and variety in moral witness. Many great social evils have been overcome because Christians even disagreed with and worked against each other, for example, in regard to slavery, segregation, and the status of women.

To aid the process of moral change, Christians need an increased knowledge of the social sciences in order to gain an understanding of how much their views and opinions are affected by their social conditions and circumstances. James Davison Hunter (2011) has performed a great service is showing the complexity of bringing about socio-cultural change. It requires much more than simply "changing individual hearts and minds" or their "world views." The United States is a demonstration that religious, ethnic, cultural, and even regional diversity are important for mutual correction in societies, as well as in Christian churches and institutions themselves.

The Church has struggled and continues to struggle with how to apply God's compassion (Proposition 2.3) to both individuals and to societies. In the nineteenth century evangelicals were active in many social causes. The "Social Gospel" associated with Walter Rauschenbusch (1919 [1912]) had an evangelical base, but in the twentieth century it acquired a "liberal" tag as Christians divided over whether to express compassion primarily toward individuals or by changing social conditions, the latter being an emphasis of the "Social Gospel." "Peace and justice" ministries became associated with the liberal churches, as the "Social Gospel" became the unofficial theology of mainline church executives (Thuesen 2002:41). However, in recent decades, conservative churches, which seek to carry the evangelical label, have taken up "mission as transformation" (Samuel and Sugden 1999), reclaiming the nineteenth century evangelical heritage. This emphasis has come to a great extent because of insights gained from overseas where missionaries encountered both the material plight of new believers and the call of local Christian leaders for transformation of whole communities.

Western history demonstrates that the struggle against social evils is long-term and in many ways never-ending. Evil has a way of reappearing in new forms. This is the principle of the reappearance of anti-Christ or evil after an advancement of good over evil. Evil has a way of reappearing in new and virulent forms after periods of advance of the gospel of Christ. Modern racism and the Holocaust are examples of the reappearance of evil. Nevertheless, the missiological implications of the importance of the Person of Jesus Christ in the spread of Christianity is that missions must never cease to relate all things to Jesus Christ, and that major efforts should be made to continually interpret and apply the Bible to life ("teaching them to obey everything that I have commanded you" Matthew 28:20). Evil will then be restrained and even be seen to "fall like lightning" (Luke 10:18).

DEVELOP VITAL CONGREGATIONAL LIFE

3.1 *Religions with voluntary organizations to which people make personal commitments are necessary for religions to spread, while religions with involuntary and/ or transient followers will not ordinarily spread.*

3.2 *Religions are able to spread widely because they organize open gatherings in which people can interact around important symbols of the divine that provide solidarity and emotional energy for life.*

3.3 *Religions spread only when there are carriers to take the religions to new people in new areas.*

These Propositions and the supporting evidence for them from Chapter 3 strongly support the need for missionaries, if they are to spread the faith, to work to establish and maintain vital congregations. In the Gospels, it is clear that Jesus Christ gathered followers around him and placed great emphasis on sustaining and training them. He identified a core group of twelve apostles, but there were other followers, including a number of women. Shortly after his death and resurrection, a group of some one hundred twenty, meaning "a large group," gathered at Pentecost. Many new followers soon augmented the original group as followers began to be added "day by day." The numerous groups of followers that developed in many locations indicate not only the wisdom, but the necessity in missionary strategy of gathering a group in every new setting who will encourage and support one another through mutual love and the sharing of gifts, each contributing to the whole. At the Last Supper Jesus said, "I give you a new commandment, that you love one another," and then he added, "By this everyone will know that you are my disciples, if you have love for one another" (John 13:34, 35). These sayings demonstrate that being a Christian means having a common life with other believers in a strong and mutually supportive fellowship. Many pastors of congregations are constantly considering ways of making congregational life more vital and reflective of mutual love. Missionaries and missiologists likewise need to be thoroughly acquainted with the principles that make for vital congregational life, as well as for broad Christian networking.

The emphasis on strong Christian group life builds directly on what was said about the importance of focus on Jesus Christ and all that is related to him in the Bible that applies to faith and moral life. The sequence is not choosing to believe in Jesus Christ and then choosing to join a Christian fellowship. Rather, believing in Jesus Christ and becoming related to him places one simultaneously in relationship with other believers. "Joining a church" is expressing a reality that already exists when one relates to Jesus Christ. What is called "church shopping" should really be like a fish out of water trying desperately to find a place to swim in order to live. The New Testament is very concerned with what it means to belong to "the body of Christ," particularly how highly diverse people can work together.

In this regard, a great many words (Romans 12, I Corinthians 12, 13, 14, Ephesians 4) are used to teach that every Christian is given a gift to bring to the group for the benefit of all.

Recognizing the centrality of congregational life in Christianity and other religions, American sociologists of religion have given major attention to congregational life. A large body of literature has been developed with which mission planners should be aware. Major examples of sociological investigations of congregational life are the work of Carl Dudley (1997) and Nancy Ammerman (1997, 2005), individually and together (2002), and also both of them with Jackson Carroll and William McKinney (1998). There are, of course, many other studies by sociologists of religion of congregations since congregational studies have been a major focus of the discipline. The writings of religious authors have their place, but they need to be checked against the more systematic and empirically based studies of the social scientists.

In her most recent extensive study of congregations, Ammerman (2005) first makes clear that the spiritual work of worship and fostering spiritual growth is widely recognized by local leaders as central to what they are doing. However, she points out (2005:272):

> The religious groups that spend the least organization energy on worship and religious education are the Mainline Protestant ones...While all the other traditions have some particular organizational effort that supports the spiritual nurture of their members, white Mainline Protestants seem to be putting all their eggs in the basket of Sunday morning worship and children's Sunday School.

She goes on to state, "Whether this minimalist organizational structure can support robust spiritual lives is questionable."

W. Bradford Wilcox (2002:293) points out that many American parents sought out mainline churches in the 1950s, "not because they had strong Christian convictions but because they wanted to provide their children with religious and moral training." He states:

> These parents adhered to what one study called "lay liberalism"—a combination of vague religious beliefs, cultural tolerance and a belief that religion's primary function is to support good behavior (e.g., the Golden rule). This lay liberalism meant that many mainline parents didn't have a strong religious identity to pass on to their children: the boomers of the 1960s and 1970s. Thus, when conventional norms on behalf of churchgoing were questioned, many young adults from the mainline decided they had no need for the church (Hoge, Johnson, and Luidens 1994:175-202).

Although still not able to hold their young people as well as conservative churches, mainline Protestants may have improved their ability to hold their young people (Smith with Denton 2005:36). Ammerman (2005:276) describes how mainline churches can join more conservative churches and become strong communities of faith by learning to talk to each other and reclaim and revitalize their faith traditions through the stories of their individual members:

In doing this work, they tap deep resources from within their faith community, but in the act of learning to communicate the stories to newcomers, they develop accessible ways of defining their own traditions and practice, creating a language that bridges between inside and out. At the same time that each particular local community of believers creates and tells stories that are theirs alone, their conscious Acknowledgment of their debt to larger traditions reminds them that no single community's story is sufficient to encompass us all.

Robust religious traditions are kept alive, then, in the work of thousands of local congregations. They are kept alive because those congregations spend most of their energy on worship, religious education, and building a place where modern wanderers can find a meaningful, even if temporary, home. This basic congregational work requires constant voluntary investment if any local community of faith is to thrive.

These conclusions based on an extensive study of congregations are very consistent with the earlier study by Smith (1998) of evangelicalism. Smith developed a "subcultural identity theory," elaborating the theory of Finke, Stark, and Ianaccone that pluralism can often have a positive effect on religion. Smith (1998:119) shows that religious strength is shaped "depending on how ordinary people utilize their religious traditions' cultural tools more or less effectively to construct distinctive, meaningful, satisfying social identities." This means that "meaning-content of theologies, customs, world views, and rituals" of Christian groups actually matter, a view this book supports and that is consistent with the previous section emphasizing the importance of transmitting the content of what is the meaning of faith in Jesus Christ.

The empirical work by sociologists of religion shows that religious group strength requires an effective transmission of the content of religious faith and practice and at the same time effective transmission of faith and practice requires strong religious groups. This is an ongoing circular process. It is a major challenge for Christian communities on the local, regional, national, and international levels. The challenge requires focusing on essentials within and between Christian communities and practicing mutual tolerance and acceptance without weakening deep commitment to Jesus Christ and his kingdom. A key step is strengthening local Christian communities.

George G. Hunter (2000:30) has written of how Celtic Christianity spread effectively through a communal approach to Christianity: "This affected the way in which–in parish churches, communities, tribes, and families–the people supported each other, pulled together, prayed for each other, worked out their salvation together, and lived out the Christian life together." This pattern may be seen in the work of Patrick and the many missionaries that followed him and carried the gospel to the Picts, the Germanic peoples who had invaded England, and to peoples across Europe. Hunter (2000:95-121) also discusses how the "Celtic" method can be used today for the "New Barbarians," many of whom are secular, as well as caught up in various kinds of addictions. In the "Celtic" approach people are welcomed into communities, brought into a ministry of conversation, and included in imaginative worship, which has indigenous forms and expressions. In such communities the faith of the followers of Jesus Christ is essentially "caught" and addictions are conquered.

Researchers have examined many aspects of congregational life, but there are new directions for research that were opened up by Collins' (2004) work on "interaction ritual chains" and the development of emotional energy that can also contribute to moral energy. Proposition 3.2 deals especially with the implication of his work. Congregations offer numerous opportunities for people to interact. In addition, the symbols found in the Christian faith are unusually powerful in generating emotions since they point to such matters as redemption, support in trial and suffering, mutual caring, sacrifice leading to victory, numerous precious memories, and everlasting life. Congregational worship is often deeply emotional because it lifts up these symbols in preaching and the sacraments. The worship site itself with its numerous symbolic objects and especially with the presence of a body of believers can be very inspiring. Large-scale gatherings can also be especially powerful in the production of emotional energy. All of this points to the fact that vital congregational life is a strong mission force in drawing people to the faith.

In many respects the creation of vital congregations requires a miracle in which people, who ordinarily would not mix and mingle, come together and stay together. It requires the miracle of mutual forgiveness since in any group of people, feelings get hurt and jealousies and resentments arise. People outside of vital congregations will intuitively recognized that the congregation is held together by more than simply "common interests" or "social and cultural similarity."

In addition to drawing people, vital congregations support mission work outside of themselves. One of the strongest movements in the last decades has been the localization of the bases of mission efforts. Countless congregations or networks of congregations are sending mission teams to foreign countries to carry out mission projects and to participate in local congregational worship and life. These teams return with a new vision of their faith gained from the enthusiastic and powerful faith of the people to whom they go, who often are living in very difficult circumstances. The short-term missionaries are able to tell inspiring stories to their home congregations of Christians in other lands. All of this increases the strength of the international networks of Christians. Congregations are inspired to support the work of long-term missionaries and overseas Christians in their efforts to spread the gospel of Christ. At the same time, it should be recognized it should be recognized that there may be special problems that develop around short-term missions. For this reason, there needs to be special attention paid to the orientation of mission teams and short-term missionaries that take into consideration potential problems.

In regard to dealing with the conflict and diversity of views that exists in all societies, one of the major contributions of Christianity is the demonstration in congregations and larger denominational communities of how people can work together for common goals through a democratic process despite great differences. Congregations and their larger networks of denominations give important political experience to people that they can apply elsewhere. Learning to debate openly and come to common decisions is based on mutual respect and love that are Divine gifts to the community of believers. The demonstration of a worshiping and serving diverse community is one of the great gifts that Christian communities can give to societies in which they exist. Many times those who have learned to work within Christian organizations have then become participants and leaders in general political and social organizational life. This leads naturally to consideration of how Christians should respond to the social factors affecting their mission.

LIFT UP THE VALUES OF SECULAR DEMOCRACY SUPPORTING RELIGIOUS FREEDOM

4.1 *In order for a religion to spread successfully people in a receiving society must have the opportunity to choose to be identified with a new religion.*

4.2 *Religions spread more easily to relatively small pre-literate societies without official religions than to large complex societies with established literate religions that have strong links to governments.*

4.3 *New religions may spread in large societies where a particular religion has not yet been made monopolistic and thus where there is relative religious diversity.*

4.4 *The spread of new religions can be greatly accelerated or blocked by governmental power, depending on whether*

> *governments seek or approve of a new religion or already have an established alliance with a religion.*
> **4.5** *The association of religions with coercive power leads to covert and overt resistance from within and outside of religions.*

It may seem strange for Christians to support a secular government, but the evidence from history and the last two hundred years in the United States is that when a government refrains from favoring any particular religion, religious vitality is a broad effect. The development of the kind of secular democracy now existing in the United States that fosters religious freedom has been a long historical process. The data supporting this and the remaining Propositions dealing with macro social factors show that there are many conditions over which individuals and even groups may have little control or influence, at least in the short term. Macro social factors are embedded in the flow of history and are often part of long-term processes. Hunter (2011) has shown this to be the typical case. It is usually necessary, therefore, to take a long range perspective and to think in terms of generations and even centuries in making macro socio-cultural changes.

Societies in which there long has been a restraint on freedom, especially freedom to make choices in religious identity, may have had such a restraining social, cultural, and political system in place for many centuries. Even when revolutions or rapid change takes place, the new order often reinstitutes the kind of authoritarian system that previously existed. Sadly, invasion, conquest, domination, and oppression by Christians or people associated in the minds of people with Christians is one of the major reasons why there may be great resistance to the Christian message over long periods of time. However, there also may be a delayed response to largely unsuccessful mission efforts after conditions have changed, for example, the large response in China in recent decades after several decades of freedom from foreign domination (not necessarily internal domestic religious freedom). Nevertheless, it is important to make a beginning in holding up the ideals of a secular democracy because changes in receptivity may actually take place at an irregular pace, sometimes slowly, but sometimes relatively quickly.

Propositions 4.1 to 4.5 deal especially with the opportunity to make religious choices and the problems arising from the association of religion with governmental power. A basic implication is that Christian missions should align themselves with democratic trends, even though it may take generations for democratic principles and especially democratic practices to be established in societies. Very often, the most important contribution Christian communities can make to societies, as pointed out in the discussion under vital congregations, is to demonstrate democracy themselves and give people experience in democratic organization. This may be as basic as conducting meetings according to parliamentary rules in which people are able to carry on orderly debate and vote on motions. Thus the belief in a noncoercive God who desires that people freely choose to accept God's grace means that Christians have a responsibility to promote democratic values in which human freedoms and rights are protected. In short, Christians have an obligation to assist in the spread of democracy, and the major means for Christianity to promote democracy is by demonstration and socialization of its own members to live and work together in mutual respect and acceptance in spite of differences among members of views and personal gifts.

One of the greatest temptations of any religion, including Christianity, is to obtain governmental help in gaining and keeping members (Proposition 4.4). Christianity fell for this temptation in the fourth century and certain denominations, especially in Europe, have continued to obtain government favor over other denominations and religions to recent years. The temptation is strong for Christian churches (or any religious group) to seek, perhaps not power anymore, but a privileged position based on an historic association with a particular society. Governments on their part find it especially tempting to provide aid and support to a single selected religion in order to obtain that religion's legitimization of governmental exercise of power, as well as to use religious ideology as a basis for the unity of the society. In this way governments agree to limit religious competitors of selected favored religions. Churches, which have official government sanction, are churches that generally have a weak mission outreach and at the same time block the access of other branches of Christianity. Any religion, including Christianity, gains immediate advantages from governmental favors. However, there is a long-term cost, which at present is most evident in Europe and in the spread of irreligion discussed in Chapter 8.

At the same time, there may be more subtle dangers demonstrated in the United States where formal separation of religion and state has existed from the founding, but where informal relationships and unrecognized cultural connections have also been continuous. The mainline churches enjoyed cultural domination for approximately a century and a half after the Revolution, but in the last few decades, independent evangelical churches have become a dominant religious influence. This new position of power for those churches that were formerly disdained by mainline churches offers special temptations to use or ally themselves with governmental power. Mainline churches need to rethink their tendencies toward being overly at "ease with the world." All Christians need to be counter cultural in a healthy fashion based on the Bible and not simply their own cultural values. It remains to be seen how the various trends among American Christians and their diverse churches with diverse emphases will ultimately unfold and affect American society and government, as well as the rest of the world.

The small pre-literate societies mentioned in Proposition 4.2 are becoming relatively rare, but the issue of domination of minorities and the sense of coercion and social pressure on minorities remain. If the pressure is not from a majority Christian population, then a minority population may be receptive to the Christian message. However, if the majority population that places pressure on a minority population is ostensibly Christian, then there may be a general resistance from the minority people to Christianity and openness to a non-Christian religion. It is important, therefore, for those carrying the Christian witness to be conscious of majority-minority relationships in the same way that they should be conscious of power relationships among the large societies.

Leaders of monopolistic religions generally oppose their societies becoming religiously pluralistic as mentioned in Proposition 4.3. In these cases a particular religious identity has usually become associated with national or ethnic identity. A moderate or transitional type of religious pluralism exists in societies, such as the United States, where one religion (Christianity) is dominant, but many varieties exist within it and foreign religions also can flourish. In these cases, considerable mutual influence takes place along with competition between the various versions of the faith. Substantial changes in attitudes toward one another takes place, for example, between Protestants and Roman Catholics, where previously there was open hostility. The change in attitudes is especially noticeable on the local level and among individuals. However, the United States is moving rapidly toward becoming not simply denominationally pluralistic, but religiously pluralistic, with the increase in the number of Muslims and followers of Asian religions. This is also true of Europe. Although some Christians may consider this a backward step from the days when they felt hegemonic and could openly place Christian or Biblical symbols (e.g. crèches and the Ten Commandments) on government property, the evidence so far is that religious pluralism causes people to think more seriously about the meaning of their faith. According to the analysis of this book, if Christians become more serious about the content of Christianity, then Christianity is more likely to spread widely. Those who want to maintain a general "Christian aura" in society are likely to be maintaining or drawn toward a superficial version of the faith represented particularly by "Moralistic, Therapeutic Deism" (Smith and Denton 2005: 162, 163).

If Christian missions are faithful in their witness to Jesus Christ, as called for in the first section above, they will resist the temptation Christ resisted in the wilderness and throughout his ministry. This was the temptation to use coercive power or any external influences and inducements to win people to faith, but rather be dependent on the power of the Word and Spirit alone. This is one of many matters to be debated in mission work. Few would argue that Christians have a right to ask for protection as part of their civil rights, as the Apostle Paul used his rights as a Roman citizen to obtain protection. However, Christians differ as to whether they should receive funding from the government to carry out social services. The most damaging kind of governmental favor, however, is when one version of Christianity is favored over another and limitations are place on those not favored. This has been a tradition in Europe and as a consequence mission work has been weakened. This is one reason this book argues that Christians need to support the development of secular democracies around the world. A secular democracy does not ordinarily interfere with the introduction of a new religion. Basically, vital Christianity does not fear competition, but does fear restriction that prevents the free proclamation of the gospel. It is true, of course, that secularization is also supported by irreligious and antireligious people as shown in the study by Smith et al (2003a). It may be that many Christian groups, particularly mainline Christian groups in the U.S.A., have not fully accepted the challenge to establish a clear Christian identity in the secular environment that has been given to them by secularization. As Christians support the development of secular democracies around the world they should also make extra efforts to create vigorous Church life in the midst of a secular context.

God has made a world in which people ignore God and still get along reasonably well. In other words, God is noncoercive. To ignore God is probably more possible today than ever before because of modern democracies with religious freedom and higher standards of living for more people than ever before. This condition gives a marvelous opportunity for those bearing the Christian message to emphasize the intrinsic blessings of the life of faith in God's redeeming grace in Jesus Christ. The reward of faith is faith and of knowing God is knowing God, as the writer of Psalm 73 discovered.

SEPARATE THE CHRISTIAN WITNESS FROM INTERSOCIETAL AND INTERGROUP DOMINATION

5.1 *Domination or threat from a sending society of a religion toward a receiving society creates resistance to the spreading religion, which may result in rejection or, if pressure is extreme, acceptance with significant change of the spreading religion.*

5.2 *When there is no domination or threat from a sending society, but rather from another nearby society (or* *societies), then a receiving society may be receptive to the spreading religion, particularly if the new religion is an aid in resisting other dominating or threatening societies.*

These propositions deal specifically with how intersocietal power relationships can affect and have affected missions. Again, as in the case of internal social conditions of receiving societies, there may be little that can be done directly and immediately in missions to change power relationships between major power centers. However, it is highly important that missionaries be conscious of the power relationships between the societies from which they are sent and the society or societies to which they go, as well as the power relationships between receiving societies and other surrounding societies. This also applies to knowing the power relationships of subgroups within societies. These relationships above the individual (micro) level may directly affect the perceptions and motives of receivers of the mission message as discussed under the Propositions that are primarily related to individuals (6.1, 6.2, 6.3, 7.1, 7.2).

While the breakup of colonialism has done much to level the nations, the legacy of the long years of Western colonialism may take many generations to lose its effect. This means that missionaries from the West to countries formerly dominated by Western countries may still be at a disadvantage in presenting the message of a coercive God and of the "lamb that was slain." An example of the lingering effect of asymmetrical power relationships (and direct oppression) is the anti-Western spirit found in much of the non-Western world, especially in the Middle and Far East. In Latin America, there is also a continuing anti-North America attitude, based on years of domination. However, if a receiving country (or subsociety) is under the domination of a nation other than the sending country, then the message of missionaries from a Western country may be received with less anti-Western feelings. People in the receiving country will be able better to perceive the power of the cross of Christ without confusing it with worldly power (Montgomery 1996:184). This was the case in Korea, where missionaries were not associated with the dominating colonial power of Japan. However, with the ongoing leveling of the powers of the nations, with small nations, such as Vietnam and Afghanistan having defeated large nations, the United States and the former Soviet Union respectively, the issue of the association of missionaries with dominating power will continue to decrease in importance.

One of the greatest influences in reversing the effect of the association of the Christian message with domination is the internationalization of the missionary force. For example, missionaries from Korea, Brazil, and African countries do not have the disadvantage of being associated with former colonial powers. An even more important influence in reversing the association of Christianity with domination is when local churches gain independence and self-governing power. This helps greatly to neutralize the issue of outside domination, as clearly seen in the case of China, where the old "three self" goal of mission (self-rule, self-support, self-propagation) has been made an official designation among Christians and the government.

However, in spite of the leveling of the power of all nations and the rising power of countries formerly dominated or threatened by Western supposedly Christian countries, there remain several important nations and areas where many people continue to be in a "defensive" mode against Christianity. The defensive mode in the West itself that did so much to develop antireligious and anti-Christian ideologies was discussed in Chapter 8. We grant that all people, including Christians, because of sinful human nature, are in a defensive mode or in resistance against God. Nevertheless, it is clear that there are historic reasons associated with Christianity that help to fortify and exacerbate this resistance in particular areas of the world. Examples of areas where there is heightened resistance to Christianity are Japan, Buddhist countries of Southeast Asia, India, and all Muslim countries. A major country, China, has lost much of its "defensive" mode because of the half-century of nonintervention from the West, along with a long history of relative religious pluralism under secularized leadership. Korea lost its "defensive mode" against Christianity in the first part of the twentieth century because of its defensiveness against Japanese domination. Of course, many minority groups in Asia never adopted a "defensive mode" and consequently were quite open to the Christian message. Native Americans have been understandably both defensive and receptive.

The creation of defensive and even hostile attitudes toward Christianity took place over centuries. On one level, Christians through their churches and other organizations, and sometimes as individuals, can seek to influence national policies related to intersocietal relationships. However, even though individual Christians may feel that they can do little to solve an issue that was centuries in the making, there is much that can be done on the micro or individual level to offset and overcome macro level influences. Beginnings can be made even though results may not be seen for many years. The next two sections will consider the micro level factors that most affect individuals and that make it possible for missionaries to be effective in spite of adverse macro social influences.

WORK THROUGH SOCIAL NETWORKS

6.1 *Social relationships can facilitate or block the spread of religions depending on the influence of those who are known and trusted and provide important emotional and material support.*

6.2 *When social relationships have been disrupted, a new religion may spread by facilitating the establishment of new relationships or a new religion may be resisted by the strengthening of former relationships.*

6.3 *Spreading religions have a universal appeal that leads to the establishment of global social networks that both aid and are aided by globalization.*

Because of the breakup of communities due to industrialization around the world, outside pressures causing strains on social networks, beginning with the family itself, have become increasingly strong. It is important, therefore, that mission efforts be carried out with a high degree of consciousness of these social networks and the efforts to maintain them and reconstruct them in spite of the strains or after their breakup. Local congregations themselves often consist of interconnected families whose relationships are strengthened by congregational life. At the same time, family networks can be both an advantage and disadvantage in church growth. Family splits can become church splits. Every congregation should be analyzed regarding the family and other social networks that exist within it. Missionaries need to gain access to social networks and then give an opportunity for the message to be transmitted along network lines. However, the particular danger for congregations is that social networks become closed rather than remaining open. In these cases, those outside of the network may feel excluded from the congregation.

The social network factor in the spread of religions relates very closely to the social nature of Christianity and most other religions discussed in connection with Propositions 3.1 and 3.2 in the third chapter. From the very beginning of the Christian faith, there was a certain tension between natural families and the new spiritual family based on loyalty to Jesus Christ and the Kingdom of God. As with any movement requiring commitment from participants, the natural family can be a hindrance to involvement. One of the "hard" sayings of Jesus is, "Whoever comes to me and does not hate father and mother, wife and children, brothers and sisters, yes, and even life itself, cannot be my disciple" (Luke 14:26). As a master teacher, Jesus knew how to get attention from his hearers and how to make clear the absolute commitment required in faith. Clearly, the attachment to God comes before all other attachments, including to the self ("life itself"). In spite of the tensions that may be felt, it is clear that the primary relationships of natural families were still regarded as potentially positive as a means for transmitting the faith both horizontally and vertically. In fact, it is clear that from earliest days, the faith spread through families. Thus the natural social relationships of families have both a potentially negative and a potentially positive effect on the formation of the spiritual family based on faith.

Because of the centrality of the family in social life, missionaries need to be students of family life. Families should be neither idealized nor considered only impediments to needed change. There are many tensions and conflicts that can exist between family members. In many traditional societies, the insecurity and uncertainty of life, make families particularly important as sources for security and protection. They may have to cling to each other when surrounded by outside forces that threaten their lives and cultural identities, and this "clinging" is usually established and supported as a major cultural-religious tradition. An authoritarian patriarchal family rule is often typical. However, many may want to escape abuse within the family or simply the domineering elders in their families. Just as individuals need a Savior to give them a focus outside of themselves, so all natural families and social groups need an outside focus and can experience great blessing by having a focus on God in Christ and the larger kingdom of God's love and power which surrounds them. Just as it is wise to recognize the close social network of both small and extended families as a source of emotional turmoil and injury, it is also wise to recognize that the gospel can be a great healing force within families for the many tensions and conflicts that exist. The spiritual family of the church is not meant in the best circumstances to replace the natural family, even though this may seem to happen in some circumstances, but to surround, transform, and bless natural family life. However, there will always be those, such as foreign missionaries, who necessarily leave their families to serve God. Such people have found that they gain new families, even lands, but also perhaps persecution (Mark 10:30)!

One of the most effective means of evangelism, therefore, is through friendship between families and individuals within extended families. Congregational life, spoken of above as one of the most important religious characteristics of Christianity, should be open and not closed. Congregational members need to make deliberate and sustained efforts to bring people on the outside into the circle of friends on the inside. People on the outside need to know that they will find acceptance and genuine friendship on the inside of congregations. It is through such personal relationships that people receive deep emotional satisfaction. The need to reach beyond the familiar network to include outsiders is a simple prescription, but one that needs sustained attention because of the tendency of all humans to be comfortable and satisfied with familiar relationships rather than seeking out new relationships.

OFFER ENHANCEMENT OF LIFE

7.1 *People will be receptive to or resist a new religion according to whether they perceive that it enhances or detracts from an aspect of their social identities which they value.*

7.2 *People will receive or resist a new religion according to whether they perceive that it heightens their emotional energy through ritual interactions.*

Nothing makes a Christian missionary sadder than to see people who do not realize the great blessings and enrichment to life that comes through faith in Jesus Christ. It is this blessing that Christians wish more than anything else to share. Mission work is essentially sharing a wonderful treasure from God. As D. T. Niles (1951:96) states, "Evangelism is one beggar telling another beggar where to get food." At the core of the great joy in the heart of a Christian is the sense of being a loved and forgiven sinner, a great joy to be shared. This reverses any sense of self-hatred or self-rejection and creates a great sense of peace and joy at being an accepted child of God ready to be of service in God's kingdom. Unfortunately, there are both internal personal factors and external social factors that keep people from perceiving the intrinsic rewards and blessings of knowing and following Jesus Christ.

Proposition 7.1 is based on the view that one of the basic human motives is to have self-esteem and that there is usually some aspect or aspects of social identities for which people have some self-esteem or would like to have self-esteem. Unfortunately, there is a tendency for people to put down others in order to build up their own self-esteem (often seen in "office politics"). There is much in life all over the world to reduce the self-esteem of people. Some factors reducing self-esteem actually may be associated with the coming of Christian missionaries who arrive from dominating or more technologically advanced and wealthy societies. Comparison with such outside societies may create a sense of loss or "backwardness" in ethnic, cultural, or national prestige or in all three aspects of social identities. Other forces reducing self-esteem may not come only from outside influences but also come from social, cultural, and economic conditions found in immediate life circumstances. The list is quite long of the categories of people who are in conditions that help to reduce their sense of worth and dignity. Women, minorities, the physically abused, the poor, the abandoned, the oppressed, the addicted, the imprisoned, the handicapped, and all those who are despised and rejected for whatever reason are subject to reduced self-esteem and self-rejection. Then there are those people who do not fit exactly into any of these categories and may outwardly appear like others, but are subject to a sense of the meaninglessness, powerlessness, and uselessness of their own lives. Educated but unemployed people in developing societies, as well as any society, are vulnerable to low self-esteem. Even successful and powerful people, although often filled with a sense of superiority over others, can suddenly realize how lacking, limited, or unworthy they are. The gospel of God's love in Jesus Christ is meant for all people, but is perceived most clearly by those who have a sense of personal limitation, weakness, and failure. This is dramatized in the story of the prodigal son, who "came to himself" and returned to the welcoming arms of his father (Luke 15:11-32).

Missionaries must first of all be aware of any associations they or their message may have with what contributes to reduced self-esteem in receivers of their message. This requires attention to both the macro level factors found especially in Propositions 4.1 and 4.2 and the micro level factors that vary according to the life circumstances of individuals. The perception that missionaries hope people will have is that Christ meets them where they are and enhances their lives with the sense of the grace of God extended to them personally. Furthermore, they need to perceive that whatever their personal and social identities may be, their identities as human beings will be enhanced by Christ. Whatever positive identities they already have or want to have, such as ethnic, national or gender identities, will be enhanced. But this is only the beginning. She or he can be a better woman or man, a better parent, husband, wife, brother, sister, or child. They can also be a better student, worker, or professional of whatever type. They can be a better citizen and representative of an ethnic or national group with important God-given places in the world with contributions to make to human advancement. If they are not clear about their own identities due to mixed parentage, abandonment, or simply minority status, or if they are keenly aware of negative views others have of them, they can know that through Jesus Christ they gain the status of a chosen child of God who can contribute to the lives of those around them. In the end, this becomes more important than what anyone or even they themselves think of themselves.

One of the most delicate and sensitive issues is the perception by hearers of the gospel of Christ of what becomes of the national, ethnic, religious, and cultural identities, which are often tied together, of people who convert to Christ. It will be difficult for Christianity to spread to resistant areas mentioned above (Japan, Southeast Asia, India, and Muslim lands–and there are others) unless there is a perception in those areas that the Christian faith is not a subtraction from but an enhancement of valued social identities. People especially have an emotional investment in their ethnic identities, which belong to them through physical and cultural inheritance. It would be most helpful from a Christian mission perspective if religious identities could be separated from national, cultural, and ethnic identities so that these identities are seen as the result of historical and individual circumstances. Then, religious identities may be seen as coming basically from personal choices. This is the advantage of secularizing and religiously diverse societies where religious groups are made up primarily of voluntary societies and there are many cross-cutting ties between various subgroups. However, for many people in the present time, their religious identity still appears to be an inherited or assigned identity along with ethnic, national and cultural identities. Is it not one of the major purposes of God in history to make the identity we obtain through faith to be based on our choice to believe, not simply or primarily on our circumstances or inherited conditions? If you were Jesus, would you not rather have followers who have chosen to follow you than followers who were assigned to you by their circumstances? The shift away from an emphasis on religious identity based on inherited circumstances ("I was born a—fill in the name of the religion") toward an emphasis on the centrality of choice has been taking place in the United States. Human planning, intelligence, or spirituality did not cause the shift, but rather it came because of the "historical accident" of the mixing of many peoples and religions in America and ongoing social and geographical mobility. Such providential changes are taking place in other lands.

In the meantime until religions become primarily voluntary groups and individual faith based primarily (never solely) on choice, we live in conditions where religions, cultures, ethnicities, and even nationalities are bound up together. Further, these identities are transmitted through personal socialization in families. Some separation of these various sources of identities has taken place in various places, but there is much more separation that is needed if religious choices are to be free. We have to ask, is it possible for Christianity to enhance Buddhist, Hindu, and Muslim identities and vice versa? There may be cultural aspects to all three of these religions which Christianity would enhance and would in turn enhance Christianity. There are already experiments underway in which people become Buddhist, Hindu, and Muslim Christians. This issue will continue to be debated by missionaries and missiologists, not to speak of individual Christians (Hunsberger 1998; Hoefer 2001; Winter 2003; Tennent 2005). What we know is that the source of any enhancement of life is not Christianity, but Jesus Christ. He will remain at the center of all aspects of life. This is where the focus on Jesus Christ becomes crucial. It is really the major basis for the spread of Christianity.

The perception of what God's love in Christ can do for the self-esteem of individuals is a work of the Spirit of God as the missionary witnesses to that love through word and deed. Of course, the search for self-esteem is a theologically ambivalent motive. Self-esteem based on some personal role or social status, including in a church, often leads to asserting superiority over others. Such a sense of self-esteem easily creeps into the consciousness of most people, including Christians. It is not the self-esteem that is built upon the grace of God. On the other hand, most personal and social identities can be viewed in the light of God's creation and grace and thereby become a basis for healthy self-esteem and self-acceptance.

Proposition 7.2 is a reminder to missionaries that the Christian gospel has provided a doorway for believers into a gathering that can be extremely rewarding and fulfilling as it brings people together in worship, fellowship, and service. The informal and formal symbols that are repeatedly employed in these various interactions in which

God's presence is invoked serve to produce profound emotions. These emotions are continually renewed in the regular meetings held by Christians in small and large gatherings ("rites of intensification"). The content of Christianity discussed in the first three chapters is the source for the rich symbols that produce the emotional and moral energy found in Christianity. This energy has carried Christianity around the world and created the largest and most widespread religion on earth. In many ways Christian missionaries do not need to seek to create the emotional energy that people desire. Rather by giving attention to the content of the faith (both belief and experience,) missionaries will enable people to find the emotional fulfillment that all people seek.

The most encouraging fact for missionaries is that people all over the world who have never heard the gospel of the love of God in Jesus Christ have come to believe it without any actual empirical proof of Christ's existence and work other than the word and example (often not that good or clear) of the bearer of this message. This is strong evidence that there exists in humans a need for Divine grace and acceptance. To obtain access to Divine grace and a personal connection with God is the underlying human need; enhancement of life with self-esteem and emotional fulfillment are outcomes of this personal connection. People come to realize that meeting the basic need to receive God's redeeming grace is followed by obtaining the outcomes of faith.

RELIGION AND IRRELIGION

After reviewing the spread of religions it may seem strange to consider irreligion, but I felt forced to do this by the fact that the modern irreligion movement arose from within a Christian context. In many ways, the irreligion movement has even exhibited religious qualities, especially in its more extreme political forms. The theoretical framework I used for analyzing the spread of religions seemed useful to apply to irreligion.

The implications of the analysis in Chapter 8 may be debated, but I believe they are that irreligion is not as dangerous to Christianity as bad religion, especially bad Christianity. Modern militant atheism is really a revival of nineteenth century naïve atheism that draws its strength from bad religion. Of course, irreligion can be extremely destructive to Christianity and all religions when it is allied with an antireligious ideology such as Communism in which coercive power is applied against all religions. It might also be argued that the secularization process so strongly supported by the irreligion movement creates an overall environment which can be very corrosive to faith. However, as we have seen, secularization is a two-edged sword. It provides an environment for a secular life-style, but it also gives freedom to create strong voluntarily based Christian communities with strong socialization and communication programs. In fact, secularization (not secularism) does not seem to have greatly injured Christianity in the United States, but rather to have stimulated its vitality. For this reason from the earliest days many Christians in the U.S.A. supported the secularization movement. It should not be forgotten that the secularization movement of the modern era was accompanied by a great Christian missionary movement.

Irreligion offers a very weak positive program. Smith with Denton (2005:181) note the fact that even if it is not understood in popular culture, the logical positivism and naïve empiricism that is an important component of the belief of irreligion has been shown to be philosophically untenable. Scientism has shown itself to be as much a belief as any religious belief. Also, people who think that they can function as completely autonomous individuals are fooling themselves and others. Attempts by individuals to be completely autonomous mean coming under the power of some hidden or unconscious drives that are often self-destructive. It has also been noted that the irreligious have a history of not being able to maintain ongoing fellowships or strong networks precisely because of the tendency of the irreligious to seek personal autonomy. The organizations that have been formed, for example, Communist, have tended to be extremely authoritarian.

However, aside from being an imitation or quasi-religion, most important, irreligion cannot offer the intrinsic rewards (not exchange or earned rewards) that come with faith in God. In the end, irreligion turns out to be an essentially negative faith whose main strength and basis of influence has been its opposition to overly authoritarian religion and societies that can be expressed on a personal level in families. When irreligion has had its best influence, it was not because of its ideas, but because humane irreligious people were joined or led by religious people in criticism of bad or unjust social conditions that were supported by other religious people.

Thus, I concluded that the greatest danger to Christianity is bad Christianity, which can infect almost all branches of the faith. When it is recognized that the irreligion movement appeared in a Christian context, then it appears that the freedoms inspired by Christianity that were placed alongside authoritarian Christianity stimulated the development of much of modern irreligion. Probably Communism would not have appeared in Europe except for the failures of Christianity to emphasize social justice during the industrial revolution. As it was, self-corrections were made in much of Europe so that Communism had its greatest successes (with the exception of Russia where it has since collapsed) primarily in traditionally authoritarian societies that were also reacting to outside domination. Going further back in history for examples of bad Christianity, would Islam have come into existence some three hundred years after Constantine if Christianity had maintained the voluntary character that it had in its first three hundred years? Instead, Islam developed when the major expression of

Christianity was as a state religion in a powerful "Christian Empire." Furthermore, it was a state religion that strongly oppressed what it considered heretical forms of Christianity that existed in the Middle East exactly where Islam arose opposing domination from both Zoroastrian Persia and Christian Constantinople.

The numerous failings of Christianity that bring shame upon it have continuing effects that are still felt and are causing great damage to the witness to Jesus Christ. Probably what has happened in Western history and in the United States to injure Christianity the most is the creation of "cultural Christianity." Of course, there are many forms of "cultural Christianity." For example, for over one hundred years after the abolition of slavery (itself a major blot on Christian history), Christianity accepted and approved the racism built into the culture of the nation, especially in the South. Smith with Denton (2005:176) discuss an ongoing particular form of cultural religion which invades Christianity in the United States through mass-consumer capitalism. David Smith (2003:124,125) refers to this as "the culture of economism" characterized by addiction to wealth and pleasure. In the self-seeking of consumerism, religion is turned into one product among others, chosen "to satisfy people's subjectively defined needs, tastes, and wants." "Moralistic Theistic Deism" (Smith and Denton 2005) easily fits into such a cultural religion.

All of these and other forms of bad Christianity are a greater danger to Christianity than irreligion because they may well convey the impression that they are genuine Christianity and thus deceive their adherents, but even worse, deceive those who are non-Christians. A wolf in sheep's clothing is a greater danger to the herd than an uncovered wolf. This view that bad Christianity is more dangerous than irreligion is conveyed by the Bible in portraying the Devil as the "Deceiver" and "Liar" and as appearing as an "angel of light" (II Corinthians 11:14).

Even more clearly, the Bible itself is the story of God focusing on his chosen people to continually correct and purify them so that God may be clearly known in the world. The apostolic word is "For the time has come for judgment to begin with the household of God; if it begins with us, what will be the end for those who do not obey the gospel of God?" (I Peter 4:17) Perhaps Christians need more than anything else a healthy fear of the judgment of God on themselves and a sense of continuous repentance (turning around) with continuous efforts to witness more clearly to Jesus Christ. Humility combined with thanksgiving is the basic apostolic view toward God.

CONCLUSION

The incarnation and atoning death and resurrection of Jesus Christ together with the spread of the gospel of Christ around the world are evidence that God desires fellowship with human beings and is at work in the world through human beings. God's work, as open and as public as it has been in Jesus Christ and in the spread of faith in him around the world, is embedded in human lives and history so that it is subject to the influence of socio-cultural conditions on earth. That is, although God took the initiative in the history of Israel and in Christ and still takes the initiative through God's Spirit, there is a real participation of humans in God's actions, making humans a secondary agency for God's work. This gives God's work a hidden quality and means that it is often hindered and blocked by human failings.

Humans are not either simply pawns of God or prisoners of the conditions in which they live. They can be true agents through their choices. God desires that humans choose to seek God's grace and fellowship and to love and serve others. For this reason, it is reasonable to believe that God's purposes are being carried out in history with the increasing opportunities around the world for individuals to make religious choices. However, physical conditions in the world, but particularly the overlapping political, economic, social, cultural, and psychological conditions created by human agency, continue to affect human responses to and participation in God's work. Some of these conditions are relatively neutral, even beautiful, in their effect, representing human diversity. Other conditions are clearly negative in their effect because they harm and destroy human lives and, when Christians are involved, injure the witness to Jesus Christ.

Through faith in Christ and with the power supplied by God's Spirit, humans can come to perceive what God has done for them in Jesus Christ. Furthermore, through continuous study of God's word, fellowship with God's people, the sacraments, and prayers (Acts 2: 42) –the "means of grace"–the perception of what God has done for us will grow and be combined with joyful praise and thanksgiving. The most important mission strategy may well be worship itself. This is a basic recommendation of Ammerman's (2005) study of congregations. In his inspiring discussion of the Apocalypse (the Book of Revelation), Smith (2003:113,114) also makes worship central to mission strategy. He adds Christian imagination (as revealed in the Apocalypse) that needs continual purging and renewing as it encounters powerful cultural influences, and finally the practice of discipleship, which was shown by Jesus to be costly.

This best way to end this book is with the words of praise from the Apostle Paul after exposing his wrestling in Romans 9, 10, and 11 to express God's work in history with Israel and the Gentiles:

> O the depth and the riches and wisdom and knowledge
> of God! How unsearchable are his judgments and
> how inscrutable his ways!

> "For who has known the mind of the Lord?
> Or who has been his counselor?"
> "Or who has given a gift to him,
> to receive a gift in return?"

For from him and through him and to him are all things. To him be the glory forever. Amen

(Romans 11:33-36. From the New Revised Standard Version)

REFERENCES

Ahmed, Akbar S. 2003. *Islam Under Siege*. Cambridge, UK: Polity Press.

Alexander, Jeffrey C. 2003. *The Meaning of Social Life: A Cultural Sociology.* New York: Oxford University Press.

Alland, Alexander, Jr. 1980. *To Be Human: An Introduction to Anthropology*. New York: John Wiley & Sons, Inc.

Allison, Scott T. and George R. Goethals. 2011. *Heroes: What They Do & Why We Need Them.* New York: Oxford University Press.

Althusser, L. 1971. *Lenin and Philosophy and Other Essays*. London: New Left Books.

Ammerman, Nancy T. 1997. *Congregation and Community*. New Brunswick, NJ: Rutgers University Press.

_____. 2005. *Pillars of Faith: American Congregations and Their Partners*. Berkeley, CA: University of California Press.

Ammerman, Nancy T., Jackson W. Carroll, Carl S. Dudely, and William McKinney, eds. 1998. *Studying Congregations: A New Handbook*. Nashville: Abingdon.

Ammerman, Nancy T. and Carl S. Dudley. 2002. *Congregations in Transition*. San Francisco: Jossey-Bass.

Armstrong, Karen. 2000. *Islam.* New York: The Modern Library.

_____. 2001. *Buddha.* New York: Penguin Putnam, Inc

Arnold, Thomas. 2006 [1896]. *The Spread of Islam in the World: A History of Peaceful Preaching.* New Delhi: Goodword Books.

Ashford, S. and N. Timms. 1992. *What Europe Thinks: A Study of West European Values*. Dartmouth: Aldershot.

Bacon, Francis. 1952 [1605]. "Advancement in Learning." In *Great Books of the Western World,* ed. Robert Mayard Hutchins. 1-101. Chicago: Encyclopedia Britannica, Inc.

Bainbridge, William Sims. 2005. "Atheism." *Interdisciplinary Journal of Research on Religion.* 1(2): 1-26.

Barnett, H. G. 1953. *Innovation, the Basis of Cultural Change*. New York: McGraw-Hill Company, Inc.

Barrett, David B. 1982. *World Christian Encyclopedia*. Nairobi: Oxford

University Press.

Barrett, David B., George T. Kurian, and Todd M. Johnson. 2001. *World Christian Encyclopedia: A Comparative Survey of Churches and Religions in the Modern World*. New York: Oxford University Press.

Barrett, David B. and Todd M. Johnson. 2001. *World Christian Trends AD 30 – AD 2000*. Pasadena, CA: William Carey Library.

Barrett, Justin L. 2004. *Why Would Anyone Believe in God?* Walnut Creek, CA: Altamira Press.

Basham, A. L., ed. 1989 [1975]. *A Cultural History of India*. Delhi: Oxford University Press.

Beckford, James A. 1978. "Accounting for Conversion." *British Journal of Sociology*. 29(2): 249-262.

_____. 1983. "The Restoration of 'Power' to the Sociology of Religion." *Sociological Analysis*. 44:11-33.

Bellah, Robert N. 1969 [1964]. "Religious Evolution." In *Sociology and Religion*, eds. Norman Birnbaum and Gertrud Lenzer. 67-83. Englewood Cliffs, NJ: Prentice-Hall, Inc.

_____. 1985 [1957]. *Tokugawa Religion*. New York: The Free Press.

Benz, Ernst. 1976. "Buddism in the Western World." In *The Cultural, Political, and Religious Significance of Buddhism in the Modern World*, ed. Henrick Dumoulin. 305-322. New York: Macmillan.

Berman, Harold J. 1983. *Law and Revolution: the Formation of the Western Legal Tradition*. Cambridge, MA: Harvard University Press.

Beyer, Peter. 1999. "Secularization from the Perspective of Globalization: a Response to Dobbelaere." *Sociology of Religion*. 60(3): 289-301.

Beyerlein, Kraig. 2003. "Educational Elites and the Movement to Secularize Public Education: The Case of the National Education Association." In *The SecularRevolution*, ed. Christian Smith. 160-196. Berkeley, CA: University of California Press.

Bird, Frederick. 2002. "Early Christianity as an Unorganized Ecumenical Religious Movement." In *Handbook of Early Christianity*, eds. Anthony J. Blasi, Jean Buhaime, and Paul-André Turcotte. 225-246. Walnut Creek, CA: AltaMira Press.

Bowen, Kurt. 1996. *Evangelism and Apostasy: The Evolution and Impact of*

Evangelicals in Modern Mexico. Montreal: McGill-Queen's University Press.

Branscombe, Nyla R., Naomi Ellemers, Russell Spears, and Bertjan Doosje. 1999. "The Context and Content of Social Identity Threat." In *Social Identity*, eds. Naomi Ellemers, Russell Spears, and Bertjan Doosje. 35-58. Oxford, UK: Blackwell Publishers.

Brinton, Craine. 1967. "Enlightenment." In *The Encyclopedia of Philosophy,* ed. Paul Edwards. 519-525. New York: Macmillan Publishing Co., Inc.

Bruce, Steve. 2002. *God is Dead: Secularization in the West.* Oxford, UK: Blackwell Publishing.

Buckley, M. J. 1987. *At the Origins of Modern Atheism.* New Haven: Yale University Press.

Campbell, Colin. 1972 [1971]. *Toward a Sociology of Irreligion.* New York: Herder and Herder.

Carmichael, Joel. 1967. *The Shaping of the Arabs, a Study of Ethnic Identity.* New York: Macmillan.

Carnes, Tony and Fenggang Yang, eds. 2004. *Asian American Religions: The Making and Remaking of Borders and Boundaries.* New York: New York University.

Casanova, Jose. 1994. *Public Religion in the Modern World.* Chicago: University of Chicago Press.

_____. 2003. "Beyond European and American Exceptionalisms: Toward a Global Perspective." In *Predicting Religion*, eds. Grace Davie, Paul Heelas, and Linda Woodhead. 17-29. Burlington, VT: Ashgate Publishing Company.

Ch'en, Kenneth K. S. 1973 [1964]. *Buddhism in China, A Historical Survey.* Princeton, NJ: Princeton University Press.

Cohn, Norman. 1961. *The Pursuit of the Millennium.* New York: Harper & Row.

Collins, Randall. 1999. *Macro History: Essays in Sociology of the Long Run.* Stanford, CA: Stanford University Press.

_____. 2004. *Interactive Ritual Chains.* Princeton, NJ: Princeton University Press.

Conn, Walter. 1986a. *Christian Conversion: A Developmental Interpretation of Autonomy and Surrender.* New York: Paulist Press.

———. 1986b. "Adult Conversion." *Pastoral Psychology.* 34(4):225-236.

———. 1987. "Pastoral Counseling for Self-transcendence: The Integration of Psychology and Theology." *Pastoral Psychology.* 36(1):29-48.

David, Barbara and John C. Turner. 1996. "Studies in Self-Categorization and Minority Conversion: Is Being a Member of the Out-Group an Advantage?" *British Journal of Social Psychology.* 35(1):179-199.

Davie, Grace. 1994. *Religion in Britain Since 1945: Believing Without Belonging.* Oxford: Blackwell.

———. 2000. *Religion in Modern Europe.* Oxford: Oxford University Press.

Davie, Grace, Paul Heelas, and Linda Woodhead, eds. 2003. *Predicting Religion.* Hampshire, England: Ashgate Publishing Limited.

Deanesly, Margaret. 1981 [1925]. *A History of the Medieval Church 590-1500.* London: Methuen.

Demerath III, N. J. 2001. *Crossing the Gods. World Religions and World Politics.* New Brunswick, NJ: Rutgers University Press.

Dobbelaere, Karel. 1999. "Toward an Integrated Perspective of the Processes Related to the Descriptive Concept of Secularization." *Sociology of Religion.* 60(3): 229-247.

Douglas, Mary. 1986. "The Social Preconditions of Radical Skepticism." In *Power, Action and Belief: A New Sociology of Knowledge? Sociological Review Monograph No. 32,* ed. John Law. 68-87. London: Routledge & Kegan Paul.

Drake, H. A. 2000. *Constantine and the Bishops: The Politics of Intolerance.* Baltimore, MD: The Johns Hopkins Press.

Drekmeier, Charles. 1962. *Kingship and Community in Early India.* Stanford, CA: Stanford University Press.

Dudley, Carl S. 1997. *How Churches Launch New Community Ministries.* Bloomington, IN: Indiana University Press.

Durkheim, Emile. 1965 [1915]. *The Elementary Forms of the Religious Life.* New York: The Free Press.

Ebaugh, Helen Rose. 2002. *Religion Across Borders.* Walnut Creek, CA:

Altamira Press.

Ebaugh, Helen Rose and Janet Saltzman Chafetz, eds. 2000. *Religion and the New Immigrants: Continuities and Adaptations in Immigrant Congregations.* Walnut Creek, CA: Altamira Press.

Ecklund, Elane Howard. 2010. *Science vs. Religion: What Scientists Really Think.* New York: Oxford University Press.

Ecklund, Elane, Jerry Z Park, and Katherine L. Sorrell. 2011a. "Scientists Negotiate Boundaries Between Religion and Science." *Journal for the Scientific Study of Religion.* 50(3): 552-569.

Ecklund, Elane and Elizabeth Long. 2011b. "Scientists and Spirituality." *Sociology of Religion: A Quarterly Review.* 72(3): 253-274.

Ecklund, Elane and Kristen Schultz Lee. 2011c. "Atheists and Agnostics Negotiate Religion and Family." *Journal for the Scientific Study of Religion.* 50(4): 728-743.

Epstein, Seymour. 1985. "The Implications of Cognitive-Experimental Self-Theory for Research in Social Psychology and Personality." *Psychological Bulletin.* 98:513-537.

Ernst, Carl W. 2003. *Following Muhammad.* Chapel Hill, NC: The University of North Carolina Press.

Esposito, John L. 2010. *The Future of Islam.* New York: Oxford University Press.

Evans, John H. 2003. "After the Fall: Attempts to Establish an Explicitly Theological Voice in Debates over Science and Medicine after 1960." In *The Secular Revolution*, ed. Christian Smith. 434-462. Berkeley, CA: University of California Press.

Feldman, Kenneth A. and Theodore M. Newcomb. 1970. *The Impact of College on Students.* San Francisco: Jossey-Bass.

Finke, Roger and Patricia Wittberg. 2000. "Organizational Revival from Within: Explaining Revivalism and Reform in the Roman Catholic Church." *Journal for the Scientific Study of Religion.* 39(2): 154-170.

Flory, Richard W. 2003. "Promoting a Secular Standard: Secularization and Modern Journalism." In *The Secular Revolution*, ed. Christian Smith. 395-433. Berkeley, CA: University of California Press.

Fox, Robin Lane. 1987. *Pagans and Christians.* New York: Alfred A.

Knopf, Inc.

Freston, Paul. 2001. *Evangelicals and Politics in Asia, Africa and Latin America*. New York: Cambridge University Press.

Friedman, Thomas L. 2002. "Iraq Upside Down," Op Ed. September 18, 2002. *New York Times*.

_____. 2005. *The World is Flat: A Brief History of the Twenty-First Century*. New York: Farrar, Straus, & Giroux.

Froese, Paul. 2005. "Secular Czechs and Devout Slovaks: Explaining Religious Differences." *Review of Religious Research*. 46(3): 269-283.

_____. 2008. *The Plot to Kill God: Findings from the Soviet Experiment in Secularization*. Berkeley, CA: University of California Press.

Froese, Paul and Steven Pfaff. 2005. "Explaining a Religious Anomaly: A Historical Analysis of Secularization in Eastern Germany." *Journal for the Scientific Study of Religion*. 44(4): 397-422.

Gard, Richard A., ed. 1962. *Buddhism*. New York: George Braziller.

Garma, Carlos. 2002. "Religious Affiliation and Conflict in the Indian Municipalities of Chiapas." *Social Compass*. 49(1): 29-42.

Garroutte, Eva Marie. 2003. "The Positivist Attack on Baconian Science and Religious Knowledge in the 1870s." In *The Secular Revolution*, ed. Christian Smith. 197-215. Berkeley, CA: University of California Press.

Geertz, Clifford. 1956. *"The Development of the Javanese Economy: A Socio-cultural Approach."* Cambridge: Center for International Studes, Massachusetts Institute of Technology.

General Social Survey. 1988. National Opinion Research Center. University of Chicago.

Ghozzi, Kamel. 2002. The Study of Resilience and Decay in Ulema Goups: Tunisia and Iran as an Example. *Sociology of Religion*. 63(3): 317-334.

Gill, Robin, C. Kirk Hadaway, and Penny Long Marler. 1998. "Is Religious Belief Declining in Britain?" *Journal for the Scientific Study of Religion*. 37(3): 507-516.

Goffman, Erving. 1967. *Interaction Ritual*. New York: Doubleday

Gooren, Henri. 2010. *Religious Conversion and Disaffiliation: Tracing Patterns of Change in Faith Practices*. New York: Palgrave

Macmillan.

Guest, Kenneth. 2003. *God in Chinatown*. New York: New York University Press.

Gunn, T. Jeremy. 2003. "Shaping an Islamic Identity: Religion, Islamism, and the State in Central Asia." *Sociology of Religion*. 64(3): 389-410.

Hajime, Nakamura. 1989 [1987]. "Mahayana Buddhism." In *Buddhism and Asian History*, ed. Joseph M. Kitagawa and Mark D. Cummings. 215-239. New York: Macmillan Publishing Company.

Hanciles, Jehu J. 2003. Mission and Migration: Some Implications for the Twenty-first-Century Church. *International Bulletin of Missionary Research*. 27:4. 146-153.

Harper, Susan Billington. 1995. "Ironies of Indigenization: Some Cultural Repercussions of Mission in South India." *International Bulletin of Missionary Research*. 19(1): 13-20.

Hecht, Jennifer Michael. 2004. *Doubt: A History*. San Francisco: Harper.

Hefner, Robert W. 1993. *Conversion to Christianity*. Berkeley, CA: University of California Press.

Herbrechtsmeier, William. 1993. "Buddhism and the Definition of Religion: One More Time." *Journal for the Scientific Study of Religion*. 32(1): 1-18.

Hiebert, Paul G. 1985. *Anthropological Insights for Missionaries*. Grand Rapids, MI: Baker Book House.

Hirst, Rob. 2003. "Social Networks and Personal Beliefs: An Example from Modern Britain." In *Predicting Religion*, ed. Grace Davie, Paul Heelas, and Linda Woodhead. 86-94. Burlington, VT: Ashgate Publishing Company.

Hoefer, Herbert. 2001. *Churchless Christianity*. Pasadena, CA: William Carey Library.

Hoge, Dean, Benton Johnson, and Donald A. Luidens. 1994. *Vanishing Boundaries: The Religion of Mainline Protestant Baby Boomers*. Louisville, KY: Westminster/John Knox Press.

Hogg, Michael A. and Dominic Abrams. 1990 [1988]. *Social Identifications*. London: Routledge.

_____. and _____. 1993. "Toward a Single-Process Uncertainty-

Reduction Model of Social Motivation in Groups." In *Group Motivation*, eds. Michael Hogg and Dominic Abrams. 173-190. New York: Harvester Wheatsheaf.

Horrell, David G. 2002. " 'Becoming Christian': Solidifying Christian Identity and Content." In *Handbook of Early Christianity,* eds. by Anthony J. Blasi, Jean Duhaime, and Paul-Andre Turcotte. 309-335. Walnut Creek, CA: Altamira Press.

Hourani, Albert. 1991. *A History of the Arab Peoples.* New York: Warner Books Edition.

Huff, Toby E. 1993. *The Rise of Early Modern Science. Islam, China, and the West.* Cambridge, UK: Cambridge University Press.

Hunsberger, George R. 1998. "Conversion and Community: Revisiting the Lesslie Newbigin-M. M. Thomas Debate." *International Bulletin of Missionary Research.* 22(3):112-117.

Hunter, George G. III. 2000. *The Celtic Way of Evangelism.* Nashville, TN: Abingdon Press.

Hunter, James Davison. 1991. *Culture Wars: The Struggle to Define America.* New York: BasicBooks.

_____.2010. *To Change the World: The Irony, Tragedy, and Possibility of Christianity in the Late Modern World.* New York: Oxford University Press

Huntington, Samuel P. 1996. *The Clash of Civilizations and the Remaking of World Order.* New York: Touchtone.

Jaffarian, Michael. 2003. "The Demographics of World Religions Entering the Twenty-first Century." In *Between Past and Future: Evangelical Mission Entering the Twenty-first Century,* ed. Jonathan J. Bonk. 249-271. Pasadena, CA: William Carey Library.

Jaspers, Karl. 1949. *Vomursprung und Zeit der Geschichte.* Munich: R. Piper.

Jelen, Ted Gerard and Clyde Wilcox. 2002. *Religion and Politics in Comparative Perspective.* Cambridge, UK: Cambridge University Press.

Jenkins, Philip. 2002. *The Next Christendom: the Coming of Global Christianity.* Oxford, UK: Oxford University Press.

_____. 2011. *Jesus Wars: How Four Partiarchs, Three Queens, and Two Emperors Decided What Christians Would Believe for the Next 1,500 Years.* New York: HarperCollins Publishers.

Johnson, Todd M., David B. Barrett, and Peter F. Crossing. "Christianity 2012: The 200th Anniversary of American Foreign Missions." *International Bulletin of Missionary Research.* 36(1): 28-29.

Johnstone, Patrick and Jason Mandryk. 2001. *Operation World: 21st Century Edition.* Pasadena, CA: Cary Library Publishers.

Kaelber, Lutz. 1998. *Schools of Asceticism. Ideology and Organization in Medieval Religious Communities.* University Park, PA: The Pennsylvania State University Press.

Kane, Danielle and Jung Mee Park. 2009. "The Puzzle of Korean Christianity: Geopolitical Networks and Religious Conversion in Early Twentieth-Century East Asia." *The American Journal of Sociology.* 115(2): 365-404.

Kapleau, Philip. 1979. *Zen: Dawn in the West.* Garden City, NY: Anchor Press.

Keay, John. 2000. *India.* New York: Atlantic Monthly Press.

Kemeny, P. C., 2003. "Power, Ridicule, and the Destruction of Religious Moral Reform Politics in the 1920s." In *The Secular Revolution*, ed. Christian Smith. 216-268. Berkeley, CA: University of California Press.

Kim, Sebastian C. H. 2005 [2003]. *In Search of Identity: Debates on Religious Conversion in India.* Delhi, India: Oxford University Press.

Koestler, Arthur. 1976. *The Thirteenth Tribe, the Khazar Empire and its Heritage.* New York: Random House.

Kosmin, Barry A. and Ariela Keysar. 2006. *Religion in a Free Market: Religions and Non-Religious Americans, Who, What, Why and Where.* Ithaca, NY: Paramount Market Publishing.

Kraft, Charles H. 1979. *Christianity in Culture.* Maryknoll: Orbis Books.

Kurtz, Lester R. 1995. *Gods in the Global Village: the World's Religions in Sociological Perspective.* Thousand Oaks, CA: Pine Forge Press.

Kwon, Ho-Youn, Kwang Chung Kim, and R. Stephen Warner. 2001. *Korean Americans and Their Religions.* University Park, PA: The

Pennsylvania State University Press.

Lamb, Alastair. 1989 [1975] "Indian Influence in Ancient South-East Asia." In *A Cultural History of India,* ed. A. L. Basham. 442-454. Delhi: Oxford University Press.

Lambert, Yves. 1999. "Religion in Modernity as a New Axial Age: Secularization or New Religious Forms?" *Sociology of Religion.* 60(3): 303-333.

Lapidus, Ira M. 2005 [1988]. *A History of Islamic Societies. Second Edition.* Cambridge, UK: Cambridge University Press.

Latourette, Kenneth Scott. 1937. *A History of the Expansion of Christianity. The First Five Centuries. Volume I.* New York: Harper & Brothers.

_____. 1938. *A History of the Expansion of Christianity. A Thousand Years of Uncertainty. A.D.500-A.D. 1500. Volume II.* New York. Harper & Brothers Publishers.

_____. 1939. *A History of the Expansion of Christianity. Three Centuries of Advance A.D. 1500-A.D. 1800. Volume III.* New York: Harper & Brothers Publishers

_____. 1943. *A History of the Expansion of Christianity. The Great Century in the Americas, Australasia, and Africa A.D. 1800-AD 1914. Volume V.* New York: Harper & Brothers Publishers.

_____. 1945. *A History of the Expansion of Christianity. Advance Through Storm. A.D.1914 and After, with Concluding Generalizations. Volume VII.* New York: Harper & Brothers Publishers.

_____. 1953. *A History of Christianity.* New York: Harper & Brothers Publishers.

_____.1956. *The Chinese, Their History and Culture.* New York: The Macmillan Company

Le Fait Missionnaire. Social Sciences and Missions. Lausanne, Switxerland.

Lee, Martha F. 1988. *The Nation of Islam, an American Millenarian Movement.* Lewiston: NY: Edwin Mellen Press.

Legge, J. D. 1964. *Indonesia.* Englewood Cliffs, NJ: Prentice-Hall, Inc.

Lewis, Bernard. 1993. *Islam in History.* Chicago: Open Court Publishing Company.

_____.1994 [1993]. *Islam and the West.* New York: Oxford University

Press.

Lien, Pei-te and Tony Carnes. 2004. "The Religious Demography of Asian American Boundary Crossing." In *Asian American Religions: The Making and Remaking of Borders and Boundaries*, eds. Tony Carnes and Fenggang Yang. 38-51. New York: New York University Press.

Lightman, B. V. 1987. *The Origins of Agnosticism: Victorians Unbelief and the Limits of Knowledge.* Baltimore, MD: John Hopkins University Press.

Lofland, John. 1966. *Doomsday Cult: A Study of Conversion, Proselytization, and Maintenance of Faith.* Englewood Cliffs, NJ: Prentice-Hall.

Lofland, John, and Rodney Stark. 1965. "Becoming a World-saver: A Theory of Conversion to a Deviant Perspective." *American Sociological Review*. 30(6): 862-875.

Lubis, Mochtar. 1990. *Indonesia, Land Under the Rainbow*. Singapore: Oxford University Press.

Luzbetak, Louis J. 1963. *The Church and Cultures, an Applied Anthropology for the Religious Worker.* Techny, IL: Divine Word Publications.

MacMullen, Ramsey. 1997. *Christianity & Paganism in the Fourth to the Eighth centuries*. New Haven, CT: Yale University Press.

Mamiya, Lawrence H. 1982. "From Black Muslim to Bilalian: the Evolution of a Movement." *Journal for the Scientific Study of Religion*. 21(2):138-152.

Mannheim, Karl. 1936. *Ideology and Utopia*. Trans. Louis Wirth and Edward Shils. New York: Harcourt, Brace & World, Inc.

Marr, John R. 1989 [1975]. The Early Dravidians. In *A Cultural History of India*, ed. A. L. Basham. 30-37. Delhi: Oxford University Press.

Martin, David. 1978. *A General Theory of Secularization*. Oxford, UK: Blackwell.

_____. 1990. *Tongues of Fire: the Explosion of Pentecostalism in Latin America*. Oxford, UK: Basil Blackwell.

McGavran, Donald A. 1957 [1955]. *How Churches Grow*. New York: Friendship Press.

McGrath, Alister. 2004. *The Twilight of Atheism: The Rise and Fall of Disbelief in the Modern World.* New York: Doubleday.

McLeod, Hew. 1989 [1975]. Sikhism. In *A Cultural History of India*, ed. A. L. Basham. 294-302. Delhi: Oxford University Press.

Meander, Keith G. 2003. " 'My Own Salvation': The *Christian Century* and Psychology's Secularizing of American Protestantism." In *The Secular Revolution*, ed. Christian Smith. 269-309. Berkeley, CA: University of California Press.

Meeks, Wayne A. 1993. *The Origins of Christian Morality: The First Two Centuries.* New Haven: Yale University Press.

Mehl, Roger. 1970 [1965]. *The Sociology of Protestantism.* Trans. James H. Farley. Philadelphia, PA: Westminster Press.

Merton, Robert K. 1973 [1942]. "The Normative Structure of Science." In *The Sociology of Science,* ed. Norman W. Storer. 267-278. Chicago, IL: University of Chicago Press.

Moffett, Samuel Hugh. 1992. *A History of Christianity in Asia, Volume I: Beginnings to 1500.* San Francisco: Harper.

Montgomery, Robert L. 1991. "The Spread of Religions and Macrosocial Relations." *Sociological Analysis (*now *Sociology of Religion). * 52(1): 37-53.

_____. 1996. *The Diffusion of Religions: A Sociological Perspective.* Lanham, MD: University Press of America.

_____. 1999. *Introduction to the Sociology of Missions.* Westport, CT: Praeger.

_____. 2002. *The Lopsided Spread of Christianity.* Westport, CT: Praeger

Mullins, Mark. 1998. *Christianity Made in Japan.* Honolulu: University of Hawai'i Press.

Nadeau, Kathy. 2002. "Peasant Resistance and Religious Protests in Early Philippine Society: Turning Friars Against the Grain." *Journal for the Scientific Study of Religion.* 41(1): 75-85.

Newport, Frank. 2010. "Americans' Church Attendance Inches Up in 2010." *Gallup Wellbeing.* June 25, 2010. www.gallup.com.

Ng-Quinn, Michael. 1993. "National Identity in Premodern China: Formation and Role Enactment." In *China's Quest for National*

Identity. eds. Lowell Dittmer and Samuel S. Kim. 32-61. Ithica: Cornell University Press.

Niles, D. T., 1951. *That They May Have Life*. New York: Harper & Brothers.

Norris, Pippa and Ronald Inglehart. 2006 [2004]. *Sacred and Secular: Religion and Politics Worldwide*. Cambridge, UK: Cambridge University Press.

Noss, John B. 1949. *Man's Religions*. New York: The Macmillan Company.

Nutting, Anthony. 1964. *The Arabs*. New York: The American Library.

Oliver, Douglas L. 1951. *The Pacific Islands*. Garden City, NY: Doubleday & Company.

Orru, Marco and Amy Wang. 1992. "Durkheim, Religion, and Buddhism." *Journal for the Scientific Study of Religion*. 31(1): 47-61.

Ornstein, Martha. 1975 [1913]. *The Role of Scientific Societies in the Seventeenth Century*. Chicago: University of Chicago Press.

Pagels, E. 1979. *The Gnostic Gospels*. New York: Random House.

Pannenberg, Wolfhart. 1988. *Christianity in a Secularized World*. London: SCM Press.

Park, Chris C. 1994. *Sacred Worlds*. London: Routledge.

Parker Gumucio, Cretian. 2002a. "Religion and the Awakening of Indigenous People in Latin America." *Social Compass*. 49(1): 67-81.

_____. 2002b. "Les Noubelles Formes de Religion dans la Societe Globalisee: un Defi a L'interpretation Sociologique." *Social Compass*. 49(2): 167-186.

Parsons, Talcott. 1964. "Introduction." In *The Sociology of Religion* by Max Weber, trans. Ephraim Fischoff. xix-lxvii. Boston, MA: Beacon Press.

Perry, Ronald W. 1992. "Diffusion Theories." In *Encyclopedia of Sociology*, eds. Edgar F. Borgotta and Marie L. Borgotta. 478-492. New York: Macmillan.

Petran, Tabitha. 1972. *Syria*. New York: Praeger Publishers.

Philip, T. V. 1998. *East of the Euphrates, Early Christianity in Asia*. Delhi, India: ISPCK.

Phipps, William E. 1991. *The Shepherds and Lapsley: Pioneer Presbyterians in the Congo*. Louisville, KY: Presbyterian Publications.

_____. 2001. *William Shepherd: African American Livingston*. Louisville, KY: Geneva Press.

_____. 2004. *Clerical Celibacy: The Heritage*. New York: Continuum.

Pollack, Detlef. 2003. "Religiousness Inside and Outside the Church in Selected Post-Communist Countries of Central and Eastern Europe." *Social Compass*. 50(3): 321-334.

Rambo, Lewis R. 1993. *Understanding Religious Conversion*. New Haven, CT: Yale University Press.

_____. 1999. "Theories of Conversion." *Social Compass*. 46(3): 259-271.

_____. 2003. "Anthropology and the Study of Conversion." In *The Anthropology of Religious Conversion,* eds. Andrew Buckser and Stephen D. Glazier. 211-222. Lanham, MD: Rowman & Littlefield Publishers.

Rahula, Sri Walpola,. 1959. *What the Buddha Taught*, Revised Edition with a Forward by Paul Demieville and a collection of illustrative texts translated from the original Pali. New York: Grove Press.

Rauschenbusch, Walter. 1919 [1912]. *Christianizing the Social Order*. New York: The Macmillan Company.

Renou, Louis, ed. 1962. *Hinduism*. New York: George Braziller, Inc.

Reynolds, Frank and Charles Hallisey. 1989 [1987]. "Buddhist Religion, Culture, and Civilization." In *Buddhism and Asian History,* eds. by Joseph M. Kitagawa and Mark D. Cummings. 3-28. New York: The Macmillan Publishing Company.

Rogers, Everett M. 1995. *Diffusion of Innovations*. New York: The Free Press.

Samuel, Vinay and Chris Sugden. 1999. *Mission as Transformation: A Theology of the Whole Gospel*. Carlisle, CA: Regnum.

Sanneh, Lamin. 1991a. *Translating the Message*. Maryknoll, NY: Orbis Books.

_____. 1991b. "The Yogi and the Commissar. Christian Missions and the New World Order in Africa." In *World Order and Religion*, ed. Wade Clark Roof. 173-192. New York: State University of New York Press.

_____. 1996. *Piety and Power: Muslims and Christians in West Africa*. Maryknoll, NY: Orbis Books.

_____. 2003. *Whose Religion is Christianity? The Gospel Beyond the West*. Grand Rapids, MI: William B. Eerdmans Publishing Company.

Scott, John. 2001. *Power*. Malden, MA: Blackwell Publishers, Inc.

Shapin, Steven. 1994. *A Social History of Truth: Civility and Science in Seventeenth Century England*. Chicago: The University of Chicago Press.

Sharot, Stephen. 2001. *A Comparative Sociology of World Religions*. New York: New York University Press.

_____. 2002. "Beyond Christianity: A Critique of Rational Choice Theory of Religion from a Weberian and Comparative Religions Perspective." *Sociology of Religion*. 63(4): 427-454.

Shaw, Douglas, ed. 2007 [1997] *Ten Thousand Lotus Blossoms of the Heart: Dharma Master Cheng Yen and the Tzu Chi World*. Taipei, Taiwan: Tzu Chi Communications and Culture Foundation.

Shenk, Wilbert R. 2005. "New Wineskins for New Wine: Toward a Post-Christendom Ecclesiology." *International Bulletin of Missionary Research*. 29(2): 73-79.

Shills, Edward. 1972. *The Intellectuals and the Powers*. Chicago, IL: University of Chicago Press.

Sikkink, David .2003. "From Christian Civilization to Individual Civil Liberties: Framing Religion in the Legal Field, 1880-1949." In *The Secular Revolution*, ed. Christian Smith. 310-354. Berkeley, CA: University of California Press.

Smith, Christian. 1998. *American Evangelicalism: Embattled and Thriving*. Chicago: The University of Chicago Press.

_____. ed. 2003a. *The Secular Revolution: Power, Interests, and Conflict in the Secularization of American life*. Berkeley, CA: University of California Press.

_____. 2003b. *Moral, Believing Animals: Human Personhood and Culture*. New York: Oxford University Press.

_____. 2006. "Review of *Sacred and Secular: Religion and Politics Worldwide,* by Pippa Norris and Ronald Inglehart.*" Journal for the Scientific Study of Religion*. 45(4): 623-624.

_____. 2010. *What is a Person: Rethinking Humanity, Social Life, and the*

Moral Good from the Person Up. Chicago: The University of Chicago Press.

Smith, Christian with Melinda Lunquist Denton. 2005. *Soul Searching: The Religious and Spiritual Lives of American Teenagers.* New York: Oxford University Press.

Smith, Christian with Patricia Snell. 2009. *Souls in Transition: The Religious and Spiritual Lives of Emerging Adults.* New York: Oxford University Press.

Smith, David. 2003. *Mission After Christendom.* London: Darton, Longman, & Todd.

Smith, Jesse M. 2011. "Becoming an Atheist in America: Constructing Identity and Meaning from the Rejection of Theism." *Sociology of Religion.* 72(2): 215-237.

Spiro, Melford. 1982 [1970]. *Buddhism and Society: A Great Tradition and Burmese Vicissitudes.* Berkeley, CA: University of California Press.

Stark, Rodney. 1995. "Reconstructing the Rise of Christianity: the Role of Women." *Sociology of Religion.* 56(3): 229-244.

_____. 1996. "Why Religious Movements Succeed or Fail: A Revised General Model." *Journal of Contemporary Religion.* 11(2): 133-146.

_____. 1997 [1996]. *The Rise of Christianity.* San Francisco, CA: Harper.

_____. 1999. "Secularization, R.I.P." *Sociology of Religion.* 60(3): 249-273.

_____. 2001. *One True God. Historical Consequences of Monotheism.* Princeton, NJ: Princeton University Press.

_____. 2003. *For the Glory of God.* Princeton, NJ: Princeton University Press.

_____. 2005. *The Victory of Reason: How Christianity Led to Freedom, Capitalism, and Western Success.* New York: Random House Trade Paperbacks.

Stark, Rodney and William Sims Bainbridge. 1987 [1996]. *A Theory of Religion.* New Brunswick, NJ: Rutgers University Press.

Stark, Rodney and Roger Finke. 2000. *Acts of Faith.* Berkeley, CA: University of California Press.

Steinberg, Stephen. 1974. *The Academic Melting Pot: Catholics and Jews in American Higher Education.* New York: McGraw-Hill.

Stenmark, Mikael. 2001. *Scientism: Science, Ethics, and Religion.* Burlington, VT: Ashgate Publishing Company.

Swatos William H. and Kevin J. Christiano. 1999. "Introduction – Secularization Theory: The Course of a Concept." *Sociology of Religion.* 60(3): 209-228.

Schweitzer, Albert. 1968 [1906]. *The Quest of the Historical Jesus.* New York: Macmillan Publishing Co., Inc.

Tabor, Charles R. 2000. *To Understand the World, to Save the World: The Interface Between Missiology and the Social Sciences.* Harrisburg, PA: Trinity Press International.

Tajfel, Henri.1972. "La Categorization Sociale [Social Categorization]." In *Introduction a la Psychologie Sociale,* ed. S. Moscovici. 272-302. Paris: Larousse.

_____. 1974. *Intergroup Behavior, Social Comparison and Social Change.* Unpublished Katz-Newcomb Lectures at the University of Michigan, Ann Arbor, MI.

_____. 1981. *Human Groups and Social Categories.* Cambridge, UK: Cambridge University Press.

Taylor, Charles. 1989. *The Sources of the Self: The Making of Modern Identity.* Cambridge, MA. Harvard University Press.

Tennent, Timothy C. 2005. "The Challenge of Churchless Christianity: An Evangelical Assessment." *International Bulletin of Missionary Research.* 29(4): 171-177.

Thalheimer, Fred. 1973. "Religiosity and Secularization in the Academic Professions." *Sociology of Eduction.* 46:183-202.

Thapar, Romila. 1969 [1960]. "Asoka and Buddhism." In *Sociology and Religion*, eds. Norman Birnbaum and Gertrud Lenzer. 43-51. Englewood Cliffs. NJ: Prentice-Hall, Inc.

Thomas, George M., Lisa R. Peck, and Channin De Haan. 2003. "Reforming Education, Transforming Religion 1876-1931." In *The Secular Revolution*, ed. Christian Smith. 355-394. Berkeley, CA: University of California Press.

Thuesen, Peter J. 2002. "The Logic of Mainline Churchliness: Historical Background Since the Reformation." In *The Quiet Hand of God,* eds.

Robert Wuthnow and John H. Evans. 27-53. Berkeley, CA: University of California Press.

Tilly, Charles. 1984. *Big Structures, Large Processes, Huge Comparisons.* New York: Russell Sage Foundation.

Tippett, Alan R. 1971. *People Movements in Southern Polynesia, a Study in Church Growth.* Chicago: Moody Press.

Toennies, Ferdinand. 1957 [1887]. *Community and Society.* Trans. Charles P. Loomis. E. Lansing, MI: Michigan State University Press.

Toyoda, Maria A. and Aiji Tanaka. 2002. "Religion and Politics in Japan." In *Religion and Politics in Comparative Perspective,* eds. Ted Gerard Jelen and Clyde Wilcox. 269-286. Cambridge, UK: Cambridge University Press.

Tsukamoto, Zenryu. 1942. *Shina Bukkyoshi Kenkyu, Hokugi-hen.* Tokyo, Japan.

Turner, John C. and Rina S. Onorato. 1999. "Social Identity, Personality, and the Self-concept: A Self-categorization Perspective." In *The Psychology of the Social Self,* eds. Tom R. Tyler, Roderick M. Kramer, and Oliver P. John. 11-46. Mahwah, NJ: Lawrence Erlbaum Associates, Publishers.

Upadhye, A. N. 1989 [1975]. "Jainism." In *A Cultural History of India*, ed. A. L. Basham. 100-110. Delhi: Oxford University Press.

van der Veer, Peter. 1994. *Religious Nationalism. Hindus and Muslims in India.* Berkeley, CA:University of California Press.

van Leeuwen, Arend Th. 1964. *Christianity in World History.* New York: Charles Scribner's Sons.

van Niel, Robert. 1963. "The Course of Indonesian History." In *Indonesia,* ed. Ruth T. McVey. 272-308. New Haven, CT. HRAF Press.

Volf, Miroslav. 2011. *Allah: A Christian Response.* New York: HarperCollins.

Voye, Liliane. 1999. "Secularization in a Context of Advanced Modernity." *Sociology of Religion.* 60(3): 275-288.

Wagner, M. B. 1983. "Spiritual Frontiers Fellowship." In *Alternatives to American Mainline Churches,* ed. J. H. Fichter. New York: Rose of Sharon Press.

Wallace, Anthony F. C. 1956. "Revitalization Movements." *American Anthropologist*. 58:2. 264-281.

———. 1967. *Culture and Personality*. New York: Random House.

Walls, Andrew F. 1976. "Toward Understanding Africa's Place in Christian History." In *Religion in a Pluralistic Society: Essays Presented to Professor C. G. Baeta,* ed. J. S. Pobee. 180-189. Leiden: Brill.

———. 2002. The C*ross-cultural Process in Christian History*. Maryknoll, NY: Orbis Books.

Walzer, Michael L. 1965. *The Revolution of the Saints*. New York: Atheneum.

Warner, R. Stephen. 1997. "Convergence Toward the New Paradigm." In *Rational Choice Theory and Religion,* ed. Lawrence A. Young. 87-101. New York: Routledge.

———. 1998. "Introduction: Immigration and Religious Communities in the United States." In *Gatherings in Diaspora: Religious Communities and the New Immigration,* eds. R. Stephen Warner and Judith G. Wittner. 3-34. Philadelphia, PA: Temple University Press.

Weber, Max. 1958 [1904]. *The Protestant Ethic and the Spirit of Capitalism*. Translated by Talcott Parsons with a Foreword by R. H. Tawney. New York: Charles Scribner's Sons.

———. 1972 [1922]. *The Sociology of Religion*. Trans. Ephraim Fischoff. Introduction by Talcott Parsons. Boston: Beacon Press.

———. 1967 [1946]. *From Max Weber*. Translated, edited, and with an Introduction by H. H. Gerth and C. Wright Mills. New York: Oxford University Press.

Webster, John C. B. 2003. "Dalits and the Conversion Controversy in India." *Cross Culture, a Newsletter of The Association of Presbyterians For Cross-Cultural Mission.* 46:1-3.

Willaime, Jean-Paul. 2004. "The Cultural Turn in the Sociology of Religion in France." *Sociology of Religion*. 65(4): 373-389.

Wilcox, W. Bradford. 2002. "For the Sake of the Children? Family Related Discourse and Practice in the Mainline." In *The Quiet Hand of God,* eds. by Robert Wuthnow and John H. Evans. 287-316. Berkeley, CA: University of California Press.

Winter, Ralph. 2003. "Eleven Frontiers of Perspective." *International Journal of Frontier Missions.* 20(4): 78.

Wittgenstein, Ludwig. 1976. *Philosophical Investigations.* Trans. G. E. M. Anscombe. Oxford: Basil Blackwell.

Woodberry, Robert D. 2004. *The Shadow of Empire: Christian Missions, Colonial Policy, and Democracy in Postcolonial Societies.* Ph.D. Dissertation, Chapel Hill, NC: University of North Carolina.

_____. 2006. "Reclaiming the M-word: The Legacy of Missions in Nonwestern Societies." *Faith and International Affairs.* 4(1): 3-12.

Woodhead Linda, Paul Heelas, and Grace Davie. 2003. "Introduction." In *Predicting Religion*, eds. Grace Davie, Paul Heelas, and Linda Woodhead. 1-39. Burlington, VT: Ashgate Publishing Company.

Wright, Arthur. 1971 [1959]. *Buddhism in Chinese History.* Stanford, CA: Stanford University Press.

Wuthnow, Robert. 1985. "Science and the Sacred." In *The Sacred in a Secular Age*, ed. Philip Hammond. 187-203. Berkeley, CA: University of California Press.

_____. 1987. *Meaning and Moral Order: Explorations in Cultural Analysis.* Berkeley: CA: University of California Press.

Yang, Fenggang. 1999. *Chinese Christians in America.* University Park, PA: The Pennsylvania State University Press.

_____. 2006. "The Red, Black, and Gray Markets of Religion in China." *The Sociological Quarterly.* 47(1): 93-122.

Young, Lawrence A., ed. 1997. *Rational Choice Theory and Religion.* New York: Routledge.

Zrinscak, Sinisa. 2004. "Generations and Atheism: Patterns of Response to Communist Rule Among Different Generations and Countries." *Social Compass.* 51(2): 221-234.

Zurcher, E. 1959. *The Buddhist Conquest of China.* Leiden: E. J. Brill.

NAME INDEX

'Abd al-Qadir, 65
Abrams, Dominic, 17, 265, 284
Abu Bakr, 185, 252, 253
Abul Abbas, 285
Abu Lahab, 252
Abu Midyan, 65
Abu Sufyan, 252, 253
Abu Talib, 252
Ahmad al-Badawi, 65
Ahmed, Akbar, 368, 370, 371
Al-Abbas, 251
Alexander, Jeffrey, xx, siii, 22, 332
Alexander the Great, 59, 196, 209, 365
Ali al-Husayn, 252
Al Mamoun, 285
Allison, Scott, 41
Alland, Alexander, 233
Althusser, L, 161
Ambrose, 176
Ammerman, Nancy, 395, 396, 423
Armstrong, Karen, 49, 52
Arnold, Thomas, 5, 13, 138, 139
Ashford, S., 299
Ashoka, Emperor, 68, 81
Attila, 201
Augustine, 3
Augustine from Rome, 132, 202
Ayatolla Khomeni, 66

Bacon, Francis, 304
Bainbridge, William Sims, xxiii, 17, 27, 160, 236, 249, 267, 319, 330
Barnabas, 128
Barnett, H. G., 278
Barrett, David B, xix, 13, 14, 220, 343
Barrett, Justin, 319, 340
Bartolome de Las Casas, 95, 213
Beccaria, 315
Beckford, James, 260, 261
Bellah, Robert, 9, 77, 114, 120, 151
Benz, Ernst, 274
Berman, Harold J, 180

Beyer, Peter, 185
Beyerlein, Kraig, 331
Bird, Frederick, 127
Boniface (Winfrith), 132, 203, 247, 250
Boris, King, 206
Bowen, Kurt, 351
Branscombe, Nyla R., 266
Brinton, Craine, 315
Bruce, Steve, 184, 226, 267, 298
Buckley, Michael J., 389
Buddha, 43–46, 48, 54–57, 61, 68, 71, 81–84, 86, 87, 101, 123, 166, 195, 244, 245, 272, 363

Campbell, Colin, 295, 297
Candragupta, 81
Carmichael, Joel, 209
Carnes, Tony, 8, 281
Carroll, Jackson, 395
Casanova, Jose, 184, 311, 324
Chafetz, Janet Saltzman, 8
Charlemagne, 178, 203
Chaumette, Pierre, 316
Ch'en, Kenneth, 44, 154, 244
Cheng, Yen Master, 86, 105
Christiano, Kevin J., 184
Clovis, 178, 201
Cohn, Norman, 311
Collins, Randall, 18, 116, 117, 124, 169, 235, 269–271, 314, 332, 346, 347, 353–355, 360, 361, 398
Condercet, 315
Confucius, 54
Conn, Walter, xix, 261
Constantine, 131, 157, 174–176, 178, 198, 203, 204, 208, 267, 421
Crossing, Peter F., 13, 14, 343
Cyril (Constantine), 205, 206, 277
Cyrus the Great, 58, 156

D'Alembert, 315
David, Barbara, 267
Davie, Grace, 12, 295, 299, 366

Deanesly, Margaret, 205, 208
De Haan, Channin G., 331
Demerath, N. J., 160, 282
Denton, Melinda Lunquist, 255, 301, 332, 338, 366, 387, 396, 405, 419, 421
Descartes, Rene, 307
Diderot, 293, 315
Diocletian, 174
Dobbelaere, Karel, 184
Doosje, Bertjan, 266
Douglas, Mary, 312
Drake, H. A., 173–176
Drekmeier, Charles, 163
Dudley, Carl, 395
Durkheim, Emile, xxii, 4, 46, 111, 270

Ebaugh, Helen Rose, 8
Ecklund, Elane Howard, 302
Ellemers, Naomi, 266
Engels, Friedrich, 311
Epstein, Seymore, 259, 260
Ernst, Carl, 2, 15, 50, 101, 102, 140, 141, 369
Esposito, John L., 51, 137
Ethelbert, 132
Evans, John H., 331

Fa Hsian (Hian), 164, 165
Fatima, 252
Feldman, Kenneth A., 302
Feuerbach, Ludwig, 311, 327
Finke, Roger, xxi, 27, 131, 236, 249, 301, 318, 397
Flory, Richard W., 331
Fouche, Josephe, 316
Fox, Robin, 92
Francisco de Vitoria, 213
Freston, Paul, 22
Freud, Sigmund, 327
Friedman, Thomas L., 268, 357
Froese, Paul, 296, 300, 303, 318, 329

Gandhi, Mahatma, 56, 123

Gard, Richard A., 125
Garma, Carlos, 282
Garroutte, Eva Marie, 331
Geertz, Clifford, 287
Ghozzi, Kamel, 66
Gill, R., 298
Goethals, George, 41
Goffman, Irving, 270-271
Gooren, Henri, 9
Govind Singh, 57
Grotius, Hugh, 3
Guan-yin, 45
Guest, Kenneth, 8, 351
Gunn, T. Jeremy, 52, 142

Hadaway, C. K., 298
Hallisey, Charles, 3
Hanciles, Jehu, 6
Haroun, 285
Harper, Susan Billington, 218
Hashem, 251
Hassan (Hussein) 253
Hebert, Jacques, 316
Hecht, Jennifer Michael, 293, 294, 306, 316
Heelas, Paul, 12, 296, 366
Hefner, Robert, W., 112
Helvetius, 315
Henley, W. E., 310
Herbrechtsmeier, Willilam, 46
Hiebert, Paul G., xix
Hirst, Rob, 254
Hoefer, Herbert, 417
Hoge, Dean, 396
Hogg, Michael A., 17, 265, 284
Holbach, 293, 315
Horrell, David G., 89, 127
Hourani, Albert, 49, 65, 69, 104, 135, 140
Hsuan, Tsang, 165, 246
Huff, Toby, 131, 180
Hunsberger, George R., 417
Hunter, George G., 398
Hunter, James Davison, xx, 333, 392, 401

Huntington, Samuel P., 368, 369
Hussein of Jordan, 251

Iannaccone, Lawrence, 397
Ibn Khaldun, 371
Ignatius, the Patriarch, 206
Igor, King, 208
Inglehart, 320, 321, 350, 363
Irenaeus, 129
Isaiah, 88, 156, 383

Jaffarian, Michael, 13, 343
James, 321
Jaspers, Karl, 154
Jelen, Ted Gerard, 22
Jenkins, Philip, 1, 130, 177, 368, 372
Jeremiah, 88
Jesus Christ, 48, 63, 64, 66, 68, 69, 71, 88, 91, 94, 99, 100, 129, 132, 237, 363, 372, 380–391, 393, 394, 397, 398, 405, 406, 411, 413–415, 417, 418, 421–423
John, the Apostle, 68, 90, 91, 389, 394
John the Baptist, 68, 246
Johnson, Benton, 396
Johnson, Todd M., xix, 13, 14, 220, 343
Johnstone, Patrick, xix
Justin Martyr, 276

Kaelber, Lutz, 130, 248
Kang Xi, Emperor, 219
Kane, Danielle, 216, 280
Kant, Immanuel, 4
Kapleau, Philip, 274
Keay, John, 121, 164, 165, 242, 243
Kemeny, P. C., 331
Keysar, Ariela, 303
Khadija, 252
Khalid Ibn Walid, 252
Kim, Kwang Chung, 8, 352
Kim, Sebastian C.H., 170–172
Koestler, Arthur, 47
Kosmin, Barry, 303
Kraft, Charles, xix

Kurian, George T., xix
Kurtz, Lesster R, 367
Kwon, Ho-Youn, 8
Lamb, Alastair, 121
Lambert, Yves, 184, 332
La Mettrei, 315
Lao Zi, 55
Lapidus, Ira, 53, 222
Latourette, Kenneth Scott, 91, 93, 123, 132, 181, 185, 201–203, 206–208, 211, 213–215, 217, 244, 246, 247, 279, 213–215
Lee, Martha F., 287
Legge, James, 95
Legge, J. D., 165, 224, 286, 287
Leo I, Pope, 201
Lewis, Bernard, 49, 137, 138
Licinius, 174
Lightman, B. V., 297
Locke, John, 306
Lofland, John, 236, 249
Louis X1V, 314, 315
Lubis, Mochtar, 165, 166
Luidens, 396
Luke, 321, 393, 411, 414
Lull, Raymond, 132
Luzbetak, Louis J., xix
Lydia, 237, 238

MacMullen, Ramsey, 62, 177, 199
Mahavira, 55–57, 122
Mamiya, Lawrence H., 287
Mandryk, Jason, xix
Mani, 59, 60
Mannheim, Karl, 311
Mao Zedong, 281, 293
Mark, 68, 88, 321, 373, 385, 412
Marler, 298
Marr, John R., 121
Martin, David, 226, 280, 324, 325
Martin of Tours, 131, 132, 200
Marx, Karl, 41, 311, 327
Mary, the Virgin, 63, 68
Matthew, 88, 127, 383, 387, 393
Mawlay Idris, 65

McGavran, Donald A., xix
McGrath, Alister, 294, 316, 318, 329, 334
McKinney, William, 395
McLeod, Hew, 126
Meander, Keith G., 331
Meeks, Wayne, 73, 90–92
Mehl, Roger, xix
Meiji, Emporer Mutsuhito, 215
Merton, Robert, xxv
Methodius, 205, 206, 277
Moffett, Samuel Hugh, 14, 60, 126, 209, 264, 276
Morier-Genoud, Eric, xix
Muhammad, son of Abu Bakr, 253
Montesquieu, 293
Montgomery, Robert L., xxv, 14, 155, 156, 194, 408
Muawiya, 253
Muhammad, 48–52, 54, 57, 58, 66, 69, 70, 71, 105, 136, 137, 142, 185, 186, 251–253, 284, 363
Muller, Max, 5, 13
Mullins, Mark, 85, 274

Nadeau, Kathy, 214
Nanak, 57
Newcomb, Theodore M., 302
Newport, Frank, 300
Ng-Quinn, Michael, 168
Nichiren, 274
Nietzsche, Friedrich, 311, 327
Niles, D. T., 413
Norris, Pippa, 320, 321, 350, 363
Noss, John, 45, 55, 56, 58
Nutting, Anthony, 223, 251,285

Olaf Haraldsson, 93,204
Olaf Tryggvason, 204
Olga, Queen, 208
Oliver, Douglas L., 279
Omar Ibn Khattab, 252, 285
Onorato, Rina, 263–264
Orru, Marco, 46
Ornstein, Martha, 313

Osama bin Laden, 370
Osiris, 198
Othman Iban Khattab, 252
Othman Ibn Affan, 252
Othman (Ottoman), 187
Otto I, 206

Pagels, E., 113
Pannenberg, Wolfhart, 389
Paramesvara, 224
Park, Chris, 6
Park, Jung Mee, 216, 280
Parker Gumicio, Christian, 282
Parsons, Talcott, 34
Pascal, Blaise, 322, 388
Patrick, 132, 201, 398
Paul, the Apostle, 90, 102, 128, 129, 237, 246, 251, 389, 405, 423
Peck, Lisa R., 331
Perry, Admiral, 215
Perry, Ronald W., 5
Peter, the Apostle, 89, 90, 385, 422
Petran, Tabitha, 276
Pfaff, Steven, 296, 303, 318
Philip, T. V., 126
Phipps, William, 94, 95
Pollack, Detlef, 299, 318

Qosiy, 251

Rambo, Lewis, xix, 118, 148, 237, 259, 260, 261
Ratislav, 205
Rauschenbusch, Walter, 392
Reynolds, Frank, 3
Robespierre, 316
Rogers, Everett, 5, 18
Rousseau, 315
Rukayya, 252

Saladin, 187
Samuel, Vinay, 392
Sanneh, Lamen, 51, 139, 140, 278, 368, 386
Sava, 207

Name Index

Savarkar, Vinayak, 282
Schweitzer, Albert, 89
Scott, John, 160
Severius, 205
Shapen, Steven, 312
Sharot, Stephen, 16, 40, 43, 62, 64, 77, 163, 169
Shaw, Douglas, 86
Shehu Shaykh 'Uthmanb, Fudi, 140
Shils, Edward, 308
Shiva –Buddha, 166
Sidi Mahraz, 65
Sikkink, David, 331
Simeon, King, 206
Smith, Christian, xx, xxi, 4, 7, 18, 22, 41, 74, 78, 84, 232, 255, 258, 259, 301, 308, 309, 318, 322, 330, 331, 332, 335, 337, 338, 365, 366, 386, 387, 396, 397, 405, 406, 419, 421
Smith, David, 385, 421, 423
Smith, Jesse, 297, 312
Snell, Patricia, 255
Spears, Russell, 266
Spiro, Melford, 44, 86, 162
Stark, Rodney, xx, xxi, xxiii 1, 3, 4, 15, 17, 22, 27, 42, 46, 47, 48, 92, 126, 113, 118, 128, 134, 160, 163, 177, 184, 236, 247, 249, 258, 267, 277, 301, 303, 318, 387, 397
Steinberg, Stephen, 301
Stenmark, Mikael, xvii, xxii, 307
Stephen, King, 207
Sugden, Chris, 392
Swatos, William, 184

Tabor, Charles R., xix
Tajfel, Henri, 18, 263, 266
Tanaka, Aiji, 169, 170
T'an-yao, 244, 245
Tatian, 276, 277
Taylor, Charles, 314
Tennent, Timothy C., 417
Teresa, Mother, 258
Thalheimer, Fred, 301
Thapar, Romila, 81, 82, 122, 162

Theodore, 93
Theodosius, Emperor, 175, 176
Thomas, George M., 331
Thomas, the Apostle, 389
Thuesen, Peter J., 392
Tilly, Charles, 359–361
Timms, N., 299
Timothy, 89
Tippett, Alan R., xix
Titus, 89
Toennies, Ferdinand, 254
Toland, John, 306
Toyoda, Maria, 169, 170
Tournon, Papal Legate, 219
Tsukamoto, Zenrya, 244
Turner, John, 263, 264, 267

Ulfilias, 200, 277
Upadhye, A. N., 122
Urban II, Pope, 187
Urban-Mead, Wendy, xix

van der Veer, Peter, 52, 65, 141
van Leeuwen, Arend Th, 40, 151
van Niel, Robert, 166
Vishnu, Lord, 164
Vladimir, 208, 283
Volf, Mirosalv, 104, 105
Voltaire, 293, 315
Voye, Liliane, 184

Wagner, M. B., 113
Wallace, A. F. C., 100
Walls, Andrew, 210, 220, 221, 368
Walzer, Michael, 306
Wang, Amy, 46
Warner, Stephen, xxi, 8, 332, 352
Weber, Max, 21, 34, 53, 55–57, 135, 160, 286
Webster, John, 171
Wilcox, Clyde, 22
Wilcox, W. Bradford, 396
Willibrord, 132, 202, 203
Winfrith (Boniface), 132, 203, 247
Winter, Ralph, 417

Wittberg, Patricia, 131
Wittgenstein, Ludwig, 312
Wittner, Judith G., 352
Woodberry, Robert, 388, 391
Woodhead, Linda, 12, 296, 366
Wright, Arthur, 83, 84
Wu Hou, Empress, 185
Wuthnow, Robert, xx, 22, 301, 332, 335, 373–376

Yang, Fenggang, xxi, 8, 352
Young, Lawrence A., 17

Zoroaster, 57–59, 68
Zrinscak, Sinisa, 300, 318
Zurcher, E., 154

SUBJECT INDEX

A

atheism
  accepted and rejected in French
    Revolution, 316
  as "luxury of elite," 340
  not caused by conflict of science
    and faith, 337
  seen as liberator, 316
  seen as oppressive, 316
  "twilight of," 318, 329

B

Buddhism
  accepted by invaders,
    106, 138, 139, 197
  accepted by ascendant rulers,
    83, 84, 154, 197
  accepted in period of turmoil
    in China, 83, 197
  alliances with governments by, 155,
    167, 168, 173
  appeal of literature in,
    165, 167, 168, 173
  appeal to intellectuals of,
    197, 273
  as additional religious layer,
    85, 246
  as enhancing self-esteem,
    273, 274
  as least ethnically bound of
    Asian religions, 13, 14, 87
  as offering a single dominant
    figure, 24, 35
  as sectarian movement,
    81, 122, 123, 195
  bodhisattvas in,
    45, 86
  compared in size to Hinduism,
    13, 343
  compassion in, 45
  competition with Hinduism in
    Southeast Asia by, 13, 83,
    164–166, 196
  contribution to capitalism of
    missionary orders of, 124
  dhamma/dharma in,
    10, 68, 81–83, 123, 162, 163
  elevation of Buddha in,
    44–46, 68
  exemplary prophecy in,
    55, 56
  gentry literati Buddhists in,
    83, 154, 244, 273
  Goddess of Mercy in, 45
  international drive in, 246
  Lamaism in, 273
  made official in Japan, 85, 169
  made official in Korea, 85
  Mahasanghika initiation of
    Mahayana in, 44
  Mahayana in, 44, 45, 84–86, 124,
    154, 274
  "middle way" in, 57, 87
  missionaries in, 123, 246
  morality in, 81–87
  not associated with outside
    domination, 198
  not in direct competition with
    Christianity and Islam as spread
    in Asia, 13, 343
  offer of single dominant figure in,
    43
  organized groups in, 120, 123, 245,
    275
  pilgrims to India in, 164, 165,
    246
  popular religion in, 43, 44
  provided moral order, 54, 55,
    138
  replaced by Confucianism in
    government favor, 85, 186
  rival to Taoism, 34
  sanghas in, 120, 123, 244, 245,
    275
  sects in, 124, 125, 274
  spread of where caste system not
    established, 244
  Theravada in, 44, 45, 86, 273

Tzu Chi (CiJi) movement in, 86, 87
Young Men's Buddhist
 Association in, 125

C

caste system, 61, 83, 121, 122, 125,
 163, 165, 167, 195, 239, 242, 243
Cathars/Catharism, 60, 129, 130, 180,
 248
"catnet," 359–361
Christianity
 acceptance of by invaders or
  dominant from dominated of,
  199–204
 acceptance by minorities/minority
  groups, 96, 159, 217, 227, 266,
  289, 409
 acceptance, but with creation of
  distinctive expression of, 200,
  208, 213–215, 282
 acceptance of non-Christian high
  moral standards by, 90–95
 acceptance by small societies of,
  131, 153, 156, 197, 208
 alliance with governments by, 93,
  388
 as a non-Western religion, 11, 14
 as associated with coersion, 130,
  211–215
 as associated with support against
  outside threat, 211, 216
 as caught and then taught, 389, 398
 as counter cultural, 387
 as enhancing female status and
  identity, 277, 278
 as enhancing identities of
  indigenous people, 276–279
 as detracting from identity of
  indigenous people, 281–283
 as missionary religious movement,
  127
 as monopoly religion, 175
 as state religion, 174–177
 anti-Christ principle in, 393
 bad Christianity as greatest danger
  to, 419, 420
 baptism as mark of identity in,
  90, 127
 categorization of as a caste in
  Hindusim, 170
 centrality of Jesus Christ in, 382,
  389, 390, 417
 coercion in, 176, 180–183, 211
 communal ("Celtic") approach in,
  398
 concern for reputation in, 89
 congregational life in, 393–399
 contrasting response to, xiii
 contribution of translation to
  enhancing identities in, 277, 278,
  386
 co-option of religious innovation
  by, 180
 "conversion" and "proselytizing"
  in, 385
 conversion through force by rulers
  to, 203, 204
 damaging effect of governmental
  favoritism to, 405, 406
 defensive mode against, 278, 409
 denominations in first 300 years in,
  128, 129, 178
 disputes over authority in,
  63, 64
 distortion of doctrine of noncoercive
  God in, 372
 divisions in, 63
 ebbing of, 132
 effects of in first five hundred years,
  91–93
 encouragement of nationalism by,
  278
 evangelical and liberal versions in,
  48, 298, 392
 evangelical movement in,
  48, 64, 94, 133
 family relationships in early,
  246, 247
 "Gentile baggage" in, 63
 global (international) relationships

in, 251
gnosticism in, 113, 128, 129
growth of after disassociation from domination of, 219, 220
inclusion of paganism by, 63, 199
"interaction ritual chains" in, 116, 117, 283
intrinsic blessings in, 406, 413
Jewish congregationalism in, 127
lack of Biblical knowledge in, 387
"little Constantines" in, 131, 157, 178
loss of voluntary spirit in, 93, 94, 108
majority outside of West of, 11, 14
message and method of from Jesus Christ, 382, 383
missionary mandate in, 48, 127, 128, 142, 384, 387
missionary monks in, 131–133, 159
missionary orders in, 132, 133
missionary societies in, 133, 134
mixed witness in, 384
mixing of religion andmorality in, 90, 91
movements against spiritual and moral laxity of, 129
not a new morality in, 90–93, 390
offer of new moral energy in, 390
other religions (Buddhism, Hinduism, and Islam) within, 416, 417
orthodoxy of heart and mind in, 388
participation in and opposition to social evils by, 221, 384, 391
peregrine monks in, 132
Pietistic movement in, 64, 94, 116, 182, 322
popular religion in, 63
provision of emotional energy by, 283
receptivity to when not associated with threat, 198, 199, 209–221
regaining of voluntary spirit in, 133
resistance movements in, 63, 180
resistance to when associated with threat, 209–221
revitalization of culture by, 276
"rites of intensification" in, 127
social gospel in, 392
social networks in, 246–251, 410–413
supplementary intercessors and intermediaries in, 63, 385
suppression of inovations in, 180
surrender to dominant cultural values by, 388
translation of the Bible in, 200, 278, 386
Virgin Mary in, 63
voluntary spirit atrophied in, 116
voluntary spirit revived in, 108, 109
worship as source of emotional energy in, 398, 399, 423
Communism
greatest success outside of West of, 317, 318
strongest in West in Southern Europe of, 317
Confucianism
clear division between elite and popular religions in, 61
clear distinction between morality and religion in, 78
disillusion with, 83
founder, a sage, not a savior in, 43, 54, 55
morality in, 78
opposition to heterodox religions by, 61
reassertion of, 85
rejection of doctrines of salvation by, 54, 55
spread of, 45, 55, 106
"superior person" in, 78
"cultural defense," 97, 226, 267, 268
"culturalism," 349

D

democracy
  advantages of secularization of, 401–406
  lack of experience with in traditional societies, 349
  multiple and ancient sources of, 347–348
  much more than elections, 348
  need for independent judiciary, free press, right of assembly in, 349, 350
democratization, theories of, 346, 347

E

emotional energy, 18, 28, 117, 142, 235, 236, 240, 269–271, 283, 288–290, 361, 398, 399, 413, 418
"existential security," 320, 350, 363

G

government as religious institution, 174

H

Hinduism
  appeal to rulers of, 163, 167
  as embedded in society, 122, 241, 242
  brahmans in, 120–123, 163–165
  competition with Buddhism in Southeast Asia, 13, 165–167
  debate over conversion in, 171–172
  "Great Tradition" in, 121, 123, 126
  incorporates popular religion, 42
  more than twice as many followers than Buddhism in, 13
  nationalism in, 171, 282
  no single savior figure in, 42, 46
  peaceful spread of, 121, 196
  Sanskrit literature in, 121
  spread hindered by attachment to local expression of, 79
  three pillars of "Aryanized" society in, 242
human figures as means of access to God and salvation, 48, 60, 66, 70
humanities
  demonstration of human need for meaning in, xxi
  need to incorporate sciences by, xxi

I

idealized national identity, 168
Indianization of Southeast Asia, 113
interaction ritual chains, 18, 116, 235, 269–271, 351, 398
irreligion
  belief and morality system of, 309–312
  current data on, 298–303
  definition of, 295–297
  desire for freedom and resistance to authoritarianism in, 305, 314–316, 334
  idol of autonomous individual in, 307, 308, 310, 334
  idol of science in, 305–307, 310
  ineffectiveness when associated with power of, 315, 317, 336
  influence of on selection of professional field, 334, 335
  informal networking in, 315, 316, 329, 330, 333, 340
  not as dangerous as bad religion, 418, 412, 422
  origin of in French Europe, 294, 315, 316
  rewarded in certain fields, 334, 335
  romantic movement and, 308, 310
  participation by intellectuals in, 301–303, 308, 334
  political activism in, 309–311
  preparatory movement for, 304–306
  promotion of new humanity and society, 311, 312
  relationship to standard of living of, 319, 320

secular priesthood in, 334
subjective philosophical expression of in Germany, 311
two types of organization in, 316, 317
Islam
  acceptance in Persia of, 222–223
  appeal to tribal people of, 100, 101
  asabiyya (cohesion) and *hyper-asabiyya* in , 391
  as authoritarian and egalitarian, 136
  as egalitarian community, 135–138
  as not spread by the sword, 139
  as revitalization movement, 100, 135, 284
  associated with support against outside threat by, 222–226
  coercion in, 188
  coercion not successful in, 187
  community (*umma*) in, 135–136
  decline of Arab power in, 100, 101, 187, 285
  dhimmi system in, 186, 190
  elevation and centrality of Muhammad in, 49–51
  family relationships in, 251–253
  five Pillars in, 51, 64, 136
  flowering of civilization in, 103, 187, 284, 285
  fusion with governmental power in, 100, 185, 186, 286
  importance of social network in, 251–253
  liberation or support of dominated by, 222, 287
  means of renewal and empowerment for many peoples by, 100
  migration to Europe and North America of, 7
  missionaries in, 13, 15, 52, 53, 139, 142
  mixing of religion and morality in, 100
  multiple centers of power in, 286
  need to understand sources of anger and frustration, 268
  "no compulsion in religion" in Qur'an, 373
  not accepted by ruled, 157, 187
  not spread by force, 138, 139, 187
  organization of, 135–143
  popular religion in, 62, 64–66, 142
  Qur'an in, 49, 52, 101, 102, 135, 373
  riddah wars in, 49
  sacralizing of commercial economy in, 286, 287
  saints in, 65
  scholars (*ulema*) in, 64, 66, 137, 138
  struggles over authority and leadership in, 136
  Sufi missionary work in, 50, 52, 53, 140, 141
  Sufi saints in, 65
  Sunni-Shia dispute in, 186, 253
  tribal character of, 136
  upward mobility in, 223, 224, 284

J

Jainsm
  a*hismsa* (universal love) in, 123
  developed with Buddhism, 55, 56
  emphasis on asceticism in, 123
  founder of, 55, 122
  influence in Indian culture of, 56
  Mahavira an "exemplary" prophet in, 56
  no single savior figure in, 43, 54
  popular religion in, 56
Judaisim
  congregations in, 127
  Diaspora of, 6
  early, but not sustained ability to spread widely, 47, 80
  expectation of exclusive loyalty to God by, 3
  impact of morality of, 80, 106
  mother religion of Christianity and

Islam, 47, 53, 54
  popular religion in, 62, 64

M

Manichaeism
  confused with Christianity, 60
  dualism in, 60
  founder, Mani, but no single savior in, 59, 60
  influence on Catharism (attempt to purify religion) by, 60
  suppression of, 59
  *w*ide spreading of, 59, 60
Marxism, 4, 184, 281, 309, 325, 365
missionaries
  cooperation away from home of, 265
  creating emotional energy, 418
  desire to enhance lives by, 415
  importance of personal action in bureaucratic systems by, 319
  increase in, 132–135
  internationalization of, 135, 408
  need to be students of family life by, 411
  number of not necessarily correlated with conversions, 119
  receptivity to message of, 418
  translation of scriptures by, 277, 278
missionary religions
  Buddhism, Christianity, and Islam as, 13–15
  definition of, 5
  necessary beliefs of, 47, 48
  necessary gathering and organization in, 114. 117
  necessary morality in, 80
missions
  accelerated by emphasis on centrality of Jesus Christ, 63, 64, 68
  aided by religious pluralism, 404, 405
  as affected by family relations, 410
  as affected by majority- minority relations, 404
  as transformation, 392
  "Celtic" method in, 398
  delayed response to, 6, 401
  demonstrating democracy in, 191, 306, 349, 388, 402
  disadvantage of domination by sending country in, 401, 402
  evangelical movements as catalyst for, 64
  for those vulnerable to low self-esteem, 413, 414
  internationalization of, 135, 408
  localization of, 399
  release of energy in, 182
  resistance over long time to, 182
  still affected by colonialism, 407
  weakened by church association with government, 402, 403
modernization processes, 346
monotheism
  limits of, 42, 46, 47, 62
"Moralistic, Therapeutic, Deism," 332, 366, 387, 405
morality
  affected by beliefs in salvation and compassion for all, 75, 77, 94, 107
  blots in, 98, 99
  breakdown of, 75
  definition of, 73
  energy in, 75
  guidance and energy in, 75–77
  progress through diversity and disagreement in, 98, 99, 391
  secularization of, 77, 78, 97
  separation from religion of, 73, 77, 82, 88
  voluntarism provides energy for, 108, 109
motivations
  ambiguity of, 257, 258
  basic difficulty in studying, 261
  variety of, 259–261

O

ontocracy, 45, 151
opinion leaders, 18, 234, 238, 240

P

pluralistic field among tribes, 150, 152
prophecy
   ethical, 53–57
   exemplary, 53–57

R

"reflective pluralism," 374–376
religion
   as incorporating resistance to God, xxiii, xxiv
   as independent, as well as dependent variable, 19, 32
   carriers of, 28, 112, 118, 119, 142, 198, 210
   civility in, 375
   definition of, 2–4
   distinction from magic of, 3, 4
   elite and popular, 17, 39–42, 63, 161, 380, 381
   ethicalization in, 77, 79
   exclusive, xxiv, 2, 10, 125, 367
   five stages of, 9, 10
   freedom of, 11, 12, 149–153, 156, 157, 159, 162, 170–173, 189, 191, 200, 322, 324, 325, 341, 347–349, 351–354, 406
   founders of,
      Buddha, 54, 55,
      Confucius, 54,
      Lao Zi, 55,
      Mahavira, 55, 56,
      Mani, 59, 60,
      Nanak, 57,
      Zoroaster, 57–59
   "Godless" religion, 4
   identification by descent with, 116, 353, 416
   increasing attention to content of, 362–367
   leaders in, 66, 67, 113
   missionaries in, 118, 119
   missionary, 7, 13,
   monopolistic, 29, 79, 97, 102, 108, 115, 133, 168, 175, 190, 191, 211, 324, 326, 340, 348, 349, 352, 373, 377, 381, 404
   "native" as polemical tool of, 1, 10
   opportunities for choice of, 148–150
   primal, primitive or animistic, 9, 12, 39, 101, 151, 152, 189
   prophets in, 54, 55, 57, 58, 88, 140, 357, 387
   rewards in, xxiii, xxiv, 17, 60, 336, 337, 378, 413
   seen as only dependent variable, 19, 32
   seen as independent variable, 32
   shift from inherited to chosen, 416
   use of coercion by, xxiv, 130, 139, 176, 177

S

science
   and the humanities, xxi, xxii, xxv, 301, 331
   and theology, xvi-xviii, xxv, xxvi, 31, 32
   as aimed at producing theory, xiv, xxv
   as corrective to thought, including theology, xvii, xix, xxv
   as "indirect theology," xxii
   as self-limiting, xxiv, xxv
   ethos of, xxv
   institutionalization of, xvii
scientism, xvii, xx, 4, 307, 308, 310, 419
secularization
   as aid to life of faith, 416, 419
   as distinct from secularism, xxiv, 295, 320, 419
   as religious movement, xxiv, 95, 184, 191
   as resistance to dominating

Christianity, 184
   not weakening Christianity by, 416, 419
self categorization theory, 264
self-esteem motivation ambivalence of, 414, 417
   importance in social identity and rational choice theories of, 266, 267
   recognized importance in international relations of, 268
Sikhism
   identified with certain castes, 126
   last guru, Govind Singh in, 57
   Nanak, founder of, 57
   nine gurus in, 57
   no single savior figure in, 43, 57
   writings of gurus (Granth) in, 57
small societies
   nonofficial religion in, 150
   pluralistic religious field among, 150–152
social identity theory, 18, 263–267
social networks as re-enforced by rites and festivals, 235
   effect of disruption of, 238, 239, 290
   importance for conversion or blocking conversion of, 236, 238
social sciences
   as study of God's activity in the world through humans, xvi, xvii
   birth of, xvii
   divisions within, xix, xx
   relationship to humanities of, xx–xxii
   theory in, xxv, 33, 34
   throwing light on, not replacing theological understanding, xvii, xviii
sociology
   historical, 32–35
   of emotions, 267, 268
   macro, micro, and meso level factors in, 26
   rational choice approach in, 17, 18, 258, 259, 263, 267, 271
   reversed causation in, 67–70
   simulated experimental method in, 32–34
   study of beliefs in, 34, 35
   "turn toward culture" of, xx, xxi, 21, 22, 332, 365
   variables in, 33, 34
sociology of missions
   as focused on theory, xvi, xxv, 6
sociology of religion
   little study of missions in, xx, 1, 2
   new paradigm in, xxi
societies
   differences for religious choices between large and small, 150–153
spread of religion
   by conversion ("expansion diffusion"), 6–9
   by migration ("relocation diffusion"), 6, 7
   crossing boundaries in, 6, 7
   definition of, 6, 7
   elevation of a human being a key factor in, 47, 53, 54
   need for theory of, 11–16
   opinion leaders in, 18, 234, 238, 240
   process of, 6
   proselytizing in, 7, 237, 285
   subcultural identity theory, 332, 333, 387, 397
   theoretical framework for, 19–27

T

Taoism
   Lao Zi as sage in, 55
   no single savior figure in, 43, 55
   rival with Buddhism of, 13, 55
theology
   and anthropology, xix
   and psychology, xix
   and science, xvii–xix
   and sociology, xvii, xviii, xix, xx
   theoretical propositions, 27–30

Z

Zoroastrianism
　ethical, not exemplary,
　　prophecy in, 57
　migration of, 6
　no single savior figure in, 54
　opposition to popular religion in, 58
　rising tide of popular religion in,
　　58–60

ABOUT THE AUTHOR

Robert L. Montgomery was born in China of missionary parents. After graduation from Rhodes College and Columbia and Princeton Theological Seminaries, he returned to the Far East and served as a Presbyterian missionary in Taiwan for sixteen years. His work was among the aboriginal people, primarily the Amis language group. The movement to Christianity of the aboriginal people spurred Montgomery to obtain a PhD in Social Scientific Studies of Religion at Emory University. Through a number of articles and books, he has sought to develop the field of sociology of missions, while also contributing to the religious field of missiology.

www.ingramcontent.com/pod-product-compliance
Lightning Source LLC
Chambersburg PA
CBHW051811090426
42736CB00011B/1432